Hegel's Political Philosophy

problems and perspectives

A COLLECTION OF NEW ESSAYS

EDITED BY

Z. A. PELCZYNSKI

Fellow of Pembroke College, Oxford

CAMBRIDGE

At the University Press

1971

Published by the Syndics of the Cambridge University Press
Bentley House, 200 Euston Road, London NWI 2DB
American Branch: 32 East 57th Street, New York, N.Y.10022

Library of Congress Catalogue Card Number: 71-160096

ISBN: 0 521 08123 8

Printed in Great Britain by
The Eastern Press Limited
of London and Reading

Hegel's Political Philosophy
problems and perspectives

Contents

v

Preface

Hegel was born on 27 August 1770, and the present volume was originally planned to appear in 1970 to commemorate the bicentenary of his birth. It appears a year later owing to the unforeseen and probably unavoidable difficulties of collecting and editing original essays by contributors scattered over two continents. Among the many thankless tasks of an editor of such a volume is to have to refuse, on various grounds, many attractive offers of contributions or to solicit contributions from unwilling or very busy authors. I would like once more to apologize to the former and to thank those of the latter who yielded to my entreaties.

I was very fortunate to have had the assistance of Professor John Plamenatz, Mr W. L. Weinstein and Dr Shlomo Avineri in the early stages of the project; the first two gave me valuable editorial help also in its later stages. I am indebted to John Havard for his meticulous editorial assistance, and to Roger Hausheer for translating two of the essays into English, and also helping me with the editorial work. The help of Pembroke College secretarial staff, especially Lady Alison Sinclair and Miss Elizabeth Stokes, must also be gratefully acknowledged. My own contribution benefited greatly from the critical comments of Mr J. R. Torrance, whom I would like to thank cordially.

The essays included in this volume cover all the major political works of Hegel, and the topics chosen by the contributors deal with central or particularly controversial issues in Hegel's political philosophy. A wide spectrum of approaches is combined with a sympathetic, though by no means uncritical, attitude to Hegel's works and ideas. What inspired the editor and the contributors alike was a common belief that Hegel's political philosophy is exciting, significant and impressive, and that its study amply repays the effort needed to understand it. We hope that we have succeeded in communicating this belief to our readers.

Oxford, August 1970   Z. A. PELCZYNSKI

Abbreviations

The titles of Hegel's works most frequently referred to in this volume, published in German or in an English translation, are abbreviated as follows:

Phänomenologie	*Phänomenologie des Geistes*
Phenomenology	*The Phenomenology of Mind*, trans. J. B. Baillie
Philosophie des Rechts	*Grundlinien der Philosophie des Rechts oder Naturrecht und Staatswissenschaft im Grundrisse*
Philosophy of Right	*Hegel's Philosophy of Right*, trans. T. M. Knox
Philosophie der Geschichte	*Vorlesungen über die Philosophie der Geschichte* (The title of G. Lasson's edition (Leipzig, 1917–20) has *Weltgeschichte* instead of *Geschichte*, but is the same work.)
Philosophy of History	*Lectures on the Philosophy of History*, trans. J. Sibree
Political Writings	*Hegel's Political Writings*, trans. T. M. Knox

The German works have had different editions and have been reprinted in various years. The English translations have also been printed more than once. The edition used and/or the year of reprint is stated by each contributor in his essay.

The Hegelian conception of the state

Z. A. PELCZYNSKI

The ideas of Hegel, as of any other political philosopher, can be discussed in a variety of ways. One can approach the ideas genetically, tracing their evolution from the earliest, generally simple, and often rather different formulations in some youthful work through various intermediate works to the author's *chef-d'oeuvre*. One can take an idea or a cluster of ideas of a political philosopher and trace its development in the history of political philosophy. One can compare the ideas of one thinker with those of another or several others. One can look at political ideas as reflections of broad currents of thought or of contemporary controversies; as a thinker's responses to the social processes or political events of his time and place; as expressions of mainly individual factors such as personal prejudices or escapist flights from the unpleasant realities of the historical situation. Or one can look at ideas simply as they are stated and developed in one particular work, especially a work that is the most authoritative or mature expression of a political philosopher's position, without asking how or why it was that he came to have them. All these approaches are perfectly legitimate; all have their limitations; they are all – as it happens – represented in this volume of essays. They reflect the personal interests and predilections of their authors, and also the intellectual traditions to which they belong.

However, if the study of past political philosophers is, so to speak, to earn its keep in the field of political and social science, rather than history of philosophy or general intellectual history, it must have some relevance to the concerns of political and social theorists of our own time. It need not necessarily influence their theorizing though it sometimes may do so by suggesting concepts, models or approaches. But it should at least illuminate their own activity by showing them the failures and successes of other minds grappling with similar problems. It is probably the last of the approaches just mentioned – the examination of ideas for their own sake, irrespective of their origin and background – which is then the most valuable. But one should not be too dogmatic about procedures; any one which promises results may be fruitfully combined with the narrow analytical approach. One other condition, however, must be satisfied before the full benefit of such an approach can be gained. The concepts, arguments or theories of past political philosophers must be translated into a language which contemporary political and social theorists will understand. In the case of Hegel this is a particularly difficult task: both because his political philosophy is a part of a general philosophical system, and because modern political and social theory is committed to logical and empirical thinking, while Hegel, at least at first sight, appears to have nothing but contempt for empiricism and non-dialectical logic. That such a reinterpretative approach to Hegel is nonetheless possible has been shown by at least one political theorist, and one can only wish that more would follow a similar path.[1]

I

In this essay I wish to examine one of the most important, and at the same time most obscure and controversial of Hegel's political ideas – his concept of the state. There is little need to stress its importance. The fundamental concept of any political philosophy is the concept of the body politic. There are few, if any, problems in political philosophy which do not, sooner or later, raise the question what sort of thing the body politic is. Problems of political obligation, of the rights of subjects against the government, of citizens' rights to political participation, and of the proper end or scope of governmental action necessarily involve some conception of the political entity within which they arise. But although Hegel's concept of the state has all these ramifications, my primary purpose is to discover what Hegel actually means by ' the state ', to express its meaning and to discuss the use he makes of it in terms which should be intelligible to social and political theorists, and to suggest the reasons which may have prompted him to adopt the concept of the state as we find it in the *Philosophy of Right*. It is my belief that by his concept of the state Hegel hoped to convey something about social and political reality which was original and important, and that his concept is obscure because he tried to put more meaning into it than it is safe for any single concept to carry. It is only when one ' decomposes ' it (to use a term which Max Weber employed) into its constituent elements that one does justice to it, and also removes a large part of the obscurity which surrounds it.

Clarity and simplicity are obviously great virtues in political philosophy, and one might venture to guess that a large part of the current and almost obsessive preoccupation with Hobbes' political philosophy, despite its numerous and patent defects,[2] is due to the clarity of Hobbes' concept of the ' commonwealth ', and in fact to the clarity of his argument as a whole. But the price of clarity may be shallowness, and this is something which Hegel certainly escapes.

It is noteworthy that the concept of the state as Hegel first elaborated it has all the clarity and simplicity of Hobbes' ' commonwealth ' without several of its defects. In his unpublished essay on the German constitution,[3] he was concerned

---

[1] See J. Plamenatz's essay in this collection and his *Man and Society* (2 vols., London, 1963).
[2] A brief list would include Hobbes' untenable materialistic philosophy, the belief that Gallilean geometry can be usefully applied to politics, the notion of the contract, the ambiguity about the basis of political obligation (force, prudence, natural law or the command of God), the thoroughly ahistorical and asocial conception of political life, and the long argument (occupying half of *The Leviathan*) that the conclusions of his political philosophy coincide with the Christian Bible.
[3] Written at the turn of the eighteenth and nineteenth centuries, but first published by G. Mollat in 1893. Translated into English by T. M. Knox and published in *Hegel's Political Writings*, with an introductory essay by Z. A. Pelczynski (Oxford, 1964).

to show that, contrary to the contention of many learned jurists and widespread illusions of ordinary Germans, the Holy Roman Empire of the German Nation was no longer a state.

A multitude of human beings can only call itself a state if it be united for the common defence of the entirety of its property. What is self-explanatory in this proposition must nonetheless be stated, namely that this union has not merely the intention of defending itself; the point is that it defends itself by actual arms, be its power and its success what they may . . . If a multitude is to form a state, then it must form a common military and public authority.[4]

What distinguishes a people which is a state from one which is part of a state or forms a collection of separate states – the latter, Hegel maintains, is virtually the position of the German nation – is its subjection to a common supreme public authority or state power (*Staatsgewalt* or *Staatsmacht* in the original). This authority is organized according to a constitution, and exercised through rules or orders possessing a universally binding character. Hegel insists in his essay that the commands of the public authority must be enforceable, must actually produce the intended results, and hence must be backed by all sorts of organized power (military, fiscal, legislative, etc.). Only then do the commands deserve the name of laws, the organization of the public authority the name of constitution, and the people united in allegiance the name of the state.

Although Hegel stresses force or power (*Macht* or *Gewalt*) as the necessary prerequisite of a state, there is nothing in the essay to substantiate the view that for Hegel force rather than law is the essence of the state (in German terminology that he subscribes to a *Machtstaat* rather than a *Rechtsstaat* conception of the state).[5] The supreme state power acts through universal laws within its territory. It is organized into separate bodies or authorities according to constitutional laws, and in contemporary Europe typically consists of a limited, constitutional monarchy and a representative body voting taxes and sharing in the monarch's legislative power.[6] What Hegel advocates (while doubting whether it can be achieved without forcible reunification) is precisely the replacement of power politics by the rule of law between the various parts of the disintegrating German Empire.

Although Hegel defines the state as merely a union of men for communal self-defence, even at this early stage of his political thinking he is quite clear that

[4] *Ibid*. pp. 153, 154.
[5] The charge was first made in H. Haller, *Hegel und der nationale Machtstaatsgedanke in Deutschland* (Leipzig-Berlin, 1921) and repeated in F. Meinecke, *Machiavellism : The Doctrine of Raison d'Etat and Its Place in Modern History* (London, 1957). It is true, however, that Hegel's views on international affairs in that early work are already marked by a thoroughgoing realism. He denies that there is any system of law or morality which effectively regulates relations between states and can achieve the Kantian ideal of ' perpetual peace '. (Cf. *Political Writings*, p. 208 and footnote.) The subject is discussed in D. P. Verene's essay, pp. 168–80.
[6] Cf. *Political Writings*, pp. 150, 160, 201, 202, 206, 217, 234, 235, 241.

such political union is not a contract of previously independent individuals motivated by fear or enlightened self-interest. It is the result of an evolution of generations of individuals forming a historical community; it is the product of their communal life, developed gradually in response to changing circumstances, and bearing the stamp of past crises.[7] A people or a nation, in the course of history, develops and perfects a machinery for common defence and for the regulation of its internal affairs. The state power is thus the creation of a nation, and the nation, through its subjection to that power and through common historical experience, is welded into a political community. The misfortune of Germany, Italy and Poland (Hegel points out), in contrast to England, France and Spain, was to fail to adapt their feudal public authorities to the needs of the modern world. As a result the first two disintegrated into separate states, and the third was partitioned by neighbouring powers. Hegel does not share Burke's optimism that a nation can find in its political tradition the necessary answers to all its pressing political problems. But he fully shares Burke's scepticism about the possibility of building a stable state on *a priori* principles, divorced from the historical experiences and traditional values of a people.[8]

What is nonetheless striking is that Hegel prefers to conceive the state in the narrowest possible way, as the legal and political framework of a community (which he generally called *Volk*, occasionally *Nation*). The specific characteristics of the community – its social structure, ethnic divisions, religious beliefs, customs and morals – while they may and do influence the constitution of the central public authority and the nature and degree of popular participation in government – fall outside his concept of the state. On the one hand there is the people, nation or community with all its manifold characteristics and ' internal social arrangements . . . made by the free action of the citizens '.[9] On the other hand there is its political organization – the supreme public authority with its specialized component bodies, and the laws and institutions emanating from it, by virtue of which the people, nation or community constitute a political union or a state. The two are conceptually separate and distinct, although socially and historically intertwined and interdependent. This way of looking at the state the Hegel of *The German Constitution*, unlike the Hegel of the *Philosophy of*

---

[7] Nowhere in the work is this better expressed than in the following passage (*ibid.* p. 146):

' The organisation of this body called the German constitution was built up in a life totally different from the life it had later and has now. The justice and power, the wisdom and courage of times past; the honour and blood, the well-being and distress of generations long dead; and the relationships and manners which have perished with them; all these are expressed in the form of that body.'

[8] See *ibid.* pp. 161–4. A detailed comparison of Hegel's and Burke's ideas on revolution and tradition will be found in J.-F. Suter's essay, pp. 52–72.

[9] *Political Writings*, p. 161. This and some other passages in the work anticipate Hegel's later concept of ' civil society '.

Right, shares with most subsequent political theorists, including contemporary ones.[10]

II

Why then did Hegel later abandon this conception of the state? Why did he find the concept of the people so thoroughly unsatisfactory that in the *Philosophy of Right* he treats it with the utmost contempt? [11] Why did he replace it with the concepts of ' civil society ' and ' the state ', and give to the latter a meaning different from that it had in the early essay? It is beyond the scope of this essay to trace in any detail the development of his thinking about the state between *The German Constitution* and the *Philosophy of Right*. This much, however, may be said. Soon after writing the draft of the essay Hegel went to teach at Jena University, and it was during the so-called Jena period of his life that he both rethought his political ideas and formulated his own philosophical system in conscious opposition to his previous philosophical masters: Kant, Fichte and Schelling.[12] Hegel became deeply dissatisfied with the individualistic conceptions of natural law and morality, and with the corresponding views about human nature, of his philosophical predecessors, who seemed to him unable to do justice to important aspects of ethical, social and political life, and he turned again to the philosophy of Plato and Aristotle and the examination of the Greek polis and its culture.[13] The insight which he gained from the analysis of ancient Greek

[10] Compare, for example, the definitions of ' state ', ' nation ', ' community ' and ' society ' in Ernest Barker, *Reflections on Government* (Oxford, 1942), pp. xv, xvi.

[11] Cf. Hegel's *Philosophy of Right*, trans. T. M. Knox (Oxford, 1942), pp. 182–3, 195–6, 198.

[12] The various stages of the development of his political thought are reflected in an essay on natural law (published as an article in 1802–3), a roughly contemporary draft of ethical theory published posthumously under the title *System der Sittlichkeit*, two courses of university lectures delivered in 1803–4 and 1805–6 and published posthumously under the title *Jenenser Realphilosophie* i and ii, and Hegel's first published book, *The Phenomenology of Mind* (1807). The development was completed in the *Science of Logic* published 1812–16 and in *The Encyclopaedia of the Philosophical Sciences* published in 1817. The *Philosophy of Right* (published in 1821) was an expanded version of the part of the *Encyclopaedia* dealing with ' Objective Spirit '. M. Riedel's and J.-F. Suter's essays deal with some aspects of Hegel's philosophical development during those years. A fuller treatment of its ethical, political and social aspects can be found in M. Riedel's collection of essays, *Studien zu Hegels Rechtsphilosophie* (Frankfurt am Main, 1969). For the most recent English study of Hegel's philosophical development, see Walter Kaufmann, *Hegel : Reinterpretation, Texts and Commentary* (Garden City, New York, 1965; London, 1966), which includes an excellent chronology and bibliography of Hegel's works. A shorter account of the development of the Hegelian system up to the *Logic* is in I. Soll, *An Introduction to Hegel's Metaphysics* (Chicago-London, 1969). Some aspects of Hegel's philosophy which bear on his political thought are explored in G. A. Kelly, *Idealism, Politics and History : Sources of Hegelian Thought* (Camb. 1969).

[13] His interest in ancient Greece was even earlier than the Jena period as is shown by his so-called early theological writings. But only in Jena did Hegel achieve a synthesis of the ancient and modern philosophical traditions, which was the hallmark of his own mature philosophy.

For the powerful impact of Greek thought on him at the time of the *Phenomenology*, see J. N. Shklar's essay; for the analysis of the final synthesis in Hegel's *Philosophy of Right*, see K.-H. Ilting's essay.

philosophy, history and literature was that men form genuine communities only when they share the same conceptions of the good life, and identify themselves wholeheartedly with the basic moral ideals of their country or culture. These shared and universally accepted conceptions and values, which are alive and operative in actions and attitudes of community members, and (so to say) incapsulated in the customs, laws and institutions which regulate their relations, Hegel calls *Sittlichkeit* (usually translated into English as ' ethical life ', ' social ethics ', ' concrete ethics ' or ' social morality ').[14] Hence a people or a nation form a genuine community when and in so far as their interrelations are animated and pervaded by *Sittlichkeit*. Greek political institutions were not something apart from the ethos of the polis, but part and parcel of its ethical life, indeed almost its most important part. A polis was an ethical community which had a political aspect, not a community on which political institutions were so to speak superimposed from outside. Laws and government were only some of the many bonds linking a people into a community. This idea of polis as an ethical community Hegel applied to the modern state during the Jena period.

Although Hegel's conception of ethical life and the model of the state as an ethical and not merely political community were derived from Greek antiquity, he is well aware of some fundamental differences between the ancient Greek and the modern European cultures.[15] Indeed he takes great care to emphasize the differences in his writings, and always insists that the modern state cannot be conceived simply in terms of the polis, whose specific ethical ideas and social and political institutions are simply inapplicable to the modern world. One obvious difference, which he noted early, is the vastly increased size of modern nation-states and their vastly more complex system of economic and social relations. These factors necessitate the existence of a permanent, specialized and highly organized system of governmental bodies – the supreme public authority or state power (*Staatsgewalt*). Unlike the amateurish and direct involvement of the citizens of ancient Greece in the public life of the polis, the government of the modern state permits popular participation only through representative institutions, and requires that a large part of its work is carried on by full-time politicians and professional administrators.[16]

But an even more important difference lay in the nature of the ethical bond between the individual and the community which is typical of the two cultures. The Greek polis absorbed its members so completely and its ethos was so sacro-

---

[14] The French translations of *Sittlichkeit*, some of which stress another aspect of the concept, are *ethique*, *morale vivante*, and *morale realisée*. The word *Sittlichkeit* comes from *Sitte* (custom, ethos).

[15] A culture, called ' realm ' or ' empire ' (*Reich*) by Hegel, was a collection of communities which, though distinct, shared the same basic values. There was thus a family resemblance between the ethical life of all communities within a culture although historical influences gave each community a characteristic configuration of ethical concepts and values.

[16] See *Political Writings*, pp. 158, 160, 202–3, 206.

sanct that it was inconceivable to them to question the fundamental principles of the polis or to assert any claims to the satisfaction of their own particular interests when they participated in politics. Moreover, the citizens' identification with the community was unconscious and spontaneous. It was brought about by customs, traditions and civic education, and reinforced by art, literature, philosophy and religion, which were all integral parts of the Greek way of life or ' the spirit of the people '.[17]

The peculiarity of modern European culture, on the other hand, largely due to Roman law and modern natural law doctrines, is that men conceive themselves not just as members of communities but also – and sometimes primarily – as bearers of private rights against the state and possessors of legitimate particular and group interests. In Hegel's view Christianity had an equally profound effect on European culture, especially after it had been developed by the Reformation and secularized by the Enlightenment. Under its influence men came to regard themselves as moral agents, acknowledging no higher authority than their own conscience or reason. Hegel calls the first tendency ' particularity ' and the second ' subjectivity '; the two together constitute the peculiarly modern and European phenomenon of individualism. While individualism had very deep roots, it was only since the French Revolution that it has taken on the form of a dominant cultural force and begun reshaping social and political reality. Hegel was convinced that the influence of the Revolution was inescapable although he recognized that there were parts of Europe where its effects were still rather slight in the early nineteenth century. Even in the three most advanced countries – France, England and Germany – some sections of the population were far more affected by the spirit of individualism than others. Long before Tocqueville and Marx, Hegel perceived that it was the bourgeoisie which formed the chief social base of individualism and through whom the traditional, community-conscious Europe of the Middle Ages had been undermined.[18]

What Hegel in the *Philosophy of Right* calls ' civil society ' is the positive creation of individualism, and he specifically calls it the achievement of the modern world.[19] It represents the growing recognition by the community that its members have legitimate rights and interests also as particular, private

[17] Hegel more than once acknowledged his debt to Montesquieu for making him see laws and political institutions as something intimately bound up with and expressive of the spiritual life of a people. Cf. *Philosophy of Right*, pp. 16, 161, 177–8.

[18] In *The German Constitution* Hegel speaks of ' the *bourgeois* sense, which cares only for an individual and not self-subsistent end and has no regard for the whole '. When the bourgeoisie became a political power through the growth of imperial cities its spirit became one of the main causes of the decline of the German Empire. Cf. *Political Writings*, pp. 190, 191.

[19] Cf. *Philosophy of Right*, § 182 Addition. In § 185 and Addition Hegel contrasts the recognition of particularity in the modern world with its denial by Plato (whose *Republic* he regards as an interpretation of Greek ethical life; *Philosophy of Right*, p. 10). In the same paragraph Hegel mentions Roman law and Christianity as the ultimate causes of individualism.

individuals and not merely as members of one of the traditional groupings of the community. It also represents the recognition that individuals have personal opinions on a wide range of issues which are entitled to respect and to free expression even when they are different from the established beliefs and values. Indeed to be acceptable to the modern man those traditional principles must take the form of a rational but subjective conviction, just as ethical life must appear to the individual not as something alien and hostile to his particular interest, but as something which is inextricably bound up with it, and on which indeed his private interest in the last resort depends. Indeed it is a moral as well as a prudential duty of the supreme public authority, in whosoever hands it is placed, to further the satisfaction of particular interests and to permit the expression of subjective opinions and wishes.[20]

In his writings after the Jena period Hegel sharply differentiates ethical life and relations from other kinds of normative principles and rules which regulate human conduct in modern society. In particular he distinguishes *Sittlichkeit* from *Recht* and *Moralität*. By *abstraktes Recht* he means the general principles of law concerning such personal rights as the right to life and property, and various personal liberties. Derived from Roman law and developed and rationalized by generations of later jurists and exponents of natural law it forms, Hegel believes, a body of abstract principles which necessarily underlies all positive legal systems of civilized countries in so far as the systems were rational.[21] By *Moralität* Hegel means the Kantian type of morality in which the value of a man's action depends on the goodness of his motive, and the conscience of the individual in the last resort determines how he should treat other individuals.[22] While the sphere of right is objective and concerned with the conformity of external conduct to the letter of the law, irrespective of motive, morality is a sphere where the personal judgement of a moral subject has primacy over the requirements of the kind of rules with which the individual is faced in his social life (conventional morality, customary law or state legislation). Hegel recognizes the validity of both kinds of normative orders in certain limited spheres, but he is convinced that by themselves they are unable to bind individuals into a cohesive and lasting community. The law-abiding citizen can legitimately contract out of civil society when the principle of reciprocity is violated or his interest unreasonably neglected or sacrificed. The moralistic individual (like an extreme type of contemporary conscientious objector) can question all of society's or the state's

---

[20] For an anticipation of this point of view in *The German Constitution*, see *Political Writings*, pp. 159–64.

[21] The Hegelian concept of *Recht* (usually translated as 'right' rather than 'law', as in the *Philosophy of Right*) is discussed in the essays of G. Heiman, K.-H. Ilting and M. Riedel.

[22] K.-H. Ilting's essay deals also with Hegel's concept of 'morality' and some of its political consequences. For a recent analysis of Hegel's ethical views and especially his critique of Kantian morality, see W. H. Walsh, *Hegelian Ethics* (London-New York, 1969).

rules.[23] The ethical man, the member of a true community, can and will do neither since he recognizes no other values than those of his community and culture which have passed the test of rational scrutiny. Only ethical as opposed to juristic and moralistic ties are capable of forming the basis of a true community. Neither a society of reasonable men restricting their selfish actions for the sake of peaceful coexistence, nor a society of moral agents guided by their individual consciences, but only a society of men sharing in, and guided by, a common ethical life can therefore properly speaking be considered a community. Hegel in fact believes that ethical life, although not always in its fully conscious form, is the actual, operative mode of human conduct, and that abstract right and morality are merely one-sided abstractions into which the critical philosophy of the Enlightenment has dissolved the concrete social ethics.

Corresponding to the three types of normative order Hegel distinguishes three types of freedom. In fact the problem of freedom was in the forefront of his mind when he was formulating his ethical, social and political theory. In the sphere of right a man is free when he can do what he wants provided he respects the same right in other men, that is, acts within the limits of reciprocity. In the sphere of morality freedom consists in the autonomy of the individual conscience *vis-à-vis* all the external rules and standards which demand conformity. The highest type of freedom – freedom in the ethical sphere – is the guidance of one's actions by the living, actual principles of one's community, clearly understood and deliberately accepted, and in secure confidence that other community members will act in the same way.[24]

III

Hegel's political and social concepts are obscure and difficult to grasp because they are immensely complex. This complexity is the result of his conception of the true philosophical method, which ought to conceptualize various forms of human experience and relate them to each other as necessarily connected. A concept (*Begriff*) in Hegel's own, special sense is necessarily complex because it is a dialectical synthesis of contrary forms of experience.[25] His concept of the state, therefore, as we find it in its mature form in the *Philosophy of Right*, con-

---

23 A striking example of such extreme non-conformity, produced by a reaction against Hegel's own ideas, is discussed in E. Fleischmann's essay on Stirner, Marx and Hegel.

24 J. Plamenatz in his essay explores fully the Hegelian concept of freedom and its relation to the social and historical context of ethical action. The connection between freedom and rational law in Hegel's thought it discussed by M. Riedel.

25 For a brief exposition of the nature of Hegel's philosophical concepts, see the essays of D. P. Verene, pp. 173–5 and R. N. Berki, pp. 200–1. A brief explanation of Hegel's philosophical methodology is to be found in the translator's foreword to T. M. Knox's translation of the *Philosophy of Right*. A more detailed recent account is J. N. Findlay, *Hegel : A Re-examination* (London, 1958). Unfortunately, Findley's views on Hegel's political philosophy are remarkably superficial and show a lack of proper appreciation of Hegel's passionate interest in, and wide-ranging knowledge of, man's political experience.

tains, in a highly condensed way, diverse experiences, observations, intellectual influences and so on, some of which have been already outlined. It is this mature and highly complex concept of the state which I now wish to analyse and then use to illuminate certain features of Hegel's political theory. The subject will be approached by considering two concepts which Hegel explicitly distinguishes, and then subdividing the second further into two distinct concepts, which Hegel distinguishes only incidentally and often not at all.

In the *Philosophy of Right* Hegel makes a basic distinction between ' civil society '[26] and ' the state '. The former is also a kind of state or rather an aspect of the state; in Hegel's own words, it ' may be prima facie regarded as the external state, the state based on need, the state as the Understanding envisages it '.[27] Civil society is the modern state conceived as a system of public authorities and autonomous bodies existing to further the private interests of individuals or their more or less organized groups, to protect their legal rights of person, property, contract, and so on, and to enforce their mutual obligations. But it is also a network of spontaneous, private relations established within the framework of the law by individuals pursuing their particular ends (' the system of needs '), which Hegel considers to be an essential aspect of ' civil society '.

To say that ' civil society ' is ' the state as the Understanding envisages it ' is a Hegelian way of saying that there is another, more adequate mode of conceiving the state. The complex of activities, attitudes, rules and institutions which make up ' civil society ' is only one aspect of political and social life ' abstracted ' from a wider, richer or more ' concrete ' system by a process of formal, abstract thinking which Hegel calls the understanding.[28] The ' abstract ' character of ' civil society ' can be appreciated without a thorough grasp of Hegel's terminology. The laws guaranteeing individual rights to life, liberty and property, which are the normative basis of ' civil society ', presuppose a person or body of persons who enact them − a legislator or a legislative assembly. The regulatory and welfare functions of the public authority active in ' civil society ' presuppose a superior public authority which determines the scope of these functions, lays down structures and procedures, appoints and supervises their personnel, and so on. The associations of individuals formed in ' civil society ' (' corporations ' and ' estates ') likewise presuppose at least the recognition of their autonomy or privileges by some higher body. Finally there are certain vital political activities, such as foreign relations, defence and the maintenance of colonies, which ' civil

[26] The term ' civil society ' had been used by writers such as Locke, Hume, Smith and Ferguson, as well as by some of their contemporaries in France, whom Hegel had read. Ultimately it is traceable to Aristotle's *koinonia politike* and Cicero's *societas civilis*. See ' Der Begriff der " Bürgerlichen Gesellschaft " und das Problem seines geschichtlichen Ursprungs ' in Riedel, *Studien zu Hegels Rechtsphilosophie*.

[27] *Philosophy of Right*, § 183.

[28] See *ibid.* translator's foreword, pp. vii, viii, x, xi, for the technical difference between ' understanding ' and ' reason ' in Hegel's philosophy.

society ' is not organized to perform, and which therefore fall outside its scope. All those activities and institutions which transcend ' civil society ' come within the scope of ' the state ' or rather (as Hegel puts it in § 267 of the *Philosophy of Right*) within ' the strictly political state and its constitution '.

The chief organs of this ' political state ' are the ' crown ' (hereditary monarchy), a collective executive (cabinet) appointed by and responsible to the monarch, and a representative body (' the Assembly of Estates ') which shares the monarch's legislative, fiscal and supervisory powers. Together they form the supreme public authority (*Staatsgewalt*) which Hegel had already distinguished in his essay on the constitution of the German Empire. But an essential part of the ' political state ' is also public opinion, that is, the ensemble of views and beliefs about the state, its organization, functioning, policies, and so on, which are held and expressed by the subjects of the public authority. Political opinion represents what Hegel calls the ' moment of subjectivity ' in the ' political state ', and is guaranteed by laws permitting free speech, freedom of the press and publishing, and freedom of assembly for purposes of political discussion.[29]

In two respects Hegel's distinction between ' civil society ' and the ' political state ' is open to criticism. It involves splitting up the public authority, which forms a highly integrated system of bodies and individuals acting in an official capacity, into two separate spheres: the supreme public authority of the ' political state ', and the law courts and the ' police ' (subordinate public authorities) of ' civil society '. It could have been possible, indeed it would be more natural, to view the two sets of authorities as just two parts of one and the same system of public authority, just as their activities could be viewed as phases or stages of the same governmental process. (Thus, for example, laws enacted by the monarch and the Estates in the ' political state ' are enforced by law courts and various administrative authorities, which are organs of ' civil society '.) Hegel in fact admits that in practice the two sets of institutions are ' organically connected ', that is, interacting and interdependent. But ' organism ' implies also differentiation or ' articulation ', and it is because the purposes which they serve seem so different to him that the two kinds of authorities, and the two areas of activity, are so sharply distinguished by Hegel. Civil authorities serve primarily individual or group purposes; political authorities primarily those of the people as a whole. This difference determines differences not just on the institutional level, but also differences in outlook, qualifications, the character of rights and duties, their universality, and so on, of the men who act in both spheres. The membership of 'civil society ' is equally open to all sane adults; that of the ' political state ' (as Hegel conceives it) selective and hierarchical. A property owner is free to dispose of his property as he thinks fit, at least within wide limits; the law allows him to be silly or capricious in his action. Those who participate in the political process

29 *Ibid.* §§ 315–20 and Additions.

are on the contrary expected to show a sense of responsibility and a devotion to public good.

The other questionable feature of Hegel's distinction is that it is not just a distinction between two kinds of public authorities and relations regulated by law. ' Civil society ' and ' political state ' are areas of activity which include the private actions and subjective attitudes of their respective members, as well as objective laws and institutions. They are thus both manifestations of ethical life, and although Hegel tries to contrast the two spheres sharply, the distinction becomes rather blurred in the end. For instance, Hegel speaks of ' civil society ' as the antithesis of ethical life; but at other times he admits that it produces and encourages at least some ethical attitudes.[30] Similarly the ' political state ' is not an exclusive preserve of ethical attitudes since, as we have seen, public opinion is essentially subjective and capricious. At least one class of ' civil society ', the ' universal estate ' of civil servants, finds in public service the satisfaction of their particular needs and interests in the sense that they derive their income and social prestige from public service. Hence in the non-institutional respect there is also no clear-cut separation of the two spheres.

Hegel stresses heavily one other difference between the ' political state ' and ' civil society ', but again fails to draw a logically tight distinction. Both are systems or orders of activity which produce, on the one hand, specific results (for example, security of property or national independence), and on the other, a certain kind of unity or cohesion or (in the language of modern sociology) social integration. As Hegel points out the unity of ' civil society ' is of a rather low kind because of the individualism dominant in it. ' Individuals in their capacity of burghers in this " civil state " are private persons whose end is their own interest.'[31] Moreover, such unity as ' civil society ' possesses comes about largely unconsciously and automatically. Men are linked together by the production and exchange of goods and services, by taking part in the social process of the division of labour. Although they aim directly at their own interest, they indirectly promote the interest of other members of ' civil society '. Hegel accepts the ' invisible hand ' theory of Adam Smith only partially because he sees that public authorities must intervene into the operation of the market and into social life in general, when automatic processes fail to produce the expected results. Unlike civil (or social) order, political order is brought about largely consciously and deliberately, by rules and institutions adopted for this end, manipulated by men whose interest and duty lie in promoting national unity and cohesion.[32]

---

[30] Cf. *Philosophy of Right*, § 184: ' it is the system of ethical order, split into its extremes and lost ' and in which ' particularity . . . [has] the right to develop and launch forth in all directions '. Yet in § 254 Hegel calls the corporation ' the second ethical root of the state ', and compares its influence to that of the first root, the family. [31] *Ibid*. § 187.

[32] ' The state knows . . . what it wills and knows it in its universality. Hence it works and acts by reference to consciously adopted ends, known principles and laws which are not merely implicit but are actually present to consciousness; and further it acts with precise knowledge of existing

The effect of these rules and institutions, Hegel adds, is reinforced by spontaneous patriotism or ' political sentiment ' (*politische Gesinnung*), which may vary from mere ' trust ' to ' educated insight '. These feelings, ideas and attitudes make the ordinary citizens, and especially those with a significant share of ' state power ', identify their private interest with the public good.[33] In both spheres, therefore, integration is promoted by a mixture of conscious and deliberate actions of the public authorities, and of spontaneous feelings and activities of private individuals, although the proportion of both elements is different in each sphere.

It is in the same § 267 of the *Philosophy of Right*, in which Hegel distinguishes the subjective nature of patriotism and the ' objective world ' of laws and institutions as two complementary aspects of the state, that he uses the expression ' the strictly political state and its constitution '. The original German phrase ' *der politische Staat* ' is also used by Hegel in §§ 273 and 276 of the book, but is rendered as ' the state as a political entity ' in Knox's translation. The seemingly odd phrase ' political state ' is of the utmost importance in understanding the Hegelian conception of the state. It suggests that apart from ' civil society ' (' the state as the Understanding envisages it ') and ' the strictly political state ' (which, though more adequate, is still an abstract concept) Hegel has yet another, even more complex concept of the state, ' state ' *sans phrase*, ' state ' without any qualification, ' state ' properly so called. It is this state which Hegel calls ' the actuality of the ethical Idea '[34] or ' the actuality of concrete freedom ', and on which he heaps all the seemingly exaggerated superlatives for which the *Philosophy of Right* is notorious. The state in this sense means the whole population of an independent, politically and ' civilly ' organized country in so far as it is permeated by ' ethical life ' and forms an ' ethical order ' or ' ethical community '. Within this wide (' universal ') community to which all inhabitants *qua* ethical beings belong, there are what Hegel calls in § 145 of the *Philosophy of Right* separate ' moments ', aspects or spheres of ' ethical life '. These ' moments are the ethical powers which regulate the life of individuals '; they are the family, ' civil society ' and the state by which Hegel presumably means the state in the strictly political sense (' political state '). Through the framework of rules and authorities of the ' political state ' the nation-wide ethical community acquires a stable, structured political form, an orderly system acting on the historical world within and outside its borders, and an individuality *vis-à-vis* other national communities. In § 267 Hegel calls ' the strictly political state and its constitution ' ' the organism of the state '. But this organism or organization [35]

conditions and circumstances, inasmuch as its actions have a bearing on these.' *Ibid.* § 270. But this can also be said of the activities of law courts and the ' police '.

33 *Ibid.* §§ 267–8 and Additions.

34 In § 257 and 260 of the *Philosophy of Right* respectively.

35 Hegel largely equates the two. *See* Knox's note 9 to § 267, *ibid.* p. 364, where Knox also stresses the distinction just made and defines ' state proper ' as ' the totality of human life so far as it is the life of moral beings united in a community by tradition, religion, moral convictions, etc.'

must not be confused with the ' state ' as such; a part or aspect of a whole, however vital, is still just a part. Hegel has been so frequently misunderstood because he fails to make a clear and explicit distinction between ' the state ' in the comprehensive sense and ' the strictly political state ', and because he uses the single term ' state ' both when he has only the political aspect in mind, and when he thinks of the political together with the ethical aspect. While it is true, as Knox writes,[36] that ' failure to realise this [distinction] has been responsible for numerous misrepresentations of Hegel's position and his attitude to " the state " ', surely a large part of the blame must rest on the shoulders of Hegel himself.

IV

It is possible to express the various ideas that make up Hegel's conception of the state in the following way. Men form communities of various kinds in which they find – or rather achieve by more or less conscious endeavour – the satisfaction of their physical needs and the needs of their spiritual nature, that is, their nature as creatures capable of thinking and willing. Among these communities, one in particular, the state, is of paramount importance to them. Looked at in one way a state is merely a certain population settled within a definite territory and subject to the rules and commands of men in authority, who themselves acknowledge no superior authority within or outside the borders of the state. Thus one essential bond between members of the state is their common subjection to a supreme and independent public authority. This authority generally acts through statutes, but sometimes through prerogative orders which, like statutes, have universal legal validity within the confines of the state. It may also possess various subordinate authorities for carrying out its orders or applying its laws in various special – local or functional – spheres. In other words, legal rules and commands enforced by authorities are one way in which the population of the state is integrated into a community.

But though this is a very important bond, it is not the only one. Members of the state establish and maintain by their own free activity a nexus of relations, which though regulated by law, is in no way a direct product of the legal order. These relations are the result of individual decisions motivated by self-interest or at least some private conception of what is good for men. They may be once-for-all exchanges or repeated transactions or more or less permanent institutions such as marriage or the corporation.[37] In contrast to the first or political bond Hegel would call this bond ' civil ', but we would prefer to call it social.

There is finally a third kind of bond, the ethical one. In so far as the members of the state share the same concepts, principles or ideals of the good life, which

---

[36] In his note to § 267 quoted above.
[37] The social relations also give rise to classes, but Hegel is not concerned with them unless they have acquired an official status in the eyes of the public authority, in which case they become estates '.

have been handed down from generation to generation (though not necessarily in an unchanged way), they form a community in a third sense, an ethical community.[38] In addition to ethical concepts there are other ' spiritual ' factors such as common language, culture, religion or national consciousness, which may bind the members of the state when all of them share them, but also divide them when they do not. And these same forces may bring all or some members of different states together into a wider, more diffuse kind of community. But whatever their effect Hegel does not attach as much importance to them as to the other types of integration. This ought perhaps to be qualified in the case of religion for Hegel sees the Christian religion as closely connected with ethical life, strengthening it when it is protestant and militating against it when it is Roman catholic.

The three kinds of communal bond Hegel takes into account, although conceptually distinct, do not operate independently of each other. He believes that they are interdependent and organically connected. Laws further the interests of society members and they express ethical convictions of community members. The bonds as they exist in practice can also work against each other, and produce social disharmony, political instability, as well as confusion and uncertainty in individual minds. This state of affairs is something of which men as rational beings strongly disapprove and seek to avoid. They try to adjust ethical attitudes, social relations, and legal and political institutions in such a way that the maximum of harmony is achieved in the national community. But the only form of integration which is subject to deliberate and direct manipulation is the legal or political order. It is laws and the authorities which issue and enforce them which are under the direct control of men, who of course may vary from a small minority to the majority of the population according to the character of the public authority. ' Civil ' activities of state members, although regulated by law, depend in the last resort on their own subjective opinions and desires, and cannot be directly influenced. The ethical order changes slowly and its change depends on wider cultural developments, which proceed according to their own laws of development; in the short run it has to be taken for granted and may only be made more explicit and effective through deliberate action. The political order is thus the most controllable form of social integration; the community which possesses a supreme public authority with all its necessary powers will be in a better position to maintain the harmony and the stability of its communal life, and to rationalize ethical and social relations, than a community which is either wider or narrower than the state, and hence deprived of such advantages. It is

---

38 Within this state-wide community there are many narrower ones like families, corporations and churches. There may also be wider and looser ethical ' families ' consisting of members of independent countries who belong to the same culture or civilization and accept similar ethical values. Also the social and economic relations typical of ' civil society ' sometimes transcend state boundaries and connect members of different states into a loosely textured network of relations. Hegel ignores this aspect, which has become increasingly important since his time.

therefore reasonable for men to want to form politically organized communities, to accept the sacrifices and restrictions which membership of the state involves, and to strive to the utmost to improve its organization and to preserve its independence and integrity. This, I believe, is the gist of the Hegelian conception of the state. It is not expressed in the way Hegel expresses it in his major political work, but it remains faithful to the spirit of his political theory and it enables us to see more clearly some of the things which are obscured by Hegel's use of two rather than three basic concepts.

V

In § 260 of the *Philosophy of Right* Hegel states his view that the modern state is a synthesis of two opposing tendencies within modern society and concludes as follows:

The modern state has prodigious strength and depth because it allows the principle of subjectivity to progress to its culmination in the extreme of self-subsistent personal particularity, and yet at the same time brings it back to the substantive unity and so maintains this unity in the principle of subjectivity itself.

In this passage Hegel makes a point that is both original and important. The modern state as an ethical, civil and political community draws strength from two separate and incompatible sources. One is the universal and objective ethical life (an ' ethical substance ') which faces the individual as something given and inescapable, the world of historically evolved values and ideals into which he is incorporated whether he wants it or not through the operation of ethical institutions such as the family, corporations, estates, and so on. In so far as the supreme authorities of the ' political state ' express this ethical life in their rules and activities, and are seen as its preservers and defenders, they enjoy far more support than they would if, for instance, they were thought to be merely the product of a natural lust for power by some men over others or just an instrument of domination over the mass of the people by some privileged and powerful minority. The second source of strength are the twin tendencies of ' subjectivity ' and ' particularity ', which nowadays we would describe simply as individualism. This is the tendency of men in modern times to look at all social values, rules and institutions as derived from the agreement of individuals, and existing for the sake of purely individual self-satisfaction and self-assertion. These two separate and antithetical tendencies are balanced, harmonized and integrated into a social synthesis by and within the ' political state '. Thus the Hegelian conception of the state combines the liberal conception of the state as the servant of individuals with the very different conception of the state as the guardian of the community. The ' ethical community ' and ' civil society ' may be conceived as dialectical opposites which are reconciled by the institutions, laws and actions of the state power – the supreme public authority of the ' political state '.[39]

[39] Cf. K.-H. Ilting's essay for a similar conclusion reached by a somewhat different route.

The Hegelian conception of the state

For cultural and historical reasons which have already been mentioned modern man finds repugnant the total and blind surrender to the community which in Hegel's view was typical of earlier ages and civilizations. Nor does modern man accept values, however ancient and hallowed by tradition, without question. His conscience refuses to abdicate moral judgement, and his ego rejects the idea of one-sided self-sacrifice. Man's relation to the ' ethical whole ' is now or rather tends increasingly to become self-conscious, it is mediated by his reason and will. Hence a compromise – or in Hegel's language a dialectical solution – is reached. Through the organs of ' civil society ' the state recognizes and promotes private interests, but in the process individuals learn to recognize public interests as their own basic interests and acquire the will to promote ' the universal ' even when it negates ' the particular '. The process of political education (*Bildung*) begins in ' civil society ' and continues in the ' political state '. Its organs and the methods of their operation – especially the Assembly of Estates, and its elections, publicity of debates, freedom of the press and public opinion, rationalization (that is, codification) of laws, and so on – offer citizens the chance of gaining insight into the ethical basis of policies and legislation and thus of voluntary submission to what the citizens now perceive as right and necessary. The result will be a widespread conviction of their righteousness and necessity, and a willing acceptance of sacrifices or restrictions. But it is also possible that the opposite will result. The people, their representatives, and the journalists, pamphleteers, writers and so on, who express and articulate public opinion, might disapprove of some measures, reject them as unjustified and actually resist them in practice. In an extreme case (as happened in France in 1789) the whole fabric of society and government might be condemned and overthrown.

The words ' strength and depth ' in the passage from the *Philosophy of Right* quoted above give us a clue to a major, perhaps the fundamental, political concern of Hegel. Living in an age in which states and empires rose and fell, some disintegrated while others were welded successfully together, and when some governments embarked on ' tremendous political experiments '[40] while others stubbornly clung to traditional institutions, Hegel sought to work out a political theory which would reveal the secret of the strength and stability of the modern state. The particular structure of the modern state – ' the strictly political state and its constitution ' mentioned in § 267 of the *Philosophy of Right* – must be understood as Hegel's attempt to do justice to the two tendencies inherent in modern society: the mainly integrating one of shared ethical life, and the mainly disintegrating one of ' subjectivity ' and ' particularity '.[41] It is worth while

[40] *Political Writings*, p. 159.

[41] It would be misleading and oversimplified to characterize the two tendencies in too sweeping a manner. Ethical life integrates in so far as men are conscious of shared ideals and assent to them. But it may also divide and separate when the community (like the France of the *ancien régime* analysed in Tocqueville's masterpiece) is ridden with ancient laws, traditional privileges, out-of-date social hierarchies and so on, which are felt to have lost their validity. The individualism

17

looking briefly at some of the features of the constitutional structure of the 'political state' from this point of view, and emphasizing those of its elements which are shaped by the one or the other tendency.

VI

There are, Hegel maintains, three dangers which can threaten the 'ethical community' and which it is the function of the supreme public authority – the organized state power – to repel. The first is its disintegration into a number of separate and independent communities as happened in the case of the Holy Roman Empire of the German Nation. It collapsed and dissolved because the bulk of politically conscious Germans had ceased in practice to regard themselves as belonging to one German nation, one German community, and the supreme public authority, despite an ancient and elaborate constitutional framework, was powerless to prevent it. Hegel believed that the process had become irreversible, but he nevertheless sketched out a constitutional plan for the empire consisting of an effective supreme public authority combined with a federal structure, which would allow the provinces to enjoy far-reaching autonomy in matters not of universal concern.[42] The preservation of the 'ethical community' within the framework of one state, therefore, does not in the least exclude the existence of particular communities with far-reaching autonomy, provided they do not have the power to press their particular interests and viewpoints to the point of endangering the political unity of the wider community.

The second danger is the loss of political independence, and therefore of the ethical individuality of a nation. As a collection of private individuals the people may have nothing to lose if their country is conquered and forcibly annexed by another state, provided their civil liberties are respected and continue to be protected by the new central government. But its basic ethical values, moulded and developed by diverse historical influences peculiar to itself, might well be imperilled by incorporation into another ethical community. This, however, need not necessarily happen. If the conquering country belongs to the same culture and shares broadly similar ethical values, and if it also provides a large measure of autonomy for the newly acquired territory, it is difficult to see why the loss of independence must be ethically disastrous.

It is in the context of independence that Hegel propounds his view that wars are a test of the ethical soundness of a people. The supreme public authority presumably might be able to defend the country in wars of some kind or in the

---

underlying 'civil society', on the other hand, turns into its dialectical opposite by bringing about a network of relations, a system of interdependence, created by men who have to cooperate to satisfy their needs. This network forces them to pursue trades and professions for which there is a social demand; it transforms particular individuals into actors of social roles, and educates them to recognize that they are members of society and not merely individuals.

[42] *Political Writings*, pp. 238–42.

early stages of any war even when the nation was apathetic or unpatriotic, but Hegel doubts whether in the long run, and in conditions of international anarchy, a state can survive as an independent political entity unless it has the inner strength which comes from being an ethical community as well.[43]

Hegel's concern with the strength of the state power as a guardian of national independence explains the peculiar status of the military in his political theory. Not only are the armed forces placed under the command of the monarch and insulated from the political influence of particular interests entrenched in the representative body. Military service itself is treated by Hegel as a particularly lofty occupation, loftier even than that of the ' universal class ' of professional civil servants. For in wartime, while ordinary citizens normally have to forego only some of their liberty and property, the military are called upon to risk and sacrifice life itself.[44] By doing so voluntarily and showing courage in the face of death they do more than set an example of patriotism to their fellow-citizens. They confirm in deeds (' actualize ') the superiority of the ethical values of their community over the private and mainly material concerns of its members.[45]

The third danger to the ethical community is that the objective side of ethical life stagnates and ossifies in customs, laws and institutions, which get out of tune with new ethical demands and ideals. The function of the supreme public authority is to adjust the old external structure to the new subjective attitudes. If they fail to do so, as the *ancien régime* did in France, the new ideals will become formulated by ideologues and demagogues without practical political knowledge, and will tend to assume the form of abstract, *a priori* ideas. The more they are opposed by the established public authority, the more they will tend to develop into the criticism or rejection of the whole political and social *status quo*, together with the traditional ethical life embodied in old customs, laws and institutions.[46] This aspect of the interaction between the ethical community and the system of political power deserves special attention.

[43] In his early years Hegel had doubts about the viability of Prussia as a state, and viewed it as an artificial creation of a monarch of genius, and devoid of an ethical basis. (Cf. *ibid*. pp. 163, 164.) His view was at first confirmed by the shattering defeat of the Prussians at Jena by Napoleon, backed by the ethically regenerated French people. The thoroughgoing reforms introduced in Prussia by the Stein ministry after the defeat, and the subsequent military recovery of Prussia, made Hegel change his mind after 1815. Hegel explained the collapse of the Napoleonic system in France and other Latin countries by the incompatibility of the rational principles of the French Revolution with catholicism; in his view political and ethical emancipation presupposed religious emancipation. (See *Lectures on the Philosophy of History*, trans. J. Sibree (New York, 1944), pp. 452–3.) For Hegel's protestant prejudice in his philosophy of history, see the essay by W. H. Walsh.   [44] Cf. *Philosophy of Right*, Addition to § 327.

[45] Hegel's views on war and the military are discussed at length in D. P. Verene's essay.

[46] Cf. Hegel's fragment on Wurtemberg where the cleavage between the established, ' positive ' constitution and popular attitudes is particularly well expressed (*Political Writings*, pp. 242–5). Cf. further his comments on France and England, *ibid*. pp. 325, 328–30; on the French 1789 and 1830 revolutions in *Philosophy of History*, pp. 446 ff., 449–52; and on the former in *Philosophy of Right*, p. 157.

VII

It will be remembered that ethical life in Hegel's conception is a complex of concepts, rules and principles which, as it were, pervade the minds of community members. Those who share a common ethical life are related to each other rather like members of a linguistic community who have been born into it, and taught to use its language in order to communicate with each other. Ethical life, like language, is not the product or property of single individuals, but of the community as a whole. Like language, ethical life may develop and be transmitted in an almost unconscious way, as something customary, traditional or ' positive ' (to use Hegel's favourite expression). Nevertheless it has a peculiar logic and structure of which men, as rational beings, sooner or later become conscious. In the process of becoming conscious of the concepts, rules or principles of their ethical community, men also become aware of contradictions, incongruities and ambiguities within the structure, and since reason abhors contradiction and obscurity they strive to remove them, to refine or formulate ideas, and to give unity and clarity to the whole. This is the peculiar task of intellectuals: journalists and pamphleteers, authors of historical, scientific and literary works, and above all philosophers, whose proper vocation is to express the ethical and other ideas of their age and culture in a systematic and intellectually satisfying way.[47] It is most important that their activities should influence and shape public opinion at large and for this reason Hegel advocates freedom of speech and publication.[48] But the impact of intellectuals is naturally greatest and most direct on the educated sections of the community, which include among them the men who exercise authority in the ' political state ' – the monarch, ministers, civil servants and Estates deputies.

The organization of the state power and the functioning of public authorities plays a crucial role in the process of communication, clarification and systematization of ethical life. Bills prepared by the executive and the civil service, and submitted to the legislature for approval, frequently raise ethical issues; debates in representative institutions help to make them explicit and thus perform important educative functions. Public debates of government policies may also give rise to new ethical claims, and they generally involve the justification (or condemnation) of measures in terms of generally accepted values. Hence the Estates Assembly is a vital part of the modern state power since ' it is through " the Estates " that the state enters the subjective consciousness of the people; and . . . the people begins to participate in the state '.[49] By becoming more fully

---

[47] Hegal clearly believes that his *Philosophy of Right* is a significant theoretical contribution to the task: see the preface. But he nowhere states that a perfect harmony of ethical principles has been achieved in practice anywhere or that it will be achieved anywhere in the future. As rational beings men can, and indeed must, strive for unity of their ethical life; whether they succeed or how far they succeed only history can show *ex post facto*.

[48] Cf. *ibid*. §§ 314–20 and Additions.

[49] *Ibid*. Addition to § 301. See also Addition to § 315.

aware of the ethical principles of their community men become more conscious and involved members of it.

The organs of the ' political state ' perform a perhaps even more important function with regard to what Hegel calls the ' objective side of ethical life ', that is, laws and institutions. Ethical life is never wholly static. It changes and develops as circumstances change; traditional values become extended to new situations or categories of people; new ethical principles become appreciated and gradually accepted. Some of the established customs, laws and institutions are now seen as untenable and requiring reform. But they seldom, if ever, just wither away to make room for new ones, which are more in accord with the changed demands of ethical life. Their resistance to reform is all the greater when they are buttressed by vested interests of privileged classes, religious bigotry, national pride in ancient institutions (' the wisdom of forefathers ') or simply prejudices of an ignorant, uneducated multitude, sometimes economically or socially dominated by the privileged minorities. In such circumstances the resort to state power is the only satisfactory way to get rid of the ballast of the past, and to give actuality to new ethical concepts or principles. This can be done either by the exercise of royal prerogative, say, issuing a decree abolishing serfdom or authorizing a new civil or criminal code, or by the enactment of the measure by a representative body acting in the name of the people.[50] By bringing laws and institutions into line with concepts and attitudes the public authority plays a crucial role in making the ethical life of the community more coherent and systematic, and hence more rational.

It is, then, in Hegel's view, a part of man's rational nature, at least at some stage of mankind's development, to strive to grasp ethical principles theoretically, to be guided by them rather than simply by tradition or fiats of political authorities, and to make external circumstances correspond to those principles. Hegel believes that after the outbreak of the French Revolution European countries entered a new stage of development in their laws and institutions. Instead of the occasional intervention of the public authority to remove some glaring injustice or abuse, the continental states led by France embarked on a policy of transforming their constitutional and legal structure into intelligible and internally consistent systems of rules derived from fundamental principles. Although it was the French Estates General which initiated the change by its declaration of the rights of man and citizen and the adoption of a new constitution, the lead in France and elsewhere soon passed into the hands of the executive, which was dependent on more or less authoritarian monarchs. In 1831 Hegel

---

[50] The second alternative would seem preferable since it was nearer the ideal of a conscious and deliberate act of the ethical community as a whole. But as Professor Ilting points out in his essay, while the logic of Hegel's conception of the ethical community, and the ancient Greek source from which he derived it, would seem to lead to that conclusion, Hegel argues instead that in this, as in various other public matters, the community acts through the monarch as the apex of the constitutional structure of the ' political state '.

attributed the backwardness of Britain in respect of constitutional and legal reform primarily to the weakness of the monarchical element *vis-à-vis* Parliament, in which a privileged landed class was strongly entrenched. A secondary factor was the lack of a class of professional administrators marked by ' theoretical study, scientific education, practice and experience in affairs '.[51] Hegel regards a professional civil service as an absolutely necessary institution of the modern state. Only where a class of public administrators exists, does the community possess a body of its most educated members who are specially trained and maintained at public expense to serve the community as their primary social function. Hegel stresses that ' knowledge and proof of ability ', are ' the sole condition of appointment ' and ' [guarantee] to every citizen the chance of joining the class of civil servants '.[52] The higher educational background of the civil servants enables them to grasp the fundamental principles of ethical life which they combine with practical experience of legislative and administrative requirements. They are thus well equipped for the task of constant re-examination and revision of laws and institutions in the post-revolutionary age.

VIII

As has already been mentioned, the ' ethical life ' affects not only the ' political state ' but also ' civil society '. It does so at first without men's knowledge and consent, by forcing them, on penalty of legal and moral sanctions, to play social roles prescribed by the system of needs and their satisfaction. In the process they learn the value of co-operation and recognize their mutual interdependence. This process of education is also carried on by other means. The publicity of judicial proceedings and the jury system enable members of ' civil society ', including those who are found guilty of crimes and punished, to uphold the majesty of law and of the ethical life of which it is an expression.[53] In the agricultural estate individuals learn to submit to a higher (although merely natural) necessity, while as administrators, local officials or officers of corporations they acquire ' political consciousness '.[54] As ordinary members of corporations men learn the concept of a limited common good, and of the need to make sacrifices on its behalf.[55] And yet Hegel believes that all those influences are insufficient and have to be supplemented by the deliberate intervention of the public authority

---

[51] *Political Writings*, p. 310. See also *ibid*. pp. 300, 330. Hegel has in mind Napoleon's reforms and German practice.

[52] *Philosophy of Right*, § 291. Cf. also *ibid*. § 205 and Addition to § 297 where Hegel admits that in practice the bulk of the civil service will be recruited from the middle class.

[53] For an analysis of Hegel's theory of punishment, see the essay by D. E. Cooper.

[54] For a narrow definition of ' political consciousness ', see *Political Writings*, p. 257. A rather wider conception is put forward in *Philosophy of Right*, § 268.

[55] The ethical influence of the corporation membership is dealt with at length in G. Heiman's essay, pp. 124–9.

to solve problems which ' civil society ' is incapable of solving or which it tries to solve by methods that contradict the principles of ethical life.[56]

The task of keeping ' civil society ' within its proper bounds as one ' moment ' of the ethical whole thus ultimately devolves on the political organization of the ' ethical community '. This organization has to be responsive to the legitimate claims of ' particularity ' and ' subjectivity ', yet independent and strong enough to resist their excessive pressure and escape the danger of being dominated by them. At first Hegel was chiefly pre-occupied with the strength of particular interests as they had developed over the ages and had acquired a host of traditional, outdated privileges.[57] While he remained aware of this to the end of his life, Hegel seems to have become increasingly sensitive to a different danger that ' civil society ' entails. He views its development in the contemporary European countries as a dynamic historical process which not only transforms legal relations of a traditional, sometimes feudal, kind in the social and economic sphere (which he wholeheartedly welcomes), but which also so to speak invades the political sphere and affects men's political relations. This is dangerous because if the individualistic point of view characteristic of ' civil society ' gains too strong a foothold in the ' political state ', the state power may cease functioning as the guardian of the community, ethical life may become subordinated to the free play of particular interests and subjective opinions of individual citizens, and the state-wide ' ethical community ' may eventually dissolve into the much looser kind typical of ' civil society '.

Hegel's fears can be illustrated by a passage in his *Proceedings of the Estates Assembly in Wurtemberg 1815–1816* (published in 1817). Virtually the only thing which he criticizes in the constitutional charter submitted by the king to the Estates for approval is the voting qualifications for election to the Wurtemberg Diet, which consisted simply of a minimum age and income qualifications.

The most striking thing about it is that, according to such dry, abstract provisions as both of those cited, the electors appear otherwise in no bond or connection with the civil order and the organisation of the state as a whole. The citizens come on the stage as isolated atoms, and the electoral assemblies as unordered inorganic aggregates; the people as a whole is dissolved into a heap. *This is a form in which the community should never have appeared at all in undertaking any enterprise; it is a form most unworthy of the community and most in contradiction with its concept of a spiritual order.* Age and property are qualities affecting only the individual himself, not characteristics constituting his worth in the civil order . . . Atomistic principles of that sort spell, in science as in politics, death to every rational concept, organisation and life.[58]

---

[56] Cf. especially the section on ' Police ' in *Philosophy of Right*, §§ 231–48; also *Political Writings*, pp. 160–1, 261–3, and ' The English Reform Bill ', *ibid. passim*.

[57] This aspect is pronounced in the minor political works. Cf. passages in *Political Writings* mentioned in the previous note.

[58] *Ibid.* pp. 262–3 (my italics).

Hegel thus saw post-Napeolonic France as the hotbed of individualism, which in this respect had spread to his native country. By the time the July 1830 French Revolution occurred, and another one seemed to threaten in Britain over the parliamentary reform bill, Hegel became convinced that ' the French abstractions' and ' atomistic principles' had become a militant bourgeois ideology, which undermined the stability and strength of the state power, and threatened the cohesion of the community itself. The overcoming of the influence of that ideology in theory and practice seemed to him the chief historical problem of his own time and the future.[59]

In the light of these quotations it is easy to understand Hegel's views on the rational organization of the supreme authority, and his determination, on the one hand, to insulate it from too much influence of ' civil society', and on the other, to strengthen the communal elements in its structure. One may begin with the Assembly of Estates, which is the main link between ' civil society' and the ' political state'. The agricultural estate, by which in the *Philosophy of Right* Hegel seems to mean landed nobility with entailed estates, is exempt from election and given a chamber of its own on the ground that their ' ethical life is natural', that is, that the method of inheritance, the family responsibilities, and the entailed ownership of land curb their ' particularity' and make them more community-minded.[60] The other chamber is the domain of the middle class, in which this most individualistic element in civil society is represented by deputies. But the deputies are not elected by, and do not represent, numerical groups of individuals, but ' circles of associations . . . [which] are already communities'.

Since these deputies are the deputies of civil society, it follows as a direct consequence that their appointment is made by society as a society. That is to say . . . articulated into associations, communities and corporations, which although constituted already for other purposes, acquire in this way a connection with politics.[61]

---

[59] Cf. *ibid*. pp. 313, 315, 324–6, 329–30, 299–300. In his *Philosophy of History* (p. 452), Hegel equates the bourgeois ideology with liberalism : ' Not satisfied with the establishment of rational rights, with freedom of person and property, with the existence of a political organisation in which are to be found various circles of civil life each having its own functions to perform, and with that influence over the people which is exercised by the intelligent members of the community, and the confidence that is felt in them, " *Liberalism* " sets up in opposition to all this the atomic principle, that which insists upon the sway of individual wills; maintaining that all government should emanate from their express power and have their express sanction. Asserting this formal side of freedom – this abstraction – the party in question allows no political organisation to be firmly established . . . Thus agitation and unrest are perpetuated. This collision, this nodus, this problem is that with which history is now occupied, and whose solution it has to work out in the future.'

Cp. with this passage the end of the ' English Reform Bill ', *Political Writings*, pp. 328–30, which was also written under the impact of the July Revolution.

[60] See §§ 305–7. In his other works he recognizes that peasant farmers may also deserve representation. Cf. *Political Writings*, pp. 313–14.

[61] *Philosophy of Right*, § 308. The phrase just before that comes from § 303. Cf. also *Political Writings*, pp. 262–3.

Moreover, the lower chamber's 'political consciousness' is increased by the presence of corporation officials, town councillors and civil servants whom Hegel expects to form a significant proportion of deputies.[62]

The hereditary character of the monarchy and the power of the crown in the constitution of the supreme public authority also become more intelligible now. Hegel's metaphysical deduction of the necessity of hereditary succession is both obscure and implausible.[63] What seems to lie behind it, however, is the desire to anchor one element of the public authority to something independent of choice, and therefore make it immune to arbitrary subjective opinions and the influence of ' particularity '. By leaving the designation of the person of the monarch to the natural phenomenon of birth, the constitution guarantees an indispensable minimum of stability and security within the public authority. Hegel regards elective monarchy as ' the worst of institutions ' because ' the nature of the relation between king and people implies that the ultimate decision is left with the particular will, and hence the constitution becomes a Compact of Election, *i.e.* a surrender of the power of the state at the discretion of the particular will '.[64] Hegel justifies in a similar way his vesting of the ultimate constitutional authority in the monarch rather than in a representative assembly or the whole citizen body. The constitution – the organization of the ' political state ' – is thus taken out of the arena in which particular interests can play their dangerous games and weaken the state power at its source. It also apparently acquires sanctity by being lifted out of the category of things which can be manufactured at will.[65] The monarch's exclusive prerogatives over the executive, the civil service and the armed forces, and his right to veto the Estates' legislative proposals, are all explicable by Hegel's eagerness to prevent their domination by the forces of ' particularity ' and ' subjectivity ', and by his belief that only the monarch's ultimate personal control can guarantee that they all remain first and foremost organs of the ' ethical community '.[66]

[62] Cf. *Political Writings*, pp. 255–62, where Hegel discusses the subject at length. Although civil servants come from the middle class, their recruitment, training, organization and *esprit de corps* all bias them towards ' the state's ' rather than ' civil society's ' point of view. Their main sphere of influence is, of course, the executive. Cf. *Philosophy of Right*, §§ 290–7.

[63] On this subject, see Marx's scathing critique, discussed in R. N. Berki's essay, p. 218.

[64] *Philosophy of Right*, § 281. Hegel was profoundly influenced by the demise of two great political entities with elective monarchs, which he witnessed during his early years, viz. the Kingdom of Poland and Lithuania and the Holy Roman Empire of the German Nation.

[65] Cf. *ibid*. §§ 273, 274 Addition. This is inconsistent with Hegel's general position that laws and institutions should not be seen as ' natural ', but as creations of the human spirit.

[66] The connection between the authoritarian character of the political system outlined in the *Philosophy of Right* and the antagonistic features of Hegel's ' civil society ' was pointed out by Herbert Marcuse in his *Reason and Revolution : Hegel and the Rise of Social Theory* (London, 1941; 2nd ed., London, 1955): cf. 2nd ed., ch. 6, especially pp. 202 ff. However, Marcuse seems to me to exaggerate the conservative role of the Hegelian state towards ' civil society ', and fails to distinguish the two senses of ' the state ' in Hegel.

25

IX

Because Hegel patently does not mean by 'the state' what ordinary men as well as social and political theorists normally mean by this term,[67] he is immune from many of the criticisms which are traditionally levied against him. It is worth considering three of them. The target of one of the major criticisms has been the Hegelian notion of freedom as obedience to the state. If the 'state' in the proper or main sense of the word means for him not just a 'political entity', but a peculiar kind of 'ethical community' a great deal of what Hegel says about the 'state' makes perfectly good sense. 'The individual finds his liberation in duty [to the state]' because 'in an *ethical* community, it is easy to say what man must do, what are the duties he has to fulfill in order to be virtuous: he has simply to follow the well-known and explicit rules of his own situation'.[68] It is a truism that 'the state in and by itself is the ethical whole, the actualization of freedom'.[69] Hegel of course conceives 'freedom' in a special sense, different from mere absence of restraints, and there may be good arguments against his usage.[70] That true freedom is to be found in 'the state' (conceived as a kind of 'ethical community') is a completely different proposition from one that equates freedom with subjection to the 'political state', its supreme authority and laws or the lesser public authorities and their orders. Hegel's concept of 'freedom'

---

[67] C. J. Friedrich is one of the few interpreters of Hegel who have clearly seen and emphatically stressed the point:

'Hegel's view on law and ethics, involving as it does also his view on politics and history, is basically at variance with prevailing views, the concept of the state being that of the community rather than of an institution (*Anstalt*). The failure to grasp this divergence of the concept of the state, as Hegel uses it, has been the source of most of the misunderstandings. For if the prevailing modern concept of the state as primarily a government, an institutional manifold comprising those who exercise command functions *in* the community is substituted for Hegel's essentially Aristotelian conception of the state as the highest community, there arise immediately authoritarian, not to say totalitarian implications which are far removed from the essential liberalism of Hegel's conceptions.'

See the Introduction to *The Philosophy of Hegel* (New York, 1953), p. xliv. The communal character of the Hegelian state is also recognized by J. Plamenatz. Cf. his essay in this book, and *Man and Society*, vol. II. The Aristotelian influence on Hegel's concept of the state is discussed by K.-H. Ilting, pp. 99–102.

[68] *Philosophy of Right*, §§ 149, 150.

[69] *Ibid*. Addition to § 258.

[70] Cf. I. Berlin, 'Two concepts of liberty' in his *Four Essays on Liberty* (Oxford, 1969) and W. L. Weinstein's discussion of the Hegelian concept of freedom with reference to T. H. Green in 'The concept of liberty in nineteenth century English political thought', *Political Studies*, XII (1965). A defence of the Hegelian concept of freedom from a non-Hegelian viewpoint may be found also in H. J. McCloskey, 'A critique of the ideals of liberty', *Mind*, LXXIV (1965); G. C. MacCallum Jr, 'Negative and positive freedom', *The Philosophical Review*, LXXVI (1967); and S. I. Benn and W. L. Weinstein, 'Being free to act and being a free man', *Mind*, LXXX (1971). For a discussion of Hegel's concept of freedom from the standpoint of his philosophy, see R. N. Berki, 'Political freedom and Hegelian metaphysics', *Political Studies*, XVI (1968). J. Plamenatz's essay in this book is an exposition and a qualified defence of the Hegelian notion of freedom from a non-Hegelian point of view.

is as complex and rich in meaning as his concept of ' the state ', and it includes one idea which is more frequently associated with Marx than with Hegel. This is the idea that to be really free a community of men must have the means of so ordering their relations that they correspond to their rationally held conceptions of ethical life. This power men acquire by having a properly organized public authority, which can further their ethical ideals as well as particular interests, that is, by being not merely an ' ethical community ' or ' civil society ' but also a ' political state '. But this authority (the ' political state ') must not only exist, but it must also act in a certain way. To be compatible with freedom, or rather to constitute freedom in another Hegelian sense, the laws, customs and institutions of the ' political state ' and the actions of those acting on its behalf must correspond, and must be seen to correspond, to the principles of ethical life. This is precisely the ground on which Hegel denies that the British of his day are truly free while admitting that they enjoy wider freedom of political speech, writing and action, and more freedom from the central government's intervention in social and local affairs than any other nation in Europe.[71]

It is another misconception that Hegel's view of the state involves an unconditional duty to obey whatever the government commands. The ' political state ', its ruling bodies and laws, of course possess legal, ' positive ' authority; whether they also possess authority in some other, moral, sense is open to question. People do often obey on the assumption that ' positive ' laws correspond to ' rational ' laws, that is, such as would be seen to be compatible with ethical life when examined, but Hegel frequently stresses that the rationality of positive laws should never be taken for granted, and may in fact be often lacking.[72] Hence while Hegel admits that law abiding, like patriotism, is in many cases a matter of ' sentiment ' or ' trust ' rather than ' educated insight ', it is the latter which produces firm conviction that, say, a governmental action actualizes ethical values or serves the interest of the ' ethical community ' in a specific way.[73] The fact that the supreme public authority possesses a capital of trust and sentiment does not mean that it will or should always be obeyed. When it becomes self-interested, corrupt and generally unethical, it loses its moral legitimacy. Hegel is no more able to specify when precisely it is right to rebel than other political philosophers, but he quite clearly recognizes the right to rebel in certain circumstances: reputedly to the end of his life he drank a toast on the anniversary of the storming of the Bastille.[74] Men have definite moral rights against the ' political state ' and ' civil society ', first and foremost to be treated as members of the ethical com-

---

[71] Cf. *Political Writings*, ' The English Reform Bill ', pp. 300, 310–12, 324–5, 330.

[72] Cf. *ibid*. ' The Wurtemberg Estates ', pp. 281–3.

[73] Cf. *Philosophy of Right*, § 268. Interestingly Hegel denies that patriotism means only ' readiness for exceptional sacrifices and actions '. ' Essentially . . . it is the sentiment which, in the relationships of our ordinary life and under ordinary conditions, habitually recognizes that the community is one's substantive groundwork and end.'

[74] Cf. *Philosophy of History*, p. 447 on his eulogy of the outbreak of the French Revolution.

munity. It is the duty of those exercising public authority, supreme or subordinate, to treat subjects in that way and themselves to behave as ethical men. Men's obligation to the 'political state' and 'civil society' is conditional, not absolute – as indeed most other political philosophers have maintained.

Within the terms of reference of the Hegelian concept of ethical life the question whether an individual has any right to disobey or question the fundamental ethical principles of the state ('the ethical order') is far more difficult to answer. One can certainly question particular principles on the ground that they are incompatible with others, which are universally held valid in a community. Thus slavery in the southern states of the United States could have been said to contradict the preamble of the Constitution that all men were created equal. But only an ethical genius, such as Socrates or Jesus, can question all the basic values of a community and thus transcend its ethical life.[75]

A third, and as far as this essay is concerned, final misconception should be cleared. Hegel's conception of the state as the highest form of human community has sometimes been criticized for having the effect of arresting the moral progress of humanity at the level of the nation-state, and for being incompatible with a supra-national conception of morality. But it has already been pointed out that Hegel does recognize a wider, if rather looser, ethical community of countries belonging to the same culture.[76] The fact that he frequently compares Germany, France and Britain, and criticizes their practices, laws and institutions, implies that he has an ethical yardstick which he believes can be applied to all of them. He sees these countries as belonging to an ethical family, and although such relationship does not eliminate armed conflicts between sovereign political communities, it does in his view modify their severity and impose certain standards of behaviour in war. Hegel's conception of the nation-state as the highest community does not exclude the possibility of a federation of states belonging to the same civilization and sharing similar interests. It only excludes the union of states at different stages of civilization or embodying radically different ethical ideals. Hegel would not deny that such a union was intrinsically impossible since it could be achieved by force. But he would argue that it was undesirable and probably could not endure for long without collapsing or damaging the ethical life of some of the states.[77]

What Hegel insists on is that ethical communities must be states if they are to protect and perfect their ethical life; he does not say that they must coincide with nations as one normally understands the term. Hegel's *Sittlichkeit* may have some resemblance to national consciousness or nationalism, but in fact is quite

[75] For a discussion of this problem, see Walsh, *Hegelian Ethics*.

[76] Cf. *Philosophy of Right*, Addition to § 339: 'The European peoples form a family in accordance with the universal principles underlying their legal codes, their customs, and their civilisation.'

[77] The possession of colonies could be justified on Hegelian principles when the dominant country thereby raised the subject ones to a higher level of civilization and ethical life.

different from it. Nationalism presupposes a linguistic, ethnic or cultural unity or at least a fervent belief that a given people has or constitutes such a unity. Being a belief it is liable to be justified or supported by irrational myths, and in general it tries to appeal to various deep-seated emotional forces. Hegel's ethical life may start as something not fully rational, as a mere trust or sentiment in favour of concepts, values or ideals which are traditional in a given nation, coupled with a spontaneous sympathy and preference for those men who happen to share them. But it is capable of becoming a rational insight, and indeed only when it has become such an insight does it cease to be a mere custom or ethos (*Sitte*) and become true ethical life (*Sittlichkeit*). What welds an ethical community into a strong and stable unity is political life and political institutions, the experience of belonging to the same state and sharing its historical fortunes. But this experience is quite different from the experience of belonging to a nation. The experience of ethical life is possible in a multi-national state or in a state that is only a part of a nation; it is thus quite independent of national consciousness. Hegel was very familiar with the strident nationalism which swept through Germany at the end of the Napoleonic period. Privately, in his correspondence, as well as publicly, in the preface to the *Philosophy of Right*, he expressed the deepest contempt for it. Although a Swabian by birth Hegel became a Prussian patriot by conviction; he was never, however, a German nationalist.[78] One can question the extent to which contemporary modern states are in fact ethical communities, just as one can question the extent to which individuals – consciously or unconsciously – share an ethical life. What one cannot do, in my opinion, is to read a sinister, nationalist meaning into the concept of *Sittlichkeit*.

[78] Cf. S. Avineri, ' Hegel and Nationalism ', *The Review of Politics*, xxiv (1962), reprinted in W. Kaufman (ed.), *Hegel's Political Philosophy* (New York, 1970).

History as the realization of freedom

JOHN PLAMENATZ

I

In England and other English-speaking countries the philosopher has turned his mind chiefly to two closely connected though not identical ideas of freedom: freedom as absence of constraint by others, and freedom of choice. What, he has asked, is to be understood by constraint, and how does it differ from persuasion? This, notoriously, is a difficult question to answer. A man who has chosen freely could have chosen otherwise than he did. But what do we mean when we say that he could have chosen otherwise? This, too, is a difficult question.

Hegel makes little or no attempt to answer these questions; he never tries to determine where persuasion ends and constraint begins, nor does he consider the situation of the man who could have chosen otherwise than he did. These favourite questions of the English-speaking philosopher mean virtually nothing to him.

It is the sociologist or the psychologist, not to speak of the historian, who would find Hegel's ideas about freedom relevant and even exciting; provided, of course, that they were translated into language more familiar to him. As Hegel sees it, it is only as a social and moral being that man is free, that freedom has meaning and value for him, that he achieves it or makes progress towards it. This progress is both in the individual and in mankind, for they both move gradually, by stages that can be distinguished from one another, towards freedom; though the individual cannot have greater freedom than social and cultural conditions allow.

It is not as a mere creature of appetites but as having purposes which he tries to achieve deliberately that man aspires to freedom, and his purposes vary with his ways of thinking about himself and the world, ways that depend on the concepts he uses, which are not peculiar to him but are shared by a community. Nor are they unchanging; they are not the same in every period of a man's life nor at all stages in the history of the community he belongs to or of mankind. How they change is determined by what men do, though the course of change is not controlled by them, nor even understood until, at a late stage of it, they have acquired the capacity to understand it. Yet the course uncontrolled by the beings involved in it is not random; it has a logic of its own and a direction; for, as soon as we understand it, we can see how each successive stage in it is a passing beyond the stage before it towards a consummation. The beings involved in it are self-conscious and self-appraising; they not only act but have ideas about

30

their actions that change the quality of what they do; so that how they see themselves affects what they are just as what they are affects how they see themselves. The course of change, for the species as for the individual, is a growth in maturity – in self-knowledge and self-control. The knowledge is of men in society; for man is essentially a being involved in what Hegel calls ' ethical life ', essentially a social being.

Man is self-conscious, rational, purposeful and moral only as a partaker in ethical or social life; and it is as a moral being that he aspires to freedom. He is, so Hegel tells us, *essentially* free; or rather, he tells us that the will is *essentially* free. But what distinguishes man from other animals is precisely his having a will – his having purposes and striving deliberately to achieve them. Who possesses a will wants to be free, and to some extent is so already; just as who thinks conceptually wants to understand and to reason correctly, and to some extent already does so. But who possesses a will partakes in ethical life and is a social being, so that the achievement of freedom is as much social as personal.

Professor Grégoire says that the central idea of Hegel's philosophy is *personality*[1]; several of the British Hegelians say it is the *concrete universal* or *identity-in-difference*, the idea of a whole that is present in each of its parts and is therefore more than the sum of them; and Sir Malcolm Knox suggests that it is the idea of the concept that ' determines itself and gives itself content '.[2]

Of these candidates for the honour of being the central idea of a notoriously difficult philosophy, the most familiar is *personality*. But the other two are not very different from it. A person, a rational and a moral being, reveals what he is in his actions, and yet is not the sum or series of them; for he is present in his every action, or at least considered action. They are *his* ways of behaving, and there is no understanding his actions apart from understanding him, nor him apart from his actions. So, too, in understanding himself, he sees his actions as proceeding from a self which is not the sum of them and yet exists only in them.

It is odd to speak of a concept determining itself and giving itself content; it is to give to the word *concept* or *Begriff* much more than its usual meaning, in either English or German. Hegel in the *Philosophy of Right*, so Knox tells us, is tracing ' the development of the will from concept to Idea '.[3] Yet Hegel in this book is not just explaining, as an historian might do, how one thing leads to another in a course of change; nor is he engaged, as a mathematician might be, in working out the logical implications of definitions and axioms. He is explaining, rather, what is involved psychologically, morally and socially in rational and purposeful behaviour. At least, this is part of what he is doing, the part most likely to interest students of society today. As he puts it himself, he

---

[1] See his *Études Hegeliennes, Les Points Capitaux du Système* (Louvain, 1958), p. 10.

[2] *Hegel's Philosophy of Right*, trans. T. M. Knox (Oxford, 1942); translator's foreword, p. viii.

[3] *Ibid.* translator's notes, p. 318.

is explaining 'how the state, the ethical universe, is to be understood'.[4] The state, as he conceives of it, is the sphere in which alone fully rational and moral action is possible; it is 'the ethical universe', the highest form of the ethical life in which alone *will*, as distinct from mere impulse and appetite, is conceivable.

The ideas 'central' to Hegel's philosophy all apply more readily to human beings, and even to human communities, than to anything else – as Hegelian scholars have often noticed. Hegel himself, though he did not apply them to everything, did apply them to the totality of things, to reality as a whole. He was aware that natural scientists do not apply them to what they study, and never implied that they ought; for nature, as the natural sciences explain it, is only an aspect of reality, and therefore to understand it at that level, we need not apply these ideas to it. But to understand the whole of which nature is an aspect, and therefore to understand how nature is an aspect of it, we must use these ideas.

It has often been objected that the idea of personality applies only to human beings and not to communities of men. The objection is sound, though Hegel might not admit it. Yet we all speak at times of communities as if they were persons; or, rather, there are ways in which we speak about persons and communities, or even groups of persons, and not about other things. Nor is it fortuitous that we do so. How much further Hegel went than we all do in speaking of communities as if they were persons, I do not know. He thought of reality as a whole as essentially spiritual, and thought of this universal spirit as revealed, at certain levels, in the activities of men and communities of men. But this, in strict logic, does not entail that he attributed personality to communities, either in the ordinary sense in which a man has it or in the peculiar sense in which he ascribed it to reality as a whole. From the proposition that an all-embracing spirit is manifest in the activities of men and human communities, it does not follow that communities are persons, either in the sense that men are so or in the sense that this spirit is. It was perhaps more to the all-embracing spirit than to states and other communities that Hegel attributed personality.

But this is a matter of little interest to the social and political theorist. More important to him is Hegel's belief that it is only as a partaker in ethical life, as a social being, that the individual is truly a person, has a sense of his own identity, has purposes as distinct from mere appetites and impulses, has reason and will. Hegel's point is not just that the individual acquires these capacities as a result of being in society with others but that there is something essentially social about the exercise of them. Even Crusoe, alone on his island, is a social being. His condition is not that of an animal that has been taught to do certain things, and can do them, when appropriately stimulated, even when it is alone

[4] *Ibid.* p. 11.

and has no memory of being taught. Crusoe, to be able to think and act as he does when alone on his island, must not only have lived in society; he must carry with him into his solitude ideas and attitudes that he acquired by living with others.

I said earlier that Hegel's account in the *Philosophy of Right* of what is involved in being a person, a self-conscious, rational and purposeful being, is not an explanation of how man acquires personality. It is neither an historical account nor a theoretical model, a deducing of consequences from precisely formulated definitions and assumptions. Rather, it is an attempt to make explicit what, according to Hegel, is implicit in specifically human, or rational and purposeful, behaviour. To some of his critics it has seemed that Hegel, as he makes this attempt, draws his readers into dark regions in which they can no longer see what he is up to, and he can play tricks on them; but to him it seemed otherwise. He claimed to be bringing out the implications of ordinary experience; and the claim might be to a large extent well founded, even though it should require an effort altogether out of the ordinary to understand him.

In the preface to the *Philosophy of Right*, on the heels of one of the most often quoted of Hegelian aphorisms (' What is rational is actual, and what is actual is rational '), there come, in Knox's rather free translation, the words: ' On this conviction the plain man like the philosopher takes his stand, and from it philosophy starts its study of the universe of mind as well as the universe of nature.' [5] Though Hegel in fact speaks of the impartial or ingenuous consciousness (*unbefangene Bewusstein*) rather than the plain man, his meaning is clear enough; philosophy, he would have us know, does not reject the assumptions that lie behind ordinary unsophisticated experience but makes a start by examining their implications. This respect for common sense would no doubt have seemed admirable to G. E. Moore, who wrote a *Refutation of Idealism*, aimed chiefly at Hegel's British disciples.

In the *Philosophy of Right* Hegel explains both what is involved in being a person and the essential character of a community, especially the community that is the state. These two explanations, as he makes them, are at bottom but two aspects of one: for a person is necessarily a member of a community, and a community consists necessarily of persons. Though the *Philosophy of Right* traces no process of development, *The Phenomenology of Spirit*, which appeared some fourteen years earlier, in 1807, does so, for it explains the progress of spirit from lower to higher levels of consciousness, reason and will. This progress, as Hegel presents it to his readers, is dialectical; he shows how one aspect of things is necessarily connected with another, which is opposed to it, and how the two

---

[5] *Philosophy of Right*, p. 10.

are reconciled at a higher level – higher because it includes and transcends them, being more than merely the two taken together.

If we take either an individual or a community, we can distinguish both between different aspects and between different levels of his or its activities. For example, we can distinguish between a man's impulses or desires and his will. Unless he had desires, he could not have a will, but in having a will he is aware of his desires, and this awareness affects him. Like the other animals, he is appetitive, and yet his appetitiveness is different from theirs because he is also purposeful. So, too, if we consider his development, the process whereby he becomes a self-conscious, purposeful, rational person, we can see how one phase of it passes into the next; for the adult is not just the effect of his past but is also the summation of it. It lives on in him; ways of thinking and feeling acquired in the past continue into the present, though their effects and significance change. In one sense the adult ceases to be a child, but in another, his childhood survives in him. He can still feel and think as a child – for, if he could not, he would not know what it is to be a child – and yet, being no longer a child, he can understand, as no child can, what it is to be a child.

As it is with individuals, so it is, according to Hegel, with communities or, as he sometimes likes to call them, ' ethical universes '. Earlier forms of communal life, earlier practices, attitudes and sentiments, survive into later stages, and yet are no longer what they used to be, partly because they are related to different things and partly because they are understood differently. The supersession of the earlier by the later phases in the progress of spirit, in the course of social and cultural development, is not just the disappearance of some things and the appearance of others; it is a change in the quality of feeling, action and thought resulting from reflection upon them and the action inspired by that reflection. It is, as Hegel conceives of it, change that comes of a sense of inadequacy or restriction on the part of whoever is involved in it; it is a process that includes self-awareness, self-frustration and self-transcendence – a striving to pass beyond one's limitations which, when it succeeds, brings with it a deeper understanding of oneself and the limitations.

This idea of progress makes good enough sense applied to the mental and moral development of the child, though even here it can be delusive. It appears to make less sense when applied to communities and other social groups, though it is often applied to them, and sometimes usefully.

II

Desire, Self-Consciousness and Will

The essential attribute of the self-conscious being is that it develops its capacities in the process of exercising them. By its actions it transforms itself. It is ' selfcreative ', not in the sense that it strives deliberately to recreate itself to a model clear to it before the striving begins, but in the sense that it gradually acquires self-knowledge and self-control as it acts and reflects on its actions and their results. A self-conscious being does not grow to mental and moral maturity in the way that a plant or mere animal grows to physical maturity; it educates itself by its own activities, raising itself from level to level of understanding and control. Yet this process, though it leads to self-knowledge, cannot, at least in its earlier stages, be understood by the being involved in it. The child feels, thinks and acts in childish ways, but to understand childishness must grow up to be an adult. The child does not know itself for what it is; or, as Hegel might put it, is not *for* itself what it is *in* itself.

The self-conscious being does not develop in isolation from other such beings. Indeed, it could not do so; it could not even be fully self-conscious unless it were conscious of others. Self-consciousness, as Hegel speaks of it, involves *necessarily* not only a discrimination of the self from what is external to it but also an awareness of other selves. This point, though it is made more clearly in the *Phenomenology*, is implicit in the general argument of the *Philosophy of Right*. It is as a partaker in ethical life that the individual comes to be aware of himself as a person, but to partake in ethical life is to stand in social relations to others, to recognize that they too are persons. In the *Phenomenology*, Hegel, when he explains what spirit essentially is, says of it that it is ' a plurality of Egos '.[6]

The spirit that Hegel here speaks of is not the individual human being; it is what he calls ' this absolute substance ' or ' the unity of different . . . self-consciousnesses '.[7] We need not stop to inquire what Hegel means by ' absolute substance '; it is enough that we should notice that he thinks of spirit as a plurality of self-conscious beings, that he calls it the ' I which is a We, and the We which is an I ' (*Ich, das Wir, und Wir das Ich ist*).[8] He is attributing to something that he conceives to be greater, more comprehensive, than the individual human being the property of being a self – and this is more than many of his critics can take; but he is also saying that there is no self-consciousness except where there is a plurality of self-conscious beings closely involved with one another – which almost any social theorist will take, though he may prefer to put it in different words.

In the *Philosophy of Right* Hegel explains how will, as distinct from mere desire or impulse, involves self-consciousness. He says,

Every self-consciousness knows itself (i) as universal, as the potentiality of abstracting from everything determinate, and (ii) as particular, with a determinate object, content and aim. Still, both these moments are only abstractions; what is concrete and true . . . is the universality which has the particular as its opposite, but the particular which by its reflection into itself has been equalized with the universal. This unity is individuality.[9]

---

[6] *The Phenomenology of Mind*, trans. J. B. Baillie, 2nd ed. (London, 1931), p. 227.
[7] *Ibid.* p. 227.   [8] *Phänomenologie des Geistes*, ed. J. Hoffmeister (Hamburg, 1952), p. 146.
[9] *Philosophy of Right*, p. 23.

I interpret this as meaning: every self-conscious being can distinguish itself from its particular actions (and I here use the word *action* in a broad sense to include mental activities that do not lead to overt actions that others could observe), and yet is aware that it exists only in its actions. Its idea of itself as distinct from its particular actions, and its ideas of its particular actions as distinct from the self, are mere abstractions. The self is self-conscious (aware of being a self) only in its particular actions, and is present only in them. What Hegel calls the 'particular reflected into itself' is merely self-conscious action, and its 'equalization with the universal' is the self-awareness involved in it. To be an individual, in the sense that Hegel here gives to the word, is to be aware of yourself as an agent, an enduring self present in your actions. Yet the self, he implies, is nothing apart from its actions.

To be able to form purposes and take decisions, an agent must be aware that he is one; he must be self-conscious. As Hegel puts it: 'An animal too has impulses, desires, inclinations, but it has no will and must obey its impulse if nothing external deters it. Man, however . . . stands above his impulses and may make them his own.' [10] This is a far cry from Hobbes's account in *Leviathan* of the will as 'the last appetite in deliberating', an account that in England was still accepted in all essentials by Hegel's contemporary, James Mill. A decision or act of will, as Hobbes and the elder Mill describe it, is merely being moved to action by the appetite (or aversion) that survives a comparison of alternatives; whereas for Hegel it is a commitment of the self.

Committing oneself consciously – and commitment is essentially conscious – to an impulse or desire is an act of will. But the commitment may be an act of what Hegel calls the 'immediate' or 'natural' will; it may be 'arbitrary' and not 'rational'. Far from denying that the arbitrary will is free, Hegel admits that it is so, in one sense of freedom; for he says that 'at this stage, the freedom of the will is arbitrariness'. But he immediately goes on to say:

If we hear it said that the definition of freedom is ability to do what we please, such an idea can only be taken to reveal an utter immaturity of thought, for it contains not even an inkling of the absolutely free will, of right, ethical life, and so forth. Reflection, the formal universality and unity of self-consciousness, is the will's abstract certainty of freedom, but it is not yet the truth of freedom, because it has not got itself as its content and aim, and consequently the subjective side is still other than the objective; the content of this self-determination, therefore, also remains purely and simply finite. Instead of being the will in its truth, arbitrariness is more like the will as contradiction.[11]

Let us consider in some detail this rather long passage, for it throws considerable light on Hegel's ideas about freedom and its connection with the will and

[10] *Ibid*. Addition to § 11, p. 229.
[11] *Ibid*. p. 27.

with reason, with purposeful and rational action. Committing oneself to action – or, as Hegel puts it, standing above one's impulses and making (or not making) them one's own – is a necessary part of freedom. This commitment is possible only to a self-conscious being able to look upon its impulses and desires as things it can accept or reject; it cannot wish them away but it can frustrate them. This, presumably, is what Hegel has in mind when he calls reflection ' the will's abstract certainty of freedom '. The creature who, when subject to desire, can say to himself, ' Shall I, or shall I not? ', has this abstract certainty. The arbitrary decision, no less than the rational, involves *reflection*; it involves taking notice of alternatives, discriminating between them. The mere animal does not make arbitrary decisions; for the arbitrary decision, though not rational, is still a decision that only a rational being, in the sense of one that is self-conscious and discriminating, can take.

Hegel speaks of the will having itself for its content and aim; and this, taken literally – or, at least, taken out of context – scarcely makes sense. How can the will will itself? Yet this is what Hegel here implies that it can do; and elsewhere he says it in so many words, just as he says that the individual can be ' his own end '. But how can he be that?

A man can have enduring purposes, and can discipline his desires and impulses in their service, and his idea of himself is bound up with them and their pursuit. In pursuing them he can be said to make himself ' his own end ', for he has himself very much in mind as he pursues them – himself as he thinks he is or himself as he would like to be. It is in pursuing them, rather than in satisfying his random desires and impulses (those not connected with any ' image ' of himself as he is or would like to be), that he ' affirms ' or ' asserts ' himself. Man, so Hegel tells us, stands above his impulses and desires, making them his own or refusing to do so – that is to say, controlling them; and when he does this, he acts wilfully. Presumably, then, when his ' will wills itself ', he does not merely control his impulses and desires on particular occasions; he makes this control his purpose, he aspires to self-control. But he cannot aspire to it *in vacuo*; he must control himself or his impulses and desires, in the service of purposes other than self-control. These purposes are related to some idea he has of the sort of life he wants to live and the sort of person he wants to be; so that in pursuing them, he makes himself ' his own end '. Thus when the ' will wills itself ', man is ' his own end '; and it is then that he passes from ' the abstract certainty of freedom ' to ' the truth of freedom '. As a mere chooser who may or may not, as he pleases, commit himself to action, he has a sense that it depends on him whether or not he acts, but he has not yet attained the freedom which is the ability to lead an ordered life cf his own choosing. Hegel, when he contrasts ' the abstract certainty of freedom ' with ' the truth of freedom ', is not just making a distinction between two senses of freedom or two conditions of man, he is also saying that whoever is free in the first sense or is in the first condition aspires to the second, or at least is not satisfied unless he achieves it. That is why he says that 'the arbitrary will' is the will 'as contradiction'. In saying it, he has, presumably, more in mind than that people who act arbitrarily often frustrate themselves; he also implies that the self-conscious being, the chooser, just because he is self-conscious and a chooser, aspires to an ordered life in which he can form purposes whose pursuit satisfies him.

Speaking of the 'contradiction' in the arbitrary will, Hegel says that it 'comes into appearance as a dialectic of impulses and inclinations; each of them is in the way of every other – the satisfaction of one is necessarily subordinated or sacrificed to the satisfaction of another, and so on. An impulse . . . has no measuring rod in itself, and so . . . its subordination or sacrifice is the contingent decision of the arbitrary will'.[12] He also says, in a passage added to this one, 'if I neglect all the others [impulses] and put myself in one of them . . . I have surrendered my universality, which is a system of all impulses. But it is just as little help to make a mere hierarchy of impulses . . . since no criterion is available here'.[13] And he speaks of what he calls a 'common sense' demand for the 'purification of impulses', saying that 'the truth behind this vague demand is that the impulses should become the rational system of the will's volitions. To grasp them like that, proceeding out of the concept of the will, is the content of the philosophical science of right'.[14]

Notice that Hegel says here that it is 'little help to make a hierarchy of impulses'. He means, presumably, that if we deal only with impulses (or, as Bentham would put it, with desires) comparing them with one another, there is no point to preferring some to others when they conflict. This, though it is not a refutation of utilitarianism (since there is here no argument directed against it), is at least a rejection of it. Hegel might have said that, at this level, it is impossible to make such a hierarchy for sheer lack of relevant criteria, but he says only that it is no help to do so. It is no help, presumably, to anyone who aspires to act rationally, and therefore no help to the philosopher who wants to explain what rational behaviour is. Hegel denies by implication what Bentham and his disciples assert. For, according to Bentham, if we want to behave rationally, we have to compare impulses – or, rather, desires – taking account of their relative strengths, frequencies, and so on, because to act rationally is to act in the way best calculated to ensure that desires are as fully satisfied as possible.

Man, Hegel tells us, is a *universal* being; that is to say, he is aware of himself as the enduring subject of all his actions. He does not seek, let alone find, happiness in satisfying as many desires as possible over a period of time; nor is it the function of social rules and institutions to encourage kinds of behaviour

12 *Philosophy of Right*, p. 28.
13 *Ibid*. p. 231.
14 *Philosophy of Right*, pp. 28–9.

ensuring that, on the whole, men's desires are satisfied as far as possible. The activities that bring happiness, or at least the sense of a life well spent, are governed by principles that are not utilitarian. A man in charge of a dog might reasonably try to 'maximize' the satisfaction of its desires, or if he were in charge of kennels might do the same for a whole company of dogs; but what a man may reasonably do for his dog, it is not reasonable that he should do for himself; for he, unlike his dog, is a moral being aspiring to freedom.

III

The Will and Ethical (or Social) Life

Hegel distinguishes between the will of the individual and what he calls the universal will that finds expression in the laws and conventions of the community or communities that individuals belong to. This Hegelian notion of a universal will is a difficult one, but before we discuss it, we must look again at what he says about the individual will when he calls it a ' rational system of volitions ' – that is to say, of purposes and decisions, and perhaps also dispositions to act, in so far as they are effects of past deliberations and decisions.

If we consider how a child develops mentally and morally, we do not see it learning *first* to distinguish between its desires, observing the consequences of acting upon them, and then *later* coming to accept certain rules of conduct as it learns by experience that obeying them ensures that its desires are more fully satisfied. The child does not become first a utilitarian self-discoverer and afterwards a moral being. Its desires, by the time that it can distinguish between them and reckon the consequences of indulging them, are already the desires of a moral being – or, perhaps I should say, a being in the process of becoming moral. And, in any case, they are the desires of a social being; that is to say, of a being that not only has enduring relations with others of its own kind but is aware, at some level of awareness, that it has them, and could not have them unless it were aware. In the language of the sociologist, such a being is already sustaining a variety of social roles that form part of a system of such roles; or, in the language of Hegel, it belongs already to an ' ethical universe ', is already a partaker in ' ethical life '. A child belongs to a family as a pet dog does not, not because, unlike the dog, it is born of human parents, nor even because it is better loved or looked after, but because it is a moral being. It is true that Hegel, at one point in his argument, says that the child lacks ' a moral will '; but the context makes it clear that he means only that the child accepts unquestioningly the rules and standards prescribed for it by its elders. There are, for Hegel – as indeed for all of us – levels of morality, just as there are levels of self-awareness and understanding.

The capacity to make decisions and to act rationally is essentially the capacity of a moral being. The individual acquires purposes that he can pursue intelligently, and for whose sake he needs to discipline his desires, in the process of acquiring a sense of what is permissible and what is not. This sense he acquires, to begin with, by being controlled by others – provided that the control is not arbitrary but is governed by principles that are ' universal ', that apply to every-one in like circumstances. The child becomes moral as it learns that there are good reasons for its having to do what its elders require of it. The will is essentially moral, not in the sense that whoever has a will (whoever is capable of forming purposes and acting upon them) always behaves morally or even wants to do so, but in the sense that he has some notion of obligation and right, that he makes claims and admits obligations as he pursues his purposes. There is, so Hegel tells us (if I have understood him rightly), no hierarchy of mere desires or impulses; there is only a hierarchy of purposes. But whoever has purposes, some of which take precedence over others, is a self-conscious being and belongs to an ' ethical universe '.

In Hegel's philosophy of man, three human attributes are closely related to one another, self-consciousness, personality, and capacity for rights; and he does not, so it seems to me, suppose that any is prior to the others. As he puts it: ' In personality, therefore, knowledge is knowledge of oneself as an object, but an object raised by thinking to the level of simple infinity . . .'; and he goes on to say, on the same page ' Personality essentially involves the capacity for rights '.[15]

By ' infinity ' Hegel appears to mean, in this context, self-determination or the capacity to make decisions. Knowing yourself as an ' object ' entails being aware of yourself in an enduring environment, in a world of which you are a part; but to be aware of yourself in this way is to be aware of yourself as a person. There-fore being a person entails being aware that you are one. This, of course, does not mean that you are able to define what it is to be a person; for it is the business of philosophy and not of common sense to attempt such definitions. It means only that there are implicit in your behaviour assumptions which, though you may be unable to define them, would, if made explicit, reveal what it is to be a person.

Among the rights that Hegel discusses in the *Philosophy of Right* is property; and he says two things about it that throw light on the connection between rights, on the one hand, and reason and will, on the other. ' My will ', he says, ' as the will of a person, and so as a single will, becomes objective to me in property '[16]; and then again, ' In his property a person exists for the first time as reason '.[17] That is to say, I acquire a will, a hierarchy of purposes, as I learn to make claims (in this case, to external things) that others recognize. To make a claim is not to give vent to an appetite; it is not to be demanding in a way that even an animal can be. It is to make a moral gesture understood by others capable

[15] *Philosophy of Right*, p. 37.
[16] *Ibid*. p. 42.
[17] *Ibid*. pp. 235–6.

of making them, a gesture that has meaning only between persons who recognize one another as persons.

Though Hegel says that the ' rationale of property is to be found . . . in the supersession of the pure subjectivity of personality ',[18] he does not mean (I think) that the sense of being a person comes temporally before the making of claims; he means, rather, that the sense of being a person that finds expression in making them is confirmed to the maker when others recognize his claims. The adult, when he makes claims that others do not recognize, may be sure of himself, for he has been for years a maker of claims that have been recognized, even though these particular claims are not so; but the child, when it makes its first claims on others, is making its entrance into the ' ethical world ', and when the claims are recognized, it feels itself accepted in that world, a person among persons. So, too, when Hegel says that ' a person must translate his freedom into an external sphere in order to exist as Idea ',[19] he does not mean that a man first aspires to freedom and then tries to realize his aspiration in the world; he means, rather, that his aspiration to freedom, to self-direction, emerges along with his endeavour to make a mark in the world. The creature that aspires to freedom is a social being and can get what it aspires to only in society – or, in the language of Hegel, it belongs to an ethical universe and can achieve freedom only inside it. But this does not ensure that the way to freedom is clear, straight and easy; for, as we shall see, it is tortuous and painful, if only because the creature that moves along it learns to see clearly only as it comes closer to its destination.

Where there is ethical life, there is what Hegel calls a universal will ' manifest' in the laws, customs and conventions that govern social intercourse. Laws and conventions exist only in so far as they are used, and men use them to control one another's behaviour and to guide their own. They use them deliberately, and their usefulness depends on their being in general use in some community or within some social group to which the persons who use them recognize that they belong. That, presumably, is the point of calling them a *universal will*. No doubt, men are restrained by them, but only because other men (or they themselves) use them to impose restraints. Social rules are not external to human behaviour, but are a part or an aspect of it, which would not be specifically human without them.

Hegel often speaks as if the rules current in a community formed a consistent whole; and this, in the eyes of the social theorist, is perhaps his worst fault.[20] He is most inclined to speak in this way of the state, especially when he calls it

---

18 *Ibid.* p. 235.
19 *Ibid.* p. 40.
20 The philosopher might object more strongly to other of his faults : to his running together ideas that ought to be kept distinct, and to a variety of category mistakes – to his speaking of ideas as if they were things or even persons, or of communities as if they were individuals.

an ethical universe. He is not content to speak of it as a community that controls and includes all others (which is already to exaggerate); he also speaks of it as if it were pre-eminently rational – as if its structure and modes of operation were such as to ensure that its policies and other acts are products of a comprehensive understanding of relevant problems and facts, and a wise application of consistent principles. Admittedly, when he speaks in this way, he has in mind above all the state as it ought to be, and as he thinks it tends to become in the course of history; but he does also suggest that even an imperfect state is likely to be wiser than any individual or group subject to it with whom it comes into conflict.

To speak in these ways is profoundly misleading. If by the state we mean a hierarchy of persons having authority of a certain kind over everyone within a given territory, it is clear that it does not control everything that men do within that territory. Not even the most ambitious state aspires to do that, or to come near to doing it; and when we call the state sovereign or supreme, we do not imply that this is what it does or wants to do. And if by the state we mean, not a hierarchy of persons, but certain kinds of activity – as, for example, the exercise of ' public ' as distinct from other sorts of authority, obedience to public authority, attempts to ensure that it is held by specific persons or used for specific purposes – then, clearly, the activities that fall outside it are only to some extent controlled or affected by it.

The social rules governing the behaviour of the citizens of a state do not form a consistent whole, whether we take only the rules administered by the state or all the rules that apply within its territories. The state has, over everyone within those territories, rights that no other organized body has; and it has, over all such bodies, rights that they do not have over it, or indeed over each other. But none of this ensures that the rules it administers form a coherent system well adapted to the needs of its citizens. The state is not necessarily more rational, in this sense, than any other organized body, and there is no need to assume that it is in order to explain its peculiar and important functions.

Nor can we attribute to society taken generally the properties that Hegel attributes to the state. For what is society, thus conceived? It is not any particular community or association or other identifiable social group. Nor is it, presumably, the whole of mankind. If we take a man at any one period of his life, we find that he belongs to many distinct social groups; and if we take him over the whole of his life, to many more. If the society in which he becomes a rational and moral person, and acts like one, consists of all these groups and them alone, then it is not, for him, what it is for anyone else, even a close neighbour. If by society in relation to any man, we mean all the groups that form his mind, and in which he lives his life, then it would seem that no two men belong to quite the same society, nor even to two quite similar societies. Nor do the rules current in the social groups he belongs to, either at any one period of his life or over the whole of it, form a coherent whole. What, then, is the universal will which he must make his own, if he is to be rational and free?

Hegel, though he shows little sign of being aware of it, is caught up in a contradiction that he fails to resolve. If a man is to be rational and free, he must do more than merely conform to the universal will, than follow custom and convention and obey the law; he must make the universal will his own; he must accept on rational grounds principles of conduct in keeping with that will, and must want and be able to live by them. As we shall see later, when we come to the last part of our argument, he must challenge, or at least question, authority, if he is to achieve freedom; he must both challenge it and be reconciled to it, and the challenge and reconciliation must change both him and the universal will. No doubt, when 'the ethical universe' is all that it ought to be, when it is fully rational, the individual who challenges it and is then reconciled to it does not change it but himself only. The challenge and reconciliation are then necessary only to his becoming rational and not to the state's (or society's) becoming so. But the fully rational state is the product of a long course of social and cultural change, and therefore, presumably, of conflicts whose resolution serves to make the ethical universe and not only the individual more rational. It is modern man and not primitive man, nor even the ancient Greek so much admired by Hegel, who is rational and free, or comes nearest to being so. And if the claims he makes and the obligations he recognizes differ greatly from those made and recognized by the primitive man or the ancient Greek, so too does the type of society he belongs to differ from theirs. The universal will that is there for him to make his own was undreamt of in their time.

Now, if we are to believe, not Hegel, but the sociologist and the social anthropologist, it is in the simple, primitive society that the social experience of different persons is most likely to be similar, and that the rules they are required to obey are most likely to be consistent with one another. If that is so, and if by a universal will we mean a set of mutually consistent rules that men can use to control one another's and their own behaviour, then it is in primitive societies that we are most likely to find such a will. But Hegel, given his conception of freedom, does not and cannot allow that man is nowhere more free than in primitive societies. On the contrary, he does (and must) insist that he is much nearer being free in the type of society in which the modern state flourishes; for it is there, as we shall see more clearly later, that man is most consciously a moral agent, claiming the right to live by principles that he accepts on rational grounds. Thus, it is precisely in the type of society in which the individual makes this claim that the social rules he is required to observe are least likely to form a coherent system. For, as we have seen, he belongs during the course of his life to many different social groups, of which some are ephemeral and none is unchanging. Consistency, to be sure, is not, in the eyes of Hegel, the only attribute of the universal will in its developed state, for that will is then also better adapted to the needs of a moral agent aspiring to freedom; but it is an essential attribute.

Indeed, it could be argued against Hegel that the need for the modern state arises in large part because in our type of society there is no universal will; because, of all types of society, it is the most diversified and quickly changing and therefore the least likely to have rules and standards that form a coherent system. If we argue in this way, we need not deny that the modern state can function properly (by its own standards, whatever they are) only because its citizens observe willingly rules on which that functioning depends. For these rules do not make up the whole of what Hegel understands by a universal will, so that their general observance is quite consistent with citizens having incompatible principles and standards – with moral and cultural disharmony, and not just diversity. The state whose laws are the most widely understood and obeyed is not necessarily the state whose citizens are least frustrated, or are nearest to having clear and consistent principles to live by.

Yet Hegel's account of the universal will in relation to the moral will of the individual and his aspirations to freedom is not altogether misleading. For it is in the process of learning to use social rules and to respond to their use by others that the individual acquires his sense of having a place in society and the more settled purposes whose pursuit makes freedom precious to him. This is so whether or not his ' acceptance ' of the rules is uncritical. He does not first acquire his purposes and then ' accept ' the rules as experience teaches him that, in the long run, they serve his purposes in a world in which he is not the only purposeful being. He does not become rational first and then moral afterwards; he becomes both together in childhood as he learns to behave as others require him to and to discern the rules that govern their requirements. This, of course, does not prevent his coming later to see how the rules serve his purposes; or when they fail to do so, his rejecting the rules for the sake of the purposes or the purposes for the sake of the rules. Yet his purposes have no meaning apart from a system of social relations governed by social rules.

This, presumably, is at least part of what Hegel has in mind when, speaking of ' the ethical substance and its laws and powers ', he says, ' they are not something alien to the subject. On the contrary, his spirit bears witness to them as to its own essence in which he has a feeling of self-hood and in which he lives as in his own element which is not distinguished from himself ' [21]; or again, when he says, ' in dealing with ethical life, only two views are possible: either we start with the substantiality of the ethical order, or we proceed atomistically and build on the basis of single individuals. This second point of view excludes mind . . . Mind, however, is not something single, but is the unity of the single and the

[21] *Philosophy of Right*, p. 106.

universal '.[22] That is to say, a man's sense that he is an individual is bound up with his awareness that he is a social being, a partaker in ethical life, and his ability to reason and to will come of his assimilating a culture, or learning to use in dealing with others ideas and rules that are at once products of social intercourse and aspects of it.

Hegel is right in seeing a close connection between the modern state and the idea of freedom as we now have it; for it is in this state that for the first time the individual is assumed to have rights by reason of his mere humanity, independently of any particular social role. The doctrine of the rights of man gives to some rights or liberties precedence over all others precisely on the ground that everyone should have them whatever his place in society. Again, it is in the era of the modern state that men have aspired to reform society deliberately to suit their ideas of what it should be. The largest claim for the mere individual and the boldest attempts to reconstruct society go naturally together; they express man's increased confidence in himself, in his ability to live as it seems good to him. Where the modern state flourishes, society is more varied and more quickly changing than ever before, the individual has a wider choice of occupations and ways of life, and men collectively have greater power to change society deliberately. If we understand freedom as Hegel understood it, not as mere absence of constraint but also and above all as the ability to live by principles and in pursuit of aims willingly and deliberately accepted, then it makes sense to say that the modern state, when true to its own ideals, enlarges freedom.

IV

The Progress of Spirit towards Freedom

It is in the *Phenomenology* and in the *Lectures on the Philosophy of History* that Hegel explains the progress of spirit or – to speak less pretentiously – of mankind towards freedom; and of these two works the *Phenomenology*, though much the more difficult to read, is also much the more impressive.

In the *Phenomenology* Hegel presents this progress in two aspects, distinguishable but inseparable: as a movement of the individual from one point of view or attitude to another, and as a movement from one type of society to another. But, before he goes on to explain this two-sided progress, he discusses consciousness and how it differs from mere sensation. Consciousness involves distinguishing a self that is conscious from what it is conscious of; it involves self-consciousness and therefore discrimination, which involves thought or the use of ideas. But where ideas are used, there is always, implicit in their use, some view of the world or philosophy, even when the user cannot (or does not) define the ideas he uses; for his ideas form a system, and behind his use of them

---

[22] *Ibid.* p. 261. Both these passages say or imply more than I have read out of them, and only a part of what they mean is acceptable.

there are assumptions about the world to which they are applied. Thus the thinker, the being capable of understanding (and misunderstanding), is necessarily world-conscious as well as self-conscious; there lies behind his use of ideas some conception of a coherent world of things and of himself as a part of it.

It is implicit in much of the argument of the *Phenomenology* that ideas and the assumptions behind the use of them are necessarily shared; for, when Hegel speaks of consciousness, self-consciousness, reason and spirit, he seems always to have in mind either the individual related to others, or else some community or group. The individual comes to know himself through confrontations with others of his own kind, and his sense that he is a person has to be confirmed to him by them. As Hegel, speaking of a confrontation between self-conscious beings, puts it, they

have not yet revealed themselves to each other as existing for themselves, i.e. as self-consciousness. Each is indeed certain of its own self, but not of the other, and hence its own certainty of itself is still without truth. For its truth would be merely that its own individual existence for itself would be shown to it to be an independent object . . .[23]

The 'certainty' that is 'still without truth' clearly falls short of knowledge and does not satisfy the creature that has it; it is not what we ordinarily understand by certainty but a kind of precarious assurance seeking confirmation; it is a putting oneself to the proof. The self-conscious individual must be recognized for what he is by another, and must recognize him in turn, if he is to be sure of himself. The self-conscious, self-assertive being approaches his own kind boldly and yet also fearfully.

The individual reveals what he is in his actions; but this self-revelation is essentially 'an exposing of what is one's own in a universal element, where it comes to be and has to be "fact" for everyone'.[24] The universal element is universal because it is shared with others, because it is public; it is speech or some activity analogous to it. The individual may be unique but the media in which alone he can express himself, can be himself and know himself, are common to him with others. In asserting himself he 'publishes' himself to others.

Yet he is also a private person, opaque to others and to himself, who not only may but (so Hegel implies) must be 'estranged' from society as he makes progress towards freedom. This estrangement from society is also an estrangement from himself; for it is in society, in the activities that constitute social intercourse, that he expresses himself. Progress towards freedom, as Hegel imagines it, is a long course of change in which man begins by accepting unquestioningly the social order and his place in it and therefore also the idea of himself that 'reflects' that place, then becomes estranged from it and withdraws into

[23] *Phenomenology*, p. 232.
[24] *Ibid.* p. 437.

himself and his fantasies, until at last he is reconciled to it and to himself inside it. This movement is at once intellectual, moral and social; it is a growth in understanding, self-awareness and self-control, and also a gradual coming into existence of social forms suited to the needs and aspirations of intellectually and morally mature persons.

This course of change produces estrangement and then surmounts it because the beings involved in it are self-conscious; for the self-conscious are also self-critical. They develop their powers in being active, and in developing them acquire needs they cannot satisfy and only half-understand; the world is a mystery to them, and they are mysterious to themselves. They put questions they cannot answer, and aspire to more than they can have, and their questions and aspirations rest on illusion. Because they are self-conscious and questioning, and reach out for more than they can grasp, whether in thought or action, they are self-frustrating and self-deluding. Yet these same qualities in them ensure that in the end they come to know themselves and their aspirations for what they are, which involves coming to know the world, and especially the ethical universe, the world of their own activities, in which they reveal what they essentially are, and the course of history, of which they and that world are products. Self-knowledge and self-control, with the ability to form and to follow ideals and principles that are coherent and realistic, grow along with the understanding of society, in which alone ideals and principles have meaning.

When man, the self-conscious being, ceases to accept uncritically the ethical world he belongs to, when he becomes estranged from it and from himself, this estrangement finds expression in a succession of states of minds or attitudes that are philosophical or religious: in Stoicism and Scepticism, in the religions of what Hegel calls the Unhappy Consciousness (Judaism and Christianity), in certain kinds of individualism, in rationalist philosophy, and in moral theories of the Kantian type. These forms are stages in the progress towards a deeper understanding and fuller control of the self and the ethical or social world in which alone the self has its being.

The Stoic withdraws from the world into himself, aspiring to self-knowledge and self-mastery in a kind of spiritual independence of society; he lives in the greater world as a stranger and tries to preserve his private world from contamination by it. But this withdrawal and independence, this refuge in the private and the pure, are illusions, for what he rejects as alien to him is indissolubly connected with him, and he draws from it what makes him himself. The Sceptic takes refuge in doubt, proclaiming that nothing can be known and nothing matters, but while he lives he belies his creed; for to live is to act, and all action rests on assumptions about the world and is purposeful. The Unhappy Consciousness, frustrated and unvalued in this world, seeks compensation in

47

fantasy, in hopes of getting in another world what is out of reach in this one; but such fantasies are marks of impotence and no cure for it.

These philosophies and religions of man who does not yet understand his essential needs (the needs of a self-conscious and rational being) and cannot satisfy them in the world as it is, and especially in the ethical world of his own activities; these creeds in which he seeks relief or compensation for his sense of estrangement in the real world, are more than mere effects of his predicament; they are also reflections of it, expressing his sense of what it is while he is as yet incapable of seeing it clearly. The philosophical historian sees revealed in them the condition of the being that resorts to them. For each illusion or fantasy is a clue to the condition that produces it, but a clue that can be read only when the illusion or fantasy is dissipated.

Man aspires to freedom long before he understands what it is and how to achieve it; he seeks it, half blindly at first, and later with increasing discernment; he frustrates himself, for the world as it appears to him and in which he is estranged is the product of his own activities, of human history; he suffers in it and takes comfort in illusion and fantasy. But, as his understanding grows, he rids himself of his illusions; he takes up the position that finds sophisticated expression in rationalist philosophy, which assumes that everything can, in principle, be explained in terms of precisely formulated laws. Yet he still, at this stage, falls short of the truth because he rejects illusion and fantasy without explaining them, without revealing what they signify. He is unhistorical, and therefore does not understand the course of change, the progress that has made him what he is. It is a sign that the self-conscious being has achieved self-knowledge that he understands how he has come to be what he is, how his past is related to his present, not just temporally and causally, but as one phase to another in a course of spiritual change, in a movement towards a true knowledge of what it is to be the sort of being he is, and towards the freedom that comes of this knowledge. For the self-conscious being is a product of history in the peculiar sense that the past lives on in him; he could not be self-conscious, and could not have knowledge as distinct from mere sensations, impulses and habits, unless this were so.

Man, estranged from the ethical world he belongs to and therefore from himself, makes claims on his fellow men that cannot be met because they rest on illusions. Hegel discusses in the *Phenomenology* several kinds of individualism which seem to him self-defeating. One kind is the deliberate pursuit of one's own pleasure, a pursuit that cannot bring happiness; for the creature engaged in it, just because he is self-conscious and rational, is caught up in relations with other creatures of his own kind such that he cannot get happiness by pursuing ends that are purely self-regarding. Another kind Hegel calls 'the law of the heart'; it is the claim of the individual who has ceased to take convention for granted that he should be allowed to follow 'the dictates of his heart', to do what he feels intuitively is right. But the dictates of other hearts may not accord with those of his own; and when that is so, he must either renounce his claim or deny to others what he claims for himself. A third kind Hegel calls ' the virtuous consciousness '; and he means by it the uncompromising claim to live by the principles of a true morality, disregarding conventional obligations that conflict with them. This harsh and assertive virtue, says Hegel, is ' not merely like the combatant whose sole concern in the fight is to keep his sword polished but . . . has . . . started the fight simply to preserve its weapons '.[25] This kind of virtue, because it treats ' the world ' as an enemy to be defied and defeated, disregards the actual needs and feelings of men, the realities to which moral rules ought to apply; it is dogmatic and rhetorical, a self-righteous and rigid adherence to forms of words, to the letter that kills. But true virtue is a discipline that enriches life and does not impoverish it.

The revolutionary demands that the world – presumably the human or social world – should be in keeping with men's ideas of justice and their claims to freedom; and he wants to change the world to ensure that it is so. This demand is not unjustified, and its making is a step towards the achievement of freedom; and yet, in the form that it takes initially, it is misconceived, for no society can be changed according to plan to satisfy doctrinaires whose ideas about how it should be organized are always inadequate and unrealistic – always vague or inconsistent or excessive, given the resources, material and human, available at the time. The transformation of society to bring it into harmony with ideas about justice and freedom is a long process, and in the course of it these ideas change as much as the laws and institutions that are supposed to realize them; and what emerges at any stage of the process is not the achievement of any one group of privileged possessors of the truth.

Sophisticated moral theories of the Kantian type, and the attitudes to which such theories give expression, appear at a late stage of the progress towards freedom. They emphasize man's claim to act on principles that are his own because he has accepted them on rational grounds, and yet also universal because his reasons for accepting them, if they are good, are good for all men. Yet these theories, so it seems to Hegel, are too abstract; the rational grounds that they put forward are not closely enough related to life. The theories apply to rules of conduct criteria of validity that would make any set of such rules valid, provided they were consistent with one another and anyone acting upon them could wish everyone else to do so as well. The true criticism of rules of conduct is the attempt to live by them; an attempt which, if it is to give us a morality that is satisfying and not just logically consistent, will move us to modify our principles and to change our institutions and other practices.

If freedom is to be achieved both these claims – the revolutionary claim made

25 *Phenomenology*, p. 407.

on behalf of the people generally that the world (the social order) should be as they would have it, and the 'Kantian' claim for the individual that he should act on consistent principles accepted on rational grounds – must be made and 'transcended'. For these claims, like others that are made for all men by reason of their humanity, take to begin with forms in which they cannot be satisfied, and are afterwards altered as men learn by experience how to satisfy them. Just as it is the nature of man, the self-conscious and rational being whose activities develop his powers, to put questions he barely understands and cannot answer and then, as he tries to answer them, to learn to put intelligible and answerable questions, so it is his nature to want more than he can get, without quite knowing what it is he wants, and then, as he tries to get it, to learn to want what he can get and what satisfies him; it is his nature first to over-reach himself and then to recover himself.

Life is the only effective criticism of doctrines about how men should live, or – as the Marxist might put it – practice is the only effective criticism of theory; though practice, if it is to teach anything, if it is to do more than strengthen habit, must be the practice of a being who produces theories and tries to live by them. Only where theory guides practice, does practice correct theory; but the practice of human beings is always so guided, even when they deny that it is. To be free, as Hegel conceives freedom, men must know how they want to live and must be able to live that way; they must learn painfully lessons that are slow in the learning, and must learn them together.

Since man is a partaker in ethical life, a social being, there are connected with these philosophies, these outlooks on the world, types of society that succeed one another; but we need not consider them in detail to get the gist of Hegel's idea of freedom as the achievement of mankind. In the Greek city-state before the days of the Sophists and of Socrates, the individual does not yet challenge conventional morality or subject it to radical criticism, though he is already more sharply self-conscious and more self-assertive than he was in the oriental kingdoms; but this self-assertion is more aesthetic than moral, a form of self-display rather than a claim to follow one's conscience, and freedom is still the right to take part in running the community.* Then later, in the Hellenistic world and the Roman Empire, in what Hegel calls 'the soulless community' the citizen gives way to the mere subject – but to one who, unlike the subject of the oriental king, is a possessor of rights precisely defined, a legal person. At his reflective best, he has a private life, a life of thought and affection, a sanctum of freedom, into which he withdraws; and it is this escape, more symbolic than real, from the world that takes the form of Stoicism. For the Stoic, without defying the community or seeking to change it, retreats into himself and into the circle of his family and friends, as into a walled garden.

* *Editor's note* – Hegel's analysis of the Greek city-state is the subject of J. N. Shklar's essay.

The soulless community gives way to ' the world of culture ' lasting from the falling to pieces of the Roman Empire to the eve of the French Revolution; it is the world of the Unhappy Consciousness, of spirit estranged from itself, and of Christianity – the religion of man deeply and painfully self-aware and concerned for himself, longing for what is still out of reach, still seen obscurely though felt more keenly and closer at hand. It is in this world, in which feudalism changes gradually into absolute monarchy, that one kind of individualism after another flourishes; and its end is marked by the triumph of a rationalist philosophy that expresses man's sense that the world is no longer a mystery to him but is the place whose measure he can take and in which he can achieve his ends, and by the revolution inspired by that philosophy. For man is not satisfied with knowing the world; he must also use it for his own purposes, must affirm himself in it. Or, rather, he cannot know it, or himself either, except through the long endeavour to affirm himself in it.

Whether Hegel believed that mankind, or any part of it, had achieved freedom in his day or was close to doing so is a question still in dispute. Perhaps it will never be settled, and perhaps is not important. Far less important, surely, than his ideas about freedom, which are admirable in spite of the obscurities and perversities of the philosophy that enfolds them. Though we deny that the movement of history is inexorably towards freedom, and do not think of freedom quite as he did, we can admit that his account of it goes a long way towards explaining how it is that men care so strongly about freedom.

Burke, Hegel, and the French Revolution

J.-F. SUTER

I should like to bring out the close similarities between the political views of Burke and Hegel, and to go on to stress the importance of Burke's linking role in the political discussion that began with Rousseau and culminated in Hegel.[1] To start with, I shall examine the opposition of both Burke and Hegel to Rousseau's moral and political doctrine, and their critiques of the French Revolution. I shall go on to show the coincidence of certain of their views on society and the state. To finish, I shall say something on their points of disagreement, in particular touching the significance of tradition and revolution.

Critique of Rousseau and of the French Revolution

According to Burke, Rousseau's moral ideal is abstract, subjective, vague and indeterminate.[2] In placing the spring of moral life exclusively in the heart or in the conscience, Rousseau makes the individual the only judge of the validity of his acts. Now the content of a private conscience may be good just as it may prove to be bad.[3] Man may be satisfied with his good intentions, be his actions as evil as they may. Burke thinks that one cannot abandon important moral decisions to the arbitrary will of the individual.[4]

Burke reproaches Rousseau for having perverted the true relationship between natural feeling and reason.[5] In the spirit of the British moral tradition, in particular of Shaftesbury and Adam Smith, Burke tries to reconcile a legitimate self-interest with a regard for the general good. He believes that passions can be useful to society if they are suitably educated and tempered by laws and manners. By contrast, Rousseau, in his moral fanaticism, tends to sacrifice all natural sentiments to the alleged requirements of patriotism or of humanity.[6] For the natural and rational ties, such as family love and public feeling, he substitutes

---

[1] Although Hegel does not expressly mention Burke's writings, it is likely that the *Reflections on the Revolution in France* (1790) would have come to the notice of someone so carefully observing English and French affairs. Moreover, the text had been published in a German translation by Gentz, in 1793.

[2] VI, 31–40. (Roman figures refer to the volumes, arabic to the pages, of the edition printed for F. and C. Rivington, 16 vols, London, 1803–27.)

[3] ' Men are full as inclined to Vice as to Virtue ', H. V. F. Somerset, *A Notebook of Edmund Burke* (Cambridge, 1957), p. 96.

[4] VI, 204–7.

[5] VI, 34–41.

[6] Leo Strauss, *Natural Right and History* (Chicago, 1953), p. 301.

' a speculative benevolence '.[7] However, as Burke notes, ' that sort of reason which banishes the affections is incapable of filling their place '.[8] Abstract reasoning destroys the natural harmony between moral and instinctive life. While individuals are prompted by natural sympathy to good moral action, Rousseau's artificial morality leads to ' an unsocial independence '.[9]

In the hands of his disciples, Rousseau's moral doctrine becomes a political weapon to subvert the existing order. Under the pretext of reconstructing the whole fabric of society, they ' commence their schemes of reform with abolition and total destruction '.[10] Burke vigorously attacks the doctrinaire mentality which sets out to realize an ' ideal ' or ' imaginary ' state as if there did not already exist a state in the world.[11] To his mind, it is absurd to look for *a priori* foundations of political life as if human existence were not already organized according to rules and laws.[12] ' I cannot conceive how any man can have brought himself to that pitch of presumption, to consider his country as nothing but *carte blanche*, upon which he may scribble whatever he pleases.' [13]

Burke sees in Rousseau the intellectual father of the French Revolution.[14] In his writings, he says, the French Revolutionaries have found ' this fundamental and fatal principle ' of their new scheme of government, ' that in every country the people is the legitimate sovereign '.[15] Burke does not reject the view that all authority has its ultimate source in the people, but he disputes that the people's rights are absolute and inalienable.[16] Rousseau's doctrine of popular sovereignty tends, in his opinion, to the subversion of all the principles of morals and politics, as it makes the authority of government dependent on the mere will of the multitude.[17]

Burke rejects Rousseau's doctrine concerning the people as contradictory and self-destructive. First, it is dangerous constantly to set one part of the constitution, the electorate or the legislature, against another part, the government.[18] Such a mechanical view of politics leads to conflict and anarchy where one should find collaboration and harmony. Secondly, it is absurd to locate the supreme power in a single organ of the constitution, because the role of the supreme power is precisely to coordinate the different powers and functions of the state. For Burke, the state cannot exist for the benefit of one of its parts only, since these parts exist only for the advantage of the whole.[19] The state is a ' multifarious thing ', pursuing various ends and permitting the greatest diversity of interests.[20]

---

[7] v, 285. [8] v, 152. [9] vi, 33. [10] v, 303.

[11] ' You had all the advantages in your ancient states; but you chose to act as if you had never been moulded into civil society, and had everything to begin anew ', v, 82.

[12] v, 310–11; vi, 258.

[13] v, 285. [14] vi, 38–9. [15] vii, 270–1.

[16] vi, 147. [17] vi, 148, 203–4. [18] v, 336.

[19] ' The government is the point of reference of the several members and districts of our representation. This is the centre of our unity. This government of reference is a trustee for the *whole*, and not for the parts ', v, 336. [20] v, 97.

The British state, in particular, is a mixed monarchy, in which three principles – monarchic, aristocratic, and democratic – are balanced and unified.[21] Neither the king, nor the aristocracy, nor the people possesses absolute power. But for Burke the ' people ', as a collection of individuals, is not properly qualified to rule; an ' uncollected multitude ' is unable to control governmental action.[22] It is only as an organic part of the constitution, as a corporate body, acting through its representatives in Parliament, that the people can participate in political decisions.[23] When it is not organized, not governed, it degenerates into a formless mass and the state becomes the prey of factions. Thus Burke warns, at an early stage of the Revolution, that the Parisian populace will become the determining factor in government, and that mob-inciting Revolutionaries will impose their will on the rest of the nation.[24]

In the chapter of the *Phenomenology of Mind* called ' Absolute Freedom and Terror ', Hegel argues a close relationship between Rousseau and the French Revolution.[25] He interprets Rousseau as the philosopher of an epoch in which, the external order being abolished, every man was free to transform his inner conviction into a political reality. In that epoch freedom was ' absolute ' because there was no community any more, only isolated individuals, private persons. The state existed only in the imagination of the citizens, in their projects of a constitution.

In Hegel's view, the attempt to realize Rousseau's abstract ideal of freedom led necessarily to a ' fury of destruction '.[26] The French Revolutionaries not only repudiated all differentiation of society into particular classes but they regarded ' all differences in talent and authority as being superseded '.[27] But the necessity of government requires that the ' general will ' be concentrated in one individuality and that a single will be put at its head.[28] Then the community resolves itself into a universal will represented by the mass of the people and a particular will represented by the government. This leads to a perpetual opposition of the government and the people, for no intermediary power is in a position to ' mediate ', to stand between them.[29] Thus the assertion in France of absolute

---

[21] VI, 113–14; VIII, 252.

[22] VII, 271. Cf. also VI, 210–11, 216; X, 95.

[23] VI, 210–11.

[24] V, 23–4, 111, 137, 350–1. But Burke saw clearly that this state of anarchy was transitory and that political authority would re-establish itself and impose some extreme form of despotism. In 1790 he made the striking prediction that the French Revolution would end in a ' military democracy ' with a general at its head. Cf. V, 390–1.

[25] *The Phenomenology of Mind*, trans. J. B. Baillie, 2nd ed. (London, 1931), pp. 599–610.

[26] *Ibid.* p. 604. Cf. also *Hegel's Philosophy of Right*, trans. T. M. Knox (Oxford, 1942), § 5, p. 22.

[27] *Ibid.* Addition to § 5, p. 227.

[28] *Phenomenology*, p. 605.

[29] The union, abstractly conceived, of the multitude into the state leads in fact to their separation. It is an example of what Hegel calls ' bad infinity ', an attitude characterized by a relationship

individual freedom necessarily involved the suppression of other individuals, and authoritarian rule over the citizens.[30]

In the *Philosophy of Right*, Hegel denounces once again the pernicious role which Rousseau's political doctrine had played in the French Revolution.[31] He begins by giving Rousseau credit for having rid political thought of empiricism, that is of the hypothesis that there is a social instinct or a divine authority.* He reproaches him, however, for having stopped at an abstract definition of the state. In his philosophy, individual wills and the general will are not really united except by the artificial device of the social contract; in the notion of contract it is still the subjective will which prevails over the general will: the contract is only valid for those who explicitly recognize its authority over them, it is not normative or objective in a universal sense. Consequently, the philosophy of Rousseau, if put into practice, yields no stable or durable state, but rather the rule of arbitrary interest. The notion of contract cannot give birth to a well-constituted state; it can only produce a shapeless aggregate of private initiatives, which will lead sooner or later to revolution. Hegel asserts that a reasonable philosophy of the state cannot promote a situation in which everything is destroyed in order that an entirely new society be built up out of nothing. One may criticize a state, but one can never arrive at its total rejection.

Hegel's critique of the French Revolution does not mean that there cannot exist a dissociation of individuals and society, a chasm between ideals and institutions; it implies, however, that this dissociation cannot last *for ever*. One may be dissatisfied with political life, one may even propose to destroy it, but one may only do so in order to create a new political reality, more satisfying than the old.[32] Subjective conscience is valid insofar as it finds an objective realization in social institutions; it must not irresponsibly condemn the actual state without putting something equally concrete in its place.[33]

of reciprocal exclusion between the individual and the universal. On the one hand, the individual rejects all particularizations of the universal as unacceptable barriers on himself. Thus the French Revolutionaries destroyed even the institutions they had themselves created (*Philosophy of Right*, Addition to § 5). On the other, the government stifles all individual initiatives and inevitably becomes despotic, since it cannot count on the cooperation of the citizens. By contrast, ' good infinity ' consists in the process of mediation, by which the individual and the state are united and reconciled. In Hegel's system, the social forms of *Sittlichkeit* (the family, the corporations of civil society, and the state) serve as mediations between the objective demands of the collectivity and the subjective claims of the individual.

[30] *Phenomenology*, pp. 605–6.

[31] *Philosophy of Right*, § 258, pp. 156–7.

* *Editor's note* – Another analysis of Hegel's critique of Rousseau is to be found in the essay by M. Riedel, pp. 138–41.

[32] Cf. Burke: ' The subversion of a government, to deserve any praise, must be considered but as a step preparatory to the formation of something better, either in the scheme of the government itself, or in the persons who administer it, or in both ', VI, 96.

[33] *Philosophy of Right*, § 106, p. 75.

Hegel takes issue with the French Revolutionaries for not willing the positive reality of their ideals. They imagine that they wish universal freedom and equality, but, in fact, they do not want anything particular and articulate.[34] Only by destroying something do they feel themselves to exist.[35] Rather than sacrifice the ideal purity of their conscience, they resort to violence to eliminate all the obstacles to the realization of their projects. Hegel's criticism of abstract individual freedom is sharply formulated in the following remark:

On the religious level, it is the freedom of the void, which in the Hindu ideal of pure contemplation, gives rise to the ascetic negation of the world. On the political level, it is the fanaticism which ends in the destruction of the whole political order, in the elimination of all suspicious individuals, and in the annihilation of any new attempt at organization.[36]

In acknowledging the failure of the Revolution and in condemning the Terror which followed it, Hegel does not take up a reactionary position, but remains a firm supporter of the Revolutionary principles.[37] He does not criticize the French Revolution for having proclaimed the principles of freedom and equality, but only for having failed to put them into practice. Hegel insists on the great advance the Revolution has made in asserting the right of the individual to obey only laws and institutions which conform with his subjective demands.[38] In the modern age, he thinks, no system of laws can remain in force unless man recognizes in it his own free aspirations and is prepared to die for it. The French Revolution was, for Hegel, a major achievement insofar as it made men aware of their rights and taught them to act consciously and thoughtfully in politics; its failure was in not conceiving and implementing some *durable* political solution.

This already suggests a difference, to which we shall return, between the political standpoints of Burke and Hegel. Whereas the former interpreted the Revolution as a complete break with the past, as a radical challenge to all traditional systems of authority, the latter looked upon it as a new and important stage in the creation of the modern state. For Hegel the French Revolution

---

[34] *Ibid.* Addition to § 5.

[35] *Ibid.* § 5, p. 22. Cf. Burke: ' Something they must destroy, or they seem to themselves to exist for no purpose ', v, 118.

[36] *Ibid.* § 5, p. 22.

[37] It is remarkable that Hegel retains his faith in the Revolution in spite of the Terror. In a passage written in 1803/4 we find him even justifying the Terror as a necessary transition from the old regime to a new epoch in world history. Hegel seems to think that Terror was needed to break the resistance of the ancient society and to allow Napoleon to erect the modern state upon the ashes of the Revolution. But once the Revolution has accomplished its necessary work of destroying all laws and institutions not founded on reason, it becomes anachronistic. After Napoleon, who knew how to reconcile civil freedom and strong government, there was no need to start again from scratch and the attempt to do so could only lead to chaos and disorder. It was reforms which from now on had to take the place of revolutions. Cf. *Sämtliche Werke*, ed. J. Hoffmeister (Leipzig, 1937), vol. xx, pp. 247–8.

[38] *Lectures on the Philosophy of History*, trans. J. Sibree (New York, 1956), p. 447.

represented a turning-point in history, because it marked the first attempt to achieve consciously and willingly the freedom of all men, the freedom of every individual.[39] The efforts of men in the past had often tended to realize freedom, but it was only after the French Revolution that these efforts had become conscious.[40] While Burke saw in the Revolution only a will to destroy, Hegel viewed it also as a positive attempt to reconstruct society on a new basis, namely on the *idea* of universal justice. Unlike Burke, Hegel clearly perceived that after the French Revolution the state could no longer depend for its maintenance simply on the wisdom of the ruler or the privileged few, but that its existence was now grounded on the principle of universal equality.[41]

Living Morality and the Dialectic of Social Life

Burke contrasts with abstract individualism the concrete manners of a whole people, the living morality that a nation preserves in the form of beliefs, prejudices and moral dispositions. Social habits and conventions seem to him superior to the decisions of an individual because they crystallize the historic mentality of a nation. Traditional morality represents a higher form of ethical life than subjective opinions because it is composed of a multitude of individual convictions. The social order, Burke says, is the cumulative ' result of the thoughts of many minds, in many ages '.[42] For this reason, he condemns the monstrous pride of the Parisian legislators who set up the authority of their personal convictions against the millennia throughout which the same law and the same institutions have united men.[43]

Burke does not banish reason altogether from politics. He does not despise reason as such, but abstract reason only: he denies individual reason the power to reject all that has been realized in the past and recognized by everyone as legitimate forms of the communal life of man. In a well-known passage in the *Reflections* he praises his fellow-countrymen for seeing more clearly than the French *philosophes* that reason must operate within a tradition, must make use of the prejudices and common opinions of the age:

Many of our men of speculation, instead of exploding general prejudices, employ their sagacity to discover the latent wisdom which prevails in them . . . They think it more wise to continue the prejudice, with the reason involved, than to cast away the

---

[39] *Ibid.* pp. 447–54.

[40] According to Hegel, the principle of subjective freedom first arose in religion with Christianity and was later developed and propagated through the world by the Reformation, but only as an inner value which was still compatible with submission to a given order. In the Reformation, this principle remained abstractly conceived as the liberty of conscience. The French Revolution completed the work of the Reformation, emancipating the individual from all forms of bondage and inequality. Cf. *ibid.* pp. 333–5, 416–17, 447.

[41] *Philosophy of Right*, § 273, pp. 177–8.

[42] VI, 261.

[43] V, 125.

coat of prejudice, and to leave nothing but the naked reason; because prejudice, with its reason, has a motive to give action to that reason, and an affection which will give it permanence . . . Prejudice renders a man's virtue his habit; and not a series of unconnected acts. Through just prejudice, his duty becomes a part of his nature.[44]

Prejudice, as understood by Burke, is not 'destitute of reason'; on the contrary, it involves a 'profound and extensive wisdom'.[45]

Here Burke approaches the position of Aristotle, who also had regarded morality as being made of acquired habits, of the stable dispositions of citizens living in a well-constituted state.[46] The essence of ethical life lies, for Aristotle, in the moral attitude, something which becomes an unconscious habit for the individual, rather than in the consciously thought out decision. Burke adopts the Aristotelian concept of habitus (ἕξις), according to which morality is real when it moulds the life of the individual and not when the individual serves as the absolute standard of right and wrong, as in the case of Rousseau's moral idealism.[47] For Burke as for Aristotle, morality must not give way to self-questioning, but must spring from the ensemble of customs and attitudes arising out of education and communal living.

Burke refuses to accept that the formation and continuing existence of a community depend on men's joining together, casting their votes and thus expressing the general will by a mere majority.[48] For the abstract notion of general will, he substitutes the idea of the nation as a product of history: 'A nation is not an idea only of local extent, and individual momentary aggregation, but it is an idea of continuity, which extends in time as well as in numbers, and in space.'[49] The constitution of a nation is not made by 'any sudden and temporary arrangement'; 'it is made by the particular circumstances, occasions, tempers, and moral, civil, and social habitudes of the people, which disclose themselves only in a long space of time'.[50]

Burke criticizes the notion of the sovereignty of the people because it implies that only the present generation is sovereign: 'present conveniency' becomes the only 'principle of attachment' to the constitution.[51] By insisting that the constitution is a work of centuries and is justified by its long duration, Burke is attacking the *primacy of the present*, which is characteristic of the philosophy of the Enlightenment.[52] Since they absolutize the present, the philosophers of the

---

44 v, 168–9.

45 v, 176.

46 *Nicomachean Ethics*, 1103 a–b.

47 III, 112; VI, 39–40.

48 VI, 211–13.

49 x, 97.

50 x, 96–7.

51 v, 169. Cf. Strauss, *Natural Right*, p. 299.

52 For Hobbes, there is no right of prescription; the sovereign is the present sovereign (*Leviathan*, ed. M. Oakeshott (Oxford, 1948), ch. XXVI, p. 175). For Locke, men are at liberty to accept or reject the political regime in which they are born (*Second Treatise of Civil Government*, § 73). Rousseau maintains in the *Contrat Social* (bk III, ch. 2) that the 'law of yesterday does not oblige today' and, therefore, that its validity rests on the presumption that the present sovereign confirms it tacitly when it does not repeal it.

Enlightenment are unable to understand the specificity of the past and are tempted to reject it as an age of darkness. On the other hand, Burke's critical attitude towards his own time allows him a more sympathetic insight into the institutions of the past. Whereas the rationalists of his day such as Voltaire fail to account for the duration of religious and political institutions, Burke seems to have perceived that the survival of these institutions was due to their capacity to transform themselves so as to answer the needs of each epoch and to adapt themselves to the mentality of each society.

Burke claims to correct the excesses of abstract individualism by giving it a *historical* base. Abstract principles of natural right must be ' embodied in some manner or other ', must be successfully institutionalized before it is possible to decide on their merits.[53] Political reflection presupposes an already existing state, and the state cannot be deduced from the existence of a stateless man, as the natural law theorists would like. A political theory is always the projection of the ideas of a living morality, the historical expression of a way of life.[54] Political philosophy does not create a state, it originates in a state that has become what it is in history – more exactly, through the successive attempts of men to understand and to transform it. To Burke society is always structured and ordered, and one of the important functions of the philosopher is to understand the positive and preserving factors that history has created from within itself. The philosopher will identify the spirit of the laws, the reason which is immanent in social institutions; the mass of the people will recognize the rule of the state as the embodiment of their personal wishes and aspirations.[55]

It is in his essay on natural law, published in Jena in 1802, that Hegel's position comes closest to Burke's.[56] Here Hegel directs sharp criticism at the political individualism of his predecessors and develops an organic conception of the state.

Hegel first sets out to differentiate his political philosophy from the *empirical* doctrines of natural right, as well as from the *formal* approach of Kant and Fichte. Both methods are inadequate because they fail to take into account the *whole* of political reality. The error of the first method is to reconstruct an anarchic primitive state by abstraction of all that belongs to ' particular customs, history, civilization and the state itself '; that of the second is to ignore the freedom which has been realized in existing laws and institutions and to reject all the singular and contingent ' under the shameful name of empirical '.[57]

---

[53] *Speeches*, III, 475.

[54] v, 311; vi, 258; x, 99.

[55] vi, 261–2. Burke's awareness of the importance of social opinion and long-adopted prejudices comes from Montesquieu's *Esprit des Lois*. See in particular Burke's magnificent eulogy of the great Frenchman in *Appeal from the New to the Old Whigs* (1791), vi, 263–4.

[56] *Wissenschaftliche Behandlungsarten des Naturrechts, Sämtliche Werke*, ed. G. Lasson, vol. VII (Leipzig, 1923), pp. 327–411.   [57] *Ibid.* pp. 335, 336, 346, 349.

Surprisingly, Hegel proves more indulgent towards the deficiencies of empiricism than towards those of formalism. He even justifies the claims of *Empirie* against those who pretend to have made a 'philosophical revolution' in expressing abstract notions of freedom, equality and humanity.[58] He sympathizes with those who do not appeal to the rights of man, but to experience and history. He also appreciates the efforts of the pragmatic historians of the Enlightenment such as Montesquieu, who do not 'deduce' the state abstractly, but grasp its true essence intuitively.[59] The approach of these historians was already philosophical because they did not explain the state by its origin, but as the result of its process, as the outcome of a long evolution.[60] The true empiricists, for all the defects of their methods, seem to come nearer an *organic* vision of politics than abstract moralists.

Finally, Hegel develops his own conception of politics. He intends to overcome the Kantian dualism between right and duty and to show that both are united in what he calls 'ethical life' or 'living morality' (*Sittlichkeit*), to distinguish it from the 'abstract morality' (*Moralität*) of Kant and Fichte.[61] The unity of law and moral life resides, for Hegel, in the ensemble of customs and traditions which constitute a people.[62] The people is that 'moral substance' in which there is no opposition between subjective demands and social prescriptions. Through his participation in the ethical life of the people, the individual is harmoniously integrated into the society to which he belongs.

This harmony between the individual and society seems to Hegel to have been realized in the Greek city-state.* He refers to the Greek notion of 'ethos', the intimate union of law and subjective dispositions.[63] Greek laws express the people's ideal of dignified and reasonable conduct. The serene national life testifies that the individual identifies himself with the community. This, of

---

[58] *Ibid*. p. 342.

[59] *Ibid*. pp. 340–1. On Montesquieu, see below, note 62.

[60] In the *Encyclopaedia* (§ 143), Hegel praises the historians for having understood that the evolution of a thing presupposes its reality. The truth of a phenomenon does not reside in something external to it (in a 'possibility' or a 'hypothesis'), but in its immanent development. For Hegel as for Aristotle, only the end of a process can explain its beginnings.

[61] *Werke*, vol. VII, pp. 368, 388–9.

[62] 'The absolute ethical whole is nothing else than a people', *ibid*. p. 368. It does not seem worth looking for a precise model for Hegel's *Volksgeist* because such an idea was a commonplace at the time and very much in the air. If one was to single out one thinker to whom Hegel's *Volksgeist* owes more than to anybody else, it would be Montesquieu. In his essay on natural law, Hegel pays a tribute to Montesquieu, whose merit, in his eyes, consists in having shown that the form of a government is not determined by a contract of private law, but by the particular character of a people. Cf. *ibid*. p. 406.

* *Editor's note* – A point discussed by J. N. Shklar, pp. 80–7.

[63] *Ibid*. pp. 388–9; *Philosophy of Right*, § 151, p. 108, and Hegel's own marginal note on this paragraph, where he translates ἦθος as *Sitte*, custom. Cf. *Grundlinien der Philosophie des Rechts*, ed. J. Hoffmeister, 4th ed. (Hamburg, 1955), p. 417.

course, is the substance of morality in its unreflected and unconscious state; here tradition is accepted without question. As yet there is no sign of that conscious approval of social morality which, in the *Philosophy of Right*, Hegel regards as the salient feature of the communal life of his day.[64]

In the *Philosophy of Right*, Hegel gives penetrating reasons why it is not possible for a community to stop at a relationship of mere trust between governors and governed.[65] Trust, though it is for the individual the essential manner of belonging to the collectivity, is too subjective and personal a feeling to guarantee the permanence and cohesion of the modern state. A healthy political life cannot be built on faith and loyalty alone, for such dispositions are easily transformed into their opposites. Faith and trust already contain seeds of doubt and of distrust, for to be trusting implies the beginning of a split between a state of affairs and a judgment on that state. To each favourable judgment corresponds the possibility of its negation. Trust is already a form of thought, though still rudimentary and inadequate: unable to say *why* one approves some given social state, one's trust may easily turn to doubt.

At Jena, Hegel seems, however, to overlook the fact that loyalty and obedience represent only an elementary form of reconciliation between the individual and the state, which must also be supported by the free and reflective activity of its individual members. He is inclined to depreciate the importance of the self-conscious activity of the subject, in order to emphasize the objective conditions of political life. When he rightly insists on the positive role of manners, laws and institutions in raising the individual to the universal, he seems to understate the importance of the process by which the universal is 'particularized' and 'relativized' by the moral action of the individual. It is only, however, through the individual's moral initiative that universal freedom can begin to be realized, that the world can be changed by reason. In short, the concept of living morality that Hegel holds at this stage fails to incorporate the individual consciousness of law and morals.[66] It should not be difficult to recognize in this concept the fundamental tenet of Burke's position, the essence of which lies in the spontaneous self-identification of the individual with the state.

Hegel is also on common ground with Burke when he refuses, in the *Philosophy of Right*, to formulate theoretically a new morality. He does not see the

---

[64] *Philosophy of Right*, § 260, pp. 160–1, and § 260 Addition, p. 280.

[65] *Ibid*. § 147, p. 106. Cf. Eugène Fleischmann, *La philosophie politique de Hegel* (Paris, 1964), p. 191.

[66] At the time of his essay on natural law, Hegel is still dominated by the ideal of the Greek city-state, where there was no dissociation between private man and political community. That predisposition towards antiquity explains why he fails to integrate the individual in a satisfactory way into the state. Hegel has not yet sufficiently developed the idea of living morality: he still thinks of it as a felt, not thought, identity. It is only in the *Philosophy of Right* that he reconciles the two aspects, subjective and objective, of morality.

need to elaborate a philosophical theory of virtues, a *Tugendlehre*, as Kant did.[67] In his system, the only virtue philosophically defined is probity (*Rechtschaffen-heit*), which consists in the individual's participation in the ethical values of the community.[68] The right of individuals to act according to their subjective conscience ' is fulfilled when they belong to an actual ethical order '.[69] In order to be virtuous, man has only to conform to ' the duties of the station to which he belongs '.[70] What the individual *ought* to do is not for Hegel a moral problem; he has only to respect the law and to follow what in his society is regarded as upright behaviour.[71]

It is well known that Burke dislikes the principle of the democratic vote, preferring the hereditary character of a monarchy. In the *Reflections*, he is eager to demonstrate that the legitimacy of the British crown derives not from popular choice, but from lawful succession.[72] A hereditary monarchy appears to him a surer pledge of what is durable, free and rational in the state than the transient will of popular elections.[73] British liberties are safer under a monarchy than under a republic because the very existence of an inheritable crown depends on the permanence of the institutions of the country. In a word, the regular succession on the throne of the same family is the best guarantee of the historical continuity of the state.[74]

Hegel is just as unwilling to accept the doctrine of popular sovereignty.[75] To invest an undefined, amorphous mass with sovereignty is to surrender the state unconditionally to the discretion of private interests.[76] Hereditary succession is a good deal less capricious than popular election. Hegel is of the opinion that the collective decision of an assembly is irresponsible.[77] In case of a serious crisis, a majority in an assembly can less easily be held responsible for its policy than a single identifiable ruler who is impelled to act prudently because of his personal responsibility. For Hegel, the individuality of the state must be represented by an individual monarch who symbolizes its unity and continuity.[78]

Burke deplores the presence in the French National Assembly of so many men of poor and obscure condition and the absence of men worthy of consideration by virtue of their independence and wealth. He remarks that the best of them were merely ' men of theory '.[79] These were capable enough of criticizing the state, but, in his opinion, lacked the practical experience to reform it. The

[67] *Philosophy of Right*, § 148, pp. 106–7.
[68] *Ibid.* § 150, p. 107.
[69] *Ibid.* § 153, p. 109.
[70] *Ibid.* § 150, p. 107. Cf. Burke: ' The situation of man is the preceptor of his duty ', IV, 44.
[71] *Philosophy of Right*, § 150, p. 107.
[72] V, 51–8.
[73] V, 64.
[74] V, 66.
[75] *Philosophy of Right*, § 279, pp. 182–3.
[76] *Ibid.* § 281, pp. 185–6.
[77] *Ibid.* § 279, pp. 181–2.
[78] *Ibid.* § 280 Addition, pp. 288–9.
[79] V, 90.

majority of the Assembly was made up of small lawyers, recently arrived from the provinces where they had spent their lives worrying about trifling matters.[80] How could they possess practical insight into the affairs of a great country?

From this starting point, Burke develops an interesting dialectic between talent and property, between those who have nothing apart from their native gifts and natural ability (lawyers, doctors, traders, writers) and those whose influence in the state comes from inherited wealth (aristocrats, squires, clergymen). According to Burke, society must recognize the importance of both groups, but not in the same proportion. To preserve the equipoise of the state, it is necessary to impose restrictions on the activities of the men of talent as the more energetic and enterprising group. Since property is a ' sluggish, inert, and timid ' principle, it must predominate in the state; it must be protected from the ' invasions ' of that ' vigorous and active ' principle, ability.[81]

In Burke's opinion, a well-ordered commonwealth has to ensure an equilibrium between the individual creativity of talented men and the social stability provided by landed property. The ' solid substance of land ' must counterpoise the superior skill and vigour of the burghers. Its fortune being newly acquired, the bourgeois class is willing to innovate and more prepared for political adventure.[82] This justifies, in Burke's eyes, the existence of the House of Lords, and also the large proportion of big landowners among the members of the House of Commons.[83]

Similarly, for Hegel, it is the class of the big landowners which is best fitted to exert a benevolent and stabilising influence on the body politic.[84] By their patriarchal life and inherited wealth, they possess a powerful moral authority which induces the other citizens to put their trust in them. They are able to mediate between the monarch, with whom their birth gives them an affinity, and the people, whose interests they may plead before the king. Furthermore, the fortunes of that class are largely independent of the state and of the fluctuations of economic life, which permits them to have a moderating effect on political life.[85] The great landowners do not owe their social position to the favour of the king, nor to popular election. They are even protected against their own self-destructive caprices, for they inherit and transmit their estates according to the rules of primogeniture.[86] It follows that landed property-owners are particularly qualified to take an active part in legislation. As the solid foundation of their existence, the land, is inalienable, there is no objection to the transmission by inheritance of their legislative functions.[87] In short, the landowning class is the

[80] v, 91–2.

[81] v, 107.

[82] v, 95–6, 206–10. Burke saw in French Jacobinism a revolt of the country's enterprising talent against property (VIII, 170). This revolt found its most visible expression in the emergence of a new type of writers, the ' political men of letters '.

[83] v, 108–9.

[84] *Philosophy of Right*, § 305, p. 199.

[85] *Ibid.* § 306, p. 199.

[86] *Ibid.* § 306 Addition, p. 293.

[87] *Ibid.* § 307, p. 199.

bulwark of both the people and the royal power. It should therefore form one of the chambers of Parliament.[88]

Just as that class, in the Upper Chamber, represents the conservative and static element, so, in the Lower Chamber, the other classes, mobile and dynamic like society itself, are represented through deputies.[89] Both chambers complement each other in a legislative body where all the vital interests of the nation are wisely balanced.[90] In outlining this constitutional scheme, Hegel implicitly criticizes Rousseau, who had required that *all* citizens should participate in political deliberations. To Hegel this is an abstract view of the state, as it presupposes that society be composed of isolated individuals.[91] In modern states, moreover, the citizens cannot take part directly in legislation, because of their number and of the nature of their activities. But they are grouped by interests, and it is sufficient that these interests are represented.[92] Whereas the decision of the landed proprietor is guaranteed by the independence of his patrimonial good, the virtue of the deputy consists in his personal talent and his experience acquired in the service of the public interest.[93]

Hegel's and Burke's conceptions of monarchy and representation, though strikingly similar in some aspects, differ completely in others. While both favoured limited monarchy, Hegel was less willing than Burke to identify this regime with feudal monarchy, based on the maintenance of the traditional rights and privileges of king and nobility.[94] To Hegel the sovereignty of the monarch was not grounded on a purely positive or prescriptive title, but on the ' rationality of the constitution '.[95] To him it concretely meant that a single monarch was legitimate only in so far as he respected the ' public freedom ' of which the nation was the *real* holder.[96] While accepting the principle of inheritance, Hegel sought to restrict the power of the monarch to a level which we may identify with that of the power of a constitutional ruler or of a president in a present-day republic.[97] He insisted that nobility and wealth were not a sufficient title to public office: every citizen had the right to hold a governmental post, if he possessed the required qualifications and had proved his competence.[98] He admitted, however, that the financial independence of the landowners could facilitate their dedication to the service of the state.[99] But Hegel nowhere identified the landowning class with the nobility of the old regime. In the *Philosophy of Right*, he did not even mention the nobility and spoke ambiguously

[88] *Ibid.* § 307, pp. 199–200.

[89] *Ibid.* § 308, p. 200.

[90] *Ibid.* § 312, p. 205.

[91] *Ibid.* § 308, pp. 200–1.

[92] *Ibid.* § 309 Addition, pp. 293–4.

[93] *Ibid.* § 310, p. 201.

[94] *Ibid.* § 273 Remark, pp. 177–8; *Encyclopaedia*, § 544.

[95] *Philosophy of Right*, § 281, p. 185, § 286, pp. 187–8.

[96] *Ibid.* § 286, p. 188.

[97] *Ibid.* § 280 Addition, pp. 288–9.

[98] *Ibid.* § 291, p. 190.

[99] *Ibid.* § 306 Addition, p. 293.

of landowners.[100] This makes it plausible that for him a landowning class based on primogeniture and entailed estates was a historical survival which would gradually disappear with the establishment of rational institutions.

Tradition and Revolution

We may sum up our previous discussion by saying that Burke and Hegel set up against abstract individualism an organic conception of the state. This conception implies that there is a close connection between the form of the state and the political life on the one hand, and on the other what Hegel, following Montesquieu, calls customs (*Sitten*) and ethical life (*Sittlichkeit*) – what was known to Burke and to ancient philosophy as laws and manners. A state is always the creation of a particular tradition just as a tradition is always the creation of a particular state. Hence it is meaningless to impose on a people a constitution which does not accord with its moral insight and its feeling for justice.[101]

---

[100] *Ibid.* § 307, p. 199. In his essay on natural law, Hegel had in view not the nobility of the old regime, but a class created upon the model of Napoleon's parliamentary and military aristocracy. See Georg Lukács, *Der junge Hegel* (Zürich, 1948), pp. 289, 479–80, 495, 497, 531. Hegel's mature political ideas bore a close resemblance to those of the Prussian reformers who advocated a reform of the Prussian nobility to end their isolation from the other classes and to make them suitable leaders of public opinion. It is even likely that the *Philosophy of Right* was conceived by Hegel as a political act to further the liberal views of Humboldt against the reactionary policy of Hardenberg.

It is important to stress that Hegel describes political institutions which did not yet exist at that time in Prussia (his demand for a permanent representative assembly was not fulfilled there until 1848); for the point has often been badly understood, and authoritarian, even totalitarian tendencies wrongly attributed to his political thinking. In Hegel's entire work, there is not to be found even the slightest hint that he thought the Prussian state of his day had realized this constitutional scheme. In some respects Hegel's system of representation bore the mark of English institutions; in others it followed the pattern of the various Napoleonic assemblies. While condemning the system of corruption and the absurdities of representation in Britain, Hegel also praised the British Parliament as a model of rational organization and procedure. See *Hegel's Political Writings*, trans. T. M. Knox, with an introductory essay by Z. A. Pelczynski (Oxford, 1964), pp. 85–6, 90, 321–30. Besides, we know that his idea of a two-chamber system was strongly influenced by British experience. See Karl Rosenkranz, *Hegels Leben* (Berlin, 1844), p. 133. On the other hand, we learn from his letters that Hegel was favourably struck by the parliamentary character of Napoleon's regime (at least in the first period of his rule), and by the obvious desire of the French emperor to convince his fellow-citizens of the rightness of his policies. See *Briefe von und an Hegel*, ed. J. Hoffmeister (Hamburg, 1952), vol. I, pp. 185, 218–19. To the end of his life Hegel seems to have regarded the constitution Napoleon gave to the kingdom of Italy as a model of judicious representation in a monarchical state. See *Political Writings*, p. 314.

[101] According to Hegel, one cannot coerce a people into freedom when by its manners and habits it is unprepared for it: ' Napoleon could not coerce Spain into freedom any more than Philip II could force Holland into slavery ', *Philosophy of History*, p. 453. Cf. also *Philosophy of Right*, § 274 Addition, pp. 286–7. Thus Rousseau was wrong in thinking it possible to force a people to be free (*Contrat Social*, bk I, ch. 7).

Hegel would agree with Burke that a constitution cannot be made or fabricated; it is a living and historical reality.[102] Men always live in an organized, constituted society, and the constitution is prior to any political theory. Since, however, the constitution is to Hegel the rational organization of the state, there is absolutely no contradiction in supposing that it may, or even must, lag behind the political consciousness of the epoch.[103] That each constitution is related to the particular character of a people does not prevent it from being altered and remodelled according to reason.

Let us now compare Burke's and Hegel's attitudes to the law.

According to Burke, law is identical with custom. It is an extension of it. Manners form the concrete foundation of legislation.[104] The lawmaker's task is to preserve and to consolidate the traditional ways of the community. One must beware of tampering with existing laws, for in them are crystallized ancestral beliefs and deep-rooted modes of behaviour. Burke sees no reason for abrogating or altering a law unless it is clear to everybody that it no longer answers the purpose for which it was originally adopted. He considers that, in general, the positive existence of law is sufficient proof of its validity. A law's antiquity provides a strong presumption in its support.[105]

The traditionalist attitude of Burke stems from his scepticism about the power of individual reason. For him, a system of law is not the outcome of the conscious calculation of one man but represents the experience and learning of several generations. Burke has a veneration for law as an expression of the *reason* of a community. He contrasts the traditional British constitution and the new French republic as the embodiments of two types of reason. In the first, he sees the store of the ' collected reason of ages ', the second he regards as the product of the ' naked reason ' of a few ambitious men.[106] The long existence of the British constitution justifies its authority in Burke's eyes: for it is the product of a continuing consent and rational choice on the part of generations of Englishmen, not simply the result of brute force nor the creature of chance events.[107]

Hegel does not believe the antiquity of a law to be sufficient argument for its preservation. Present importance, not past evolution, can alone serve to justify a law. Hegel criticizes Hugo and Savigny * for confusing a historical with a philosophical understanding of law.[108] He would assess a law by its rationality, not its positivity. He does not regard tradition as an adequate basis of law; on

[102] *Philosophy of Right*, § 273, p. 178; § 274 Addition, pp. 286–7.
[103] *Ibid.* § 273 Addition, p. 286. Cf. also § 298, pp. 193–4; § 298 Addition, p. 291.
[104] VIII, 172.
[105] V, 119, VIII, 187.
[106] V, 182, 168.
[107] X, 96–7.
  * *Editor's note* – The relation between Hegel and the historical school is examined more fully by G. Heiman, pp. 113–15.
[108] *Philosophy of Right*, § 3, p. 17. Cf. also § 211, p. 136.

the contrary, he argues in the *Philosophy of Right* that the laws of a civilized nation must cease to be 'merely implicit' and must be made known and consciously recognized.[109]

While Hegel condemns traditionalism as an attitude, he nevertheless accepts tradition as a positive value when it is given a restricted sense. To him a traditional order has validity to the extent that it crystallizes the moral sense of a nation. The individual will readily fulfil the obligations prescribed to him by the community if he sees his own aspirations embodied in its institutions. Then, instead of looking on the state as a formal authoritarian structure, he will find in it an assurance of his freedom. In other words, the law will have become so internalized that it will have ceased to act as a constraint and will have turned into a habit, a way of life.

We are back again with the Hegelian notion of ethical life, or, as he calls it in the *Encyclopaedia*, the 'objective spirit'.[110] But ethical life is now the unity of both subjectivity and law.[111] It is not enough for a man to recognize the rule of law; he must also be given a chance to see the grounds on which the law stands. To be valid, tradition must cease to be purely external and become permeated with the thoughts and conscious approval of individuals.

Hegel recognizes a moral and political value in custom and tradition, but, unlike Burke, he considers that customary laws are inferior to statutory laws because they do not derive their validity from clear thinking but from external circumstances. For Hegel, a legal system must take the form of general statutes or universally obligatory laws; laws must be expressly stated and formulated and their knowledge must not be confined to a narrow group of men, lawyers or politicians.[112] It is out of the question to make a system of laws that is entirely new in content; one can only examine and revise existing laws in the light of reason. Codification is one way of achieving this rationalization of laws. The formulation of laws in a code brings to light outdated privileges and legal discriminations. The publicity of laws implies that the citizens will protest against them when they are unjust. This dialectic of free thought and tradition is the spring of historical advance.[113]

In his last essay, devoted to the English Reform Bill, Hegel reaffirms his old revolutionary beliefs in the cause of rational law and attacks the traditionalist attitude opposed to it.[114] England is far behind the civilized nations of the continent because her system of laws is still based on purely positive rights and

---

[109] *Ibid.* § 270, p. 165. Cf. also § 316 Addition, p. 294: 'What is to be authoritative nowadays derives its authority, not at all from force, only to a small extent from habit and custom, really from insight and argument.' Cf. also *Political Writings*, pp. 282, 283.

[110] *Philosophy of Right*, § 33, p. 36; § 144, p. 105. *Encyclopaedia*, §§ 483, 513–14.

[111] *Philosophy of Right*, § 141, p. 104; § 144, p. 105.

[112] *Ibid.* § 211, pp. 134–6, and Addition, pp. 271–2.

[113] *Ibid.* §§ 212–16, pp. 136–9.

[114] *Political Writings*, pp. 295–330.

not yet framed on rational principles.[115] English backwardness in apprehending general principles Hegel attributes primarily to that reverence for antiquity and to that devotion to positive law, in which Burke had seen the quintessence of British virtue.[116] While admitting that the Bill undermines the position of the nobility and represents a reawakening of reason and justice, he maintains that a much more thorough-going reform is required to remove the various unjust privileges and social inequalities in England.[117] The contrast between the general misery of the people and the enormous wealth of a few individuals may lead to violent popular upheavals and to the overthrow of the constitution.[118] In the absence of a strong governmental power and an independent civil service, England runs the risk of seeing a struggle for power between the ' new men ' – the demagogues and the radicals – to whom the Bill opens the way to the House of Commons, and the traditional ruling class.[119] Hegel seems to think, however, that the practical sense of the English people, its distrust of abstract principles, and its reform-mindedness may save England from the instability periodically caused in France by precipitate reforms and abstract views of freedom.[120]

Burke considers the state as the expression of the historic nation, and accepts the concept of the nation as a spirit of time and place. His idea of a nation held together by a long tradition excludes the possibility of a sudden mutation, of a jump from one stage to another brought about by a revolution. Burke realizes the necessity of alteration, but the only form he approves is a slow change analogous in its gradualness and unconsciousness to the processes of nature.[121] Here lies the reason for his anti-Revolutionary polemics: a radical alteration of the existing order would destroy the continuity of the commonwealth and the unbroken chain of generations.[122]

Burke thought that the history of English law and constitution reflected no ' fundamental change ' but a tendency to preserve the heritage of the past.[123] ' All the reformations we have hitherto made, have proceeded upon the principle of reference to antiquity '.[124] Even the Glorious Revolution was not a revolution, but a restoration; it was ' a revolution, not made, but prevented '.[125] Whereas

---

[115] *Ibid*. pp. 299–301, 311–12, 325.   [116] *Ibid*. pp. 298–9.

[117] *Ibid*. pp. 295–9, 301, 314, 324.

[118] *Ibid*. pp. 301, 325.

[119] *Ibid*. pp. 23, 309–11, 323–6, 329–30.

[120] *Ibid*. pp. 301, 315–16, 321, 326, 328–30. Hegel's view on the necessity of transforming England's public and private law into a rational and coherent system proves remarkably correct. He seems, however, to have underestimated the capacity of the English aristocracy to achieve such a transformation.

[121] v, 78–9; vi, 369–70. Cf. Letter to Richard Burke, *The Correspondence of Edmund Burke*, vol. vii (Chicago, 1968), pp. 292–3.

[122] v, 181.

[123] vi, 150, 180–1.

[124] v, 75.   [125] v, 20.

the French, in their lust for change, demolished what was established, the English wanted only ' to preserve . . . their ancient constitution '.[126]

Burke believed that a revolution may be justified in extreme circumstances, but he could not sympathize with those who made ' the extreme medicine of the constitution its daily bread '.[127] He was reluctant to accept the destruction of any established institution of government on theoretical grounds alone.[128] In the *Reflections*, he rejected the universal applicability of abstract principles as being harmful to the existing order; the definition and discussion of abstract rights might destroy the habitual disposition of men to obey their traditional authorities.[129] Admittedly it was not so much the rights themselves as their absolute quality that Burke denied; but he also placed restrictive qualifications on the people's rights on the grounds that most men were incapable of sound political judgement.[130] The mass of the people could not rationally judge of policy; they could only feel and express their grievances, but ' the real cause (of the complaint) or the appropriate remedy ' ought to be determined by ' their natural leaders '.[131] If the French Revolution had been, like the Glorious and American Revolutions, ' a general rebellion of a whole people ', led by an upper and propertied class, in the reassertion of its historic rights, and not only a revolt of the lower orders, fighting for new rights, he would have welcomed and approved it.[132]

For Hegel, the modern state is born of the efforts of men to be recognized as free and equal. It is only in so far as the individual finds in the state freedom and satisfaction that he can accept submission to its laws. Hegel insists that the modern state must grant its citizens rights as well as duties if it is not to be overthrown by revolution.[133] Whereas Burke sought political stability through imposing restraints upon the appetites and will of individuals, Hegel sought it through the satisfaction of the reasonable desires of the citizens.

Hegel is aware that modern society encourages social inequalities and produces the masses, the populace.[134] Nevertheless, he proposes to amend that society

---

[126] v, 74. Cf. v, 19; vi, 342. In *Appeal from the New to the Old Whigs* (1791), Burke invoked the historical record of Dr Sacheverell's trial to prove that the Revolution of 1688 had aimed at conserving traditional forms (vi, 174–5).

[127] v, 73–4, 127.

[128] iv, 14; Letter to Philip Francis, *Correspondence*, vol. vi (Chicago, 1967), p. 173.

[129] v, 124, 126, 175; vi, 251–2.   [130] v, 120–6; vi, 216, 308–9; viii, 162.

[131] ii, 226; vi, 346; vii, 262–3; Letter to the Duke of Richmond, *Correspondence*, vol. iii (Chicago, 1961), p. 218.

[132] iii, 170. In *Appeal from the New to the Old Whigs*, Burke's retrospective judgement was that the Americans had fought not to ' enlarge ' but to ' secure ' their liberty ' in its ancient condition ' (vi, 121–2).   [133] *Philosophy of Right*, § 261, p. 162.

[134] Hegel's main criticism of his contemporary society was that the standard of living of ' a large mass of people ' was below subsistence level. His description of the rise of the ' rabble ' (*Pöbel*), later called proletariat, strikingly anticipates Marx's condemnation of bourgeois society. Cf. *ibid.* § 244, p. 150 and Addition, pp. 277–8.

not by revolution, but by a central legislative and administrative control.[135] Since there exists in society the danger that one or more classes will dominate or oppress another, the state must intervene to restore justice and equality. Hegel assigns to the deliberate action of the government, aided by the civil service, the introduction of rational principles of justice into society. It is to the middle class, the recruiting ground of the Hegelian civil servant, that he entrusts the task of maintaining at once the smooth running of the state and the proper balance between conflicting groups.[136] Thus Hegel became one of the earliest nineteenth-century partisans of the middle class as a political force.

Hegel is the first philosopher to understand the French Revolution as the *realization of an abstraction*.[137] Political fanaticism is nothing else than a realized idealism, characterized by the violent elimination of all the differences, the diversity of the world in general.[138] While condemning this revolutionary attitude, Hegel finds in it, however, a relative justification in so far as it illustrates the power of thought to become the foundation of the state by transferring itself from subjectivity into objectivity.[139] It is an important, but one-sided element, for it remains in the grip of the contradiction between the particular and the universal, the individual and the state. Individual rights can only be realized if they are embodied in some concrete social structure. In short, Hegel approves the social order that emerged from the French Revolution, the realization of universal freedom in the form of a code of laws (the *Code civil* of Napoleon), but he condemns the ideology of the Revolution as one-sided because it failed to take account of the historical process, in which individual rights were already becoming part of the existing order.[140]

In the *Philosophy of Right*, Hegel describes and explains how a moral universal order realizes itself through the consciously willed *activity* of individuals. The moral substance of the community cannot remain static, for it exists in the subject, who struggles for the recognition of his rights by society, as well as in rather stable elements like laws and manners.

---

[135] *Ibid.* § 280 Addition, pp. 288–9; § 302, p. 197 and Addition, pp. 292–3.

[136] *Ibid.* § 297, p. 193. While Hegel's conception of the middle class as the stabilizing element in the state reminds us of Aristotle (*Politics* 1295b), the Hegelian civil servant (conceived as the main instrument of rationality) points to Lenin's professional revolutionary. Hegel's view that the people was unable to rule may have suggested to Lenin the idea that the proletariat, left to itself, would never go beyond trade unionism and would never seize power unless organized by revolutionary leaders.

[137] While clearly perceiving the ' theoretical ' aspect of the French Revolution, Burke does not see that the attempt to master the world by thought was the real motive behind the production of ' general theories '.

[138] *Philosophy of Right*, § 5 Addition, pp. 227–8.

[139] *Philosophy of History*, p. 447.

[140] *Briefe von und an Hegel*, vol. 1, pp. 185, 218–19.

More generally, the difference between Burke's and Hegel's political stand-points is that between nature and thought.* While the first sees in the state a projection of the natural order, the second regards it as a creation of human reason.

Against the 'bold experimenters in morality', the 'Parisian philosophers' and especially Rousseau, Burke never ceases to argue for a 'natural morality'.[141] By this he understands a way of life which is not prescribed by philosophers, but has been born and has developed within some community. In the same way, the English political system is in accord with 'Nature' because it has come into being not through rational planning but through the imitation of a natural process, because the method by which power is transmitted is modelled on the transmission of life in the family.[142] Burke's idea of 'a natural and just order', maintained by a 'chain of subordination' between the landlord, the farmer and the labourer, is still that of a predominantly feudal society, based on the 'natural' production of the land.[143]

To Hegel, on the other hand, history is of a higher order than nature.[144] In his unconscious existence, man is nothing else than a part of nature.[145] But by his labour he both separates himself from nature, and becomes conscious of himself and of the fact that he is free to become what he wills to be.[146] By the transformation of the given, man grasps his superiority over nature. Hegel is the first philosopher to have fully recognized the importance of the labour already performed by man in subjugating nature and humanizing the world.[147]

For Hegel, the state's true vocation is to transform a (natural) people into a (civilized) nation by codifying its laws and rationalizing its institutions. The rational nature of modern labour is already turning the 'natural' individual into a member of a civilized society.[148] Hegel insists on the process of 'socialization' of the individual which takes place in modern society as a result of imitation, fashion and convention.[149] But it is primarily by deliberate social legislation, by a growing awareness of the universal aim which is at work within it, that man frees himself from his enslavement to economic production and becomes the

---

* *Editor's note* – M. Riedel discusses Hegel's sharp distinction between nature and reason; see esp. pp. 141–5.

[141] VI, 30, 35–7.

[142] V, 77–9; VIII, 251. Cf. Strauss, *Natural Right*, p. 314.

[143] VII, 383–4.

[144] *Philosophy of Right*, § 146, p. 106; *Die Vernunft in der Geschichte*, ed. J. Hoffmeister (Hamburg, 1955), p. 42.

[145] *Philosophy of Right*, § 57, p. 47.

[146] *Ibid*.

[147] In the *Phenomenology*, Hegel insists on the part played by labour in the self-education of man towards the realization of freedom.

[148] *Philosophy of Right*, § 187, pp. 124–6.

[149] *Ibid*. § 192 Addition, p. 269; § 193, pp. 127–8; § 194, p. 128.

master of his political fate.[150] 'Primitive' nations are not doomed to remain unconscious: sooner or later they will become aware of the inherent rationality of their laws.[151] The state which wants the freedom of its citizens must act on their conscience by education, instead of imposing on them laws from without.

Hegel does not, however, believe in the possibility of equating people and state; on the contrary, he draws a sharp distinction between the people (or civil society) and the state.[152] He rejects the Revolutionary identification of the two on the ground that, in modern times, the direction of the latter demands information and knowledge that are not within the immediate reach of everybody.[153] The people has lost its substantial unity with the state and is now separated from it by a central external administration which employs the services of highly trained civil servants.[154]

To conclude, one may formulate the difference between the political attitudes of Burke and Hegel in the following way. Against the French Revolution Burke sets up *political action*, the practical wisdom of the statesman; Hegel, on the other hand, elaborates a *political theory* which takes account at the same time of the possibility of the revolution and the necessity of maintaining the state. Burke rejects the French Revolution entirely, because he sees in it an attempt to break the continuity between past and present, to destroy the 'natural' and traditional world of the state. For Hegel, on the other hand, the Revolution has not only spread destruction, but it has also given birth to the conscious organization of the modern state.[155]

---

[150] *Ibid.* §§ 210–11, pp. 134–6.

[151] *Ibid.* § 274, pp. 178–9.

[152] *Ibid.* Addition to § 182, p. 266; § 324, p. 209. Within civil society, the people is truly self-governing; within the state proper, its influence is restricted to the choice of deputies for parliament and to the expression of public opinion. Cf. *ibid.* § 301, pp. 195–6.

[153] *Ibid.* § 301, pp. 195–6. Hegel is sarcastic about the attempt of the proto-nationalist political thinker Fries to organize the state 'from below, from the people itself'. Cf. *ibid.* pref., p. 6.

[154] *Ibid.* § 289, p. 189; § 295, pp. 192–3.

[155] I am much indebted to Michael Bacharach for the hard work of revision.

Hegel's 'Phenomenology': an elegy for Hellas

JUDITH N. SHKLAR

The *Phenomenology of Spirit* as a whole is an immense funeral oration at the graveside of speculative philosophy. Inevitably the Greeks dominated Hegel's remembrances, for they had begun, set the ends and determined the form of that search for certain knowledge which had now been completed. It was now possible to know what knowing was because in looking back one could recognize that knowledge was the collective creation of those who had tried to find it. Retrospection was the only certain knowledge because it alone could reveal that men had made their knowledge and that it was the work of their own minds, and not an object to be seized. Since knowing was self-creation, it had now become self-understanding. Remembering alone could now yield that certainty that an entire literary culture had, through the medium of a shared language, struggled for. Hegel saw spiritual history as Aristotle had seen nature. It was the gradual process, by no means painless or peaceful, by which half-truths had overcome each other to reach an end that was implicit in the origin and which determined the structure of every form of thought.[1] Because the whole is now achieved it can be understood. The kind of reconstruction offered by a funeral oration was now in order: an account of the deeds and works which reveal the meaning and purpose of the life now at an end.

Hegel was convinced that his was an age of transition.[2] The French and Kantian Revolutions had brought to an end the old ethical, religious and intellectual order. A new age had been born, but it was impossible to know what form it would take. Hegel was no crystal-gazer. Instead, he devoted himself to recapturing and reliving the past, to knowing what it was possible to know perfectly. It was his answer to the old question: 'What is knowing?' This mnemonic exercise not only had to begin in Greece, but it had to follow through all the explicit and implicit generative ideas, especially of Plato and Aristotle, which had shaped the entire literary culture and philosophic language of Europe. In this collective enterprise their influence had never been absent entirely. Hegel was often very critical of Greek philosophy, especially where social ideas were involved, and his remembrances are not untinged with justice. To be sure their defects were creative, a spur to renewed intellectual effort, but Hegel did not

---

[1] *The Phenomenology of Mind*, trans. J. B. Baillie, 2nd ed. (London, 1949), pp. 83–4, 95; *Phänomenologie des Geistes*, ed. J. Hoffmeister (Hamburg, 1952), pp. 22, 31.
[2] *Phenomenology*, pp. 75–6; *Phänomenologie*, pp. 15–16.

spare them. The Greek philosophers were recalled as philosophers deserve to be remembered, with an often unflattering devotion to truth. No such judgment, however, impinged upon Hegel's vision of the ethical spirit of the ancient city as he glimpsed it through dramatic literature. Here he could feel pure regret, a sense of loss for a unique moment that could only inspire admiration and possibly serve as a model for new effort. Here was a real threnody, and it gives the whole *Phenomenology* its elegiac tone.

The funeral oration for philosophy dwells directly on political ideas only occasionally, but they are never wholly absent. For Hegel was not remembering individual men or reviewing the ' great books '. He was recalling the transforming ' moments ' of collective thought. The spiritual adventure which had begun in Greece and which was now completed and ready to be grasped by the retrospective understanding had engaged generations of thinking and communicating men. It was not a matter of successive individual works. Hegel very rarely names a philosopher, and then only by way of illustration. The general form, trend, and end of the search for certain knowledge and the immanent logic of its development comprise a collaborative effort. As such it is social by definition. The ancients were unique, certainly, in having begun, and then inspired, the whole at every turn. It is their creative impulse that has now been fulfilled in the modern age, after the long medieval silence. The phenomena of the classical spirit were not purely individual manifestations, however. Socrates expresses the individualism of the decayed polis.[3] Stoicism is the voice of men living under Roman imperial rule.[4] There is, of course, no crude linking of ideas and events in a chain of effective causality. Both are integral parts of a single process, the awareness of which is expressed in language which, as Hegel insisted often, is a social creation, the great bond of the spiritual community. A few years later he was to remark that grammar as such, and Greek grammar especially, had made abstract, conceptual thinking possible at all.[5]

The communality of rational thought would itself suffice to make political ideas major phenomena of the human spirit. There is, however, an additional, more specific reason for their importance. Hegel's *Phenomenology* is a massive assault upon the ' subjectivity ' of individualism, both epistemological and social. From the first rather flippant remarks about the upside-down world of Platonism, to the polemic against Kantian morality, individualism is the notion that has to be overcome. The greatest single obstacle to the quest for certain knowledge is the view of men as discrete entities, each one of whom must find his ends somewhere out there, when in reality they are together the creators of their selves and their common world. Neither Plato nor Aristotle is, therefore, beyond censure. Their incompleteness was, of course, necessary, and Hegel was not grading the

---

[3] *Phenomenology*, pp. 379, 747; *Phänomenologie*, pp. 258–9, 519.

[4] *Phenomenology*, pp. 244–5, 501–6; *Phänomenologie*, pp. 153, 342–6.   [5] ' On Classical Studies ', *Early Theological Writings*, trans. T. M. Knox (and Richard Kroner) (Chicago, 1948), pp. 329–30.

truth or errors of the past, but tracing the immanent necessities of philosophical change.[6]

The flaws that drove European philosophy restlessly ahead seemed especially evident to Hegel in Platonism. Generally he repeated Aristotle's criticisms of Plato's doctrine of ideas. Indeed, he was quite ready to applaud Aristophanes' caricature of Socrates retailing empty clouds that could be filled with any fancy imaginable.[7] More seriously, the ideas were, in their complete dissociation from the world of change and mutability, incapable of explaining and ordering the multiplicity of experience. To Aristotle they seemed merely to act as abstracted reproductions of actuality.[8] Hegel, looking forward to Christianity, saw Plato's ideas not as mirrors, but as inverted representations of common sense and conventional wisdom, which they are designed to indict. They are, like many utopias, reversed pictures of the world they condemn. As such the 'supersensible' and 'inner' worlds are merely the prevalent order inverted. When revenge was the justice due to one's enemies, the 'upside-down' world presented punishment as a 'cure' due to the criminal or even as a benefit to him in a world 'beyond'.[9] It is the unjust man whose soul is injured, after all. His victim suffers no comparable affliction.[10] Socrates' challenge to the amoral individualists of his day seems to be a radical transvaluation, as does his pursuit of his inner voice without concern for the legality of his conduct. In both instances he is not far from the Christian demand that enemies be forgiven rather than injured, and that good intentions alone matter even when they are expressed in criminal acts. In fact, these departures from the prevailing conventions are not as radical as they appear. For in their concentration on the person of the criminal and the effect of punishment upon him neither overcomes the individualism of justice as self-help against one's enemies. The supersensible world is just as individualistic as the actual one. Both disdain law and the general, impersonal social values which it enforces. Charity is in that respect not unlike the decadent heroic ethic of Plato's opponents. Punishment as a cure for evil-doers is perhaps an advance, in that it points to the positive value or punishing. However, the real value of punishment is not in its effect upon the law-breaker. It lies in the fact that it is an activation of the law which thus restores the balance of social rights and duties which it exists to maintain against wrongful assertions by individuals.*

Hegel was, of course, perfectly aware that Plato had recognized that ego-

---

6 *Phenomenology*, pp. 97–9, 105–6; *Phänomenologie*, pp. 33–5, 39.

7 *Phenomenology*, pp. 747–8; *Phänomenologie*, pp. 519–20.

8 *Phenomenology*, pp. 201–3; *Phänomenologie*, pp. 119–21. Aristotle, *Ethics*, I 1096 a and b; *Metaphysics*, A, 990 b–993 a; M, 1078 b–1080 a.

9 *Phenomenology*, pp. 204–6; *Phänomenologie*, pp. 122–4. The true function of law that Hegel points to is, again, very close to Aristotle's view, *Ethics*, V, 1131 b–1134 a.

10 *Gorgias*, 469, 472, 476–80, 508–9, 525, 527. Also *Crito* and *Phaedo*, *passim*; *Laws*, 860–2.

* *Editor's note* – For Hegel's views on punishment as stated in the *Philosophy of Right*, see D. E. Cooper's essay, pp. 151–67.

centricity was the great defect of the convention of revenge. No one can really know what is due one's friend or enemy or even who is one or the other. Only society as a whole can make such judgments. Hegel was to use that very argument against those who looked to inner sentiment to determine what they owed their neighbor. Only the law of the state, not unintelligent feelings of benevolence, can decide what is just and what is not.[11] Yet Platonism ignored law as the answer to the question of what is just, because it had drawn a veil between the actual world and the supersensible realm 'beyond' or 'within'. And true justice was believed to be behind that curtain, outside the Cave. Perhaps it was necessary to draw a curtain to induce men to look behind it. For only then would they know that there was nothing there, that justice was their own creation, and that the rules of society are its only authoritative form.[12]

Platonic justice for all its struggles against cupidity and egotism seemed to Hegel to retain an element of anarchism which had infected modern Europe and had found its ultimate expression in the French Revolution. For it was in the pages of the *Republic* that aristocratic Europeans had found their ideal of education, of forming perfect individuals. *Bildung* is not mere schooling. It is the effort consciously to form individuals according to a premeditated plan and model. Such an enterprise is inherently a response to social incoherence. It is an effort to do the work that law and convention perform among 'free' and 'ethical' peoples. In modern Europe this education was, moreover, explicitly an attempt to return to the fountain of civilization, to Greece. And Plato was the guide. From him came the notion of service to the state as the highest aim of aristocratic training. Nothing could seem less anti-social. Hegel, however, saw it as just that, because Platonic education expressed a deep contempt for wealth.[13] Now production, work, the creation of wealth may seem selfish, but in fact it is all eminently social. As common labor and common enjoyment this is the most genuine form of cooperative activity. Because it saw only the individual in pursuit of gain, Platonism ignored the social character of wealth. Service to the state was regarded as the very opposite of the desire for wealth, because it seemed so self-subordinating and self-sacrificing. In Hegel's view it was, however, far more self-centered because it looked to self-edification. Moreover, as an ideal of self-perfection it was inherently impossible. Timocratic man yearns for wealth as Plato had, after all, himself shown in his phenomenology of moral decline.[14] Hegel followed him there, no less than Aristotle's taunting 'who would be happy in such a Republic!' But while Aristotle had accepted wealth as a necessary means to liberality and happiness, he also treated it with some disdain, as an

[11] *Phenomenology*, pp. 443–4; *Phänomenologie*, pp. 304–5. That was, after all, the message of the first two books of the *Republic* as well.

[12] *Phenomenology*, pp. 212–13; *Phänomenologie*, pp. 128–9.

[13] *Phenomenology*, pp. 519–29; *Phänomenologie*, pp. 354–63.

[14] *Republic*, VIII, 547–64.

inferior preoccupation of merely instrumental worth.[15] Hegel, however, looked only to the 'social' contribution of cupidity, not to its bearing on personal character. The aristocratic contempt for the man of wealth was, from that vantage point, not merely deceptive, it was false. It was an anarchic preference for personal 'nobility' over the 'base' work of social man. In the offices of state performed by feudal grandees the ideology of service scarcely hides the military and class interests of the 'guardians'. Self-abnegation can no longer hide the anarchic impulse here. However, feudal 'state service' and other historical examples of 'noble' values only demonstrate what was immanent in Plato's original contrast between noble service and base wealth: service to the state is really a form of self-fulfilment while the accumulation of wealth is a contribution to social welfare. The greedy producer is less anarchic than the official educated for self-perfecting service to others.

Quite in keeping with his general design, Hegel treated the culmination of an idea as its guiding force, recognizable as such from its birth through all its historical expressions. The anarchic, indeed the suicidal impulses of Europe's ruling classes, so brilliantly displayed in the closing years of the *ancien régime*, were thus the end and the immanent principle of growth of their Platonic *Bildung* and its 'heroism of service'.[16] Very similar considerations also governed Hegel's autopsy of other aspects of heroic individualism. For the failure of the guardians is only a part of this ideal, which Hegel believed had now completed its spiritual career.

The deficiencies of heroic individualism, especially of the Aristotelian autonomous man, are above all illuminated in the most spectacular set-piece of the *Phenomenology*, 'Lord and Servant'. Here Hegel traces the path, from classical birth to Christian death, step by step, of the Aristotelian hero-as-philosopher.[17] For it is the autonomy of contemplative man, rather than of the warrior or ruler, that stands in contrast to the enslavement of the producer. To Hegel the ideal of a contemplative ruler who has been liberated from toil and care was an ill-conceived aspiration that was bound to fail, since there is nothing out there to contemplate. The man who expects truth to come to him from the beyond waits

---

15 *Politics*, II, 1264 a–1264 b; I, 1256 a–1256 b; II, 1263 a–1263 b; *Ethics*, IV, 1120 a; VI, 1141 a and b, 1144 a and b; x, 1178 a.

16 *Phenomenology*, p. 527; *Phänomenologie*, p. 360.

17 *Phenomenology*, pp. 229–40; *Phänomenologie*, pp. 141–50. The degree to which the relationship of master and slave, the man who can attain to rationality and the man doomed to pure instrumentality, dominated Aristotle's entire philosophy can hardly be exaggerated. It became the paradigm of all order, whether it be that of the cosmos or that of an individual person. Above all, the contemplative hero is always explicitly regarded as the man freed from the cares of the body and every sort of physical toil, that is the very essence of his self-sufficiency, which puts him at the apex of mankind just as surely as labor puts the slave at the very bottom. *Ethics*, v, 1138 b, VIII, 1161a–1161 b, x, 1177 a–1178 a; *Politics*, I, 1252 a–1255 b, 1260 a–1260 b, III, 1277 b. H. C. Baldry, *The Unity of Mankind in Greek Thought* (Cambridge, 1965), pp. 88–101.

in vain. By cutting himself off from creativity, action and experience, moreover, he distorts his vision. For as his own most basic experience is the contrast between his own passive superiority and the working creativity of his inferiors, he comes to see everything, from man to the cosmos, in terms of this radical dualism.

Heroic man stumbles into this spiritual blind alley almost accidentally. The hero-as-warrior has quite a clear view of himself as a man. The distinctive feature that sets men apart from the beasts is the willingness to risk one's life in order to demonstrate one's prowess to oneself and to others. To choose the possibility of death for the sake of glory is a uniquely human freedom. That is the germ also of the notion of mankind.[18] It does not go very far, for only the sense of a common fate, of inevitable death, is shared by heroes. One recalls that Homer's phrase for men is ' mortal beings ', and that moment when Achilles and Priam recognize their common humanity as they look at the dead body of Hector. The possibility of a greater social awareness is cut off by the immediate consequences of battle. The victorious hero enslaves the vanquished and he becomes a user of human tools. That ensures the continued isolation of the hero, and it also arrests his development. His defined role is now that of a man who depends on others to do all work and creating for him. He is thus not as free as he believes, for his life is really in the hands of his servants. Despising creativity, he has also denied himself the possibility of new learning and development. As he is transformed from a military to a philosophic figure he no longer contends with others for their esteem. Only the human tool and his owner compose his world, and the former is seen as a mere extension of the hand of the latter, like an axe. That is not a human relationship and it cannot give rise to one. For the lord it means that by trying to be more than a man, he has become less. He is quite alone, with nothing to do and nowhere to go.

The ideal that the lord pursues justifies and reflects this situation faithfully. Mind and body, pure form and pure instrument, spirit and matter are separated. The principle of division, tools and their owners, determines all relations of superiority and inferiority. It sets a pattern now apparently evident not only in all living creatures, but one that originates in ' the constitution of the universe ', according to Aristotle. Nothing can exist without a ruling principle and men, like all parts of the universal order, are marked from the time of birth to rule or be ruled. Nor is there any way to overcome this duality. The work of the body impedes that of the mind which alone can reach happiness in a state of perfect contemplation: the height of rationality. However, even this hero of the rational life, contemplative man, remains threatened by his body, his lower part. For as the mind cannot know anything without sense experience, so the spirit cannot live without a body, which seen as pure instrumentality impedes it. The lord in his contemplative independence cannot survive without his body-slave. He is in

---

[18] Baldry, *Unity of Mankind*, pp. 8–15.

fact not as autonomous as he thinks, for he is chained to his human tool, which is, indeed, a part of himself. That is the contradiction which undermines his whole position.

The slave as body-tool is not as immobilized by this situation as is the master. The slave learns. In his mortal fear he knows how to discipline himself. As he labors and produces for the benefit of the master, he imprints himself on the dead matter with which he works. In the process he not only creates things, but also himself. In his creative relation to objects he discovers his powers, and the really essential character of man. It is man as creator who is really self-aware and free, not the passive and dependent master. The slave achieves self-consciousness through his work. The lord, however, can come to it only in ' recognizing ' the slave and himself in the other. That the slave was an extension of himself had always been accepted. Now he comes to see in this mere appendage his own humanity. He is thus converted to the slave's point of view. That attitude is no longer one of pure submissiveness. The slave now has a mind of his own. However, as he remains a slave, his independence is merely a stubborness, the resentment that is always typical of the slave-mentality. Nevertheless, the heroic aspiration to autonomy is not lost. It is rather internalized by this, the Stoic, state of consciousness.

Although the lord has been drawn into the slave's realm of consciousness, the slave is not raised to mastery. Marcus Aurelius on his throne and Epictetus in his chains share a single philosophy. Both cherish the autonomy of their mind and will, and feel burdened and hemmed in by their body and the weight of the external world. The heroic quest has been turned entirely inward. It is less a liberation than an escape from reality – a path made altogether inviting by the oppressiveness of Roman rule.[19] The sense of a crushing external world is overpowering. It is felt in Marcus Aurelius' quoting Epictetus' saying that man was ' a poor soul burdened with a corpse ' and pitying the great warrior heroes of the past for suffering from ' an infinity of enslavements '.[20] Epictetus' own view of slavery is an inversion of actuality, not a liberation, when he remarks that slavery is not a matter of being owned by another, but of being ambitious and avaricious.[21] To be sure, the Stoic wise man has not only found his freedom, but also humanity within himself. However, he is so removed from historical life that he can only issue abstract, dogmatic rules of conduct which, directed at all men in all cases, fit no one at any time. In this he only mirrors the legal order in which he lives, which assigns only legal personality and abstract roles to the inhabitants of the empire.

The heroic, resentful withdrawal of the Stoic wise man devalues the actual world and concrete experience too radically. His balance is destroyed in a

---

19 *Phenomenology*, pp. 242–6; *Phänomenologie*, pp. 151–4.
20 *Meditations*, trans. Maxwell Staniforth (London, 1964), book IV, s. 41; book VIII, s. 3.
21 ' Of Freedom ', *Moral Discourses*, ed. H. D. Rouse (London, 1910), pp. 200–16.

skepticism which comes to distrust the evidence of the senses completely and rejects the outer world as an impenetrable maze where anything may or may not be true. Because the skeptic must continue to live by his senses and to accept social, no less than natural laws, which he regards as entirely arbitrary, his inner integrity is broken. He is aware of himself as free and unfree, as certain and uncertain, and this distraction is unendurable. He turns from this world, inner and outer, and yearns for a beyond.[22] The ' unhappy consciousness ' abandons the heroic pursuit of autonomy in what is now wholly a vale of tears. Its final term is reached when men, submitting to the mediating agency of the church, give up all their powers and reduce themselves, in their own mind, to mere things.[23]

The heroic individualism of antiquity did have its moments of glory, but it could be followed from birth to death without regret. Hegel gives one an inimitable sense of the sadness of its decline and defeat. However, he preserves his detachment in the face of these failures, for they were the inevitable consequences of self-destructive illusions. Individualism, even in its heroic, ancient form, is a fundamental misunderstanding of reality which prevents men from recognizing their essential identity, their social being, and their common humanity. The civic ethos of Athens, however, was the very opposite of individualism and its memory could only inspire longing. The world of Antigone, the memory of the spirit of a ' free people ', was a reminder of the perfection men could reach. To those who think of him as the complacent philosopher of progress, it should come as a surprise that Hegel felt that the real ' paradise of the human spirit ' had existed in the remote past, in early Athens.[24]

The happiness of the Athenians was all due to their being a free people. No tension between the private and the public self, the inner and the external world or the here and the beyond interrupted the undivided consciousness of free citizens in a free polity. They alone had laws and customs that were the creation of each and all of them. And all and every one of them expressed in his person the collective consciousness of the whole polity.[25] This integrity of spirit had only one defect. It was spontaneously lived and enjoyed without being understood. The reflective demands of the restless intellect had, therefore, to break away from this happy condition.[26] That alone must serve both as an explanation

[22] *Phenomenology*, pp. 246–51; *Phänomenologie*, pp. 154–8.

[23] *Phenomenology*, pp. 265–6, 755; *Phänomenologie*, pp. 170, 525.

[24] ' On Classical Studies ', p. 325.

[25] Although Baillie translates *Volk* as nation, Hegel obviously meant ' people ', for he used the term nation exactly once to refer to the Homeric Pantheon and the linguistic unity that bound Greeks together: *Phenomenology*, p. 731; *Phänomenologie*, p. 506. The term *Volk* is used to apply to the polis and its free citizens: *Phenomenology*, pp. 374–82, 709–10; *Phänomenologie*, pp. 255–61, 490–1.

[26] *Phenomenology*, pp. 378–9, 498–9, 747; *Phänomenologie*, pp. 258–9, 342, 519.

and as a consolation for the loss of the most perfect moment in history. It allowed Hegel some hope that newly self-aware men might yet reconstruct what they had once destroyed, but it was only many years later that he was able to provide convincing arguments to sustain such an expectation. In the *Phenomenology* he exposed the destructive character of the individualism that had undone the ancient polis and that has dominated the modern age all too effectively. There was nothing in the spirit of his own age that he could then recognize as a successor to the 'ethical substance' of the classical past. That substance was only 'a floating selfless adjective' for us.[27] Indeed, not even those aspects of the modern spirit that Hegel could admire showed the seeds of a collective consciousness akin to that of a free people. Hegel could think of the vision of ancient Athens as a possible, but certainly not as a likely future.[28] And except for an occasional lapse such as this Hegel did not allow himself to think ahead, preferring the certainty of mnemonic knowledge and the consolations of elegiac praise.

What had the happiness of Athens been? What did its freedom signify? First of all it means that the people preserves its collective autonomy and individuality against other peoples. To that end war is not only an aspect of political life, it is the supreme expression of citizenship. Indeed, war has an educative function also. It tears the citizens away from the many private associations and groups to which they belong.[29] The free people was for Hegel, as for Aristotle, not a pile of bricks, but composed of a plurality of types and groups.[30] The government, however, has the highest and prior claim upon them. For its power is 'the will, the self' of the people.[31] The laws express the active character of each individual citizen. They are not impersonal rules 'out there' that impose roles on legal persons, as in Rome. The law is such that each citizen can see himself as a particularization of its general aims. For he has willed them. That is why a free people is 'reason realized'.[32]

Law and government are not the only aspects of civic life that are rational in that the most general public activities are freely accepted by the citizens who rceognize them as their own creations. Religion is also free, because the polity is its substance. Religion, which Hegel understood to be the collective beliefs of a community, is social and this-worldly among a free people. Its supreme expression is art.[33] And it is an open public art that is not an outpouring of the artist's personal inspiration, but an expression of the spirit of a whole people.[34] The rites of such a people are a daily part of its common existence. Unlike the Olympian

---

[27] *Phenomenology*, p. 380; *Phänomenologie*, p. 260.
[28] *Phenomenology*, pp. 379, 460–1; *Phänomenologie*, pp. 259, 315–16.
[29] *Phenomenology*, pp. 473–4, 497–8; *Phänomenologie*, pp. 324, 341.
[30] *Phenomenology*, pp. 709–10; *Phänomenologie*, pp. 490–1.
[31] *Phenomenology*, p. 511; *Phänomenologie*, p. 348.
[32] *Phenomenology*, pp. 378, 731; *Phänomenologie*, pp. 258, 506–7.
[33] *Phenomenology*, pp. 709–11; *Phänomenologie*, pp. 490–2.
[34] *Phenomenology*, pp. 715–16; *Phänomenologie*, pp. 494–5.

religion over which Zeus presides, it is truly popular and local. That official pantheon is too feeble and distant, and in its unstable division of labor between gods and men it is even ridiculous.[35] The real religion of a free people remains particular, a part of its active, shared life. The people has a god to unite it, but he represents not a remote hope or a deferred fulfillment, but present, common work.[36] The drama, which is a spiritualized and universalized rite, abandons all the crudities and improbabilities of local and Olympian ritual, but it is still rooted in common experience and is shared by all.[37]

The only powers that are not encompassed by the polity itself are those ascribed to fate. Men are creative, but they are not omnipotent. Fate is the whole of that dire necessity to which men must submit. They bow before all that defeats and defies them. The common people, demos, especially aware of its helplessness, finds its voice in the chorus which, as it warns and laments, reminds men of their limits, of fate. However, fate is not a deity or an object of reverence. Eventually it is even understood to be character, and the circumstances created by men in their complexity.[38] What mattered most to Hegel was the integrity and autonomy of the religion of a free people. It was a uniting not a devisive, a common not a private, a human and not a supernatural religiosity. In short it was everything that Christianity is not.

The free people owes its conditions not to invention, but to a unique social balance. The equipoise between the kin and the city is really what maintains it. The ethical spirit which sustains freedom has its roots in a precarious arrangement by which the polity preserves the kin and the kin raises citizens fit for freedom.[39] Hegel went well beyond Aristotle here, who had only seen the family as a necessary economic base of the polis. Hegel ascribed to it a far greater and very much less material function in the life of a free people. The family (or kin) group is an ethical not just a productive unit. While the polity remains prior to the family as the only realm in which men can reach their highest ends, it could not without the ethical family create the spirit of citizenship on which its survival depended. The ethical family ties the living to the dead. Its religion is ancestor worship. As such it is less than rational, with its deep belief in the nether-world. However, it serves a truly human and social function. It protects the individual against his most awful fear, the horror of extinction. Here the dead endure among the living, who continue to fulfill their obligations to their departed kinsmen. Hence the absolute duty to bury and avenge the slain kinsman. For women this family, with its rites and duties, is the whole of the social world. The men, however, must ascend to the realm of light, the upper world of the

---

[35] *Phenomenology*, pp. 733–5; *Phänomenologie*, pp. 508–10.

[36] *Phenomenology*, pp. 723–4; *Phänomenologie*, pp. 501–2.

[37] *Phenomenology*, pp. 736–45; *Phänomenologie*, pp. 510–17.

[38] *Phenomenology*, pp. 685–6, 735–48; *Phänomenologie*, pp. 473–4, 510–20.

[39] *Phenomenology*, pp. 467–8, 481–2; *Phänomenologie*, pp. 319–20, 330.

polity, as young citizens and warriors. The women in their educative and supporting task, as the guardians of the family ethos, also make their contribution to the civic order. Indirectly but indispensably they give men the strength to become citizens.[40]

The criminal law of the city has its roots in the family. That is also the source of its strength and its social immediacy. When the civic ethos at last calms the furies, the prosecution of murderers is left to the kin of the slain citizen. The community as such does not participate on behalf of either party in cases that call for vengeance. It only sets limits to the process of retaliatory justice, but it does not deprive the kinsmen of their duties to their dead.[41] That is why they can devote themselves so wholeheartedly to the upper-realm, to the rational, distributive, man-created law of the city. It supports their familial existence, which in turn prepares them for the civic life. Again war, the necessary discipline and highest function of citizens, would be an intolerable slaughter if the warrior did not know that he would be buried and worshipped by the surviving kin, among whom he would thus remain alive.

Sooner or later the balance gives way. Sophocles' *Antigone* in Hegel's view was the dramatic recollection of that collapse. Antigone stands unwavering for the ethos of the kin. The brother must be buried and to do this is her unquestionable duty. To punish the usurper, the disturber of the public order is just as surely the task of Creon. He must assert the rules of the realm of light, indeed of reason, the human law made by human beings for their own fulfillment. If public law runs counter to the demands of the nether-world, to the ethos of family life, that is a disaster, but not one that he can avoid by giving way. The upshot is that both the family and the polity are destroyed. Fate in the form of destruction overcomes both.[42]

Now the individual ceases to see himself as wholly a social being and neither family nor city can absorb him entirely. The struggle between two social claims degenerates into the war between the sexes; a concomitant of democratic societies that Hegel was exceptionally sensitive to have recognized. In Aristophanes' comedies he found how war had ceased to be the occasion on which citizens proved their freedom and had become, in the eyes of the women, a silly escapade provoked by male incompetence and stubbornness. The actors no longer wear masks to hide their individuality and to emphasize their social, impersonal roles. Now the stage is full of specific people, each one speaking for himself or herself. The sister who preserves the ethos of the family is replaced by the wife and mother who only wants her sons and lovers to stay alive and at home. As Praxagora explains carefully, women have no use for war. Now that

[40] *Phenomenology*, pp. 468–79, 739; *Phänomenologie*, pp. 320–8, 512–13.
[41] *Phenomenology*, pp. 480–1; *Phänomenologie*, pp. 329–30.
[42] *Phenomenology*, pp. 484–96; *Phänomenologie*, pp. 330–40.

they speak as individuals and no longer as the guardians of the familial ethos, their hostility to the male world of so-called law and order and war becomes open and their weapons, ridicule and laughter, prove irresistible. They mark the dissolution of a free people, but it is an outburst of such healthy individual self-assertion that even Hegel could not solemnly condemn it.[43]

To most contemporary audiences it would seem evident that the ladies of *Lysistrata* and the *Ecclesiazusae* enjoy far more freedom than Antigone, burdened with endless ethical obligations even before her conflict with Creon. That was, however, not Hegel's view, and not because he felt sorry for Aristophanes' beleaguered males. He simply had a very different notion of freedom. What, in fact, did he mean when he spoke of a 'free people'? He certainly did not mean that its citizens had rights against the polity. Quite on the contrary, their freedom was due wholly to their being unaware of themselves as individuals apart from their social being. It is freedom conceived in spiritual and not institutional terms, moreover. Just as slavery and lordship are not discussed as economic and legal institutions, but as inter-acting psychological and philosophic phenomena, so the freedom of early Athens is not a matter of its political or religious organization. Even the ethical family, which Hegel analyses in such detail, is seen as a set of spiritual relationships among its members, dead and alive. The freedom of the people is a state of mind, both individual and collective, that is marked by an absence of tension between the demands of the polity and personal beliefs and aspirations. The very possibility of such a conflict is unknown to the free citizen, or at least obscured by the harmonious transition from family to public life. For as soon as the ethos of the family and the duties of citizenship collide, the individual is emancipated from both, and now sees himself as a discrete entity for whom society is 'out there'.

It seems that the 'free people' is more easily recognized for what it was *not* than for what it actually was. That is entirely in keeping with Hegel's purpose, which was to contrast the happiness of the socially integrated citizen, for every one of whom this was a spontaneous rather than consciously chosen role, with the unhappiness of the restless, searching individualist of the modern age. Little as Hegel liked the Middle Ages, he could scarcely have forgotten that feudalism had also been a system of kinship ties and of ancestor worship. The individualism that had followed its dissolution was the spiritual descendant of Socratic independence and Hegel viewed both with equal misgivings. That made Athens so unforgettable. In the *Phenomenology* Hegel did not concern himself with the shape of the modern state, but when he eventually did try to establish its principles of cohesion and rationality, the vision of the ancient polis was still with him. To be sure, he knew that the religious and political role of the kin was extinguished and he fully accepted this state of affairs. That made the search for the

---

[43] *Phenomenology*, pp. 496-8, 745-9; *Phänomenologie*, pp. 340-2, 517-20.

ethical and functional equivalent of the Sophoclean family a compelling enterprise for him, and one that was to mark his political philosophy deeply.[44]

The impact of the reproaching image of antiquity was heavy indeed. For Hegel used Antigone's example to expose the vanity of modern, and especially Kantian, morality. He was very far from admiring Antigone simply as a prophetess of the higher law. Indeed, when he quotes her celebrated lines about its obscure origins he made it clear that she did not understand the law that bound her, and just believed in its divinity.[45] She did not see the limits of kinship obligations and religiosity. Hegel was impressed with her ethical certainty even though he rejected her claim along with every other higher law doctrine. Justice and law can only be created by public authorities.[46] Creon's law, made by a government for a polity, was the most rational and most universal law possible. All other rules are less general and less valid because they serve lesser groups. Hegel did not think all actual laws perfect. Far from it. The effect of Roman law was clearly profoundly destructive to those who had to abide by it.[47] That did not, however, render notions of an extra-political or supra-human legality or justice acceptable to him. Law and justice, like every other idea, were entirely the work of men acting together.

The way men judge the rules that they have created for themselves, however, differs. It was Antigone's great merit that although she did not understand the origins of the law which she so heroically defended, she never thought of herself as an individual expressing a personal morality. She spoke solely as a sister within an ethical family, as a social being, fulfilling a defined role. That was the real source of her perfect certainty. She did not look into her heart or conscience to discover righteousness. She knew what had to be done, and always had known, because she was not making a moral choice, but obeying an unquestionable law.[48] That she failed to understand that law, that her allegiance to the netherworld, to the ethos of the kin, was less valid than the law of the polity that expressed the rationality of the world of light, was irrelevant here. What mattered, above all, was that she had no notion of conscience, of personal conviction, or of individuality as an inherent claim. She was right, within her limits, because she represented an ethical group and its binding values. The universal significance of Sophocles' play and its enduring power to educate and move us

---

44 Hegel believes that there is a ' universal ' civil service class arising to rationality from the middle class wholly through some undefined sort of education: and that there is a politically impartial landed aristocracy particularly suited for legislative activity because its entailed estates guarantee its ethos. (*Hegel's Philosophy of Right*, trans. T. M. Knox (Oxford, 1942), §§ 158–81, 287–307.) If there is something a little contrived about such notions, it may well be that they answered the reproving demands of Hegel's classical memories.

45 *Phenomenology*, pp. 452–3; *Phänomenologie*, pp. 311–12.

46 *Phenomenology*, pp. 467, 473–4, 493–5; *Phänomenologie*, pp. 319, 323–4, 337–40.

47 *Phenomenology*, pp. 501–6; *Phänomenologie*, pp. 342–6.

48 *Phenomenology*, pp. 452, 458, 484–6, 613–14; *Phänomenologie*, pp. 311, 314, 330–2, 423–4.

is due to its social character. The drama is true because it presents two inherently valid social moralities and two conflicting sets of social mores. To Hegel the tension between personal conscience and reason of state was trivial by comparison, a mere accident. The confrontation of two dependent yet irreconcilable social claims, which go beyond a mere judgment of individual rightness or error, is a philosophical tragedy. It is tragic not because the protagonists suffer, but because they are not mere private individuals, they are each a personification of a social necessity. Creon is not a mere tyrant, but the voice of the polity and its priority, its claim to general social rationality, the end of men's striving. Antigone is neither a criminal nor a martyr to conscience. She also asserts a social, ethical claim, the validity of which had not been challenged until it collided with the demands of the public order. That is why her certainty is rooted not in personal conviction but in historical reality. It would be unfair to Hegel to say that he was defending the supremacy of the modern state in the person of Creon. He would not have admired Antigone so profoundly if that had been his aim. He was, rather, insisting on the excellence of men and women who knew themselves to be wholly members of established social orders and who lived and died ethically, that is in response to the customs and beliefs of their peers.

The greatest difference between such free peoples and all others is in the quality of justice that renders ethical life so valid and certain. Athenian distributive justice was not an alien imposition like the law of Rome and of the modern world. It was not the haphazard outcome of the judicial resolution of individual conflicts. It had intelligible guiding principles which corresponded to the actual ' self-conscious will of all ' and thus integrated the various groups and citizens within the polity into a single whole.[49] There is no room left for the rampant self-assertion of the modern world. People find their pleasure in the family, not in the defiance of social convention. When they rise above the pursuit of pleasure, they turn to active citizenship, not to introspection. The law of their hearts is not a self-centered tyranny, but a sense of the uniformity of all hearts in an ethical society. Virtue is a civic act, not personal edification pitted against the course of the world. When men concern themselves with a cause it is a matter of concrete policy, not chimerical dreaming. They weigh actions within a stable context of law and justice, instead of forever questioning and testing the validity of the laws in terms of some purely personal or abstract rule. Instead of the ever-unsteady voice of conscience they have objective ethical laws to guide them. Not for them the ' pompous ' rhetoric about the good of all mankind and the oppression of humanity; they pursued the public good of their city, a task within their reach.[50] The conflicts that ethical people experience, like those between Antigone and Creon, are not the ' comical ' conflicts between two abstract duties. They are

[49] *Phenomenology*, pp. 479–80; *Phänomenologie*, pp. 328–9.
[50] *Phenomenology*, pp. 409–10; *Phänomenologie*, pp. 280–1.

collisions between two social groups and their respective ethical orders.[51] Antigone's claim may be inferior to Creon's, but it is the expression of a complete 'character' and of an objective social situation. That is far superior to the modern (Kantian) morality which is merely a matter of abstract knowledge. She may have been less self-aware, but she completely lived her morality; she did not have to think.[52] Modern morality with its empty and universal 'ought' forces the individual to give his duty any aim his conscience may choose. As such it hovers between tautology and arbitrariness. Antigone knows right and wrong with perfect certainty – that is her greatness and that of her society. Modern morality knows nothing of such poise. It dooms the individual to testing every law, every choice, by matching it against formal maxims that lack all specific content. This syllogistic practice reduces duty to a self-evident generality and moral action to an exercise in formal logic. In practice it can yield no guidance. The individual is left to his own confusion, apart from, and indeed opposed to, the sole source of genuine morality: social ethics.[53] It is a devastating indictment. Moreover, since Hegel was at this stage of his intellectual career neither able nor willing to show just where the present age of transition was to find its social certainties, his outburst suffers from all those faults which he was denouncing. He also was pitting himself against his own time and place, even if it was only to overcome the manifest defects of critical reason. He also, after all, was a fine example of the spiritual maladjustment of the age.

Hegel's defense of Creon and even his view of Antigone's character have rather slender ties to Sophocles' drama. The practice of using the ancients to reveal the flaws of the moderns has, however, often demanded such ingenuity. One need not go back as far as Rousseau to recall how Sparta could serve to condemn modern Europe. The German romantics, among whom Hegel had lived for years, were all deeply devoted to the memory of ancient Greece, the home of genius. The contrast between beautiful antiquity and the world that followed, their own age especially, was for them a subject of anguished reflection. Schiller had thus lamented the passing of the spirit of playfulness that had moved the Greeks to be so infinitely beautiful. He, and at much the same time Schlegel, had drawn detailed comparisons between classical and modern art, spontaneous and artificial education (*Bildung*), a capacity for realization against one for perpetual striving, and lastly a cyclical and progressive view of history. In each case the difference tended to favor the ancients.[54]

There are some traces of romantic nostalgia for Greece in the *Phenomenology*. Right at the outset Hegel spoke of the superiority of Greek schooling, which

---

51 *Phenomenology*, pp. 446–53; *Phänomenologie*, pp. 306–12.

52 *Phenomenology*, pp. 613–14; *Phänomenologie*, pp. 423–4.

53 *Phenomenology*, pp. 446–53; *Phänomenologie*, pp. 306–12.

54 A. O. Lovejoy, ' Schiller and the Genesis of German Romanticism ', *Essays in the History of Ideas* (New York, 1960), p. 215.

perfected the natural mind by raising it to general conceptions, to that of the moderns who find abstractions ready-made and have neglected concrete experience.[55] Again, Hegel was not blind to Greece as the home of beauty. If it were not for Greece we would not know what beauty is, he was to remark a few years later.[56] This for him also was the moment when the human spirit had been endowed with ' freedom, depth and serenity '. Nevertheless, there are great differences between Hegel's and the aesthetic's dream of Greece, which reflect his general contempt for romanticism. Schiller's notion of beauty as a mediator between matter and form or nature and reason and as the cure for public ills was far too irrational for Hegel. Beauty, he wrote bitterly, ' is powerless and helpless and hates the understanding '. It is too feeble to endure the destructive impact of restless inquiry which the pursuit of knowledge demands. Greek spontaneity, serenity, and ' cheerfulness of heart ' for all their beauty were intellectual defects, and in its drive toward truth the human spirit had to relinquish this happiness. Moreover, it was not the Greeks at play, but the disciplined freedom of their civic life that Hegel admired. The romantic distaste for the useful and the practical, no less than the yearning for the imaginative and so the individual and particular, were part of all that Hegel regarded as most destructive in the modern ' unhappy consciousness '.[57] It was the active, down-to-earth, collective spirit of Greece that he chose to pit against this, as against all forms of individualism. The spiritual health of the Greeks was in their ability to create collectively a religion, a polity and an art here and now. Nor was their happiness a matter of personal gratification. It also was a social state, as was their freedom. War was its highest manifestation, and not because it was enjoyable. It was the absence of romantic individuality among people who knew collective self-mastery, limited only by necessity, that appealed most to Hegel. It was no doubt for the benefit of the romantic poets that he chose to stress the religious, public character of Greek art, so remote from the modern cult of genius.

Above all, Hegel was still alone in sensing clearly the dark side of the Greek spirit. That especially made any notion of regeneration through play seem a travesty upon that true message of antiquity, which he found in Sophoclean tragedy. Indeed, Sophocles, as he knew, was also looking back to an earlier age to record its meaning for a city already in ethical decline. That in itself drew Hegel to him. And indeed the *Phenomenology* as a whole is a drama of sorts and its author more than half in love with fate. The spectacle of spiritual creations struggling with each other, all in the grip of the necessity of pushing on and on toward certain knowledge, is not unlike a tragedy. And looking back at this

---

[55] *Phenomenology*, p. 94; *Phänomenology*, p. 30.
[56] ' On Classical Studies ', p. 325.
[57] *Phenomenology*, p. 93; *Phänomenology*, p. 29. Schiller, *On the Aesthetic Education of Mankind*, trans. Reginald Snell (London, 1954), especially letters II, VI and XXVII, pp. 26–7, 42 and 138.

process we also relive a shared experience. Like the Athenian public Hegel had relived his and our spiritual past and found understanding in reintegrating into his own consciousness and that of his readers the cumulative creations of European literary culture. He had followed it from freedom to enslavement and illusion and finally to what he believed to be the grave of certainty and achievement. He might well have ended on a note of triumph, but he did not. He looked back in reverence and resignation, like an exhausted chorus, which was a measure of his devotion to ancient Greece.

The structure of
Hegel's 'Philosophy of Right'

K.-H. ILTING

It is surely strange that until now the discussion of Hegel's political philosophy has concentrated on the question whether we may recommend Hegel's political views, or ought rather to warn our contemporaries against them.[1] For it can easily be shown that Hegel's main endeavour as a political thinker was to develop and to formulate a theory of the modern state. To determine what place he gave to liberalism in his theory should therefore be more important than to decide to what extent he was a liberal. As long as we are clear about *that*, we can ignore Hegel's views on contemporary politics. They would be of merely historical interest. And as he lived in an eventful time which was entirely different from ours, it would indeed be very remarkable if we could share them all, calmly considering them from the distance of our present times.

It is true that Hegel's theory of the modern state, probably the deepest and the most comprehensive in the history of political philosophy, is extremely involved.[2] Its author intended it to form a part of his encyclopaedic system of philosophy, the structure of which is very opaque. It is also, more or less explicitly, an attempt at an exhaustive critique of ancient and modern political philosophy. Finally, in constructing his theory of the modern state, Hegel constantly refers to the politics of the period of the Continental restoration. In doing so he takes up a position on some of the burning political questions of his times.

We are, therefore, not only faced with the difficult task of interpreting the text of the *Philosophy of Right*, and so making it intelligible to the contemporary reader. We have also to analyse the theoretical foundations of Hegel's political philosophy, and to decide how far Hegel succeeds in solving the basic problems of a theory of the modern state. In this essay I shall try to analyse the composition and structure of the *Philosophy of Right* at some points of his argument which seem to me to be of special importance. It will be shown that the structure of

[1] See Rudolf Haym, *Hegel und seine Zeit* (Berlin, 1857); Franz Rosenzweig, *Hegel und der Staat* (Munich-Berlin, 1920); Hermann Heller, *Hegel und der nationale Machtstaatsgedanke in Deutschland* (Leipzig-Berlin, 1921); Herbert Marcuse, *Reason and Revolution* (London, 1941); Karl R. Popper, *The Open Society and Its Enemies* (London, 1945); Georg Lukács, *Der junge Hegel und die Probleme der kapitalistischen Gesellschaft* (Vienna, 1947); Eric Weil, *Hegel et l'état* (Paris, 1950); Joachim Ritter, *Hegel und die französische Revolution* (Cologne, 1957).

[2] For comprehensive interpretations of Hegel's *Philosophy of Right* see Hugh A. Reyburn, *The Ethical Theory of Hegel* (Oxford, 1921); Eugène Fleischmann, *La philosophie politique de Hegel* (Paris, 1964); and the translator's notes to *Hegel's Philosophy of Right*, trans. T. M. Knox (Oxford, 1942).

this work not only belies the greatness of the task which Hegel set himself, but also that it clearly indicates the limits which he was not able to transcend. Surprisingly, Karl Popper will be found to be quite right in his criticism of Hegel, although not with the outcome Popper intended: Hegel's critique of liberalism will prove itself to be well-founded and fatal to Popper's own presuppositions.

I

The first part of the *Philosophy of Right* treats of the same subject which Kant discussed in his *Metaphysics of Morals* under the heading of private law (*Privatrecht*). As a subject of political philosophy it goes back to Thomas Hobbes' theory of natural law.* Like Kant and Hobbes, Hegel assumes that man initially has rights, and only one duty: to acknowledge that other men, as well as he, have rights. In order to develop this fundamental thesis and to make its consequences as clear as possible, Hegel makes use of the same method as all his predecessors since Hobbes. He abstracts from all conditions of social life which are created by human activity itself. The background of his arguments, then, is the fiction of a state of nature without any form of established society and, above all, without the coercive power of the state. As this fiction only serves the purpose of bringing out more clearly the consequences of his approach, Hegel need not refrain from treating in this first part of his theory of the state some of the legal questions the importance of which may only be understood by reference to modern conditions. Nevertheless, in order to make it clear to the reader that this methodological fiction underlies the whole section, Hegel has given the heading '*Abstraktes Recht*' (Abstract Right) to the first part of the *Philosophy of Right*.

As we are concerned with a theory of natural law, it is not beside the point to stress what is *not* intended by this kind of theory of law. The expression ' natural law ' originally meant nothing else than a law the foundations of which were to be sought in nature rather than in arbitrary actions of men. Thomas Hobbes, the originator of modern natural law, had already turned his back upon this kind of theory of law. Unfortunately, however, he did not abandon the expression ' natural law ' and substitute for it another term, such as ' law of reason '. The modern theory of law attempts to derive all legal norms from the one fundamental norm that man must be recognized primarily as having rights, and it does not look for the ground of their validity in a supposed order of nature or of creation or in the decisions of public authorities.

Man who has such primary rights is (and nothing else is meant by the expression ' right ') at liberty to do whatever he pleases, if only he is prepared to recognize that all men who are affected by his actions have the same rights as he

---

* *Editor's note* – The development of the concept of natural law from Hobbes to Hegel forms the principal subject of M. Riedel's essay.

claims for himself.[3] His liberty never refers directly to the freedom of other men, but only to his own capability of action and to objects which do not themselves have rights, to 'things'. Indirectly, it is true, the liberty of one man can relate to the liberty of another, if both have agreed by equally free decisions upon a certain performance. Consequently the two main parts in Hegel's doctrine of Abstract Right treat of property and of contract.

Professor Macpherson has labelled the conception of man that is presupposed in this theory of law 'possessive individualism'.[4] He has admirably shown that this conception lies at the heart of the liberal theory of civil society, which we find presented in the writings of Hobbes and Locke or of Kant and Hegel in fundamentally the same way, though with varying degrees of precision and conceptual discipline. But it would be wrong to deduce from this observation of Professor Macpherson that the modern theory of rational law is nothing more than an ideology of the possessing class. Such an interpretation fails to do justice to the claims of this theory. Nor does it offer conclusive arguments why the doctrine that all men ought to be recognized as having equal rights and liberties should be nothing but the ideology of some class of society which arose under determinate historical conditions. The contrary thesis that modern rational law can serve as a safe foundation of all legal theory may be supported by strong arguments. In so far as this legal theory may be called liberal, liberalism itself will be absolved from the suspicion of being only the ideology of one class in society. It is therefore strange that one of the most prominent advocates of this kind of legal theory, Hegel, has been emphatically charged with not being a liberal.

II

Hegel's treatment of modern rational law is original not because it adds to the subject important propositions which had never before been considered or because it surpasses the acuteness of argumentation which had been reached by Kant. His aim is not so much to deduce rational law as a system of normative propositions and to recommend its acceptance, but rather to show how the exercise of these rights is a realization of human freedom. Having shown this, Hegel claims to have delivered a 'proof' of rational law.

Of course principles, especially fundamental norms, are not open to the same kind of proof as the propositions which can be deduced from them. This was quite clear to Hegel. It would be false, therefore, to suppose that Hegel was trying to give a kind of proof which he knew could not be given. What he really

---

[3] This notion of right was laid down by Thomas Hobbes: 'The right of nature, which writers commonly call *jus naturale*, is the liberty each man hath, to use his own power, as he will himself, for the preservation of his own nature; that is to say, of his own life; and consequently, of doing any thing, which in his own judgment, and reason, he shall conceive to be the aptest means thereunto' (*Leviathan*, ch. 15. In M. Oakeshott's edition (Oxford, 1946), see p. 84).

[4] C. B. Macpherson, *The Political Theory of Possessive Individualism* (Oxford, 1962).

had in mind was something not very different from the confirmation of a hypothesis. If it could be shown that the consequences of rational law implied the presuppositions of the realization of human freedom, then Hegel would have regarded this as a kind of confirmation of his fundamental norm. On the assumption that human freedom is worth striving for we may readily follow him.

Part of this context of argumentation is Hegel's thesis that man has ' an absolute right of appropriation with regard to all things '.[5] Hegel denies that this right may be derived from the fact that all things may serve to satisfy human needs. He insists that it may be derived only by showing that man creates the conditions of his free actions in the external world by declaring something to be his property.* The appropriation of extra-terrestrial space by man would certainly have been praised by Hegel as an enlargement of the possibilities of human freedom. Just as certainly he would have denounced the abolition of all private property in a community as an act in which injustice against the human personality has been raised to a universal principle.[6] In both respects Hegel shows himself to be an advocate of the freedom of property. This does not prevent him from emphasizing that, according to the fundamental norm of this rational law, only the *possibility* of private property is granted to all. It is an entirely open question what, or how much, an individual may possess as his private property. According to Hegel's analysis, the equality of the right of all to freedom and consequently to private property necessarily leads to inequality in their abilities and in their possessions under the conditions of competition in the civil society.[7]

Already at this point Hegel makes clear a fundamental limitation of the theory of modern rational law. By preserving a residue of *bellum omnium contra omnes* from Hobbes' state of nature in its individualistic premisses, it did not succeed in ' positing the sphere of abstract personality as identical with liberty '. As a matter of principle Hegel admits that ' the provisions concerning private property must be subordinated to higher spheres of law, a community, the state '.[8]

Hegel does not trace these consequences of the theory of rational law any further in the first part of his *Philosophy of Right*. This is due to the structure of argumentation characteristic of his philosophical system. Before he enters into

---

[5] *Grundlinien der Philosophie des Rechts*, ed. J. Hoffmeister, 4th ed. (Hamburg, 1955), § 44, to be compared with Kant, *Metaphysic of Morals*, pt 1 (*Metaphysical Foundations of Jurisprudence*), § 2, A57.

* *Editor's note* – Cf. J. Plamenatz, pp. 40–1.

[6] *Philosophie des Rechts*, § 46.

[7] *Ibid.* § 49. For a similar view, see Macpherson, *Possessive Individualism*, pp. 55, 251.

[8] See *Philosophie des Rechts*, §§ 46, 49, 200, 289. In these remarks may be found the point of departure of a legal theory which stresses the social obligations of property. Hegel himself sought to overcome the ' contradictions ' of the liberal civil society in the organization of corporations (see §§ 201, 249, 255, 303).

a discussion of the problems of social life in a state, Hegel sets himself the task of defining the range of this fundamental norm, that every human individual is first and foremost a subject of rights. In this respect he is more thorough than his predecessors, who had taken for granted that this principle was universally applicable.

In his analysis Hegel resorts to the method of reconstructing the scope of free actions of an individual who regards himself exclusively as having rights and is prepared to recognize other individuals as having rights in the same way. The results of this theoretical method are entirely different from Kant's. Kant tried to deduce a complete system of normative propositions from the fundamental norm of modern rational law. In so doing, he proved to be a faithful disciple of Hobbes. Like him he presupposed the unlimited validity of the individualistic approach to modern rational law. In opposition to them, Hegel insists that this approach applies only when individuals face each other as autonomous persons. In Hegel's theory this condition is only fulfilled if human individuals grant to each other the basic liberty of acting on their own arbitrary decisions or if they determine their respective rights to an external thing by an essentially arbitrary agreement. Kant's attempt to construe the legal relations between the members of a family, and especially marriage itself, as a contract entered into by autonomous persons is therefore rejected by Hegel as an ' outrage '. If one sees where Kant lets himself be led by his individualistic rational law in defining marriage as a sexual community,[9] one is likely to assent to Hegel's thesis that the construction of marriage as a contract entered into by autonomous persons cannot do justice to the concept of marriage as a social institution. Hegel excludes the treatment of the family from the first part of the *Philosophy of Right*. This implies an important limitation of applicability of modern rational law: a theoretical interpretation of the family must make use of other principles than those which are the basis of that law.

For the same reason, according to Hegel, it is not possible rationally to interpret the state as a contract of autonomous individuals. The doctrine of the social contract is an attempt to conceive the state as an association which, although necessary under the conditions of human nature, is ultimately based on the arbitrary decisions of individuals. This is as mistaken as the juristic theory of the family derived from the individualistic rational law. All these interpretations of rational law make the state something ' external, formal, and universal '. The state is regarded as a sphere in which decisions are made about the common

---

[9] *Philosophie des Rechts*, § 75. See Kant, *Metaphysic*, § 24, A106: Marriage is ' the union of two persons of different sex to possess mutually each other's sexual properties for all life '. Essentially on the same lines though, as usual, more moderate than Kant, Locke defines conjugal society as ' a voluntary compact between man and woman ' which consists ' chiefly in such a communion and right in one another's bodies as is necessary to its chief end, procreation ' (*Second Treatise of Civil Government*, § 78).

interests of citizens, but these common interests are discernible only by an impartial observer. On this theory the state confronts the citizens as something alien to them in which they do not really participate.[10] It is not because he wants to revert to earlier forms of political organization that Hegel rejects the doctrine of the social contract. Rather, he criticizes this doctrine because it retains, in some way, the theoretical basis of older, medieval legal doctrines. Hegel's theory of the state, as well as the theory of the family, is, therefore, separated from his discussion of rational law. It is treated in a later section of the *Philosophy of Right*, where Hegel has developed principles which he needs for his theory of the modern state. The structure of the *Philosophy of Right* thus allows us to see the outline of Hegel's theory. Although he starts from the liberal principle of the autonomy of the individual, Hegel (unlike Kant) is not a theoretician of the liberal state which guarantees and respects the rights and liberties of the individual. Like most contemporary theoreticians of the liberal–democratic state, he does not think that liberal principles alone are sufficient for a comprehensive theory of the modern state. So far, at least, Hegel should be praised for his clearsightedness, rather than accused of error.

III

The limitations imposed by Hegel upon the liberalistic principle in the theory of the state come out most clearly when, like all theoreticians after Hobbes, he discusses the state of anarchy. This discussion continues his treatment of rational law in the third section of the first part of the *Philosophy of Right*. More faithfully than most of his predecessors he follows Hobbes in his hypothesis that a *bellum omnium contra omnes* would break out ' if there be no power erected, or great enough for our security '.[11] Nevertheless Hegel does not accept this hypothesis as a sufficient ground for the construction of a theory of the state.

Vengeance, which in the state of nature descends ' from generations to generations, infinitely ', does not in Hegel's theory lead to the erection of a political power to enforce the individualistic rational law, as it did in the liberal theory. The outcome of vengeance is, first of all, ' the postulate of a punishing justice ', that is, the wish that there should exist some person who although an individual, no longer intends to carry out vengeance, but to inflict justice by punishment.* Such a person would no longer act as an autonomous individual pursuing his own arbitrary interests; he would make the realization of universal norms the very aim of his actions. Hence it would be impossible to derive his actions from the fundamental norm of the individualistic rational law.[12] The wish thus becomes realized in the person who has the will to realize justice instead of

---

10 For Hegel's criticisms of the social contract theory, see *Philosophie des Rechts*, §§ 29, 75, 100, 258.
11 *Leviathan*, ch. 17 (Oakeshott's ed., p. 109).
* *Editor's note* – For further elucidation of the distinction in Hegel between vengeance and punishment, see D. E. Cooper's essay, pp. 151–67.   12 *Philosophie des Rechts*, §§ 102–4.

pursuing his own arbitrary aims and seeking vengeance. The boundaries of the individualistic rational law are transcended. The system of norms which is now recognized as valid is treated by Hegel in the second part of his theory of the modern state under the heading of ' Morality '.

Hegel's position differs from that of all theoreticians of the modern state before him: he explicitly recognizes the acceptance of moral norms by the citizens as one of the necessary conditions for the existence of the modern state. Hobbes conceives the state as a system of rules which, according to his basic distinction between external and internal duties, exclusively refer to external actions. Kant goes so far as to claim that ' the problem of the erection of the state, hard as it may seem, may be solved even for a people of devils, if only they be endowed with reason '. He even claims that the state resulting from this construction is precisely the liberal state which guarantees and respects the rights and liberties of the individual.[13] Legal theory and ethical theory, the systems of legality and of morality, are strictly separated from each other in Kant's practical philosophy.

Hegel's treatment of *Rechtslehre* and *Pflichtenlehre* in his Nuremberg Gymnasium lectures [14] is formally equivalent to Kant's, though his leading ideas are in direct opposition to those of Kant. Already in his Nuremberg Encyclopaedia [15] he inserts the doctrine of morality between his treatment of the individualistic rational law and his theory of the state. In this he has made explicit his recognition of morality as one of the necessary conditions of social and political life. There is an apparent analogy between the *Philosophy of Right* and Kant's *Metaphysic of Morals*, in that both philosophers treat of legal theory and ethical theory one after the other; this analogy, however, on closer analysis proves to be an expression of a fundamental difference.

Hegel's conception of morality does, of course, differ from the ordinary, or the ordinary philosophical, use of the word. This conception is the result of his criticism of Kantian ethical theory. Hegel completed his critique of the basic tenets of Kant's ethics as early as his Frankfurt period, although he repeatedly returned to it. The essential result of this criticism was that Hegel distinguished two fundamentally different notions in the conception of morality: *Moralität*, the virtue of the individual conceived in isolation from social relations and primarily responsible to himself, and *Sittlichkeit*, the righteousness of which man is capable only as a member of a community to which he belongs and in the communal affairs of which he participates.[16] The object of this distinction in

---

[13] Kant, *Perpetual Peace*, first supplement, sect. 1.

[14] *Hegels Werke* (Berlin 1832–45), vol. XVIII, pp. 3–96 (hereafter quoted as *WW* XVIII, 3–96).

[15] *WW* XVIII, 215–23.

[16] *Hegels theologische Jugendschriften*, ed. H. Nohl (Tübingen, 1907), pp. 264–7, 388. (For an English translation of pp. 264–7, see *Hegel's Early Theological Writings*, trans. T. M. Knox (Chicago, 1948), pp. 208–12.) See also *WW* I, 396; *The Phenomenology of Mind*, trans. J. B. Baillie, 2nd ed. (London, 1931), ch. V, sect. Cc, ch. VI, sect. Ca.

Hegel's philosophy is to make clear that the problems of morality which Kant discusses in his ethics presuppose a determinate relation of the moral subject to other moral subjects, just as the questions of rational law dealt with in the first part of the *Philosophy of Right* refer to man as an autonomous person, organizing his legal relations freely and arbitrarily. It is obvious that both systems of norms correspond to each other. They both presuppose Riesman's 'inner-directed type' and complement each other; the individualistic rational law contains the norms which govern external actions, and the theory of morality supplies the principles according to which the moral subject decides on his actions.

The position Hegel assigns to morality in the structure of his *Philosophy of Right* is meant to show that the individualistic rational law of the modern era needs as its complement the morality of the moral subject who is conscious of being responsible to himself, and that both systems of norms form the necessary preconditions of the modern state. It follows from this that the liberal thesis which confines the task of the state to providing protection and security of life and property for individuals, unduly limits the scope of political theory and ought to be rejected in this respect. This is not to say, of course, that the state ought not to provide protection and security. But it should be seen that the function of the state is not exhaustively described on the basis of this liberal thesis. Hegel maintains that the state ought to guarantee the right of the moral subject ' to find himself satisfied in his aims '. One can easily recognize this thesis as the starting point of Hegel's theory of the rights of man, which in itself is an important inheritance from the liberal tradition.[17]

Hegel explicitly professes to be a follower of this tradition when he declares the proclamation of subjective liberty at the centre of rational law and morality to be the 'turning and crucial point in the difference between ancient and modern times'. He asserts that this principle has been given to the world by Christianity and has gradually been made 'the universal active (*wirklich*) principle of a new form of the world'.[18]

Hegel's acknowledgement of the principles of individualistic law and morals and his giving them a prominent place in his philosophy of history do not imply that he accepts their validity without reservations. Quite the contrary is true. Rational law and morality are confined by him to the consideration of the individual existence of man. It turns out to be necessary to overcome the individualistic basis of the modern juristic and moral philosophy in order to arrive at a theoretical foundation of the modern state: that is, at a theory of the state as a political community in which individuals no longer separately pursue their private aims, but achieve their public interests in common. The insight into this

---

[17] See *Philosophie des Rechts*, §§ 124, 132, with the important limitation in § 137.
[18] See *ibid*. §§ 124, 162, 185, 206, 299, 358–60.

task Hegel finds missing in the entire discourse of modern political philosophy. So he thinks it necessary to go beyond its boundaries and to return to the tradition originated by Plato and Aristotle.

IV

The intricate structure of argumentation of the *Philosophy of Right*, which differs from all earlier presentations of political philosophy, is a reflection of Hegel's implicit criticisms of the political philosophies advanced by ancient and modern thinkers. This thesis will be corroborated when it is shown that the composition of the third part of the *Philosophy of Right*, to which Hegel gives the heading *Sittlichkeit*, corresponds in all essential points to the structure of the political theory of Plato and Aristotle.

Hobbes and all his followers based their political theory on the principle that human individuals must be conceived primarily as having rights, and must unite into a political body in order to secure their respective spheres of right. Plato and Aristotle, on the contrary, had conceived man as a being which is primarily in need of community with other men. From this standpoint the communal order cannot be understood as something essentially opposed to the claims of the individuals. Following their principle, Plato and Aristotle sought the origin of the state in the simplest forms of human community, and then traced the gradual development of the political community out of these elementary forms. This structure of political theory is reproduced by Hegel in the third part of the *Philosophy of Right*, where he dialectically develops civil society out of the family and proceeds from civil society to the state. In the construction of this part of his political theory, moreover, he makes use of essentially the same principles as Plato and Aristotle. This correspondence is so marked that it has always been seen and stressed that the third part of Hegel's *Philosophy of Right* is 'antique' in character.[19] It is therefore remarkable that Hegel patently tries not to make the historical affiliations of his political theory too obvious, although ordinarily he tends to define his own position by explicit references to other theories.

Our analysis has yielded the following result as far as the structure of the *Philosophy of Right* is concerned. In its first two parts Hegel presents the outline of a *philosophia practica* which rests on the modern distinction of legality and morality. The theory of the state which Hegel leaves out of the first two parts of the *Philosophy of Right* appears in the third part as a doctrine of the political

---

[19] Eduard Gans in his preface to the *Philosophy of Right*, WW viii, viii; Karl Rosenkranz, *Hegels Leben, Supplement zu Hegels Werken* (Berlin, 1844), pp. 124, 129; Haym, *Hegel und seine Zeit*, p. 377; Rosenzweig, *Hegel und der Staat*, vol. ii, p. 85; Ritter, *Hegel und die französische Revolution*, p. 25; M. Riedel, *Studien zu Hegels Rechtsphilosophie* (Frankfurt am Main, 1969), pp. 19–22, 118; K.-H. Ilting, *Philosophische Jahrbücher*, LXXI (1963/64), 38–58, and *Hegel-Studien*, III (1965), 389.

community modelled on antique patterns. The *Philosophy of Right*, then, consists of two different systems of practical philosophy. This means that any interpretation of the framework of Hegel's theory of the modern state has to answer the question how the legal and moral theory of the first two parts is related to the theory of communities and social institutions of the third part. The answer is that the juristic and moral theory is meant to be understood as a methodological fiction; man abstractly conceived as an autonomous person and as a moral subject lives, in reality, in a situation of manifold social interrelations. In so far as the realization of individualistic rational law and of individual morality presupposes these interrelations, which are not created by free decisions of individuals, Hegel maintains that juristic and ethical theory achieve their true meaning and validity only in the context of the theory of institutions and communities. In this sense, the characteristics of Hegel's legal and moral theory are *aufgehoben* (negated, preserved and elevated) in his '*System der Sittlichkeit*'.[20] This establishes the precedence of ancient political theory over the modern theory of the state in Hegel's system of practical philosophy.

V

It is not only on the fundamental idea, that being a member of institutions and communities is more elementary than exercising one's rights and fulfilling one's duties as an individual, that Hegel agrees with Plato and Aristotle. Other fundamental concepts and patterns of thought of his theory of the state are also derived from Platonic and Aristotelian philosophy.

This may be seen most clearly at the decisive junctures in the structure of the *Philsophy of Right* where Hegel prepares a transition or starts a new argument. The beginning of the third section in the second part of the work is such a decisive juncture. There Hegel writes:

The good is the Idea as the unity of the concept of the will and the particular will. Abstract right as well as happiness, subjectivity of thought, and contingency of external existence are negated in it as separate, self-sufficient spheres, and, by the same act, are contained and preserved in it in their essence: it is freedom realised, the absolute and ultimate aim of the world.[21]

In the context of Hegel's theory the idea of the good, the key concept of the Platonic philosophy, is given the function of overcoming the opposition of

20 *Philosophie des Rechts*, §§ 208–10, 256.
21 *Philosophie des Rechts*, § 129. By the 'concept of will' Hegel means that manifestation of the will which is relevant in his treatment of abstract right, viz. the 'person' (*ibid*. §§ 34, 35). The 'particular will' is meant to denote the moral 'subject' which underlies his treatment of morality (*ibid*. § 106). In Hegel's dialectical representation of political philosophy abstract, right figures as 'thesis', morality as 'antithesis' (see *ibid*. §§ 5, 6; *Wissenschaft der Logik*, *WW* v, 35; *Encyklopädie der philosophischen Wissenschaften im Grundrisse*, paras. 112, 163). The 'Idea of the good' consequently stands for the 'synthesis' of right and morality.

legality and morality, manifested in the possible conflict between moral and legal claims. According to Hegel, individuals may seek to realize their legitimate striving for happiness and welfare only on condition that they take the common good into account. In the case of conflict one's legal claims, derived from the individualistic rational law, must be foregone in favour of the welfare of all or of someone else. The idea of the good Hegel talks about in this context may therefore be defined as the fundamental norm that all claims of individuals to their right and to their welfare ought to be balanced against each other. Whenever this fundamental norm is recognized and adopted as the maxim on which we act, the individualistic approach has been given up and the community of men declared the ultimate aim of action.

A group of men who had submitted to this fundamental norm could all be called free at least in this sense, that their possibilities of action were no longer dependent on an alien will. By realizing their claim to freedom in this way, they would have achieved an aim of their conduct which could no longer be conceived as a means to the realization of other aims, and was thus an ' absolute ' aim. This conception of an ultimate aim of action common to all men recaptures the essential meaning of the Platonic–Aristotelian doctrine of the idea of the good.[22]

At the beginning of the third part of the *Philosophy of Right*, Hegel returns to this conception.

Ethical life (Sittlichkeit) is the Idea of freedom, as the *living good*. The living good has its thought and will in *self-consciousness* and its actuality through the actions of self-consciousness, just as self-consciousness finds in *ethical reality* its basis, which is in and for itself, and its aim, which sets it in motion. It is the concept of freedom developed into the existing world and into the nature of self-consciousness.[23]

The idea of ethical life, the subject of the third part of Hegel's theory of the modern state, is nothing else but the idea of the good which lies at the basis of Plato's theory of the political community. While in the second part it was conceived as a fundamental norm or as a ' still abstract idea ', it is now introduced as the ' living good ', that is to say as the principle, by which a real community of men is organized.[24]

Hegel's idea of *Sittlichkeit*, then, is a pattern of thought borrowed from ancient

[22] See Plato, *Lysis*, 219 c 5–220 b 3; *Gorgias*, 468 b 1–8, 499 c 6–9; *Republic*, 505 d 5–506 a 2; Aristotle, *Nicomachean Ethics*, 1094 a 18–b 11.
[23] *Philosophie des Rechts*, § 142. In this paragraph Hegel distinguishes two aspects (or ' moments ') of the Idea of the good : the aspect of self-consciousness and the aspect of ethical reality. In the political self-consciousness of the citizens the idea of the good (that is, the idea of a political community) is actually existent; the citizens, on the other hand, conceive the idea of their political community as the basis of their political activity. In so far as it appears to them as something given and independent of their own arbitrary decisions, Hegel calls this aspect of the idea of the political community its ' ethical reality ' (*sittliches Sein*).
[24] See *Philosophie des Rechts*, § 131, to be compared with § 144.

political philosophy. Its content, too, is derived from the model of the ancient city-state. This is most easily proved from his early writings. In April 1796 Hegel wrote of the citizen of the ancient city-state: ' The idea of his country, of his state, was the invisible principle, the higher aim he worked for, which impelled him to act. This was his ultimate aim in the world or the ultimate aim of his world. He found it expressed in reality or helped, by his own actions, to express it and keep it alive.' [25] *

Hegel's antique conception of the state is, therefore, thoroughly republican. It is based on the model of a political community which is ' easy to survey' (εὐσύνοπτος),[26] in which all free citizens take a direct part in political affairs and pursue the common aim of maintaining their political community. This common aim is for them not an abstract scheme which they have still to realize. It is already realized in their political community and has become their ' existing world '. The final end, therefore, presents itself to each individual as a ' being ', as ' something objective ', or as ' concrete substance '.[27] This final end, considered as the motive for political action of each citizen, is described by Hegel as the aim which sets them in motion; or even, in an expression borrowed from Aristotle's theology, as the end which moves, but which itself is absolutely unmoved.[28]

This interpretation of the ancient city-state lies at the heart of one of Hegel's well-known formulae. In order to understand it, one should first of all see this interpretation as the result of an idealization of ancient political life. Although Plato and Aristotle would not have fully agreed to it, it is not quite without foundation in the perspective of Greek metaphysics. I have in mind Hegel's interpretation of the state as ' the divine which is in and for itself '.[29]

---

[25] *Hegels theologische Jugendschriften*, p. 222 (*Hegel's Early Theological Writings*, p. 154).

* *Editor's note* – Hegel also discusses this in the *Phenomenology*. See J. N. Shklar's essay, esp. pp. 80 ff.

[26] Aristotle, *Politics*, 1326b 24.

[27] See *Philosophies des Rechts*, §§ 130, 142, 144. In representing the political community as ' substance ' Hegel incurs the risk of conceiving the citizens merely as accidents or as qualities of substance (see *ibid*. §§ 146, 156 Addition). In this he was less cautious than Aristotle, who was anxious not to call the political community a ' substance ' (see *Politics*, 1253a 19–23). In his Jena lectures on the *System der Sittlichkeit* Hegel himself maintained that ethical life must completely destroy any particularity (*Schriften zur Politik und Rechtsphilosophie*, ed. G. P. Lasson (Hamburg, 1952), p. 464), but in *Philosophie des Rechts* this idea was given up.

[28] See *Philosophie des Rechts*, §§ 142, 152, 258. In Aristotle's theology God is the final cause which, being unmoved itself, moves the world (*Metaphysics*, 1072a 21–b 14). Hegel himself refers to this concept in the preface to *Phänomenologie des Geistes* (ed. J. Hoffmeister (Hamburg, 1952), p. 22. In Baillie's translation of the *Phenomenology*, see p. 83). As Aristotle's concept had grown up out of Plato's idea of the good, Hegel had no trouble in giving it a political interpretation.

[29] *Philosophie des Rechts*, § 258. The antique origin of Hegel's expression is evident when Hegel, alluding to Athene as the goddess of her city-state Athens, describes the spirit of a people (*Volkgeist*) as ' the divine which knows and wills itself ' (*ibid*. § 257). In his early *System der Sittlichkeit* this deification of the people is quite frequent. (See Lasson's ed. of *Schriften zur*

VI

Hegel's deification of the state is justifiably notorious. It was bound to provoke both the abhorrence of those who object to any profanation of God's name, and the hostility of all militant atheists. This conception of the state is not objectionable solely because Hegel attempted to interpret the political community in terms of the fundamental concepts of ancient metaphysics and theology. What is really questionable is that he tried to extend this interpretation explicitly to the modern state.[30] By doing this he exposed himself to easy attacks: an opportunity which, as is well known, has been energetically utilized.[31] What is more, he ran the risk of losing sight of those realities which he sought to explain in terms of the humanistic ideal of his youth. Above all, by his antique interpretation of the modern state, Hegel was induced to assume that peoples or nations are, as it were, historical personalities to which the individual man, in his historical existence, belonged unconditionally. The possibilities of enlisting Hegel's republican ideal of the state in the service of some stupid ideology of the national state are immense.

We shall misunderstand the importance of the Hegelian conception of the state as long as we are not clear that in his theory it has the function of remedying a patent defect of the liberal conception. As long as the state has but to protect and to secure the freedom and property of the individual, the exercise of power within the state remains something evil even if unavoidable. Viewed from the standpoint of the interests of the individual it is, then, ' something arbitrary to be a member of a state ' or, as Hobbes put it, men come together ' not because

---

Politik und Rechtsphilosophie, pp. 465, 467, 469, 475, 487, 488, 503. See also *WW* 1, 400.) Hegel's very notion of the divine as something ' which is in and for itself ' recalls the notion of Absolute Being in Greek metaphysics. See Parmenides, in H. Diels and W. Kranz, *Die Fragmente der Vorsokratiker* (Berlin, 1934–8, and later eds. Cited as ' DK '), B 8, 29; Xenophanes DK B 29, 1. Plato looked upon the immortality of the species as something divine (*Symposium*, 207d 1–208b 6). Alluding to this conception, Hegel expounds his notion of the divinity of the people in the *System der Sittlichkeit* (Lasson's ed., p. 449, to be compared with p. 464). Even in Aristotle's notion of the self-sufficient political community Hegel might have found some hint on its divine character, in so far as self-sufficiency was considered something divine (see Aristotle, *Politics*, 1252b 31–1253a 1 and *Metaphysics* 1091b 15–20, to be compared with *Philosophie des Rechts*, § 270 Addition).

[30] Hegel's attitude to the ' people ' is rather ambiguous, and the relation of the ' people ' of the ancient city-state to the ' people ' within the modern monarchical state not very clear in his thought. On the whole he seems to have regarded it as a concept appropriate only to conditions where a highly organized public authority did not exist. In discussing modern democratic ideas he speaks of the people with the utmost contempt (see *Philosophie des Rechts*, §§ 279, 301, 317, 318). On the other hand there are passages in the *Philosophy of Right* where he seems to equate the modern state with the people (§§ 331, 347) or with the ' spirit of the people ' (§§ 156, 274, 352).

[31] J. Ritter has admirably discussed the meaning of Hegel's deification of the ' ethical world ' in his philosophy of history, yet he has not dispelled the doubts which arise from Hegel's deification of authoritarian monarchy.

naturally it could happen no otherwise ', but ' by accident ', a statement Hegel is likely to have had in mind, when he discussed the deficiencies of liberalism.[32]

To this view Hegel opposes his conviction that individuals may overcome the limitation of their particular and private interests in only learning to take part in the political decisions of their community: ' It is the destiny of individuals to lead a public (*allgemeines*) life.' Hegel's antique ideal of the state, then, serves the purpose of overcoming the liberal conception of the state. In about the same way in almost all modern states since his time, the idea of democracy has made it a right and a task of all citizens to take part in the exercise of political power. (Here I take it for granted that a liberal state is not necessarily democratic, nor a democracy liberal.)

Why, then, did Hegel persistently refuse in the *Philosophy of Right* to join Rousseau in his method of overcoming the liberal conception of the state and in his democratic ideals? This is all the more remarkable since he had been sympathetic to Rousseau's ideas from his earliest years and especially shared Rousseau's dislike of ' the particular ' (private existence) and his admiration for ' the general life ' (public affairs). The explanation might be that this was due to political opportunism, which Hegel by no means ignored in writing his major political work.

Hegel's explicit objection to Rousseau's conception of the state concerns Rousseau's radicalism in deriving all social and political relations in his democratical state from political decisions.* Indeed, Rousseau's social contract creates ' un corps moral et collectif, lequel reçoit de ce même acte son unité, son moi commun, sa vie et sa volonté.' 'To begin all over again and to start out from thought ' means, according to Hegel, that the historical traditions out of which social institutions and political communities have developed are not just to be reformed (as Hegel would have agreed), but declared in principle invalid and abolished. This concedes more to the ' subjectivity of freedom ' than it is capable of accomplishing and is to conceive the idea of a rational state in a one-sided way.[33] So far Hegel's criticism of radical democracy is not so very different from the considerations which all over the world, a century later, gave rise to the conception of a constitutional democracy which enjoyed historical continuity.

Something that is not made explicit by Hegel in his criticism of radical democracy, but which is presupposed in it, may be even more important for a just estimate of his theory of the modern state: his fidelity to liberal principles. He did, it is true, find them insufficient as the basis of a theory of the modern state.

---

[32] *Philosophie des Rechts*, § 258; Hobbes, *De Cive* I 2 (*Opera Latina*, vol. II, p. 159). Similarly Hume admits : ' Society must be esteemed in a manner accidental, and the effect of many ages.' (*Treatise of Human Nature*, ed. L. A. Selby-Bigge (Oxford, 1888), p. 493.)

* *Editor's note* – Hegel's critique of Rousseau is also discussed by J.-F. Suter, pp. 54–5; and by M. Riedel, pp. 138–41.

[33] Rousseau, *Du Contrat Social*, bk 1, ch. 6; *Philosophie des Rechts*, § 258.

Nevertheless he attached the greatest importance to preserving them in his political theory. In Rousseau's democratic state they were on principle eliminated:
' Dans une législature parfaite, la volonté particulière ou individuelle doit être
nulle.' To this annihilation of the individual in radical democracy Hegel opposes
the postulate of uniting the liberty of the individual with the force of the community: ' The principle of modern states has this enormous strength and depth
because it lets the principle of subjectivity develop into the autonomous extreme
of personal particularity and at the same time to lead it back into the substantial
unity and preserve this unity in it.' [34] The state, it is true, may impose limitations
on the spheres of private rights and welfare, of the family, and of civil society;
but in principle it ought not to interfere with these spheres and should leave them
to be organized by the autonomous individuals through their own free decisions.
Hegel's state, then, is not meant to be totalitarian, while Rousseau's radical
democracy has often been charged with this character.[35]

The same reasons which make Hegel reject a state which proclaims an unrestricted liberty of subjecting all social and political relations to political decisions
also induce him to reject its ancient counterpart, the state of Plato, which in its
way is quite as totalitarian; the liberties of the individual are also completely
extinguished in it. Compared with Rousseau's democracy, which acknowledges
only the principle of ' subjective ' liberty, Plato's *Republic* is the other extreme of
one-sidedness in the idea of the state to have been overcome in modern history.
Plato's conception of a state is one in which the principle of ' subjectivity ' is
suppressed in favour of ' substantiality ' (the idea of the community).[36]

So we arrive at the conclusion that the core of the Hegelian conception of the
state lies in the peculiarly Hegelian union of the general with the particular, of
substantiality with subjectivity.[37] This union is to be achieved in such a way that
both principles are fully developed and yet complement each other. In Hegel's
state, then, the claim of individuals to their free development and self-determination is fully satisfied; on the other hand the political community is also recognized
as something which may not be reduced to individual and private interests alone.
The state so conceived is a ' substantial unity, in which liberty is granted its
highest right '.[38]

[34] Rousseau, *Contrat Social*, bk III, ch. 2; *Philosophie des Rechts*, § 260.

[35] This difference may well be seen in the role Rousseau and Hegel attribute to religion in their
states. While Rousseau tries to establish a civil religion the profession of which is, under the
penalty of death, obligatory (bk IV, ch. 8), Hegel's main endeavour is to secure the independence
of the state from religious influences (*Philosophie des Rechts*, § 270).

[36] See *Philosophie des Rechts*, preface, p. 14 and §§ 46, 185, 206, 299.

[37] Hegel's idea of the union of substantiality with subjectivity is expressed in the well-known passage
of *Phenomenology* (p. 80). It has been excellently analysed by Andrew J. Reck (*Studies in Hegel*,
Tulane Studies in Philosophy, IX (New Orleans–The Hague, 1960), pp. 109–33). See *Philosophie
des Rechts*, §§ 257, 258, 278.

[38] *Philosophie des Rechts*, § 258.

Hegel was not content to conceive the modern state as a union of public-spirited-ness with civil liberty, and thus to achieve a synthesis of the basic ideas of ancient and modern political philosophy. He had to define clearly his position with reference to the key concept of the modern theory of the state, the concept of sovereignty. His treatment of the problem of sovereignty, then, must show whether the synthesis of political ideas he was striving for has been successfully accomplished.*

In all modern theories of the state, the doctrine of the social contract occurs at the point in the structure of argument where it must be stated who has the right of the final decision and who is the source of all political and legal authority. This doctrine Hegel explicit rejected, and replaced by the idea of a historically con-tinuous political community which the individual finds already in existence. Precisely at the point where all older theories proceeded from the state of nature to 'civil society' (the state), Hegel inserted his doctrine of morality as a neces-sary condition of the state. In the third part of the *Philosophy of Right,* where he introduces the fundamental and most important distinction between civil society and the state, one might have expected him to pose the problem of sovereignty: and then to expound his theory of it at the point of transition from civil society to the state. But he postpones the discussion of this problem and comes to deal with it only when he treats of the different powers of the state.

The division of the three powers of the state proposed by Hegel follows (as it is often, but not always the case in the *Philosophy of Right*) a 'dialectical' order taken over from his *Logic*.[39] The legislative power has the office of 'determining the universal'; the executive power is given the task of subsuming 'the *particular* spheres and individual cases' under 'the universal'; the 'princely power' is given by Hegel the '*subjectivity* of the last decision of the will'. According to Hegel's dialectical scheme 'subjectivity' or 'individuality' is to be understood as the synthesis of universality and particularity.[40] It would follow from this that the

---

* *Editor's note* – R. N. Berki, pp. 208–10, also discusses Hegel's conception of sovereignty, and Marx's critique of it. Cf. also Z. A. Pelczynski's essay, pp. 230–2.

39 It may well be maintained, against Hegel, that the dialectical procedure in political philosophy has no real advantages. Some inconsistencies in Hegel's dialectical treatment of political philo-sophy have been pointed out by J. Plamenatz, *Man and Society* (London, 1963), vol. II, pp. 227, 232, 235. Other inconsistencies may be added, for example, the third section of the first paragraph on crime and punishment does not fit the dialectical scheme, and neither does any of the second part. The dialectic of the *Philosophy of Right* implies the idea of different stages of a fictitious journey through which the human will passes in pursuit of its final end. The dialectic is the arrangement of the stages in the sequence of 'immediacy' (= thesis), 'difference' (= anti-thesis), and 'unity' (= synthesis), as well as the necessity which urges the will to pass from one stage to the following till it reaches the final end (see *Philosophie des Rechts*, § 31). Grand as it is in itself, this programme is hardly adequate in political philosophy, as will presently be seen in Hegel's exposition of the powers of the state.

40 *Philosophie des Rechts*, § 273. For the dialectical division of this paragraph, see *ibid*. §§ 5–7.

princely power was meant to comprehend legislation and government. It might then be given the function of representing the state as a whole and of embodying the sovereignty of the state. Whether this representative of the sovereignty of the state was a monarch who possessed the trust of the citizens, or an elected head of the state, would have had no special importance in the framework of Hegel's political philosophy.

A similar interpretation of his own doctrine of sovereignty was indeed proposed by Hegel in his Berlin lectures. There he described the monarch as the state authority whose task consists in ' putting the dot on the i '.[41] Unfortunately this interpretation in no way agrees with the presentation of his doctrine in the *Philosophy of Right*. There he allows himself to make an unintelligible exception to the ' dialectical ' order of presenting his theories. In carrying out the plan of his exposition he proceeds in inverted order: he begins with the dialectical synthesis, goes on to the dialectical antithesis, and presents the thesis last. This contradiction of the rules of the dialectic, which is unique in Hegel's system, has its parallel in the prominence which is given to the princely power in Hegel's argument. The king is presented as a ruler, who needs no democratic legitimation; hereditary monarchy is ' deduced ' by dialectical logic; and the two other powers of the state, government and legislature, although dependent on the king, are assigned the task of mediating between his solitary majesty and the people.[42]

Faced after the Congress of Vienna by the hereditary monarchy of the Prussian state, and the Karlsbad Decrees on the suppression of ' demagogic ' activities, Hegel sacrificed his own conception of the modern state and allowed his theory to fall into two irreconcilable parts. It is presumably because of the obscurity of his argumentation that this decisive break in his theory – one is almost tempted to call it a betrayal of his own principles – has not yet been given the attention it deserves.[43]

---

[41] *Ibid*. § 280 Addition.

[42] *Ibid*. §§ 275 (with Addition), 279–80, 281, 287, 302. Hegel's ' deduction ' of hereditary monarchy, as Rosenzweig justly observes, is unparalleled in the history of political philosophy (Rosenzweig, *Hegel und der Staat*, vol. II, p. 139).

[43] Haym pointed out merely that Hegel (apparently, so he maintained) gave unusual importance to the subjectivity of the monarch (Haym, *Hegel und seine Zeit*, p. 382). Rosenzweig, too, failed to notice what happened when Hegel made the monarch the dialectical synthesis of the powers of the state (Rosenzweig, *Hegel und der Staat*, vol. II, pp. 139–42). Only Reyburn (*Hegel's Ethical Theory*, pp. 240 ff.) saw the problem in question, and tried to solve it, assuming that Hegel treats monarchy in §§ 275 ff. as the ' abstract ' thesis of the dialectical triad. But he failed to corroborate his interpretation by an analysis of Hegel's text.

Hegel explicitly rejected the concept of popular sovereignty in the *Philosophy of Right* (see the long discussion of the subject in § 279). But the grounds he gave for the rejection were largely of the ' empirical ' character he frequently dismissed as unworthy of philosophy, viz. that the state would be at the mercy of individual whims and caprices, etc., and no stable rational legal order would be possible. If the people is conceived as a constitutional organ through which the political community decides some of its most important affairs then the people would seem a more appropriate bearer of the sovereignty of the state than a single individual.

The inevitable consequence of Hegel's conception of the monarchical state was the destruction of the internal coherence of the 'system of ethical life'. For, after introducing the monarch as the 'top *and the beginning* of the whole ',[44] Hegel could no longer describe the state as that organization of a political community where the citizens examined and decided the general problems of the family and especially of civil society. The connection between civil society and the state is lost for some forty paragraphs. Then, after he has finished his treatment of the princely power and the government, Hegel tries to re-establish it without real success in the context of his discussion of the legislature. This deprives him of the fruits of his most worthy endeavour. The significance of his theory of civil society has become almost indiscernible.

In the history of political philosophy Hegel was the first to introduce a distinction between civil society and the state as two different spheres of public life, and to attempt to give a theoretical foundation to this distinction. Civil society, in Hegel's theory, is conceived as a context of individual activities. It is created by a multitude of individuals who primarily pursue their own aims. By entering into manifold relations with each other, they ultimately become wholly dependent on the very conditions of this network of their actions, which they themselves helped to produce. It is first and foremost a 'system of needs and wants' (*System der Bedürfnisse*), in which one is dependent on the others: the conditions of production in modern industrial society. As this system cannot exist without some regulating influence, civil society in Hegel's doctrine also contains the spheres of the administration of justice, of social welfare and of social institutions (the 'corporations ').

Hegel could include this whole sphere in his political philosophy, only because he had discovered the productive power of labour as the foundation of civil society. This insight, which lies already at the basis of Hegel's famous dialectic of master and slave in the *Phenomenology of Mind*,* is perhaps Hegel's most original contribution to philosophy. In the *Philosophy of Right* his theory of civil society enables him to analyse some problems of the modern state which would be of central importance in the history of the nineteenth and twentieth centuries.

The liberal tradition in political philosophy before Hegel contains no more than the rudiments of a theory of labour and of civil society.[45] It is so much pre-

---

44 *Philosophie des Rechts*, § 273. In his Berlin lectures Hegel tried to explain, not very convincingly, why he began his treatment of the powers of the state with the princely power (see *ibid*. § 275 Addition).

* *Editor's note* – Cf. J. N. Shklar, pp. 77–9.

45 John Locke's famous chapter on property and labour (*Second Treatise*, ch. 5), so congenial to Hegel, is of little consequence in Locke's political philosophy. On Hegel's reception of British national economy, see Paul Chamley, *Economie politique et philosophie chez Steuart et Hegel* (Paris, 1963).

occupied with the theory of individual rights and liberties that, when private property is discussed, the questions of the origin of property out of labour and of the social consequences of the division of labour are never raised. In this way, the theory of the state is reduced to a theory of the limits of rights in the state.

Human labour and the division of labour in society play an important part in ancient political theory. Plato's state develops out of the division of labour and has its basis in it. In the political community, according to Plato, men realize their common good by the work each of them contributes as his part to the preservation of their common life. But neither Plato nor Aristotle deduced from these principles of their political philosophy that human labour as such ought to have a decisive influence on the organization of the state. Even less in Plato and Aristotle than in liberal theory does human labour give direct rise to political claims and rights.

Hegel is on the way to remedying the shortcomings of those two theories when he inserts the theory of civil society between the theory of the family as the elementary human community and the theory of the state as the self-sufficient and perfect community, and when he connects it with the liberal rational law as well as with the theory of the state. This is why he is so concerned to carry over the formations of society which rest on the division of labour into the structure of the state. His odd rejection of universal and equal suffrage in favour of estate representation is due to this endeavour.[46] The relationship between civil society and the state was bound to become the crucial problem of his political philosophy.

Moreover, Hegel could really have achieved his aim of overcoming the individualistic approach of the liberal conception of the state, and applied plausibly his older republican ideals to the modern state, in only one way: by making the social character of human labour the foundation of his political philosophy. Plato and Aristotle could have taught Hegel that man is a social animal for this very reason, that he is dependent for the production of the means of life on the division of labour in society. The social or welfare functions of the state are stressed by him very clearly in the *Philosophy of Right*,[47] and the political problems which would result from the growth of the industrial proletariat are anticipated in an almost prophetic phrase: ' civil society, by its own dialectic, is driven beyond its own limits '.[48]

Hegel's political philosophy, then, was almost destined to be developed into a liberal socialism. Karl Marx saw this very early when, laying the foundation of his socialist theory, he wrote of Hegel: ' The greatness of Hegel's Pheno-

---

[46] *Philosophie des Rechts*, §§ 300–8. Hegel argues that universal and equal suffrage takes away the possibility of representing the structure of civil society in the legislative assembly and ' separates social (civil) from political life ' (§ 303).

[47] Under the old-fashioned title ' Police ' (*Philosophie des Rechts*, §§ 231–48).

[48] *Ibid*. § 246.

menology . . . lies in the fact that Hegel conceives the creation of man by man as a process . . . therefore, that he perceives the essence of labour.' [49]

Hegel failed to draw the consequences implied in his approach to political philosophy. Instead, he irremediably disturbed the structure of his theory of the modern state by treating sovereignty as the problem not of a social and democratic state, but of a monarchical ruler. The main work of his political philosophy, which could have been the basis of a really forward-looking policy if Hegel had not abandoned his own principles, was soon known as ' a servile book from the principles and doctrines of which any liberty-loving man ought to keep away '.[50]

Hegel seems to have been conscious of the fact that he had not been able, under the conditions of the Continental restoration, to accomplish a theory of the modern state which satisfied his own standards. The preface of the *Philosophy of Right* concludes on a note of resignation: ' When philosophy paints its grey in grey, some shape of life has grown old, and by grey in grey it may be perceived but not rejuvenated. The owl of Minerva begins to fly only when the dusk sets in.'

IX

K. R. Popper was not the first to make against Hegel the charge that his state is simply not a liberal state. We may suppose that Hegel would have promptly replied that his problem was exactly whether the modern state can be nothing more than liberal. Popper's attack on Hegel was, after all, understandable in a time when the defence of the liberal state against totalitarian fascism and communism was at stake. One generation later, however, it has become clear that the problems of the Third World can no longer be solved by means of liberal politics. This confirms Hegel's insight into the limitations of the liberal principle.

Nevertheless, 150 years after the first publication of the *Philosophy of Right* we cannot avoid stating that Hegel's theory of the modern state has been a failure. In some sense this must be said of all great political thinkers of modern times. None of them has developed a theory which nowadays is satisfactory, even in outline.

But Hegel, unlike his predecessors, did not fail because he had not sufficiently realized the greatness of his task. He realized it as nobody before him and, after all, nobody after him. His failure is due to his refusal to recognize the contradiction between the rational that was already actual, and the irrational which did still exist.

In a way, his political philosophy has thereby become a picture of his historical epoch, in a manner not very different from the way in which Plato's political

---

[49] So-called ' Paris Manuscripts ', fol. xxiii.
[50] Gans, *WW*, VIII, ix.

philosophy, in Hegel's own interpretation, was a picture of its time. In a deep sense, then, Hegel is ultimately right, and what he said of Plato may also be said of him: 'He has proved a great mind in that the principle on which his distinctive idea turns is just the pivot on which the imminent revolution of the world was turning in those days.' [51]

[51] *Philosophie des Rechts*, preface (Hoffmeister's ed., p. 14; Knox's trans., p. 10). The author wishes to thank Dr F. O. Wolf and the editor for their help in translating the essay into English.

The sources and significance of Hegel's corporate doctrine

G. HEIMAN

' *Omnis multitudo derivatur ab uno – ad unum reducitur.*' [1] In these words Otto Gierke summarizes the publicist and civilist doctrines of the late Middle Ages. These were the doctrines which were designed to establish the legitimacy and eventual supremacy of the political over the theological realm, the supremacy of the law of the *regnum* over that of the *sacerdotium*. In a different context but succinctly nevertheless, Gierke's sentence also serves to describe one of Hegel's fundamental postulates of politics and law. The whole, the completed state, is ultimately derived from the one, the singular, the monad. It depends for its existence and verification upon the singular just as the singular, in turn, is unavoidably dependent upon the many, the whole. The mutual recognition on the part of these polarities is the only method by which a rational and ethical (*sittlich*) community can hope to attain that unification which is the major purpose of Hegel's *Staatslehre*. Paramount to this process of recognition and mediation is Hegel's doctrine of corporatism. As will be shown, corporatism, in turn, belongs not only to the realm of right (*ius, Recht*) but more specifically its place is in the realm of law (*lex, Gesetz*), of positive legal and political action as Hegel perceived it.

The first part of this essay will deal with Hegel's attitude towards some of the intellectual trends and schools of legal and political thought in his time. The same section will also touch on the concept of corporatism as it emerged from the Roman system of law. Without taking note of these and their influence, Hegel's espousal of corporatism becomes rather meaningless. The rest of the essay will examine Hegel's own doctrine of corporatism, his use of that concept as a means of mediation and, ultimately, of the politicization of his countrymen.

I

Hegel looked upon his work as an *ex post facto* explanation, for ' a work of philosophy . . . must be poles apart from an attempt to construct a state as it ought to be '.[2] Yet despite this it can be argued that perhaps too much has been made of the owl of Minerva and its flight at dusk at the cost of disregarding the

[1] Otto Gierke, *Das deutsche Genossenschaftsrecht* (Berlin, 1881), vol. III, p. 515.
[2] *Hegel's Philosophy of Right*, trans. T. M. Knox (Oxford, 1942), p. 11. Wherever the German text is consulted and deviations from the Knox translation occur, the text used is Hegel's *Grundlinien der Philosophie des Rechts*, ed. J. Hoffmeister, 4th ed. (Hamburg, 1955).

fact that Hegel did make prescriptive statements. Indubitably he rejected the role of philosophic prophet but he was not averse to condemning and to praising certain political and legal ideas.

It is equally difficult to accept the portrait of Hegel as the brooding philosopher of the Absolute, the religious mystic, the spokesman for Prussia or even the ' idealist ' as that term is being used in the modern vernacular. He was, as his works indicate, as political as any of his contemporaries and quite possibly much more so. Moreover, Hegel's system of law and politics, and particularly his doctrine of corporatism, appears to be designed to help turn the apolitical, retiring, pietist and smug *Spiessbürger* (philistine) of his time into a more responsible political being. Considering Hegel's historical epoch – the intellectual and political turmoil of the post-Napoleonic era, when Hegel wrote his *Philosophy of Right* – the range of available legal and political schemes was far from limited.

For example, romanticism had been the predominant intellectual and artistic trend in Germany in the last two decades of the eighteenth century. It had influenced the young Hegel. But after his break with Schelling and the completion of *The Phenomenology of Mind* in 1806, Hegel turned his back on most romantic notions. Philosophically he rejected those abstractions which, in his view, the romantics pursued. Moreover, Hegel became dissatisfied with the lack of realism and apoliticism common to much of romantic thought. The work of Goethe is an illustration of the failure of the intellectual to prepare the German public mind for the political tasks confronting it in the nineteenth century.

Faust is the prototype of the active, searching Promethean mind which attempts to traverse all of history and the universality of human experience to come to terms with itself and the world. Faust is the *Tatmensch par excellence* yet at the very end of his imaginative venture he is no closer to reality than being involved with reclaiming some land from the sea. This reclaimed land is to support a ' free and active race ',[3] Faust announces. Yet such details as to their form of government, the type of law under which the free are to flourish, and their means of livelihood are not explained. Romantic poetry then, even if it came from Goethe, Minister of State in Saxony-Weimar, offered no adequate political preparation. It can be claimed of course that it is not poetry's task to do so, yet Goethe's example is typical of the romantic experience.

It would not be accurate, however, to claim that romanticism failed to contribute anything to German politics. One of its products, nationalism, was to have far-reaching consequences. It is amply clear that Hegel was unalterably opposed to zealous chauvinism, as distinct from patriotism.[4] The latter plays a modest and tempered role in his corporate doctrine. But a devastating critique of

---

[3] Goethe, *Faust*, part II, act v.

[4] For an authoritative discussion of the subject, see Shlomo Avineri, ' Hegel and Nationalism ', *Review of Politics*, XXIV (1962), 461–84. Reprinted in W. Kaufmann (ed.), *Hegel's Political Philosophy* (New York, 1970).

chauvinism can be found in Hegel's statement, ' By the simple family remedy of ascribing to feeling the labour, the more than millenary labour, of reason and its intellect, all the trouble of rational insight and knowledge directed by speculative thinking is of course saved '.[5] In short, a rational system of law in which the corporate doctrine plays a clearly assigned economic, political and legal part could not be derived from romantic and essentially irrational chauvinism.

Despite his rejection of romanticism as a whole, however, Hegel used some romantic notions, but in greatly modified form.[6] The organic view of the state, the concept of the *Volk*, and the attempt to comprehend history philosophically appear in his thinking, but the point is that he was not inclined to accept any concept which he did not reformulate in his own fashion. This also applied to Hegel's reaction to the juristic controversies of his time for they too had been influenced by romanticism.

The historical school of jurisprudence came to the fore under the leadership of Gustav Hugo,[7] Savigny, Eichorn, Thibault and Puchta, who were critical of what they considered the mechanistic and abstract legal attitude of the Enlightenment. While far from presenting a united front they agreed upon one issue, the need for a general revision of the legal systems of the German lands and the establishment of a truly indigenous jurisprudence. They sought to locate the sources of law in historical practice and precedent, in the character of the native *Volksgeist* and the language in which it expressed itself. The task appeared to them a particularly pressing one in view of the fact that the German lands were, on the whole, governed according to Roman law. This had replaced native common law by what had been called the ' *receptio in complexu* '[8] of the *corpus juris civilis*, in the sixteenth century. The case was far from being simply a matter of replacing a non-indigenous with an indigenous system. Roman law, Germanic

---

5 *Philosophy of Right*, p. 6.

6 There is little indication that the semi-legal and political writings of such romanticists as Schlegel, Haller and Adam Müller left much of an impression upon him. For his criticism of Haller's *Restauration der Staatswissenschaft*, see *Philosophy of Right*, §§ 219 and 258. It can be pointed out also that Hegel's concept of the state does not appear to be far removed from Müller's, who sees it as ' the totality of all human affairs and their mediation to the organic living whole ' (*Die Elemente der Staatskunst* (Berlin, 1809), vol. I, p. 48). But in Hegel's system the state is only a stage of the objective mind.

7 G. Rexius in his ' Studien zur Staatslehre der historischen Schule ', *Historische Zeitschrift*, CVII (1911), 508n., points out that it was a matter of contention whether Hugo belonged to the historical school. Rexius, however, is prepared to place him into the category. More importantly, so does F. C. von Savigny in his *Vom Beruf unserer Zeit für Gesetzgebung und Rechtswissenschaft* (Hildesheim, 1967) (retrographic copy of the Heidelberg 2nd ed. 1840), p. 182. Hegel, while not concerning himself with the question of whether Hugo belonged to the historical school, takes him to task for allegedly finding ' rationality ' in Roman law (*Philosophy of Right*, § 3).

8 Heinrich Mitteis, *Deutsche Rechtsgeschichte* (Munich, 1956 ed.), p. 160; Gierke, *Genossenschaftsrecht*, vol. III, p. 672.

law and canon law had become intermingled since the days of the later Roman Empire.[9]

It would be wrong to assume however that the advocates of the historical school of law, Savigny foremost amongst them, were intent upon the elimination of all Roman legal principles. Indeed he warned against removing, by over-zealous and imprudent surgery, those parts of the Roman-derived law which could still be useful.[10] But as already indicated, the historical school was far from united in its views as to how the transformation of German jurisprudence was to come about.[11] Thus when one examines Hegel's attitude towards that school it must be noted that despite his strong condemnation of Roman civilization and law, a subject which will be discussed later, and although he maintained a hostile attitude towards his colleague at the university of Berlin, he was just as cautious as Savigny ' not to wield the surgical knife with great abandon '. All the same, Hegel stood apart from much of historical legal thought, for his measure of legal validity was essentially rationalist and not historical. Long before he lectured on *The Philosophy of History* he had condemned the constitution of the Holy Roman Empire as an irrelevant old edifice.[12] In his *Lectures on the History of Philosophy* he spoke of the ' wretched German law ' being replaced by the more appropriate Frederician code.[13]

Legal positivism, the assumption that the *Volksgeist* could serve as a source of positive law, the assumed existence of some mythical ancient law, and Savigny's denial that a general civil code could be written, were the factors which set Hegel apart from the historical school.[14] Yet there are also similarities which cast some doubt on the depth of the disagreement, particularly when Hegel's attitude towards positive law is considered. Savigny showed great respect for Roman law and indeed argued that ' without the influence of Roman law the development of German law would have been impossible '.[15] In turn, Hegel stated that ' The

[9] The German case was by no means unique in the history of continental European jurisprudence. Nevertheless, what could possibly be considered as ancient common law had, since the ' reception ', been entirely overshadowed by the principles contained in Justinian's compilations, Roman-canonical tenets, and the arbitrary juridical practices of the enlightened despots who followed in the wake of the Middle Ages.

[10] Savigny, *Vom Beruf unserer Zeit*, pp. 114–15.

[11] An example of a schism within the historical school can be found in the disagreement between Savigny and Thibault on the subject of a general code. Savigny maintained that jurisprudence in Germany had not reached a sufficiently ' scientific ' level to make the compilation of a general code feasible. Indeed he even doubted that the German language itself was sufficiently advanced to allow for such a project (Savigny, *ibid.* p. 52). This provoked Thibault's criticism who insisted upon the establishment and the publication of a general civil code for Germany. On this point Hegel thoroughly disagreed with Savigny (*Philosophy of Right*, § 211).

[12] ' Proceedings of the Estates Assembly in Wurtemberg ', in *Hegel's Political Writings*, trans. T. M. Knox (Oxford, 1964), p. 248.

[13] *Hegel's Lectures on the History of Philosophy*, trans. E. S. Haldane and F. H. Simson (London, 1955), vol. III, p. 391.

[14] Avineri, ' Hegel and Nationalism ', p. 479.   [15] Savigny, *Vom Beruf unserer Zeit*, p. 38.

science of positive law has not only the right, but even the inescapable duty to study given laws, to deduce from its positive data their progress in history, their applications and subdivisions, down to the last detail, and to exhibit their implications '.[16] Again, Savigny was far from advocating the total dismissal of Roman legal principles: ' When we have learned to handle the existing legal material with the freedom and mastery of the Romans, then we will be able to do without (historical) models.' [17] Nor did Hegel hesitate to take principles from the Roman system and use them as starting points for much of his corporatism.

It appears then that despite the fact that they held different views as to the source and the validity of legal principles, neither Hegel nor Savigny could escape, even had they wanted to do so, from Roman law as an unalterable presence in German positive law and politics. To have advocated any other route to legal reform would have been a negation of the long historical process by which Roman law mixed with Germanic law. Traces of this process, well before the major ' reception ', are to be found in the *Lex Romana Visigothorum* and the *Lex Romana Burgundiorum* in the sixth century. The Carolingian rule and the establishment of the Holy Roman Empire further contributed to the inter-mingling of the very advanced Roman and the ancient and ill-defined customary law of the Germanic peoples. Attempts were made to resist the preponderance of the Latin legal sources.[18] But the influence of Roman law increased rather than waned for a number of reasons. Firstly, Roman law served as an example of a legal structure for an increasingly civilized community. Secondly, Roman law itself was not monolithic in so far as many of its principles were adaptable to a changed environment, that is adaptable to local or customary legal practices. Thirdly, and most importantly, Roman law itself underwent considerable change when the church and its canon law became its prime custodian. The idea and practice of corporatism, it may be noted, proved itself quite as adaptable as the legal body whence it originated.

The basic characteristics of corporatism emerged in republican Rome even though it led a somewhat precarious existence from its very inception. In essence, the corporations consisted of groups of like-minded individuals who had banded together for the furtherance, protection and administration of certain common, limited interests. Paramount to their existence was the fact that the corporations derived their legitimacy from the state and from no other possible source. Ever jealous of its pre-eminence, the Roman state viewed all subsidiary groups within

---

[16] *Philosophy of Right*, § 212.

[17] F. C. Savigny, *System des heutigen römischen Rechts* (Berlin, 1840), vol. 1, p. xxxi.

[18] Notably in the *Sachsenspiegel* written in the third decade of the thirteenth century and the similar *Schwabenspiegel* produced some forty years later. Mitteis, *Deutsche Rechtsgeschichte*, pp. 150–1. A brief but informative discussion of the subject in English can be found in P. Vinogradoff, *Roman Law in Medieval Europe*, 2nd ed. (Oxford, 1929), chapter 5.

its jurisdiction with marked suspicion, a tendency exacerbated during the rule of Augustus who abolished, by *fiat*, most corporations.[19]

Yet the obvious need and utility of legitimate subsidiary groups within a large empire did not escape the attention of Justinian's lawyers. The *Digest* hesitatingly but nevertheless positively acknowledged circumstances in which permission for the formation of certain bodies, whether they be called *societas* (partnership), *collegium* or *corpus* could be granted. The purpose of these groups was essentially economic, for example, tax-gathering, salt-extraction, mining and shipping.[20]

If the corporate principle cannot be said to have dominated Roman legal and political practice, it must be noted that the successors of the Roman legal *corpus*, the church and the medieval community greatly expanded it. Indeed it was the Roman state itself which acknowledged the corporate nature of the church. The Edict of Milan of 313 which terminated the persecution of Christians spoke of the 'Christian body corporate' and the 'body corporate and congregation' which was to be left undisturbed in its practices, including the ownership of its places of worship.[21] Under the protection of the state the church thus emerged as a group-entity, a legal *persona*, capable of holding rights (*rechtsfähig*) independent from those of its individual members.

Legal confirmation, however, was not the sole source of Christian corporatism for the notion received ample support from the theological side also. The church was considered *corpus mysticum Christi*, the living organic whole, representing and incorporating Christ, the priesthood and the faithful.[22] St Paul, whose doctrine greatly contributed to the organic and corporate view of the church, spoke of Jesus as the head of the Christian *corpus* which recognized the life and importance of its subsidiary members.[23] Despite its hierarchical structure, moreover, the papacy found itself obliged to cede a measure of self-administration to such organs as monasteries, orders and foundations, motivated not merely by political and geographic expediency but also in accordance with corporate practice.

The temporal side of the medieval world presented a model of even greater social, political and administrative decentralization. In the absence of a permanent unitary authority, an articulated society prevailed in which such corporate groupings as guilds, companies, fellowships (*Genossenschaften*) and associations flourished. Of particular significance were the corporations devoted to higher

[19] Theodor Mommsen, *Römisches Staatsrecht* (Graz, 1969), vol. II.2, p. 886; vol. III.2, p. 1235. Typical of the uneasiness displayed by the Roman state *vis-à-vis* the corporations was Emperor Trajan's refusal to permit Pliny, governor of Bithynia, to authorize the formation of a fire-brigade for fear that it might become a centre of political agitation. (Ernest Barker, *From Alexander to Constantine* (Oxford, 1956), p. 252.)

[20] *Digest*, 3.4.1.

[21] Barker, *From Alexander to Constantine*, p. 470.

[22] Gierke, *Genossenschaftsrecht*, vol. III, p. 108.

[23] Eph. 1.22–3; 4.11; Rom. 12.4–6.

learning for it was at such universities as Bologna and Padua that Roman law was studied and eventually transformed to meet the requirements of the secular realm. Their civilists and publicists came to represent the Italo–Roman school of law which, while concerning itself with the legal applications of corporatism, engaged the sacral realm and its canon law in a struggle for speculative autonomy. And it was this juristic *corpus* rather than ' pure ' Roman law which was ' received ' in Germany in the sixteenth century.

The subsequent centuries, however, witnessed the disintegration of the medieval world and with it the model of the articulated organic society. The modern state tending towards unitarianism and centralism showed little tolerance for subordinate bodies and corporatism played a politically diminishing role until Hegel and some of his contemporaries started to revise and rejuvenate it.

II

Does Hegel's espousal of the corporate doctrine signify his acceptance of Roman and medieval legal and political thought? Moreover, is he himself not guilty of the taint of romanticism when he arrays his corporate society against some of the models of society prevalent in his day? An examination of his attitude towards Rome and its political and legal structure, and a glance at his judgment of the France of his time, will show that these suggestions are not justified. On the other hand many of the basic assumptions of his own corporate doctrine emerge from his criticism of these two systems, leading to a form of corporatism which is nearly as far removed from the medieval version as was the Byzantine school of law from that of Bologna. We propose to examine Hegel's attitude towards Revolutionary and post-Revolutionary France first.[*]

In Hegel's view the French Revolution, or rather its advocates, failed primarily on one account; they juxtaposed the ' law of the heart ' to reality.[24] That is, disregarding given political, economic and social conditions, they pursued abstract ideals. The process was bound to shatter on the ' rocks of hard reality '.[25] Individualism and particularism carried the day, leading to a state wherein men lost control over their affairs and it passed into the hands of ' fanatical priests (and) riotous, revelling despots and their minions, who seek to indemnify themselves for their own degradation by degrading and oppressing in their turn – a distortion practiced to the nameless misery of deluded mankind '.[26]

---

[*] *Editor's note* – See the essay of J.-F. Suter for a detailed analysis of Hegel's views on the French Revolution.

[24] G. W. F. Hegel, *The Phenomenology of Mind*, trans. J. B. Baillie, 2nd ed. (London, 1955), p. 391. German edition used: *Phänomenologie des Geistes*, ed. J. Hoffmeister (Hamburg, 1952).

[25] G. W. F. Hegel, *Lectures on the Philosophy of History*, trans. J. Sibree (New York, 1956), p. 453. German edition used: *Vorlesungen über die Philosophie der Geschichte*, ed. H. Glockner (Stuttgart, 1961).

[26] *Phenomenology*, p. 397.

'Fanaticism wills an abstraction ',[27] describes Hegel's view of the whole process. Legally and politically, the process reflected the Rousseauist attempt to establish a direct citizen-to-state relationship, a relationship unhindered by intermediary organs. This appeared particularly objectionable to Hegel. To centralize all decision-making power in the hands of a few ministries, to do away with corporations and local government, a process which he observed in the France of his day,[28] could only lead to alienation, atomization and hostility between citizen and government. Unequivocally he states, ' The proper strength of the state lies in its associations '.[29] An organic articulation of political society which recognizes and indeed encourages the existence of its subsidiary members, is the most certain prevention against the atom getting lost among the multitude of other atoms. True, the Revolution eliminated a system which had been oppressive and unjust.[30] But in its fanatical preoccupation with abstract ideals it had proved itself a ' revolution without reformation '.[31] Interestingly, some of Hegel's criticism of Rome and its law are on similar grounds. But while the experience derived from France could be largely rejected as external to German experience, that of Rome could not for, as pointed out earlier, its law and the derivations of that law had become part and parcel of German legal institutions and thus of its politics. Therefore it has to be given more detailed consideration.

If Hegel's judgment of the institutional excesses of the French Revolution can be summed up by the word ' fanaticism ', then his judgment of Rome and its law can be in the term ' unethical ' (*unsittlich*). Roman civilization is the epitome of a community which failed to establish itself on the basis of ' ethical life ' (*Sittlichkeit*) without which no modern and rational state can or ought to exist, so far as Hegel is concerned. The length to which he goes to validate his judgment is considerable.

Hegel takes exception to the genesis of the Roman community which, as he sees it, was formed by a band of robbers.[32] Having been conceived in violence, Rome developed a ' harshness of manners ' which, in turn, was reflected in the composition of its society and its laws.[33] Persistent class division between patrician and plebeian emphasized the fundamental failure of Rome to form an

---

[27] *Philosophy of Right*, § 5 and Addition.

[28] *Ibid.* § 290 and Addition. For an early expression of Hegel's hostility to over-centralization and a eulogy of the corporate nature of medieval society, see *Political Writings*, pp. 159–61, 163–4.

[29] *Philosophy of Right*, § 290 and Addition.

[30] *Philosophy of History*, p. 446.

[31] *Ibid.* p. 453.

[32] *Philosophy of History*, p. 278. In contrast to Rome, Hegel displays great admiration for classical Greece. Yet he disregards the fact that many city-states adjacent to the sea practiced piracy in the early stages of their history. (Thucydides, *Peloponnesian War*, I.3.5.) It is equally doubtful that the various peoples (the Germanic tribes included) who invaded Europe during the great migrations showed any greater respect for private or public property than did the early Romans.

[33] *Philosophy of History*, p. 286.

ethical political union between members of the community and the state. As Hegel puts it, ' A state which had first to form itself, and which is based on force, must be held together by force. It is not an ethical, liberal connection, but a compulsory condition of subordination that results from that origin '.[34] The aristocracy, manipulating the combined religious, political and military powers, maintained its superiority over the plebeians.[35]

Force as a means to attain unity was and remained the tenor of Roman politics. While the later Republic granted a more meaningful role to plebeian representatives and admitted some to the religious offices, the measure was merely designed to allow the Roman state to direct its energies towards external conquests.[36] Its success inspired patriotism, but on the other hand it lead to a further schism in the Roman character, the struggle between private interests and that very patriotism;[37] and thus a meaningful body of customary ethics (*Sittlichkeit*) had no opportunity to develop. The ' unspiritual unity ', the ' cold abstraction '[38] as Hegel characterizes the nature of the Roman state, remained. Religion, due to its patrician origin, never became a strong bond between members of the community.

An additional failure of Rome, as Hegel sees it, emanated from its refusal to give scope to corporate existence. There was only one ' universality ', the state. Besides the state, or rather within it, there were only two ' incorporated ' entities, the individual when and if he was recognized as an abstract legal *persona* and the indifferent and homogeneous mass of these persons ranged against the state itself.[39] It is precisely the concept of *persona* as a private and indeed as an exclusively private right-bearing entity which Hegel finds unacceptable.[40] This approach separates the individual from political action and judgement, a condition which is indeed reflected in the Roman division between *jus privatum* and *jus publicum*.

Harshness, force, the absence of ethical ties and the relegation of the individual into the realm of legal abstraction, all these features contributed to the major shortcoming of Rome, its failure to establish an articulated society which would have prevented that trend towards ' subjective inwardness ',[41] that alienation,

---

[34] *Ibid*. p. 288.

[35] The change from monarchical to republican form of government did not heal the schism between the classes either. In fact, it was just another politically meaningless gesture extended to the majority by the ruling minority. As Hegel sees it, the expulsion of the Tarquinians was of direct benefit to the aristocracy only. It assumed the royal powers and deprived the plebeians of the protection of the monarch. *Ibid*. pp. 299–300.

[36] *Ibid*. p. 303. [37] *Ibid*. p. 307.

[38] *Ibid*. p. 308.

[39] *Ibid*. p. 107; *Philosophy of Right*, § 357. It is very doubtful that the sum total of persons can be viewed as a truly corporate entity. As Hegel's argument develops, it becomes clear that his idea of corporatism is the opposite of such an unarticulated view of the citizenry.

[40] The German text transmits Hegel's opinion more trenchantly: ' *Individuen . . . werden rechtliche Personen als Privaten* ' (p. 154). [41] *Philosophy of History*, p. 281, p. 312.

which Hegel detects in it. France had rejected organizations which could have acted as intermediaries between the individual and the state. Rome, in Hegel's analysis, failed on the same account. But the latter contains a further complication for Hegel, because the very conditions of which he was so critical led to the establishment and growth of Roman law. He argues, ' To the constrained, non-spiritual and unfeeling intelligence of the Roman world we owe the origin and development of positive law '.⁴² The origins of this positive law were reflected in its provisions.⁴³

Yet not all facets of Roman civil law appear equally bad to Hegel. He approves of the practice of codification instituted by Justinian. He notes that all advanced, civilized nations ought to have a thorough and clearly comprehensible code of law.⁴⁴ Indeed he is prepared to admit that in Byzantium civil law had ' reached the highest perfection through the labours of the great Roman juris-consults; so that the *corpus juris* . . . still excites the admiration of the world '.⁴⁵ Hegel is also prepared to perceive an element of flexibility in the practice of Roman juris-prudence when he argues that it ' is the illogicality of the Roman jurists and praetors that must be regarded as one of their chief virtues, for by dint of being illogical they evaded unjust and detestable laws, though in the process they found themselves compelled . . . to devise empty verbal distinctions . . . in order to pre-serve the letter of the Twelve Tables . . .' ⁴⁶

Hegel's critique of Rome and its law cannot be considered an idle and mean-ingless exercise directed against a legal system whose origins had been alien to Germany. It is not a chauvinistic attack upon a ' foreign ' law. Had Hegel seen it that way, he would have joined forces with the more nationalistic faction of the historical school of law. Rather, the critique is essentially designed to achieve

⁴² *Ibid.* p. 289.

⁴³ Lacking in proper ethical content and bearing the stamp of oppression arising out of the dualism which rent the Roman state, its law carried these characteristics even into the realm of family relationships.

No other feature of Roman law enrages Hegel more than the concept of *patria potestas* which, at least in early Roman law, turned the head of the family into a potential tyrant. Having the right to dispose of his children as he saw fit, even to the point of killing them or selling them into slavery (*Philosophy of Right*, § 180, and also Addition to the same paragraph), the *pater familias* could consider his descendants as ' things ', belonging to the realm of *jus ad rem* and not to the realm of *jus ad personam* (*ibid.* § 43). Hegel disagrees with the division between *jus ad rem* and *jus ad personam*, maintaining that the latter is based on the Roman concept of *status*, and as such is too narrow a conception of the individual. Even if this relationship is modified by love, which Hegel considers as the proper bond between members of the family (*ibid.* § 158), the fact remained that the absolute power of the head of the family over children and wife, who was considered to be under his ' hand ' (*manus*), illustrates, to Hegel, the fundamental irrationality of Roman family law (*ibid.* § 3).

⁴⁴ *Ibid.* § 211. A notable exception, to Hegel, is the English legal system based on case law, which he characterizes as being in a state of ' monstrous confusion '.

⁴⁵ *Philosophy of History*, pp. 337-8.

⁴⁶ *Philosophy of Right*, § 3.

one effect, the modernization of a legal *corpus* which had become indigenous to such a degree that it could no longer be removed from the body politic. It is not surprising therefore that Hegel's discussion of corporatism and those aspects of positive law which pertain to it takes Roman legal principles as its starting point.[47] Moreover, it is indicative of the prevalence of that jurisprudence that, to a certain degree, Hegel's usage of Roman terminology parallels that of Savigny.[48] The point of divergence is arrived at when Hegel, as he develops his corporate idea, rejects the ancient Roman distinction between public and private law in order to attain his end.

III

On the first glance, corporatism in Hegel's *Philosophy of Right* appears as a concept of somewhat limited scope. It belongs to the realm of civil society, where particularism could reign supreme, where ' accidental caprices ' and ' subjective desires ' come to the fore. In historical terms, Hegel's civil society was a segment of an early nineteenth-century community which was in the process of entering the industrial age with all its tensions and dislocations. According to the law of the various German lands most men, since the peasant emancipation in the first decade of the century, were ' free '. This freedom was primarily understood in the terms of Roman jurisprudence, that is, men were considered legally autonomous ' persons '. Hegel, with the examples of Roman and French society before his eyes, finds this mere legal condition quite inadequate.

On the demographic side, the structure of civil society was being subjected to considerable changes. Industrialization had led to a partial dislocation of the peasantry which moved into the cities to find employment. Torn from their customary environment, separated from village, parish and not infrequently from their family, this element of the population was in danger of becoming a ' rabble of paupers ', the prototype of Marx's proletariat.

The pietistic, apolitical and heretofore fairly uninfluential middle class, whose development in Germany had lagged behind that of France and England, was slowly and somewhat hesitatingly making its bid for political participation.

---

[47] There is little doubt that when Hegel refers to Roman law he thinks of that *corpus* which had undergone a metamorphosis since Justinian. Thus, for instance, Hegel accepts the concept of *persona ficta*, a medieval contribution to Roman legal thought and to corporate theory (Gierke, *Genossenschaftsrecht*, vol. III, p. 279). While the extensive work done by Gierke on the coalescence of the Roman law and its derivatives came after Hegel's time, he could be faulted for disregarding the pioneer work in that very field, F. C. von Savigny's *Das Römische Recht im Mittelalter* which appeared in 1815. Thus F. Rosenzweig's argument in *Hegel und der Staat* (Munich, 1920), vol. II, p. 104, that the historical school of law appeared too late to influence Hegel's concept of law is not quite correct.

[48] Savigny's *System des heutigen römischen Rechts*, was published in 1840, that is, nine years after Hegel's death. The affinity between Hegel and Savigny on certain points of Roman law is, however, of no surprise. After all, both were speaking of a ' living ' and functioning *corpus*, a fact which their philosophic disagreement could not alter.

Belonging to that strata of civil society, yet standing apart from it due to its occupation, one found the vast and complicated array of civil servants. Just as had been the case in the late Roman Empire, it was this group within society which, for all intents and purposes, carried on the affairs of state. The age of absolute monarchy was on the wane and slowly the *Obrigkeitsstaat* was being replaced by the *Beamtenstaat*. In keeping with the tradition of its environment, the impetus towards administrative if not vast political reforms came from this very group, particularly in the case of Prussia. Finally, the aristocracy and, where applicable, the monarch, completed the structure of the community within which civil society was emerging. Yet the term ' community ' may be totally incorrect to apply to this example.

The centrifugal forces which had prevented the formation of a single, coherent legal and political entity in Germany were also active within the sectional communities themselves. Neither feudal dispersion nor absolutist centralism could alleviate or were even equipped to deal with that sense of estrangement which had been a hallmark of the romantics. And while the political contributions of that movement had been minimal or unrealistic, their concept of alienation did point to severe political, social and economic shortcomings. Civil society, in which corporatism plays an important role is, as Hegel envisages it, responsible for offering some remedies to this condition of alienation.

However, civil society might appear as a most unsuitable ground for such remedies. It is the realm of ' want as well as physical and ethical (*sittlich*) degeneration ',[49] where particularism and materialism culminate in a ' system of atomism '.[50] Here the bond of love which held the family together does not exist and the individual, by sheer necessity, is forced to enter the *maelstrom* of competition, of rootlessness and passionate arbitrariness. The questions arise how, then, is this civil society to remedy the faults when they are given scope in that very sphere? Moreover, if Hegel is the ' idealist ' he is purported to be, why does he not eliminate the troublesome strata?

The explanation is found in Hegel's use of the individual will within the dialectic of history. Not only is the existence of civil society a *fait accompli*, but it can be rationally fitted into Hegel's system by emphasizing the necessary, antithetical role the particularism of civil society plays to the unity represented by the whole. Let the complex of human passions run their course. Let selfish desires and private aims have their say, for they are the effective springs of action. Without these actions, history grinds to a halt.[51] If modern man's ' asocial sociability ',[52] to borrow a phrase from Kant, is such that it leads to the atomiza-

---

[49] *Philosophy of Right*, § 185.

[50] G. W. F. Hegel, *Enzyklopädie der philosophischen Wissenschaften im Grundrisse* (Hamburg, 1959), § 523.   [51] *Philosophy of History*, p. 20.

[52] Immanuel Kant, ' Idee zu einer allgemeinen Geschichte in weltbürgerlicher Absicht ', in *Kleinere Schriften zur Gechichte, Ethik und Politik* (Hamburg, 1959), p. 9.

tion of society, then instead of counselling a utopian annihilation of the individualistic instincts of man, it appears more prudent to channel these urges within a
properly ordered articulated community. Ever wary of advocating abstract ideals,
for the advocacy of the elimination of growing civil society with all its ills would
have been just such an abstraction, Hegel uses civil society as a means of attaining
a higher degree of mediation.

Hegel is confronted with a series of problems here. On the one hand he has
accepted the centrifugal forces constituted by the members of civil society. He
has accepted them as unavoidable and therefore uses them as a dialectical
counterpart to the unity of the whole. At the same time, however, he must place
the individual within civil society under some restraint in order to avoid chaos.
Positive law is required to avoid the worst excesses but at the same time this law
may not be imposed exclusively from without or from above. To rule without
the citizens' approval in the Roman manner, or to legislate without means of
effective communication through intermediary elements within the state, is also
unacceptable. The articulation of civil society is Hegel's first step towards
meeting the problems.

Civil society itself is divided into three ' moments ': the ' system of needs ' or
the economic realm; the ' administration of justice ', and the ' Police (that is,
Public Authority) and Corporation '.[53] This scheme is further divided into the
' substantial ' (that is, agricultural), the ' reflecting ' or ' *formal* ' (business) and
the ' universal ' (that is, civil service) estates (*Stände*).[54] The corporations are
especially relevant to the second estate for it is here that the tensions are most
apparent. Yet, initially, the function of the corporations appears to be rather
limited. As Hegel sees it, their purpose is ' wholly concrete and no wider in
scope than the purpose involved in business, its proper task and interest '.[55] This
statement warrants a closer explanation.

Firstly, Hegel's word for ' business ' is ' *Gewerbe* ', a term meaning not only
business (*Geschäft*) in the current sense of the words, but also ' vocation ' and
' profession '. In effect, the corporations are relevant to all members of civil
society who do not derive their livelihood from the soil and who do not belong
to the civil service. In view of the increasing industrialization and urbanization
which was taking place, the ' business ' group (including workers as well as
managers,[56] tradesmen as well as traders, apprentices as well as professionals) is
thus very large, and represents a substantial segment of the population.

Secondly, the term ' concrete ' requires definition. In Hegel's terminology, as
indeed in modern, common usage, the word stands for the dialectic opposite of
' abstract '. ' The reasonable (*das Vernünftige*) . . . ', Hegel states, ' is still a
concrete, because it is not simple, formal unity but rather a unity of distinct

---

[53] *Philosophy of Right*, § 188.
[54] *Ibid*. § 202.
[55] *Ibid*. § 251.   [56] *Ibid*. § 204.

propositions.' [57] The sentence describes his notion of the *character* of corporatism. Fundamentally, it forms a rational unity for a certain specific purpose. Being limited, it does not encompass all the aspirations and facets of its constituent members. They remain ' distinct propositions ' as individuals, citizens, as members of their families, as religious subjects, etc. But a ' simple, formal unity ', for the attainment of certain goals, such as those usually pursued by professional groups, unions, guilds, associations and religious foundations, is in keeping with the corporate idea. The concrete unity does not eliminate the individual's existence; his ' distinctness ', rather than hindering the evolution of unity, actually facilitates it.

To Hegel the family had been the epitome of ethical unity. The dissolution of its unity was unavoidable, partially due to natural causes (that is, coming of age of the younger generation) but also due to the entry of the individual into civil society as nothing more than a legal ' person '.[58] While the natural causes leading to the dissolution cannot be altered, the legal approach can. The concept of recognizing man merely as a legal entity is unacceptable to Hegel. The individual cannot remain an ' unfulfilled empty abstraction ',[59] nor can unity be attained by a sheer plurality of such legal persons.[60] The abolition of serfdom was too recent an experience to allow Hegel to disregard the division of the Roman concept of *persona* into freemen and slaves.[61] On the other hand, the modern conception of the person as a totally independent will, externalizing itself through property only,[62] is one of the major causes of the particularism within civil society. Hence the concept of *persona* has to be substantially modified and indeed transcended.

The demands made upon the individual by the new environment had weakened his ties with the family. In consequence, the whole ethical (*sittlich*) framework of the community has suffered and there is a need for another source of cohesive strength. Therefore Hegel argues, ' As the family was the first, so the Corporation is the second ethical root of the state, the one planted in civil society '.[63] Indeed, it is now the corporation which provides the family with a stable basis [64] not only in an economic but also in an ethical sense.

IV

The corporations are effective in two interrelated but nevertheless distinguishable relationships: one refers to the individual, the other concerns the state.

[57] *Enzyklopädie*, § 82.
[58] *Philosophy of Right*, §§ 181, 238.
[59] *Phenomenology*, p. 752.
[60] *Ibid.* p. 501.
[61] Gaius, *Institutiones*, I.9; Justinian, *Institutes*, I.3.
[62] *Philosophy of Right*, § 46.
[63] *Philosophy of Right*, § 255.
[64] *Ibid.* § 253.

The initial purpose of the corporation is to bring the isolated individual into the economic, political and ethical order. The groups which receive the individual are most frequently referred to by Hegel as corporations and 'fellowships' (*Genossenschaften*).[65] These are not free associations, private clubs or 'combinations' but legally recognized, state-sanctioned organizations derived from the usual trade and vocational [66] groupings within the community.

In using the word 'fellowship', Hegel resorts to the terminology of Germanic legal tradition which held that the formation and the joining of such fellowship-groups was the 'natural' customary right of all qualified men. Hegel fails to draw a clear distinction between the idea of free association inherent in 'fellowship right' (*Genossenschaftsrecht*) which is more closely related to the right of free association, and the Roman and Italo-Roman corporate idea.[67] He follows in the tradition of the latter school which makes the legitimacy of the corporation dependent upon the state and does not recognize any 'natural' right to associate. In the spirit of what Gierke is apt to refer to as 'pure Roman law',[68] and parallel to Savigny's understanding of what the nature of a corporation consists, Hegel also considers community (*Gemeinde*) and church [69] as corporate entities. Essentially, like all other corporations, these organs are regarded as collectives, capable of holding conjoint rights and legally liable for their actions. In brief, they are legal 'persons'.[70]

Hegel must however proceed cautiously when he accepts the idea that communities are corporate entities. Princely anarchy [71] which had divided, and in his own time was still dividing the land into political fragments, could easily be adopted by the growing communities. The free cities of the Middle Ages had

---

[65] *Ibid.* §§ 251–3, 270, 308.

[66] Hegel avoids using the term *Zunft* (guild) for any trade corporation because the term is too medieval in its connotations.

[67] Otto Gierke, *Die Genossenschaftstheorie und die deutsche Rechtsprechung* (Berlin, 1963), pp. 80–1.

[68] *Ibid.* p. 80. It is noteworthy, however, that Hegel inclines towards the idea of a 'natural' right to free association in his earliest political work, *The German Constitution*. He speaks of the development of self-governing entities 'as a hallowed tradition directly from custom itself', being 'set up by native impulse' and having 'grown up of themselves'. Cf. *Political Writings*, p. 160.

[69] *Philosophy of Right*, §§ 270, 278, 295, 302, 308, 309.

[70] Savigny, *System*, vol. II, para. 86. The author distinguishes between an 'artificial' and a 'natural' legal person. Among the former he lists the guilds and trade groups (*Zünfte, Innungen*), for example, while villages and communities (*Gemeinden*) appear as examples of 'naturally formed' corporations. The distinction between natural and artificial corporation is not made by Hegel. Savigny's general term for corporation is *universitas* (vol. II, § 88) and, besides the above-mentioned groups (that is, trade and vocational corporations and communities) he is also prepared to accept the *societas* (partnership) and a *collegium* as a corporation. Unlike Hegel, however, Savigny excludes religious foundations (*Stiftungen*), arguing that while they may be considered as legal persons they are not corporations (vol. II, para. 88).

[71] G. P. Gooch, *Germany and the French Revolution* (London, 1920), p. 3.

exerted a centrifugal force no less than had the warring nobility. Yet, as Hegel views it, the strength of the state lies in its subsidiary organs, therefore a measure of local autonomy is essential. The practice corollary to this autonomy, that is, participation of the citizen in the governance of his corporation, is an essential ingredient of Hegel's doctrine. Hence, the communities must retain their corporate, semi-autonomous identities.

Hegel's attitude towards the corporate nature of religious groups, and their church organizations, is less ambiguous. In terms somewhat reminiscent of the Edict of Milan, he argues, 'When individuals, holding religious views in common, form themselves into a church, a Corporation, they fall under the general control and oversight of the higher state officials.' [72] Religion, he maintains, is essentially the 'field of the heart' and thus a model of subjectivity. The state, on the other hand, is the objective framework within which religion and its organizations develop.[73] Ideally there is no tension between the two realms, but if there is any disagreement in secular matters the church corporation is subject to the positive law of the state, just like any other similar group.

It has been argued earlier [74] that Hegel wanted to modify the Roman legal concept of *persona*. As the foregoing discussion indicated, there is little evidence that he was successful in so far as the groups within civil society are concerned. If the public authority is to supervise such entities as church and community then it is logical that they be considered in their collectivity as legally capable and responsible 'persons'. Two factors contributed to Hegel's acceptance of the notion of legal 'group-personality'. One, the obvious factor, was the predominance of Roman and Italo-Roman law in the jurisprudence of Germany. To try and eliminate the tradition which, after all, was functioning as well as being perfectly amenable to revision, could have appeared as foolhardy to Hegel. Secondly, and more cogently, in the increasingly complex and important civil society, the recognition of the legal 'group-personality' [75] prepares the ground for the negation of the concept of the individual as a mere legal abstraction. That is, by accepting and indeed advocating the legal group, be it corporation, church or community, Hegel seeks to provide the individual with the basis for the full development of his individuality well beyond the confines of that of a mere legal *persona*.

The relationship between the individual and his corporation bears out the

---

[72] *Philosophy of Right*, § 270. The German text uses both '*Korporation*' and '*Gemeinde*' as descriptive of religious groups.

[73] *Ibid.* and Addition.

[74] P. 124.

[75] H. F. Jolowicz, *Roman Foundations of Modern Law* (Oxford, 1957), p. 127, states the case admirably: 'In fact the fraction of human affairs that can be satisfactorily handled by thinking only in terms of the acts and interests of single human beings is probably smaller now than it was ever before, and the chief device in use for dealing with the remainder is still – though it may not be so in the future – the legal person.'

argument. Initially, the individual who joins a corporation or is co-opted by one, gains a measure of economic security, for the group guards against 'particular contingencies'.[76] He is also offered two forms of education. One, schooling in his chosen trade, vocation or profession and more importantly, training in the conduct of the affairs of the corporation. The latter, to which we shall return, is the essential and necessary process by which the individual becomes a politically active citizen.

'Real liberty requires . . . freedom in regard to trades and professions – the permission of every one to use his abilities without restriction . . .',[77] Hegel argues. Man's 'natural' right to exercise his skill[78] is rationalized by his corporate membership, for now it is not the case of an individual atom within society struggling for recognition. Rather, corporate membership indicates that the individual is 'somebody' who has gained rank and dignity.[79] In pursuing this line, Hegel is forsaking the concept of *status* inherent in Roman private law which distinguished between freemen and legally encumbered individuals such as slaves and minors. However, the unrestricted, though not totally arbitrary, right of the individual to exercise his skill and thereby attain status is not a mere formalistic legal argument. Serfdom and the subjection of men to arbitrary governance by their rulers were recent phenomena in Hegel's time. Therefore to declare that skill and ability and not birth or 'connection' is the proper ground for attaining status cannot be considered a meaningless assertion.

The training received through corporative membership moreover, is not confined to trades and professions only. Hegel argues that appointments to the civil service are to be made according to knowledge and ability,[80] qualities exhibited by the individual in his specific group. Indeed, the individual's experience acquired in his corporate life assures him of a measure of social mobility derived from his 'natural' right to externalize himself in skill and labour. The mobility and the participation offered by the corporations is viewed by Hegel as a guard against the calcification of civil society into a caste system. At the same time he is aware that his articulated system of corporations, communities and religious organizations presents a picture not dissimilar from that of feudal society. He rejects the comparison on the grounds that the independence of the medieval constituent groups was so great that the community, if it could be called that at all, was an aggregate of particular functions lacking any organic cohesion. Equally lacking from the medieval model was that type of sovereignty which

---

[76] *Philosophy of Right*, § 252.   [77] *Philosophy of History*, p. 448.

[78] *Philosophy of Right*, § 254.

[79] *Ibid*. § 253.

[80] *Ibid*. §§ 291, 308. Hegel does not propose that civil servants, the representatives of the 'universality' of the state, form their own corporations. In doing so, he rejects yet another Roman legal tradition which knew the corporations of such public servants as the *librarii, fiscales, censuales* and *scribae* (Savigny, *System*, vol. II, para. 88).

brings about a constitutional and legally ordered interaction between the numerous elements of the whole, an arrangement which allows for diversification yet retains the aims of the whole in sight.[81]

Hegel's individual, in his capacity as a corporation member, has learned to assess his interests both economically and, gradually, politically. The corporation offers him a measure of economic protection; it can prevent the individual from becoming a pauper, a material as well as ethical degradation, and assure him of honour and recognition as a member of a useful cell of the organic structure. According to Hegel, once the individual has recognized the full extent of his own interests he becomes aware of the fact that the protection is best afforded in the actions taken by the public authority of the state which had legitimized his corporation. The hostility to and alienation from the state which the individual may have harboured is alleviated by his corporate existence. Ultimately the immediacy of the group, the contact with his ' fellows ' and the sharing in the management of his corporation provides the foundation of patriotism and political loyalty.

Hegel's analysis of it is remarkably direct. ' Patriotism is often understood to mean only a readiness for exceptional sacrifices and actions. Essentially however, it is the sentiment which, in the relationships of our daily life and under ordinary conditions, habitually recognizes that the community is one's substantive ground-work and end.' [82] It would appear from this statement that the individual is obliged to make the ends of the state his own, but the state itself is perceived as reflecting the diverse wishes and ambitions of its citizens organized into numerous subsidiary organs. The state may be the incorporation of the divine will on earth, it may be the primary entity which history takes note of,[83] but in the realm of positive law it is merely the head of the organic whole [84] which excites the sentiment of the individual primarily for one specific reason, the protection provided for his self-interest as put forward by his group. ' This is the secret of patriotism of the citizens in the sense that they know the state as their substance, because it is the state that maintains their particular spheres of interest together with the title, authority and welfare of these.' [85]

In one of his rare lyrical moods Hegel describes the feeling entertained by the individual towards his community as an awareness of a precious possession, a sentiment which is consciously possessive about the state, its laws, its arrangements, its history and the physical features of the land.[86] But, in the prosaic

---

[81] *Ibid.* §§ 278, 286; *Political Writings*, p. 263; *Philosophy of History*, p. 399.

[82] *Philosophy of Right*, § 268.

[83] *Philosophy of History*, p. 39.

[84] The organic nature of the state is referred to by Hegel in *Philosophy of Right*, §§ 267, 269, 271, 279, 302 (the original speaks of ' *organischer Staat* ').

[85] *Philosophy of Right*, § 289.

[86] *Philosophy of History*, p. 52.

realm of positive law, patriotism is seen by Hegel as being derived from the individual's appreciation of the protection he and his group receive from the public authority. Initially, this interpretation of patriotism may not be notably lofty. But Hegel is determined to bring the individual into the sphere of legislative participation. He is not interested in making sweeping assertions about the ' rights of all men '. Rather, the goal, in the realm of positive law, is to introduce a functioning mechanism which bridges the fatal gap between Roman private and public law. Sheer emotionalism is unable to surmount the break in any rational manner. Moreover, the situation of the singular confronted by the complexity and vastness of a modern state must be improved by postulating a harmonious but nevertheless structured and articulated whole. The universality of the state is attained by the individual not by virtue of his being a singular *per se*, but only by this very individual's involvement in corporate and group affairs and thereby becoming legally and politically identifiable.[87]

V

Hegel's development of the idea of the state would not come about if he were content with leaving the individual and his corporation or group in the realm of economics. The whole argument for the highest goal, unification,[88] has to be carried past the level of civil society to the level of the state and it is precisely the corporate spirit which provides the means of mediation between the two stages. ' The corporation mind . . . is now inwardly converted into the mind of the state since it finds in the state the means of maintaining its particular ends ',[89] Hegel argues. No other sentence summarizes Hegel's point more concisely.

The state provides the individual with an opportunity of ' living a universal life ',[90] that is, the opportunity to maintain himself as an ethical unit within a larger ethical whole. The basis of this ethical elevation is not a monolithic state *per se*, but a structure which is heedful of the requirements and identities of its constituent parts. The legal existence of the parts is derived from their recognition by the state. The state enters the field not as an absolute power but as the legal authority which maintains the orderly relationship between its constituent groups. It cannot act tyranically against them, for its power depends upon the recognition by these diverse elements that their interests are protected by it.

The argument for such a typical *Rechtsstaat* could be considered highly circular, and its model a purely static one, were it not for the political education which the individual receives in his corporate capacity. This education, the

---

[87] *Philosophy of Right*, § 308. Further and valuable light on the essential role of corporations in mediating between the individual and the state is thrown by Hegel's commentary on the Constitution of Wurtemberg. Cf. *Political Writings*, pp. 262–5.

[88] *Philosophy of Right*, § 258.

[89] *Ibid*. § 289.

[90] *Ibid*. § 258.

second and more important form of training offered by the group, carries the individual from the realm of private into the realm of public law. Participation in the management of the corporation, in the administration of its affairs, in the decisions of its membership, and in the election of its representatives, all contribute to the preparation for politics. Yet as he considers these activities, Hegel shows a certain hesitancy and even disparagement. He states, ' The administration of a Corporation's business by its officials is frequently clumsy, because although they keep before their minds and are acquainted with its special interests and affairs, they have a far less complete appreciation of the connexion of those affairs with more remote conditions and the outlook of the state.' [91] In the same passage Hegel speaks of the ' foolish management of trivial affairs ', which inflates the ' self-satisfaction and vanity ' derived from it.

The tenor of these remarks casts doubt upon the value of the political education which Hegel ascribes to corporate activity, and there are two provisions which may limit the corporation's political effectiveness. First, in the traditional Roman manner, it must have the state's approval from its inception. Secondly, while corporation officers are elected by the membership, the results of the elections are subject to scrutiny by the public authority.[92] Despite the disparaging tone used by Hegel when referring to the trivialities which may be of concern to the corporations, he cannot logically deny their importance. Having denounced the examples of Rome and France as systems of atomism due to the lack of organizations which could act as intermediaries between the citizen and the state, Hegel is obliged to opt for an articulated model.

' The state . . . is essentially an organization each of whose members is in itself a group . . . and hence no one of its moments should appear as an unorganized aggregate ', he argues. Moreover, ' The circles of association in civil society are already communities. To picture them as once more breaking up into a mere conglomeration of individuals as soon as they enter the field of politics . . . is *eo ipso* to hold civil and political life apart from one another and as it were to hang the latter [that is, the political] in the air . . .' [93] The chasm between the Roman *jus privatum* and its *jus publicum* is bridged in these words. The state, as Hegel sees it, cannot deal effectively with an unorganized multitude.[94] Nor can a member of this multitude hope to be recognized on the basis of his singularity alone. Some systems had used subsidiary organs, if they had any at all, as means of controlling the multitude, thus excluding the many from effective political participation.[95] But, Hegel stresses, ' . . . it is of the utmost importance

[91] *Ibid.* § 289.   [92] *Ibid.* § 288.

[93] *Ibid.* § 303.

[94] *Ibid.* § 302.

[95] *Ibid.* § 290 Addition. This statement alone makes any equation of Hegel's corporatism with that of fascist Italy incongruous for it was the latter which used its so-called corporate structure as a means of total centralized control.

that the masses should be organized, because only so do they become mighty and powerful '.[96]

Organization means articulation and articulation stands for the political recognition of the groups, corporations and communities as well as of the estates (*Stände*); in short, of all those constituent elements of the state which contribute to its legislative activities. Ultimately, the ' private ' person becomes a ' public ', i.e. political, entity when he contributes to the decisions of the legislative assembly, or the ' law-giving power ' (*gesetzgebende Gewalt*) as Hegel refers to it.[97]

' Under modern political conditions, the citizens have only a restricted share in the public business of the state, yet it is essential to provide men – ethical entities – with work of public character over and above their private business.' [98] In these words Hegel summarizes the developing relationship between the corporations and the state. As we have argued, the corporations and other groups prepared the way for political activity by the training they offered in self-administration and decision making. ' Trivial ' though that activity may be when compared to the more complex problems faced by the executive and the legislature of the state, it is also the means by which the private person enters the realm of public (that is, political) activity.

The composition of the lower house of the bi-cameral legislature [99] is indicative of Hegel's scheme. The deputies of that chamber are the representatives elected to that office by the corporations, communities and fellowships.[100] Thus they carry with them into the legislature the interests and ambitions of their specific groups. At the same time, however, they are subjected to a further form of education, in so far as they learn to consider not only the goals of their groups but the interest of the whole public sphere. This is why Hegel argued that the corporation mind becomes the mind of the state.[101] It can be called patriotism within the context of his thought, or it can be viewed simply as the realization on the part of the delegate to the legislative assembly that his interests, and those of his group, are but one side of a complex problem manifesting itself in the debates of the lower chamber.

The duality inherent in this condition is obvious. Assuming that he has the means to do so, a deputy may attempt to force the views of his group upon the assembly. But his attempt is checked and limited by that of other groups and by philosophic as well as legal and political necessity, so he learns to subject his demands to that mediation which is the essential task of Hegel's legislative scheme.[102] The ' inner necessity ' is inherent in Hegel's philosophical view; that

96 *Ibid.*
97 *Ibid.* § 298.
98 *Ibid.* Addition to § 255.
99 *Ibid.* § 312.
100 *Ibid.* §§ 308, 311.
101 *Ibid.* § 302.
102 *Ibid.* § 302.

is, the individual, through his corporate capacity, is connected to the legislature, the moment of universality in the concept of the state. Legally and politically, the individual and his social background, civil society, are politicized by the mediation between the realms of private and public law. That the result of this mediation is not a matter of obliterating the groups, even on the legislative level, becomes obvious from observing a number of factors. As pointed out, the groups elect the representatives to the lower house. Thus the electorate does not appear as a multitude dispersed into ' atomic units ' [103] but as organized and clearly identifiable groups with clearly-stated interests. The groups, within the legislature, act as a check upon one another while, simultaneously, learning to consider their goals in the wider context of the public interest. In the extra-legislative sphere the groups act as a restraint upon the civil service. Despite the value Hegel attaches to the ' universal ' estate, he is not insensitive to the dangers of bureaucracy. Therefore he argues that it is essential that the monarch on the one hand, and the corporations on the other, should act as a guard to prevent the civil service from becoming a new aristocracy and a potential tyranny. [104] Finally, presence during and participation in the debates of the legislative assembly is an education in itself, for the representatives as well as for the attending public. [105]

Ultimately, then, all political activities, while originating with the individual's need for self-assertion and protection, are channelled through a system of group politics within the *corpus* of positive law. Considering the length to which Hegel goes to argue the case for such an articulated and balanced system, it may not be too far-fetched to say that one of the principles guiding him in this matter is the recognition of man not only *qua* man but man *qua* citizen.

VI

Aufheben means to preserve, to elevate as well as to abolish. As he perceived his doctrine of corporatism, Hegel used the meanings of the word to their fullest extent.

In drawing deeply and sometimes quite unconsciously from the late Roman, canonical and Italo–Roman legal tradition which left such a lasting mark upon German jurisprudence, Hegel preserved some of the features of the corporate idea as it emerged from that realm. The legitimization of the group by the state is one such lasting tradition. Equally traditional is the whole idea of legally sanctioned corporations, fellowships and communities organizing and ministering to their needs under the *aegis* of civil law. Taking the legal concept of *persona* as a starting point is also typical of Roman and allied law, as is the

[103] *Ibid.* § 308.
[104] *Ibid.* §§ 295, 297.
[105] *Ibid.* § 314, and Addition to § 315.

assumption that not only individuals but also legally recognized groups can be considered 'right-bearing' (*rechtsfähig*) entities. Representation in a politically effective manner, however, was not characteristic of the older systems. Neither emperor nor pope viewed the growth of a sense of independence or even traces of self-autonomy with great enthusiasm even though the church, as we pointed out, subscribed to the organic articulated view from its inception. Nor were these rulers alone in their suspicion of corporate entities. The absolutist state which emerged in the modern, the post-Machiavellian era, was determinedly centralist in its practices. Only the subsequent historical age attempted to introduce a viable alternative, the political representation of all citizens in a national assembly which would function in the name and interest of all.

The technical, if not necessarily the theoretical, shortcomings of that scheme became evident soon enough. The Revolution ended in a fanaticism which alarmed Hegel, as well as in the formation of the centralist Napoleonic Empire. Precisely because the Revolutionary theory neglected the question of the machinery of proper political representation, it cannot be claimed that it was in this respect a great deal more successful than its predecessors. Another system of representation, perhaps the most firmly established and eventually most successful, had grown up in Great Britain and in those countries which followed its example. But the irrational British electoral structure, the party system dominated by the landed interest, and the questionable electioneering practices which Hegel was able to observe, all contributed to his rejection of parliament-arianism as it was then known in England. An equally fundamental reason for Hegel's rejection of the British system was the unalterable historical fact that political parties were simply non-existent in the fragmented German lands. Thus, in Hegel's view, corporatism had to serve as the initial vehicle towards political participation and representation. But when he turned to that concept, he could not merely 'preserve' it; even an advocate of ancient practices for their own sake could not have done that. Rather he had to rejuvenate corporatism to make the concept more appropriate to the nineteenth-century milieu. In doing so, Hegel utilized the second meaning of the word *Aufhebung*, for he 'elevated' something out of the past, reformulated it, and made it relevant to the present, thus giving it a rationality which it had lacked.

Starting from the corporatism of the older legal system, Hegel turned the concept into a doctrine of group interest and group representation which might be called legal–political pluralism. This legal–political pluralism served as a model of an articulated and structured political community which was the opposite of the Rousseauist scheme. Hegel thus upheld, not the singular *vis-à-vis* the huge and complex state, but the individual as a member of a group recognized by the positive law of the community.

In keeping with Hegel's use of the word, however, *Aufhebung* also stands for 'abolition'. His reformulation of corporatism altered its nature, broadened its function and changed its content. Abolition thus relegated the old concept to the historical annals, while simultaneously producing a new and more viable legal–political pluralism. The most substantial change that Hegel made in the corporate idea was his conscious recognition and utilization of the political implications inherent in it. Rather than seeing the groups as a means to retaining a pre-Revolutionary *status quo*, Hegel used corporatism to view the conditions of the individual and his society in a different light. He eliminated the distinction between the strictly private and strictly public sector of the law by making the individual, as a member of an interest group, a political actor. That Hegel's argument should in this instance have started from the legal background was perfectly logical. It would have been most un-Hegelian to disregard the fundamental link between politics and positive law, a connection which was predominant in the continental European experience. But to see a legal institution as a method of politicizing the individual, as Hegel did, was an innovation. Equally novel to Hegel's time and background was the mobility ascribed to the individual, who could move between groups according to his interest, and within them according to his ability.

If one were to take the fallacious step of equating Hegel's corporatism or legal–political pluralism with the pseudo-corporatism of twentieth-century fascist Italy, one could argue that *étatisme* was paramount to Hegel's thought. But to do so would be to disregard the mobility, the political participation and representation offered by Hegel's scheme. It would also be to disregard the fact that while modern fascism was essentially monolithic, claiming pre-eminence in all aspects of human existence, Hegel's legal–political pluralism did not do so. As we have argued, education was one of the tasks of his corporations, fellowships and communities. There is no indication that this education involved the indoctrination of all citizens with the tenets of any civil religion. Rather than being inclusive, Hegel's corporatism was essentially exclusive. That is, in the final analysis, the groups served a certain, specific purpose. That purpose was the recognition of the individual, his protection, his political participation and his representation. However, the activities associated with man's corporate existence did not, in Hegel's view, obliterate all the ambitions, aspirations, and essential particularism of the individual. His corporate capacity was relevant only to his occupational, vocation and professional existence. It had nothing to do with the individual's private life, the development of his talents (artistic or otherwise), or his religious and philosophic leanings. These aspects of human existence were not absorbed by the state, nor its laws, nor its constituent groups. The claim that Hegel eliminated the traditional gap between the Roman *jus privatum* and *jus publicum* must not give rise to the impression that man's purpose was exhausted and totally fulfilled by his political nature and capacity. Hegel's philosophy, which envisaged the progress of the mind from its objective to its absolute stage, made it amply clear that the political was but one moment in the course of a vast development.

On a more mundane level and in keeping with the specific purpose of legal–political pluralism, it can be observed that the model of Hegel's articulated state is one in which the ascending and descending theories of government co-exist.[106] The ascendant aspect of Hegel's theory is represented by the institution of legal–political pluralism which is essentially a bid, on the part of the many, for their share of political power. The descending theme enters when the role of the state as the source of the groups' legitimacy and its role as arbitrator is considered. It is not hard to discern here a process of mediation, one inherent in the dynamic interchange between the ascending and descending power structures. But this mediation merely reinforces what could be considered as Hegel's *Leitmotif*, the view that the whole is derived from the one – and it is to that one that it eventually returns.

---

106 This theory of government is described by W. Ullmann, *Principles of Government and Politics in the Middle Ages* (London, 1961), pp. 20 ff.

Nature and freedom in
Hegel's 'Philosophy of Right'

MANFRED RIEDEL

In the preface to the *Philosophy of Right*, Hegel contrasts the theory of the ethical world developed in that work with the philosophy of nature. Everyone is prepared to agree that philosophy has to understand nature as it is; that nature is inherently rational, and that science has to explore and grasp the actual reason present in nature as her immanent law. On the other hand the ethical–historical world created by man, in so far as it is brought forth by his will and is subject to chance and caprice, is supposed to be devoid of law and reason.[1] In the second edition of the *Philosophy of Right* (1833) prepared by Eduard Gans, there is a lengthy footnote taking up this contradistinction, which is a very old one in the history of philosophy: it concerns the difference between natural and normative laws, a topic which Hegel did not deal with in the text of the work itself but only in his introductory lectures given during his time in Berlin.[2]

According to the distinction drawn in this addition, there are 'two kinds of laws, laws of nature and laws of right'. The laws of nature simply exist; their existence renders them valid, and we naturally think of the whole of nature as being determined by laws. In the sphere of laws of nature, being and validity are identical: 'These laws are true, only our view of them can be false. The measure of these laws lies outside us, and our knowledge adds nothing to them, does not modify their existence in any way; only our knowledge of them can be extended.'[3] So far they are not distinguishable from normative laws, which we likewise come to know from without as something given; and the jurist necessarily maintains this objective standpoint according to which the laws are valid precisely because they are laws. But it becomes apparent from the variety and mutability of normative laws that they are not as absolute as the laws of nature, that in their case being and validity diverge. Normative laws are laid down

---

[1] G. W. F. Hegel, *Grundlinien der Philosophie des Rechts*, in *Sämtliche Werke*, ed. H. Glockner (Stuttgart, 1927–30), vol. VII, pp. 23 ff. [The paragraphs of this edition are the same as in Knox's translation. Gans' footnote mentioned below is printed as Addition 1 in Knox's translation – *Editor*.]

[2] The basis of this remark, which Gans edited, is a passage from the lecture notes of H. G. Hotho taken in the winter term 1822/23. The notes are among the Hegel documents in the Staatsbibliothek der Stiftung Preussischer Kulturbesitz, Berlin (referred to afterwards as 'Hegel documents' . . .). They are catalogued as 'Philosophie des Rechts. Nach dem Vortrage des H. Prof. Hegel, im Winter 1822/23, Berlin', Ms. 2, pp. 1–4. Cf. also 'Vorlesungen über Philosophie des Rechts WS 1824/25, Nachschrift von Griesheim', Ms. germ. quart. 545, pp. 13 ff.

[3] Cf. *ibid.* p. 1 and *Philosophie des Rechts*, preface, p. 24.

('posited', *gesetzt*), they originate with man and depend upon his will and consciousness. Thus, while laws of nature directly determine the essence of things and are essentially immutable, positive laws, because of their dependence on man, are in a state of constant change. They have a history and for this reason man does not automatically recognize and accept them as valid, but mediates their existence and validity through himself, through the subjectivity of his will and consciousness. We cannot submit to power and authority stemming from laws issued by a law-giver in the way in which we bow to the necessity of natural laws which regulate the course of non-human things, for the measure of these human laws no longer lies outside ourselves but within our own breasts. A law of nature receives its highest confirmation from the simple fact of its existence, while in the sphere of right a law does not derive its justification from its mere existence but from the fact that it is known and willed. And for this reason it is only with laws of this latter kind that the conflict between being and obligation (*Sein und Sollen*) is possible.

The most important viewpoint which emerges from this contrast between laws of nature and normative laws is not, however, this dualism in the fundamental concept of natural law, which has been apparent since the time of Hobbes and Kant. What interests Hegel is a dualism that goes far deeper, the contrast between nature and spirit, which resolves the conflict between being and obligation by penetrating to its very root. Hegel's juxtaposition is sharpened into the following contrast: ' If we contemplate the difference between these two kinds of laws, and ask what is the basis of laws of right (*Gesetze des Rechts*, that is, normative laws), we will conclude: right proceeds solely from the Spirit, for nature has no laws of right. And so there is a world of existing nature, and a spiritual world of nature, each opposed to the other.' [4] With this in mind, Hegel says in § 4 of the *Philosophy of Right* that the basis of right is ' spirit ' and that its starting point is the ' free will ' that wills itself and possesses in the system of right the ' realm of realized freedom ' – ' the world of spirit brought forth out of itself as a second nature '.[5]

I

The world of spirit as a second nature is not the δεύτερα φύσις of Aristotle, the native custom and morality of the polis based on law (νόμος) and tradition (ἦθος), but rather a nature produced and set to work by man, and therefore closer to Hobbes' *Leviathan* than to Aristotle's *Nichomachean Ethics* or his *Politics*. In fact, almost all the adjectives used by Hegel to distinguish laws of nature from normative laws are to be found in the classical contrast between ' natural ' and ' artificial ' societies, which Hobbes, at the beginning of modern natural law theory, insinuated into both the Aristotelian theory of the natural character of the polis and the traditional sophist alternative between law and

---

[4] *Ibid.* p. 2.   [5] *Philosophie des Rechts*, introduction, § 4.

nature (*nomos* and *physis*). Concord in 'natural' societies – according to both Hobbes and Hegel the concord of animals – is 'the work of God by way of nature'. On the other hand, 'concord amongst men is artificial, and by way of covenant'.[6] And Hobbes too, in agreement with Hegel, regards the things of nature as permanent and necessary while the artificial structure of laws and contracts created by men, precisely because of its dependence on human will, is held to be arbitrary and inconstant. In the background the old conceptual problem of law and nature (*nomos* and *physis*) still stands out quite clearly: what is natural is independent of contracts and deeds (in Hegel, of will and consciousness), while what is artificial *is* thus dependent. But Hobbes draws from this contrast a conclusion which diverges from the sophist alternative and its solution in Plato and Aristotle. He no longer wishes to show that only a natural society, that is, a society ordered according to nature's yardstick, can impose obligations on individuals while an artificial society leaves them free. On the contrary, he wants to demonstrate that only a society which is in the strict sense 'artificial' can place an obligation of obedience on its citizens, for in connection with nature the concept of obligation can no longer be used meaningfully. And so as between the alternatives of *nomos* and *physis*, the idea of obligation attaching to the concepts of 'natural' and 'artificial' has shifted from the one to the other.[7]

What this shift means for the theory of modern natural law may be seen from the function of the biblical God of the Creation who, in reducing nature to the merely created, empties her of autonomy, and bases her existence in the divine will. This has the following consequences for the concept of obligation: if the natural is still to have some binding power on men, then the basis of this obligation can no longer reside in nature, but, separated from her, in the will of God. This model allows of a further transformation: an entirely new basis of obligation is now opposed to the binding power of nature, and in the process its derivation from the will of God is renounced.[8] In Hegel's view, this new step was taken not by Hobbes but by Rousseau, whom he commends in § 258 of the *Philosophy of Right*: 'by adducing the will as the principle of the state, he is adducing a principle which has thought both for its form and its content, a principle indeed which is thinking itself, not a principle, like gregarious instinct, for instance, or divine authority, which has thought as its form only'.[9] Rousseau made the 'innermost part of man', freedom as 'oneness with oneself', the foundation of right, thereby conferring on it an infinite strength *vis-à-vis* nature

---

[6] *Elements of Law*, pt I, ch. 19, sect. 5; *De cive*, pt II, ch. 5, sect. 5; *Leviathan*, pt II, ch. 17.

[7] Cf. F. O. Wolf, *Die Neue Wissenschaft des Thomas Hobbes. Zu den Grundlagen der politischen Philosophie der Neuzeit* (Stuttgart-Bad Cannstatt, 1969), pp. 82 ff.

[8] *Ibid.* p. 84, where this viewpoint is explicitly developed.

[9] *Philosophie des Rechts*, § 258 Addition.

or the will of God working through nature.[10] All the same, the contrast between nature, freedom, and right already occurs in the work of Thomas Hobbes, with whom, in Hegel's view, the real history of modern natural law begins. For he was the first to try to ' trace the framework of the state and the nature of its supreme power back to principles within ourselves, which we recognize as our own '.[11] Hobbes breaks with the assumption of a teleological law of nature (*lex naturalis*) which stands above the human will and rules over the world of natural things, a law which reason need simply reflect or copy if it is to be ' right ' (*recta ratio*) and lead to ' righteous ' action. With Hobbes the theory of right and of society still depends on the concept of nature, only in so far as the ' law of nature ' contains conditions which necessitate the abandonment of natural law. Through Hobbes an ' ambiguity ' arises in the traditional expression ' natural law ' which is of the greatest importance to Hegel, and he draws attention to it in his lecture on Hobbes: ' The expression " nature " is ambiguous in the sense that the nature of man is his spirituality and rationality; but his natural state is that quite other condition wherein he behaves in accordance with his brute naturalness.' [12]

According to Hegel, this ambiguity is sharpened in Rousseau, who widens Hobbes's initial breach with traditional natural law theory. Rousseau conceives of the ' spirituality ' and ' rationality ' of man as his freedom, which removes him from nature and is the essential mark of distinction between man and beast. While Hobbes allows the ' natural ' bond of authority of the master–slave relationship to subsist side by side with the institutional or ' artificial ' bond of authority which rests on the contract, Rousseau inquires into the ultimate justification of authority itself. And he makes neither positive law nor the fundamental natural laws of Hobbes the ultimate principle of justification – but freedom. Without regard for his predecessors of the seventeenth century – whom he places on a footing with Aristotle the apologist of human oppression and servitude, and Caligula its practitioner – and without regard for the current laws of contemporary European states, ' he replies to the above question as follows: That man possesses free will, and freedom is what is qualitatively unique in man. To renounce freedom is to renounce being human. Not to be free is to renounce all duties and rights '.[13] Rousseau's principle that man is free, and that the state built on the foundation of the ' general will ' is the realization of freedom, must, so Hegel says, be ' deemed correct '. ' Ambiguity ' occurs in Rousseau only when he allows the general will to be ' composed ' of the separate wills of individual men, their

---

10 *Vorlesungen über die Geschichte der Philosophie, Sämtliche Werke,* ed. Glockner, vol. xix, p. 527.

11 Cf. *ibid.* p. 442.

12 *Ibid.* p. 443.

13 *Ibid.* p. 527. Hegel quotes the well-known section of the *Contrat Social,* bk 1, ch. 4. Cf. also *ibid.* chs 1, 8, 11; bk iii, ch. 9. Cf. *Discours sur l'origine de l'inegalité parmi les hommes,* ed. K. Weigand (Hamburg, 1955), pp. 106 ff. Cf. also *Vorlesungen über die Philosophie der Weltgeschichte,* ed. G. Lasson (Leipzig, 1917–20), vol. iv, pp. 920 ff.

natural inclination towards freedom. The 'freedom of nature' – the spontaneity of the individual will – cancels 'thereby freedom as the utterly absolute' as it is conceived by Rousseau in his concept of the general will.[14] Yet for all that, he makes us fully aware that freedom is the utterly absolute, the very 'concept of man': 'Thinking itself is freedom; whoever rejects thinking and speaks of freedom knows not what he says. The unity of thought with itself is freedom, the free will . . . Only the thinking will is free. The principle of freedom arose and has conferred on man, who conceived of himself as infinite, this infinite strength.'[15] What the will is in itself can be grasped neither by analogy with nature and her 'laws' nor through its simple contrast with nature or naturally determined caprice. The will – and Rousseau's appeal to the 'general will' as the fundamental principle of the state reminds us of this – must break out of these opposites. It is only free when it 'wills nothing else, nothing external and nothing foreign – for then it would be dependent – but only itself; when it wills the will. To will to be free is the absolute will'. With this notion of the free will Rousseau completes the inversion begun by Hobbes of the teleology of nature – which is the basis of the *lex naturalis* of traditional natural law – into the subjectivity of the individual who thinks and wills himself. In place of the binding power of nature and the ambiguous recourse to the will of God, we are given the binding power of the will become absolute. This transformation of the Hobbesian model by Rousseau was recognized by Hegel as the most important presupposition of his own concept of right.

The absolute will consists in the will to be free. The will that wills itself is the basis of all right and of all obligation, hence of all positive laws, moral duties, and imposed obligations. Freedom of the will itself, as such, is the principle and substantial foundation of all right, is indeed itself absolute, eternal right, and the very highest, insofar as other, specific rights may be placed beside it; it is indeed even the essence of what makes man truly man, that is, the fundamental principle of spirit.[16]

It is from this point that Hegel deduces the transition to the Kantian philosophy. Kant puts an end to the 'ambiguity' still present in Rousseau's concept of natural law by making a radical distinction between the laws of nature and those of freedom, between the 'empirical' and the 'free and pure will'.[17] From the viewpoint of transcendental philosophy the 'concept' of the will attains to an understanding of itself. The 'simple unity of self-consciousness', the 'ego' dissolved from all preceding natural causes, is the

---

[14] *Ibid.* p. 528. 'These principles, expressed in this abstract way, must be deemed right; yet ambiguity soon arises. Man is free, and indeed this is the substantial nature of man. Not only is freedom not surrendered in the state, but in fact it is established there for the first time. The freedom of nature, the propensity for freedom, is not yet true freedom, for only the state is the actualization of freedom.' Cf. further *Enzyklopädie*, § 163; *Philosophie des Rechts*, § 258.

[15] *Ibid.* pp. 528 ff.

[16] *Vorlesungen über die Philosophie der Weltgeschichte*, pp. 921 ff.

[17] *Ibid.* pp. 529 ff., 552, 590.

unassailable, utterly independent freedom and source of all general determinations of thought – theoretical reason; and likewise the highest factor in all practical determinations – practical reason as free and pure will; and the reason belonging to the will aims simply to maintain itself in a state of pure freedom, to will nothing but this in all specific instances, to will right only for the sake of right, duty only for the sake of duty.[18]

' Consciousness of the spirit ' thereby becomes the foundation of the philosophy of right. It discovers ' a principle of thought for the state . . . which is now no longer some principle derived merely from opinion, like the social instinct, the need for security of property etc., nor of piety, like the divine institution of authority, but the principle of *certainty*, which is identity with my self-consciousness . . .' [19]

II

This characterization of the principle of right as it occurs in Hobbes, Rousseau, and Kant must be kept in mind if one wishes to grasp the relationship between nature and freedom in Hegel's *Philosophy of Right*, and to understand the peculiarly ambivalent position of this work at the close of modern natural law theory. Hegel stands on the ground of natural law theory prepared by Hobbes, and does so in two ways: on the one hand he adopts the concept of nature which constitutes this theory, and on the other the presupposition of a will emancipated from given natural and historical forces, a will which, through its own movement, must first come into relations with things and then adjust them to itself. The *Philosophy of Right* shares with the natural law theories of the seventeenth and eighteenth centuries an essentially restricted definition of nature from which is absent the notion of ' natural ' ends and their organization towards the realization of an ' ultimate ' end. As a part of the philosophy of spirit, the *Philosophy of Right* knows of no graduated scale of nature each of whose members occupies a natural position on it, and which, according to the scholastic notion, has its continuation in the ' realm of grace ' (*regnum gratiae*). It further knows nothing of the doctrine of pre-established harmony between the ' kingdom of nature ' and the ' kingdom of ends ', which both obey various causal laws and in which, by virtue of this harmony, the paths of nature lead automatically to the state of grace.[20] The realm of the spirit, whose realization this work presents, presupposes a teleology which is immanent in the free will itself and constitutes that movement of the ' concept ' which pervades all reality and therein wins its freedom. The graduated scale of the spirit does not fall into the category of natural

---

[18] *Ibid.* p. 922.
[19] *Ibid.* p. 924. Cf. in this connection my essay ' Hegels Kritik des Naturrechts ' in *Hegel-Studien*, IV (1967), 178 ff., now also to be found in *Studien zu Hegels Rechtsphilosophie* (Frankfurt am Main, 1969), pp. 42 ff.
[20] Leibniz, *Monadologie* (1714), § 88.

concepts; it rests upon its own essence, and for Hegel this means: on freedom which only exists as a continuing liberation from nature and the production of a 'second nature', of the world of spirit. The realm of spirit is the realm of freedom, and as such no natural hierarchy or otherworldly kingdom of spirits, but the 'world of the spirit brought forth from within itself'.[21] Within this world – this 'second nature' – nature and freedom stand to each other as does spirit to nature – in an antagonistic relationship. 'The nature of spirit may be understood from its most perfect opposite. We oppose spirit to matter. Just as weight is the substance of matter, so we are moved to say that freedom is the substance of spirit.' [22]

It is the same antagonism which affects the concept of nature as it occurs in natural law theory. This concept, which in the doctrine of the state of nature plays both a fundamental and fateful role, contains for Hegel an

important ambiguity which can lead to absolute error. On the one hand nature means our natural existence, us as we directly know ourselves in our various facets, the immediate aspect of our being. But over against this determination, and different from it, nature is also the concept. The nature of a thing is the concept of a thing, what it is from the point of view of reason, and this can be something quite other than merely natural.[23]

If nature designates the concept of a thing, then right in the state of nature must be conceived of as that form of right 'that is fitting for man according to his concept, the concept of spirit'. But this must not be confused with what the spirit is in its natural state, the state of servitude and dependence on nature. For this reason Hegel says with Hobbes and Spinoza: *Exeundum est e statu naturae*.

The a-teleological character of this utterance, seen against the backcloth of modern natural science, takes on a curious sharpness and pointedness. When nature was defined as an order moved by final ends, freedom could be related to it, and human action thought of as its continuation or imitation.* With the transformation of nature into a mathematically describable and mechanically conceived causal system, this reference back to nature becomes impossible. The idea of freedom – and Kant's *Critique of Pure Reason* makes this abundantly clear for the whole modern era – can no longer find in nature the analogy of natural ends, and therefore turns in upon itself. This is also of decisive importance for Hegel's *Philosophy of Right*. It is true that Hegel finds in the concept of gravity a kind of natural analogy for the basic concept of freedom, but here we have a category which itself has only made its mark on the conception of nature since the advent of Newtonian physics. Freedom of the will is best understood, so we are told in

---

[21] *Philosophie des Rechts*, § 4; *Enzyklopädie*, para. 387.

[22] *Die Vernunft in der Geschichte*, ed. J. Hoffmeister, 5th ed. (Hamburg, 1955), p. 55; *Enzyklopädie*, para. 381 Addition.

[23] *Die Vernunft in der Geschichte*, p. 117.

* *Editor's note* – This was Burke's position: see J.-F. Suter, pp. 52, 68, 71.

the Addition to § 4 of the *Philosophy of Right*, by 'reference' to physical nature. Freedom and gravity are 'fundamental properties' of the will and of bodies, that is, properties which are not contingent but necessary and essential, conditions of their very existence:

When one says that matter is heavy, one might suppose that this predicate is only incidental: yet it is not incidental, for it is not as though there were something about material which is heavy: material is rather gravity itself. Gravity constitutes a body and is the body itself. And the same goes for freedom and the will, for what is free is will. Will without freedom is an empty word, just as freedom is only real as will, as thinking subject.[24]

In the case of weight, natural bodies strive towards a central point, the centre of gravity of the system formed by the relative position of these bodies in space. But this centre remains permanently outside them. In the case of freedom as the fundamental determination of the will, the will refers permanently to itself. Indeed, such self-reference is precisely the essence or substance of will, which likewise strives towards a centre, but a centre which it already possesses in itself: 'It does not have unity outside itself; it finds it constantly within itself, it is in and with itself (*in und bei Sichselbst*). Matter has its substance outside itself; spirit on the other hand is self-contained being (*Beisichselbstsein*), and this precisely is freedom.'[25]

The second presupposition which Hegel shares with modern natural law theory concerns the movement of the will. It is on this that the *Philosophy of Right* rests, rather than on the teleological structure of social and political institutions arranged in complex tiers one above the other, as we know it from Aristotelian–scholastic natural law theory. Although Hegel expressly distances himself from the theoretical extremes of Hobbes, Rousseau, and Kant, the overall position of the *Philosophy of Right* remains in an important respect one of natural law: its conceptual development begins with the 'individual will of the subject' in its relations with the things of nature (property) and with other individual wills (contract).[26] It begins with a form of 'abstract' right which reproduces the pre-political condition of natural law theory. The impulse issuing from the individual will – and this is often overlooked – permeates the whole system, stretching even to the derivation of the will concentrated in the 'state' which, according to Hegel, must likewise be an 'individual' will, that of the monarch.[27] Admittedly this individual will is not 'free' in the sense of natural

---

24 *Philosophie des Rechts*, § 4 Addition.
25 *Die Vernunft in der Geschichte*, p. 55.
26 Cf. *Enzyklopädie*, §§ 400 ff.; *Philosophie des Rechts*, §§ 34 ff. Hegel repeatedly emphasized the moment of individuality which belongs to the immediacy of the free will, as for example in §§ 13, 39, 43, 46, 52.
27 Cf. *Philosophie des Rechts*, § 279 with the Remark to § 381; in addition, cf. § 190, and *Enzyklopädie*, 2nd. ed., § 514.

law, it is not the chance individual whim and impulse of each and all from whose reciprocal restriction right, the concept of the general will, arises. It is because Hegel first introduces the will as the object of the *Philosophy of Right* only after he has, in his doctrine of subjective spirit, purged it of all incidental causal determinations, that the movement of the work stems from the ' general ' will already contained in the individual will. And so the free will for Hegel is the ' unity of the rational will with the individual will, which latter is the immediate and peculiar element of the activity of the former '.[28]

Yet this does not mean any retraction of the idea of natural law; on the contrary, it means in reality an enormous intensification of it.[29] For it is no longer the individual as such, in his naturalness, who is the object and point of departure of the doctrine of right, but the individual as a rational being.* While Kant and Fichte restrict the concept of freedom revealed by them to the field of ethics, and take as a basis for natural law the naturally determined free whim and impulse of each and all, Hegel makes use of this concept in his doctrine of right as well. Right is not the restriction of the free will but its very ' being ' – ' freedom as Idea '. This new twist means for Hegel that freedom is no longer a postulate (an ' idea ' in the Kantian sense), but reality, something actually given in the historical–social world, and not just something yet to be achieved. The dialectic is necessary in order to grasp this reality, and in the introduction to the *Philosophy of Right* Hegel applies it to the natural law ' concept ' of the will. According to Hegel, Kant does discover in the principle of the transcendental ego the fundamental basis of the self-determination of the will, the moment of ' pure indeterminacy or of the pure reflection of the I into itself ', in which all limitation and every content ' given ' by nature is dissolved. But freedom of the will, considered in itself, would be merely negative. In the political sphere it would lead – as did indeed happen during the French Revolution in accordance with Rousseau's theory – to the ' destruction of all existing social order ' and the ' annihilation of all organisation striving to re-emerge '.[30] The ego as the pure concept of the will thus necessarily contains a second moment, the ' determining and positing of something definite as content and object ', whereby it posits itself as determined, that is, comes into existence. This something specific which determines and limits the will is not a given external limitation, but – according to Hegel, this is a point overlooked by Kant and Fichte – is immanent in the very act of self-determination. In the unity of these two moments, the undetermined universality and the determined particularity of the will, freedom is realized as the third moment. ' It is the *self*-determination of the ego, which means that at

[28] Cf. *Enzyklopädie*, 2nd ed., para. 485; also *Philosophie des Rechts*, §§ 2, 4.

[29] Cf. F. Rosenzweig, *Hegel und der Staat* (Munich-Berlin, 1920), vol. II, pp. 106 ff.

* *Editor's note* – The sense in which, according to Hegel, the individual as a rational being is free, is further discussed by J. Plamenatz. See especially, pp. 34-9.

[30] *Philosophie des Rechts*, § 5.

one and the same time the ego posits itself as its own negative, that is, as restricted and determinate, and yet remains by itself, that is, in its self-identity and universality. It determines itself and yet at the same time binds itself together with itself.'[31]

III

This dialectical movement of the free will which combines the moment of the universal and the particular, and reconciles both with itself into 'concrete' individuality, into the 'existence of the free will' (§ 29), is that 'nature of the thing' which we encounter in Hegel's *Philosophy of Right* as the 'concept'. The concept contains within itself the full sense of nature; it designates nothing other than that form of right which, along with all its determinations, is based on the 'free personality', on 'self-determination which is the very opposite of natural determination'.[32] The dialectical movement of the concept begins with the self-determination of the individual 'person' who is free from all 'natural' determinations. It begins with the infinite 'concept' of the free will unlimited by anything external to itself as the sole principle of right.

This connection between concept (= nature), freedom and right was repeatedly discussed by Hegel in the Berlin lectures on the philosophy of right. The first lecture given in the year 1818–19 – before the appearance of the work itself – goes into this question in § 3:

The principle of right does not reside in nature, at any rate not in external nature, nor indeed in the subjective nature of man insofar as his will is naturally determined, i.e. is the sphere of needs, impulses, and inclinations. The sphere of right is the sphere of freedom in which nature, insofar as freedom externalizes itself and gives itself existence, does indeed appear, but only as something dependent.[33]

Manifestations of freedom are all aspects of the objective, historical–social reality of man as they are represented by the *Philosophy of Right*, beginning with the outward forms of abstract right and leading to the family, civil society, and the state. It need scarcely be said that, in all of these, 'natural' relations and forms of existence play a part. The question is whether they produce out of themselves a law which rules over those forms. The necessity ascribed, for example, to the existence of the state in relation to the being of the individual, no longer means in Hegel that for the individual it is a law of nature to have to live in the state. The necessity of the state rests much more upon that law which freedom prescribes to itself. On this point Hegel's elucidation of § 3 is unambiguous:

---

[31] *Ibid.* § 7.

[32] *Ibid.* Cf. also the *Nürnberger Propädeutik, Sämtliche Werke*, ed. Glockner, vol. III, pp. 55, 71, and especially *Propädeutik*, pt III, sect. II; *Enzyklopädie*, pt III, § 181: 'The spirit as a free, self-conscious being is the self-identical I, *i.e.* that I that is first of all utterly exclusive in its absolutely negative relations, a single free being or *person*.'

[33] 'Hegel documents . . .', Ms. germ. quart. 1155, p. 9; 'Natur und Staatsrecht nach d. Vortrag des Professors Hegel im Winterhalbjahr 1818/19 von G. Homeyer.'

This paragraph is prompted by the term natural law. The unification of freedom and necessity has been brought about not by nature, but by freedom. Natural things remain as they are and have not freed themselves from law in order to make laws for themselves. But spirit breaks away from nature and produces for itself its own nature and its own laws. Thus nature is not the basis of right.

As for Kant and Fichte,[34] so too for Hegel, the term ' natural right ' is ' merely traditional '. Indeed, it is even wrong from the point of view of the ' concept ' of right itself, because ' by nature ' is to be understood (1) the essence, the concept; (2) unconscious nature (the proper meaning). The ' proper ' name of the subject should be ' philosophical jurisprudence '.[35]

Thus at the time when he was working out the system of the philosophy of right, the development of Hegel's thought leads straight back to that philosophy of freedom which the early essay on natural law (*Über die wissenschaftlichen Behandlungsarten des Naturrechts*) sought to overcome by the construction of a law of ' ethical nature '. But at the end of a long process of coming to understand the basic concepts of ' philosophical jurisprudence ' – a process which at the same time clarifies its historical relationship to traditional natural law theory – there can be no question of resort to this solution. Nature and freedom, the law of nature and the law of right, have parted company in Hegel too. He thus emphatically rejects the traditional view that the ' law of nature ', in so far as man is willing to recognize and follow it, might serve him as a ' model ' of law. The only law which governs the historical existence of man is the law of freedom, which is not given by ' nature ' but by the ' concept ' itself.[36] The concept becoming its own legislator means for Hegel the eighteenth-century idea of man's universal eligibility for rights,[37] with which philosophy rose against the existing state of affairs and broke down the façade of naturalness behind which the idea of law, that is, freedom, had until then been hidden. Positive law now becomes inseparable from the knowledge of this idea.

Admittedly, as is pointed out in the introductory lecture of 1824–5, in ' conventional natural law ', which has nature, natural needs, goals, etc., as its basis, the idea of freedom is not consciously excluded, but ' in effect it is neglected, for both principles are taken up without due assessment of their characteristic features '. Freedom cannot be thought in the form of nature but must be thought in the form of the ' concept ', which reconciles freedom with itself and nature. And if freedom comes forward with the claims of the ' concept ', which assert

---

[34] Cf. Kant, *Reflexionen zur Moralphilosophie* 7084, *Kant's gesammelte Schriften*, ed. Preussische Akademie der Wissenschaften, vol. xix (Berlin-Leipzig, 1934), p. 245; Fichte, *Grundlagen des Naturrechts*, *Sämtliche Werke*, vol. iii, p. 148.

[35] ' Hegel documents . . .', as in footnote 33.

[36] *Ibid.* p. 3; ' The concept of the thing does not come to us from nature.'

[37] *Ibid.* p. 5; ' We must find something lofty in the fact that now man, because he is man, must be regarded as possessing rights, so that his human essence is higher than his status.'

that it is only freedom ' that is at stake in matters of law and ethics, then the term natural law begins to totter '.[38] One could only retain it by conceding that freedom is the ' nature of the thing ' postulated by natural law, i.e. the ' concept '. But the expression is nevertheless ' inappropriate ', for nature, in contrast to freedom, is ' basic, not opposed to anything else. Freedom on the other hand appears to be polemical, it has opposites, and the first of these is nature itself '.[39]

IV

This opposition of nature and freedom decisively shapes the system and concepts of Hegel's *Philosophy of Right*. It determines not only the demarcation of ' philosophical jurisprudence ' and ' natural law ' in the double title of the work,[40] but also the doubling which the last and most important section of the system undergoes with the introduction of the concept of ' civil society ' beside family and state. For the difference between civil society and state has its basis in the separation of the concepts of nature and freedom, a separation which historically is thought through to an end in Hegel. True, in the course of the development of modern natural law the identity of state (*civitas, res publica*) and civil society (*societas civilis*) is dissolved. This identity of state and civil society was the characteristic hallmark of the traditional (' feudal ') theory of state and society, and received philosophical legitimation from the teleology of the *lex naturalis*, which made the natural ends (impulses, needs, etc.) of separate individuals coincide with the ethical end of the whole. But the dissolution of this identity does not lead to a permanent distinction; it is overcome time and time again.

Paradoxically, the cause of this lies in the natural law doctrine of contract, which is the catalyst both of this separation and of its overcoming. The view that the teleological order of nature transcends the individual and civil society is abandoned, but nature nevertheless enters the construction of the contract, at the point of departure of natural law theory, as the caprice (*Willkür*) of the many. It is the needs, instincts and inclinations which, contained in the category of ' free caprice ', must be restrained by the concept of law so that the capricious will of each can harmonize with the will of all under a universal law, which replaces the now discarded natural law. Here is to be sought the real motive for the polemical separation of the principles of law and freedom as against Kant and Rousseau, on which Hegel sets great store in his philosophy of right. At the same time he is also fully aware in this context of the differences between

38 ' Hegel documents . . .', ' Nachschrift von Griesheim ', pp. 9 ff. (see footnote 2 on p. 136).

39 *Ibid.* p. 10.

40 Hegel expressly refers to this in his lectures of 1824/25. Cf. Griesheim as above, p. 3; and my essay: ' Tradition und Revolution in Hegels " Philosophie des Rechts " ' in *Zeitschrift für philosophische Forschung*, XVI (1962), 206 ff. (Reprinted in my *Studien zu Hegels Rechtsphilosophie*.)

Rousseau's and Kant's conception of nature, and that of the older natural law theories. The traditional mode of treatment in which 'the two meanings' of the concept of nature are still unseparated takes as its basis the 'natural being' of man, his inclinations, needs, impulses: first, his physical needs and the necessity of their satisfaction, but then also the 'impulse towards sociability and society which is connected on the one hand with relations between the sexes, and on the other is extended into universal civil society' which in turn 'develops into the state'.[41] But it is precisely at this point that for Hegel the 'unsatisfactory nature of this connection' appears. There is no teleology of nature to reconcile the instincts and needs of individuals with the ethical–historical existence of the 'state'. All determinations deduced from the instinctual nature of man remain 'abstract' in comparison with what the state and civil society are according to the 'concept':

If we are to say that civil society and the state arise out of instinctual impulse, then at once the unsatisfactory nature of this connection, of the state arising from impulse, is apparent. The impulse towards sociability which philosophy formerly accepted as the basis of the state is something indefinite and abstract which can only furnish some of the necessary conditions for the vast and highly structured state, and which appears excessively thin beside the phenomenon it is meant to explain.[42]

To this natural principle which was first abandoned by Hobbes, Rousseau, and after him Kant and Fichte, oppose the principle of freedom. But, as Hegel says in the lectures of 1824–25, this is done 'in a manner which is not ours, and which did not permit jurisprudence to develop into a complete and coherent system'.[43] Hegel agrees with Kant that freedom under the laws of nature is impossible since nature and freedom are opposed to one another. For this reason he rejects, like Kant, the question posed by the traditional teleological conception of nature concerning the 'historical origins of the state',[44] or, to use the traditional terminology of politics and natural law, the question of the 'beginning of civil society'. For the philosophy of right is only concerned with the 'Idea of the state', with the 'thought as concept' (*gedachten Begriff*). But in Kant and Fichte, and in Rousseau before them, the principle which they make the basis of jurisprudence contradicts their exposition of it. On the one hand the principle of the state – that principle 'which is not just thought in its form, like the social instinct or divine authority, but thought in its content' because 'thinking itself' is will – excludes nature from itself. And yet on the other hand, Rousseau, Kant and Fichte reintroduce nature by placing, in the forefront of their theories, will in its specific form as the 'individual will',[45] the 'particular individual'. As a

---

[41] Cf. Griesheim as above, pp. 5–8. Cf. *Philosophie des Rechts*, introduction, § 19.
[42] Cf. Griesheim, p. 8.
[43] *Ibid*. p. 11. Cf. 'Hegel documents . . .', Hotho, pp. 7 ff. (see footnote 2 on p. 136).
[44] Cf. *Philosophie des Rechts*, § 258.
[45] Cf. *ibid*. §§ 258, 29, 182 Addition; *Vernunft in der Geschichte*, pp. 111 ff.

result of this they conceive of the ' general will ' of the ' concept ' of the state, not as the ' absolutely rational part of the will, but only as the common good (*das Gemeinschaftliche*) which emerges from this individual will '. And hence the more recent natural law theory, and with it the classical liberalism of the nine-teenth century, retreat to the viewpoint of older natural law theory, in their attitude to the ' concept ' of state and civil society. The construction of the con-tract, which in Hobbes, Rousseau and Kant presupposes the dissolution of the classical identity of *civitas* and *societas civilis*, repeats that confusion of two separate conceptual spheres which Hegel uses in § 182 of the *Philosophy of Right* as an objection to the natural law view of the state.[46]

The fact of such an objection presupposes that Hegel had drawn for himself the conclusions that follow from the approach of modern natural law theory. By radicalizing the contrast between laws of nature and laws of freedom, Hegel relinquishes, along with the traditional term ' natural law ', the term ' civil society ' (*societas civilis*). The abandonment of the latter was to prove incom-parably the richer in results. With Hegel's separation of state and civil society, a whole new perspective of problems concerning human life and will was opened up. The relations of individuals with one another and with nature were given theoretical independence and set in relative isolation, and could now be conceived of and studied as ' social ' relations. The naturally determined individual will, the ' particular individual ' and his needs, impulses and inclinations, is no longer directly and fundamentally related to the universal will manifest in the state. Precisely because of this it becomes possible for Hegel to discern in that ' system of needs ' the economic basis of modern society which had been concealed from the liberal followers of the natural law theory by the model of the social contract and its political implications. It is therefore apparent that the problem of the relationship between nature and freedom finds no satisfactory solution in the philosophy of right; on the contrary, it re-emerges on a new level. The ' freedom as Idea ', which demands the conceptual liberation of civil society from the state, descends, on this new level, from reality to appearance – ' the world of ethical appearance ', in which ethical identity cannot be thought of as freedom but only as necessity.[47] The cluster of concepts centred on the sphere of the free will is here on the verge of being transformed into the law of development of society, a law which has as its basis nature, instead of the freedom presupposed by the concept. This is the ' element of inequality ' which gives expression to the objective right of particularity of mind, and not only fails to cancel the inequality

---

[46] *Philosophie des Rechts*, § 182 Addition: ' If the state is represented as a unity of different persons, as a unity which is only partnership, then what is really meant is only civil society. Many modern constitutional lawyers have been able to bring within their purview no theory of the state but this.'

[47] *Ibid.* § 186. Cf. §§ 184–5.

given by nature, but indeed 'produces it out of spirit'.[48] Here lies one of the seminal points in Hegel's philosophy of right against which the dialectic of the concept of will strikes as against a barrier – a barrier which Hegel's most important and historically most influential pupil, Marx, sought to surmount by the 'materialist inversion' of this dialectic into the development of relations of production.*

---

[48] *Ibid.* § 200. A minimum reference to nature which is indispensable to the concept is further to be found in the deduction of hereditary monarchy (§§ 280 ff.) and in the justification of war (§ 324).

* *Editor's note* – Translated from the German by Roger Hausheer.

Hegel's theory of punishment[1]

DAVID E. COOPER

In this essay I discuss Hegel's theory of punishment for its own sake. I am not concerned with its relation to the rest of the *Philosophy of Right*, and even less with its place in the dialectic as a whole. For example, I shall not consider how the concept of punishment is meant to forge a link between the stages of Abstract Right and Morality. Detailed discussions of Hegel's theory for its own sake are, in fact, fairly rare – which is one good reason for my essay taking the limited form it does. The essay is divided into three unequal sections. In section I I consider those anti-utilitarian arguments of Hegel's that can be understood independently of his positive theory. In section II I consider his criticisms of views that might be confused with an acceptable retributivist approach – the ' revenge ' view of punishment, for example. Finally, in section III I discuss Hegel's positive theory: a theory most neatly encapsulated in the claim that punishment ' annuls ' crime. The last section is the longest and most important, for a number of reasons. First, there are less exegetical difficulties in stating those of Hegel's ideas which are discussed in the first two sections. Second, most of his points discussed in the first two sections are not novel. Kant had made similar points – so it is not in these directions that Hegel's originality lies. Finally, his most important arguments against utilitarian accounts come by way of inference from his positive theory. Those which can be stated in isolation from that theory are not the most effective.

I

A large part of Hegel's discussion of punishment is devoted to showing that utilitarian justifications are inadequate. Such accounts, he says at various points, are ' superficial ', ' irrelevant ', and ' confused '. Four points need to be made concerning his arguments considered in this section: (a) they are not his most effective; (b) they are not original; (c) they do score against some commonly held views; (d) they do not score at all against a utilitarian who confines himself to regarding utility as the General Justifying Aim of punishment – to use Professor H. L. A. Hart's terminology.[2] These arguments may be loosely divided into the ' Conceptual ' and the ' Moral '.

---

[1] Except when otherwise stated, all references to Hegel will be to *Hegel's Philosophy of Right*, trans. T. M. Knox (Oxford, 1942).

[2] See ' Prologomenon to the Principles of Punishment ' in *Punishment and Responsibility* (Oxford, 1968). By a General Justifying Aim, Hart means that which justifies the practice of punishment in general, as opposed to some particular aspect of it, such as mitigation.

The Conceptual Argument. This underlies the following passage:

The various considerations which are relevant to punishment as a phenomenon and to the bearing it has on the particular consciousness, and which concern its effects (deterrent, reformative, &c.) on the imagination, are an essential topic for examination in their place, especially in connection with modes of punishment, but all these considerations presuppose as their foundation the fact that punishment is inherently and actually just.[3]

We can ignore, until section III, what is meant by saying that punishment is 'inherently and actually just'. However, it is clear what Hegel's point is. Before any question can arise as to reforming a man through punishment, or to deterring others through it, it must be established that he did commit a crime, and in a manner deserving of punishment. (For example, he must not have been asleep when he did it.) More exactly: the reason why a given person is punished is that he has committed a crime in a certain manner – and not that he stands in need of reform or that others need deterring. The corollary of this point is that, were reform and deterrence the reasons for punishing an individual, there would be no need to require his guilt. But this is required – so reform and deterrence cannot be the reasons.

This seems perfectly correct, as far as it goes. It is not an original point. Kant had said that a man 'must first of all be found to be punishable before there is even a thought of deriving from the punishment any advantage for himself or his fellow citizens'.[4] Also, it is difficult to see what weight the point has against someone who regards utility only as the General Justifying Aim. The utilitarian could say: 'Certainly it is true that the reason given for punishing a man is that he has committed a crime. But why should this be counted as a reason? Why, that is, should the fact that men commit crimes be a reason for punishing people? Surely the answer must be in terms of utility.' Concerning the fact that we only punish the guilty, he could add: 'Either we can explain that on utilitarian principles, or we can accept it as a separate principle of justice. Either way, it is irrelevant to the claim that the practice of punishing people in general is justified in terms of utility.' To counter this reply, Hegel would have to say more about punishment's being 'inherently and actually just'. So far then he has not shown that utilitarianism involves a 'superficial attitude towards punishment'.[5]

The Moral Arguments. Hegel argues that utilitarians must take certain unethical attitudes towards punishment. This is an interesting charge, since typically it has been the utilitarian who has accused his opponents of taking a barbaric, brutal attitude. This latter accusation is unfair with regard to Hegel, who is

[3] § 99, p. 70.
[4] *Metaphysic of Morals*, quoted in Bradley's *Ethical Studies* (Oxford, 1962), p. 28.
[5] § 99, p. 70.

certainly aware of the importance of reform and deterrence. That is clear from the passage quoted above, where he says it is 'essential' to consider these, especially in connection with the 'modes of punishment'.

Hegel, in fact, brings two charges against the utilitarian – that the latter takes an immoral attitude (1) towards the convicted criminal; and (2) towards those who might commit crimes. The first charge involves Hegel's (in)famous claim that punishment is the 'right' of the criminal: that the criminal 'wills' his punishment. This claim appears in the following passage:

The injury (the penalty) which falls on the criminal is . . . his implicit will, an embodiment of his freedom, his right . . . it is also a right established within the criminal himself, i.e. his objectively embodied will, in his action. The reason for this is that his action is the action of a rational being and this implies that it is something universal and that by doing it the criminal has laid down a law which he has explicitly recognized in his action and under which he should be brought as under his right.[6]

One thing Hegel seems to mean here is false, if taken at all literally. He says that when a man commits a crime, he is thereby adopting a principle to the effect that men may be coerced: that violation of rights is permissible. Consequently, since his punishment is a form of coercion, involving loss of rights, the criminal is simply being treated under the principle he has adopted. So really he wills his own punishment. Now I think there is a sense in which we might speak of the criminal implicitly denying rights – but it is not that sense (see section III). The average criminal does not deny that his victim has rights, nor probably, does he think that coercion in the form of crime is permissible. He may well assert that it is wrong. Again, a criminal might think himself justified in coercing a victim, but deny that the authorities have a right to coerce him – Robin Hood, for example. In neither case does the criminal adopt a principle under which his own punishment falls. In the first case he acts against a principle he probably adopts. In the second case, only *his* action is justified by his principle.

Hegel's point, however, can be made in another way. If a man acts as a free, rational agent, and is aware of himself as such, then he must, in general, wish to be held responsible for the intended results of such actions. He has a right, indeed, to have his actions looked upon in this light. To treat him otherwise is to treat him like an animal or a maniac.

Since that is so, [says Hegel] punishment is regarded as containing the criminal's right and hence by being punished he is honoured as a rational being. He does not receive this due of honour unless the concept and measure of his punishment are derived from his own act. Still less does he receive it if he is treated either as a harmful animal who has to be made harmless, or with a view to deterring and reforming him.[7]

To speak to the criminal as Hegel thinks the utilitarian must speak to him would deny him the status of a rational being. The utilitarian would have to say: 'You

[6] § 100, p. 70.
[7] § 100, p. 71.

must not think we are making you suffer because of any rational decisions you have made. Any such decisions count for us only as symptoms suggesting how we should treat you. We are doing this to you simply to alter the decisions that you, and others, will take in the future.' This, Hegel would claim, is the way to talk to a typhus-carrier, and not to a rational criminal.

The point may be reinforced in the following way: consider how implausible a utilitarian account of rewards would be, which treated rewards merely as stimuli to future effort. If such an account of rewards is unacceptable, then the corresponding account of punishment is hard to accept. For it is absurd to say: 'We will only treat you as rational and deserving when you do well.' To be rational and deserving only when one does well is not to be rational and deserving at all – for there must be the possibility of choosing the wrong course if one can choose the right course. As Hegel says in an earlier work ' this possibility of making a clear-cut opposition between virtue and vice is freedom, is the " or " in " virtue or vice " . . . the one is not unless the other is '.[8]

Hegel's argument is persuasive, though it is not new. Kant had said ' a man can never be treated simply as a means for realizing the views of another man, and so confused with the objects of the law of property '.[9] Partly, of course, Hegel is repeating the earlier conceptual point that the reason for punishing an individual is that he has committed a crime in a more or less responsible manner. But he is also urging that it is wrong to encourage the criminal to think of himself as anything but a person who deserves what is happening to him as the result, solely, of a free, rational choice he has made. Many criminals would agree with him here. Mabbott quotes a prisoner as writing ' to punish a man is to treat him as an equal: to be punished for an offense against rules is a sane man's right '.[10] However, while I would myself go along with Hegel and Mabbott's prisoner, I do not know what to say against someone who insists that, on the contrary, criminals should prefer to be regarded simply as means towards social betterment. Such an attitude is common in, for example, Soviet Russia. During the Great Purge trials, those convicted were encouraged to say how consoling they found the fact that their punishment would act as a lesson to others. At the same time, the stress upon punishment as being deserved by responsible actions was played down – for the ' guilty ' usually claimed, with official approval, to have been ' dupes ' of some pernicious, foreign agency.

Whichever attitude we prefer, however, it is difficult to see how Hegel's point has any effect against the claim that utility is the General Justifying Aim of punishment. The utilitarian might agree that it is wrong to encourage the criminal to think of himself as anything but a rational agent deserving what

[8] ' The Spirit of Christianity ', in *Early Theological Writings*, trans. T. M. Knox (Chicago, 1948), p. 225.

[9] *Metaphysic of Morals*, quoted in Bradley's *Critical Studies*, p. 28.

[10] ' Punishment ', *Mind*, XLVIII (1939), 158.

happens to him – but he can deny that his justification of punishment entails thinking of the criminal in any other light. He can simply ask: why should the fact that we punish, in general, only for utility's sake entail treating the criminal like a typhus-carrier? It is clear, he might say, that criminals often freely and rationally choose to commit crimes, and because of this they are punished. Were they like typhus-carriers we would not punish them at all. No doubt men are punished in general, and typhus-carriers isolated, for similar reasons – but that does not mean treating criminals and typhus-carriers similarly. We saw earlier that a utilitarian answer to ' Why do we have the practice of punishing? ' did not involve a utilitarian answer to ' Why do we punish just those that we do? '. It can now be seen that a utilitarian answer to ' Why do we punish and treat men *in the manner* that we do? ' is not entailed by a General Justifying Aim utilitarianism. Non-utilitarian considerations of degrees of responsibility and mitigation can be allowed to enter into the answer to that question. Precisely because of that, to point out that we should treat criminals as responsible agents does not force us to reject utility as the general justification of punishment.

Hegel's second, and lesser known, charge is that utilitarians must take an immoral attitude towards those who might commit crimes. Specifically, he attacks Feuerbach's contention that punishment is justified as a threat against those who would otherwise commit crimes. However, we might regard the following passage as a criticism of anyone who regards punishment justified as a form of deterrent.

A threat presupposes than a man is not free, and its aim is to coerce him by the idea of evil. But right and justice must have their seat in freedom and the will, not in the lack of freedom on which a threat turns. To base a justification of punishment on threat is to liken it to the act of a man who lifts his stick to a dog. It is to treat a man like a dog instead of with the freedom and respect due to him.[11]

Hegel, here, sees two things wrong with regarding punishment as a threat. First, he suggests that to threaten people is to diminish their freedom, which is not justifiable. I fail to see this point. Whether we *use* the prospect of punishment *as* a threat, or merely mention it, a person is equally apprised of its existence. If his freedom of action is at all curtailed, it is done so equally by the threat and the mere mention of punishment. The second, better, point he is making is this: there is a wrong and a right way to advise a person against committing a crime. The wrong way is to say to him: ' Don't do it, because you'll be made to suffer if you do.' The right way is to say: ' Don't do it, because it's wrong – and because it's wrong, you'll be made to suffer.' It is important, that is, for men to avoid crime for the right reasons, such as thinking that crime is wrong. When Hegel speaks of treating a man like a dog, instead of with ' the freedom and respect due to him ', the important word is ' respect '. It does not respect a man to assume

[11] § 99 Addition, p. 246.

that he will only avoid crime for fear of punishment. To respect him is to suppose that he regards punishment not as that which prevents him committing a crime, but as that which he will deserve if he does commit it.

It is worth quoting Kant's similar, and more full, account:

Just as rewards ought not to be grounds for doing good deeds, so punishments ought not to be the grounds for avoiding evil deeds. If they are, a mean condition of mind tends to be set up . . . the ground for not doing an evil action should not lie in the punishment but the action should not be done because it is evil. Reward and punishment are merely subjective incentives, to be used only when the objective ones are no longer effective, and they serve merely to make up for the lack of morality.[12]

It is difficult to disagree with Kant and Hegel here – and what they say holds against certain common attitudes often associated with utilitarianism. First, clearly, they oppose the psychological egoism often underlying utilitarianism – according to which punishment would be as good a way as any other to encourage obedience to the law. Helvétius, for example, says ' tout l'art du legislateur consiste donc à forcer les hommes, par le sentiment de l'amour d'eux-mêmes, d'être toujours justes les uns vers les autres '.[13] The legislator's means, for Helvétius, is a system of rewards and punishments. Kant and Hegel insist, however, that to act rightly, to be just, is *inter alia* to act for the right reasons – and selfish hopes and fears are not amongst these. Second, what they say holds against the way some people might use the threat of punishment. It would be quite wrong for the authorities – or for a father, say – to encourage the young to keep the law simply by threatening them. Advice, reasoning, and education should come first: and threats only when all else has failed.

However, their arguments do not apply against a careful utilitarian. He need not be a psychological egoist, and he can agree that advice and education should come before carrots and sticks. All he need insist – as Kant admits – is that punishment is justified once these ' objective ' incentives fail. (Strictly speaking, it is the *threat* of punishment that deters – but then actual punishment is no doubt a precondition of that threat being effective.)

When pressed into a corner, there is a question the utilitarian will always ask : ' If punishment were utterly ineffective in preventing crime, would it not be better to abolish it, since by doing so the area of suffering would be reduced at no loss whatsoever? ' Nothing Kant and Hegel have said so far provides sufficient reason for answering this question in the negative – and it is the difficulty of answering this simple, but effective question in the negative that makes the utilitarian position strong. Hegel, unlike Kant, does not want to answer a straightforward ' No ', I believe. His position is a more subtle one, and preferable, I think, to the more straightforward utilitarian and Kantian ones. But more of this in section III.

[12] *Lectures in Ethics*, trans. L. Infield (London, 1930), p. 56.
[13] *De L'Esprit* (Paris, 1795), p. 394.

II

Two objections often brought against retributivist theories in the past have been that retributivism (a) entails the absurd ' eye-for-an-eye ' doctrine of punishment; and (b) treats punishment as a form of revenge. Hegel spends some time showing that his view of punishment contains no such elements. He himself is eager to stress the absurdity of the ' eye-for-an-eye ' doctrine – the logical absurdity, that is. ' It is easy enough to exhibit the retributive character of punishment as an absurdity (theft for theft, robbery for robbery, an eye for an eye, a tooth for a tooth – and then you can go on to suppose the criminal has only one eye or no teeth).' [14] Here he is pointing out that some crimes rule out the possibility of the punishment taking the form of the crime – for example, treason or attempted suicide. More important, though, is to show up the falsity of the principle of which the ' eye-for-an-eye ' doctrine is only an especially silly instance. The false principle is that there is some natural scale according to which each crime has its naturally fitting punishment, which can be read off from the scale quite independently of any actual legal system. Hegel is quite adamant that this principle is false: ' How any crime is to be punished cannot be settled by mere thinking: positive laws are necessary.' [15]

While the principle is plainly false, Hegel shows how easy it is to reach such a principle from acceptable, but misunderstood, premises. It is perfectly reasonable, he says, to describe punishment as an ' injury of an injury ', or to say ' punishment should equal the crime ', or that punishment ' repays ' the crime. We move from these premises to the false conclusion, according to Hegel, only if we fail to distinguish between crime and punishment as external phenomena and as concepts. More precisely, we must distinguish between ' specific equality ' and ' value '. The specific equality of two things is their likeness in external, empirically observable respects. Value, on the other hand, is ' the inner equality of things which in their outward existence are specifically different from one another in every way '.[16] What is wrong with the false principle is that it demands specific equality of crime and punishment – but this is absurd, since no scale informs us, independently of a legal system, what prison sentence is equivalent to the harm done by the thief. However, crimes and punishments are comparable in value. Hegel remarks: ' it is only in respect of that form [i.e. specific] that there is a plain inequality between theft and robbery on the one hand, and fines and imprisonment on the other. In respect of their " value " however, i.e. in respect of their universal properties of being injuries, they are comparable '.[17] So, when punishment ' equals ' or ' repays ' the crime, it does so by sharing a certain conceptual similarity to it – and not by possessing some physical, empirical aspect which is somehow similar to a physical, empirical aspect of the crime.

[14] § 101, p. 72.
[16] § 101, p. 72.

[15] § 96 Addition, p. 246.
[17] *Ibid.*

Once we consider the values of certain crimes, says Hegel, we are in a position to decide that some crimes deserve stiffer penalties than others – though we cannot by mere reflection decide what any given penalty should be. Because of this there is no merely ' arbitrary ' connection between crimes and their relative punishments.[18] We are able to do this because crimes differ in value, according to the extent to which rights are infringed.

It makes a difference to the objective aspect of crime whether the will so objectified and its specific quality is injured throughout its entire extent, and so in the infinity which is equivalent to its concept (as in murder, slavery, enforced religious observance) or whether it is only injured in a single part or in one of its qualitative characteristics, and if so, in which of these.[19]

That is, when we enslave a person, say, we infringe more of his rights than when we steal from him. This difference should be reflected in the punishments meted out by a rational legal system. Difference in values of crimes is logically independent of differences in physical harm. There can only be a contingent connection between the ' objective value ' of a crime and its external harmfulness.[20]

Hegel, then, manages to preserve what is reasonable in such claims as ' punishment should equal the crime ', while avoiding the absurdities of the ' natural scale ' principle, and the implausible suggestion that there is merely an arbitrary, conventional connection between certain crimes and their relative punishments.

Faced by the second charge, that retributivism makes punishment a form of revenge, Hegel first shows that he is at liberty to make important conceptual distinctions between the two; and then shows that what makes revenge undesirable does not also make punishment undesirable.* While he does make clear conceptual distinctions, Hegel admits that there are marginal cases. For example, when the heroes and knights-errant of old set out to redress wrong, they were neither pure avengers, nor pure instruments of punishment. In general, though, there are clear differences. In the first place, revenge is paradigmatically ' the act of a subjective will ',[21] whereas the will of those who punish is ' the universal will of the law '.[22] That is, revenge can only be sought by the injured party, or by one closely related to him in some manner. Those who punish, however, are not the injured parties, and not specially related to the injured parties. On the contrary, if a judge is personally involved in a crime, he must not sit in judgment upon the case. Second, punishment is ' the business of a public authority ',[23] whereas an act of revenge is not the act of anyone with legally constituted authority. So punishment is not merely not administered by injured parties, it is administered by persons possessing authority. Authority does not belong to the

---

[18] § 101, p. 73.
[20] *Ibid.*
* *Editor's note* – Cf. K.-H. Ilting, pp. 95–6.
[22] § 102 Addition, p. 247.

[19] § 96, p. 68.

[21] § 102, p. 73.
[23] § 219, p. 140.

avenger. Third, there is a necessary distinction between the motives involved in revenge and punishment. An act of revenge is necessarily motivated by feelings resulting from an injury to oneself or to a person related to oneself in some way. I cannot be seeking revenge if I search for the killer of a man quite unknown to me, and whose life and death I have simply read about in the newspaper. The motive behind punishing a man, however, is not the ' subjective and contingent retribution of revenge ', but the ' genuine reconciliation of right with itself '.[24] The authorities, that is, seek right for its own sake, quite independently of any emotional considerations. This is not so in the case of revenge.

Apart from pointing to these conceptual distinctions, Hegel is also able to show that some of the demerits of revenge do not belong to punishment. First, he argues, the victim of an act of revenge is likely to regard the act as a ' new transgression ', since it was not the act of any authority. Consequently he is likely to seek revenge upon the avenger. Revenge, consequently, is ' contradictory in character, it falls into an infinite progression, and descends from one generation to another ad infinitum '.[25] No doubt Hegel has vendetta in mind here. Punishment, though, since it is not carried out by individuals *qua* individuals with personal motives, will not set up such an attitude in the criminal – except in those rare cases where a released prisoner seeks out the judge or prosecutor in order to terrorize him. A second problem with revenge is this: since it is motivated by strong feelings, the avenger may not be concerned to decide just how serious the wrong done to him was, and so may carry his revenge to quite inordinate lengths. As Hegel puts it: ' the person wronged . . . views the wrong not as something qualitatively and quantitatively limited but only as wrong pure and simple, and in requiting the injury he may go too far, and this would lead to a new wrong '.[26] Since legal authorities are not similarly motivated – since they are able to assess the seriousness of a crime objectively – they will not, with any frequency, ' go too far '.

Hegel is able to show, then, that the question of whether punishment is justified is quite separate from the question of whether revenge is justified. He is also able to show that what makes revenge undesirable does not similarly make punishment undesirable. Authorities and individuals are to be judged in different ways. This, taken together with his rejection of the first charge, shows that Hegel is quite able to resist attempts to foist upon retributivism patently unwelcome implications. If a non-utilitarian view is unacceptable, it is not because it has such implications.

III

It is, of course, uninteresting to describe Hegel or anyone else as a retributivist, since that title tends to be given to anyone who rejects a utilitarian justification of

24 § 220, p. 141.
25 § 102, p. 73.   26 § 102 Addition, p. 247.

punishment. As such, the onus is on Hegel to refute the charge that he, like other retributivists, has no theory at all beyond a denial of utilitarianism, together with a bald assertion that punishment is justifiable. Such a charge would be a just one to bring against Kant, I think – but not against Hegel. So far, however, his arguments do not operate against a person who treats utility solely as the General Justifying Aim of punishment. Any effective arguments must come from the positive theory that Hegel has.

The crux of this positive theory is contained in the claim that punishment ' annuls ' crime. Hegel says, for example, that when crime is punished ' coercion is annulled by coercion '[27]: or that to punish the criminal is ' to annul the crime '.[28] He also speaks of punishment as the ' negation of the negation '.[29] Properly interpreted, these remarks form the basis of a plausible justification of punishment. Most writers on Hegel, however, have either repeated what he says in his own terms – which is unhelpful: or they have confessed to not understanding him. Benn and Peters, for example, say ' it is not easy to see how a wrong can be annulled: what is done cannot, in a literal sense, be undone '.[30] Certainly, if one does not look very closely at what Hegel says, it is possible to discover apparent nonsense. He says that crime is an ' infringement of right ', which, in turn, we are told is ' only an injury to a possession or to something which exists externally '.[31] Clearly it is absurd to speak of annulling damage to a person's body – which is part of property in Hegel's sense of ' property '. One has to look closer then.

There is one interpretation of how punishment is justified as annulment that will not do. According to H. A. Reyburn, in crime ' the negation and subordination of right by the will is intrinsically a failure: it is a self-contradiction which demands to be sublated '.[32] The ' self-contradiction ' is meant to be that between (1) the crime as an act of a free man; and (2) the crime as an attack upon free men. That there is such a contradiction is supported by this sentence in Hegel: ' force or coercion is in its very conception directly self-destructive because it is an expression of a will which annuls the expression or determinate existence of a will '.[33] So, according to Reyburn, it is because a crime is by nature ' self-contradictory ' that it requires to be ' sublated ' by punishment: that is, punishment shows the crime up for what it is, ' self-contradictory '. Frankly, I do not understand this. It seems to mean that since a crime is a piece of inconsistent behaviour, it must be punished. But even if it is inconsistent, why should it be punished? No doubt inconsistent behaviour should be brought to the attention

[27] § 93, p. 67.

[28] § 99, p. 69.

[29] § 82, p. 64.

[30] *Social Principles and the Democratic State* (London, 1959), p. 177.

[31] § 98, p. 69.

[32] *The Ethical Theory of Hegel* (Oxford, 1921), p. 144.   [33] § 92, p. 67.

of the agent – this might be the job of a psychoanalyst – but I do not see how inconsistency *per se* merits punishment. I think there is a sense in which we can speak of crime being a 'contradiction', but it is not the sense Reyburn has picked upon. Perhaps Hegel does think that crime is 'self-contradictory' in that sense, but I do not think that this is the important sense that Hegel operates with.

My account of Hegel's theory will take the following form: first, I shall sketch a justification of punishment in non-Hegelian terms. Then I shall argue that this is essentially Hegel's own justification. Finally, I shall see what replies can be given to objections against Hegel on this interpretation.

First, then, the sketch. The existence of the tree in my garden is logically independent of any person's having gone through some rule-governed, conventional (including verbal) behaviour. The existence of the vast majority of things is independent in this way. However, there are some existents of which this is not true. For example, whether or not there exists a promise on A's part to do something depends upon A's having gone through some rule-governed procedure. (He may have said 'I promise . . .', or nodded his head in reply to 'Do you promise . . .?', etc.) I shall refer to such existents as 'performatees'. This is to bring out (a) the fact that they depend upon rule-governed performances or procedures for their existence; and (b) the relation of what I am saying to certain well-known theses of J. L. Austin concerning 'performative utterances'. Austin points out that for certain performances to 'come off', such as promising, 'there must exist an accepted conventional procedure having a certain conventional effect'.[34] Similarly, there must be such procedures for certain things, performatees, to exist. Examples of performatees would be promises, marriages, guarantees, gifts, contracts, bets, names. An interesting one, also, would be sovereignty, on Professor Hart's account. Sovereignty only belongs to a person or body in virtue of certain 'secondary rules' – rules, that is, which 'confer powers, public or private . . . which lead . . . to the creation of . . . duties or obligations'.[35] At some point, in other words, rules must be stated or implicitly govern behaviour, if someone is to be counted as the sovereign.

Often the absence of a certain conventional procedure does not entail the non-existence of the relevant performatee. The position may be less clear than that. Has the person who says 'I promise . . .', with his fingers crossed, promised or not? We might say 'No', but more likely we shall say 'Yes, in a way', or 'Yes, but it doesn't count', or 'Yes and no – not *really*'. Austin gives the name 'infelicitous' to performances which fail to be paradigmatic in some way or another. A further example: the drunken vicar who 'christens' the child 'Satan' has christened 'infelicitously'. Correspondingly, we may speak of 'infelicitous performatees' – for example, the insincere promise, the vicar's christening. One way in which a performance may be infelicitous, according to

[34] *How to do Things with Words* (Oxford, 1963), p. 14.
[35] *The Concept of Law* (Oxford, 1961), p. 79.

Austin, is if certain subsequent behaviour does not take place. If I hand my friend a parcel at Christmas, and demand it back a few days later, did I make him a gift or not? Well, a very funny sort of gift. We will be particularly concerned with this type of infelicity.

Legal rights are performatees. Whether or not a person has the right to do x is logically dependent upon some rule or convention by reference to which such a right may be ascribed. The rule may exist in the form of a written statute, or implicitly in the form of judicial decisions, and other ways. Now such rules, whilst necessary for the existence of rights, are not sufficient – not sufficient, at least, for the ' felicitous ' existence of rights. A story is told of an Oxford student who insisted upon his ' right' to a pint of ale during a recent examination, on the basis of an unrepealed medieval statute. Clearly, though, there is a good sense in which the student had no such right. Again, it is not clear that people during wartime have the rights that the law states they have, even before special promulgations expressly deny them these rights.

There is one very important question to ask if we are trying to decide whether persons have rights or have them, at least, in any straightforward, paradigmatic manner. The question is: what happens to those who try to prevent these persons from doing what they have a supposed right to do? If nothing happens to them – if no attempt is made to apprehend and punish them – there is very strong reason to suppose that the persons had no such right at all. One reason for saying that people do not have their usual rights in wartime is that there is not even the presumption that the military authorities should be charged with the commission of certain crimes – as in cases of requisition, for example. Again, the fact that no one would dream of censuring the examiner who refused the student his pint of ale is a good reason for saying the student had no such right, or had it only in some jokish sense. The point is this: attempting to apprehend and punish men is a form of procedure necessary to establish that rights of a certain kind exist in any paradigmatic manner. If a man is not liable to punishment for an action, that is strong reason for supposing he committed no crime, that he infringed no rights.[36] Of course, we require a type-token distinction here. It is only failure to attempt to punish a class of actions which is strong reason for supposing that these actions are not criminal infringements of rights.

This seems to be plausible, and if it is, new light is cast upon the justification of punishment. Most people, and certainly utilitarians, regard punishment as a useful means towards the preservation of rights. But if the above view is correct, the connection between rights and punishment is not an empirical ' means–ends ' one, but is logical. Unless people are generally apprehended and punished for preventing others doing x, there is reason to suppose that the latter do not have

---

[36] This seems to me to be the element of truth in Kelsen's claim that ' Law is the primary norm, which stipulates the sanction . . .' *General Theory of Law and State* (Cambridge, Mass., 1945), p. 61.

the right to do *x* – certainly not a ' felicitous ' right. At the very least, a charge of gross insincerity could be levelled against legal authorities who stated that men did have certain rights, but made no attempt to protect those rights against violators. (Think of the ' rights ' of Jews in Nazi Germany *before* the Nuremberg laws explicitly took them away.)

If all of this is so, then the justification of punishment is very simple. It is the same as the justification of the rights which crimes violate. If it is important that men have legal rights, it is important that there be punishment – for without the latter, there could not, logically, be the former. Analogously, the justification of marriage ceremonies is one with the justification of marriage. Unless there is some form of ceremony there is no marriage. The ceremony, it should be noted, is not a means towards getting married in the way the initial courting might have been. Failure to grasp such a point might be due to the fact that one says ' We should punish him *because* he has infringed a right ', with the apparent implication that there is a complete distinction between punishment and rights. But we also say ' He's putting on the ring because he's getting married ', and we also say ' you ought to pay him because he's earned it '. And in these cases, getting married is not something distinct from putting on rings and the like : nor is one's obligation to pay a man logically distinct from his having earned it.

As I say, I find such an account plausible. Clearly, though, it would have to be expanded at much greater length to command acceptance. I have no time for that. My task is to show that Hegel had some such account in mind, and to rebut certain predictable objections. I believe we can treat Hegel as claiming, albeit in quite different terms, that rights are performatees which logically depend for their felicitous existence upon the punishment of those who infringe them. How can we superimpose Hegel's talk of ' annulment ' on to the above account?

Hegel uses ' annul ' in two senses, corresponding to the two ways in which crime may be regarded. From one point of view, a crime is an ' injury to a possession or to something which exists externally '. Annulment of the crime in this sense can only be ' the satisfaction given in a civil suit, i.e. compensation . . . so far as any compensation can be found '.[37] This is clearly a metaphorical sense of ' annul ', since compensation does not make the damage actually disappear. Also, as Hegel sees, only certain crimes can be ' annulled ' in this sense – those, namely, where compensation is possible.

Crime, however, can be looked at from a quite different point of view. The criminal is implicitly denying that his victim has certain rights. This follows from Hegel's claim that a crime is ' an injury which has befallen the implicit will ', and from his claim that to talk of the ' implicit will ' is to talk of ' the right or law implicit ' within it.[38] Rights, that is, belong to persons as free agents – in

[37] § 98, p. 69.
[38] § 99, p. 69.

virtue of their ' wills '. Any attack upon a person's property is an implicit denial of that person's rights as a free agent.

How is it that crime, regarded as an ' injury which has befallen the implicit will ', can be annulled? Hegel, let us be clear, is quite definite that crime is *annulled* – literally made nothing at all. He says that an injury to the will is ' inherently . . . nothing at all ' [39]: that it is ' only something negative ' [40]: that it has no ' positive existence '.[41] What he means here is *not* that an injury to the will did occur, and is later spirited out of existence. He means that there never was such a thing as an injury to the implicit will. The crime was, in intention, a demonstration that the victim had no rights. But the victim did have these rights, and so there never was such a thing as the demonstration that he did not have them. So, to speak of annulling the crime is to speak of whatever it is that establishes that the victim did have those rights which were implicitly denied by the criminal. What establishes this, of course, is punishment. But before going on to that, it is worth pointing out the parallel between annulment in this context, and annulment of verdicts given at trials. When the verdict of Guilty is annulled, we do not spirit away the judge's having given that verdict. Like damage to property, the verdict is part of history, and cannot be erased from it. What we do is to run through a procedure establishing that there never was such a thing as the defendant's guilt. Similarly, to establish that there never was an absence of rights on the victim's part is to annul the crime.

But how does punishment succeed in annulling the crime? According to Hegel, we must punish the crime, for ' otherwise [it] would have been held valid '.[42] In an earlier passage, he states that right, via punishment, ' makes itself actual and valid, while at the start it was only something implicit and something immediate '.[43] I can only interpret these remarks as making the same point outlined in the account given above. Only if we punish a certain class of actions is there sufficient reason to suppose that these were actual infringements of rights. To establish the felicitous existence of rights we must punish the relevant actions. Hegel, of course, does not speak of infelicitous rights: he speaks of them as ' only . . . implicit and . . . immediate ', as opposed to ' actual and valid '. Punishment serves to demonstrate that the victim did have rights, despite the criminal's implicit denial of them – a denial, therefore, which is not ' valid '. Punishment, Hegel says, serves ' to restore the right ' [44] – that is, to establish with certainty that the right exists.

It is now fairly easy to interpret some of Hegel's other well-known remarks. When a crime is punished, he says, ' right reasserts itself by negating this negation of itself '.[45] This can be interpreted quite literally. A crime involves the

[39] § 97, p. 67.
[41] *Ibid*.
[43] § 82, p. 64.
[44] § 99, p. 69.

[40] § 99, p. 69.
[42] § 99, p. 69.

[45] § 82, p. 64.

implicit assertion that the victim lacks rights. Punishment establishes the claim that he had such rights. Punishment, then, is a denial of a denial: a negation of a negation.

Hegel also remarks that punishment is ' not only right under certain conditions but necessary '.[46] This cannot mean physical necessity: nor can it mean moral necessity, since Hegel explicitly contrasts being right, and being necessary. The only plausible interpretation is that Hegel means logical necessity. Punishment must logically follow crime if we are to speak of there being rights and crimes at all.

My interpretation can be supported by glancing at some of Hegel's earlier writings. In his much earlier work, ' The Spirit of Christianity ', Hegel discusses both legal and divine punishment. At one point he states fairly explicitly what I take to be the essence of his account. ' The law cannot forgo the punishment, cannot be merciful, or it would cancel itself.' [47] While this is false if applied to a particular (token) punishment, it makes the point that, in general, rights without punishment are no rights at all, or at best infelicitous ones. Second, there is a passage in *Phenomenology of Mind* where Hegel makes the point, albeit in obscure fashion, that rights depend for their existence upon far more than the mere assertion by authorities to that effect. Supposedly he is talking of the system of rights in Antonine Rome. In this system, the official assertion of men's rights was not, apparently, backed by appropriate procedures and practices. In this state of affairs, says Hegel, ' Consciousness of Right . . . experiences the loss of its own reality: discovers its complete lack of inherent substantiality: and to describe individual as a " person " is to use an expression of contempt.' [48] J. N. Findlay interprets this passage, and subsequent ones, as making the point that ' the mere abstract assertion of personal rights pass [es] over into the doubt over the question as to whether persons have any rights at all '.[49] If so, Hegel was aware at this stage of the logical connection between rights and practices, including no doubt the practice of punishing.

Finally, before considering some objections, I shall quote a passage from Hegel without comment – for it should now be clear how this difficult passage should be interpreted. I consider it as the fullest, although one of the most obscure, statements of his view:

The nullity [of crime] is that crime has set aside right as such. That is to say, right as something absolute cannot be set aside, and so committing a crime is in principle a nullity: and this nullity is the essence of what a crime effects. A nullity, however, must reveal itself to be such: i.e. manifest itself as vulnerable. A crime, as an act, is not something positive, not a first thing on which punishment would supervene as a

[46] § 93, p. 67.
[47] In *Early Theological Writings*, p. 226.
[48] Trans. J. B. Baillie, 2nd ed. (London, 1949), p. 505.
[49] *Hegel : A Re-examination* (London, 1958), p. 119.

negation. It is something negative, so that its punishment is only a negation of the negation. Right in its actuality, then, annuls what infringes it and therein displays its validity, and proves itself to be a necessary, mediated reality.[50]

At least two objections might be raised against Hegel on my interpretation of him. The first is this: Hegel talks of crime as containing a denial by the criminal of his victim's rights. It is this aspect of the crime that is supposedly annulled. However, is it not simply false to suppose that the average criminal – as opposed to an intellectual anarchist – is denying that his victim has rights? I have already dealt with this question partially in section 1, where I agreed that the criminal need not, at any level of consciousness, be denying rights. Now it is not completely clear that Hegel did think that the criminal was doing this at any conscious level. That he did is suggested by such a sentence as '[the] sole positive existence which the injury [to the implicit will] possesses is that it is the particular will of the criminal'.[51] But whatever he meant, it is possible to lend good sense to the claim that the crime involves a denial of rights, without making reference to the criminal's actual intentions. What we can say is this: the crime is a denial of rights in that, were it to go unpunished, there would be good reason to suppose the victim did not have the rights. It would then be *as if* an explicit denial of rights had been made, and had gone unchallenged. An analogy might help. A pupil may ask his teacher a series of difficult questions with the sole intention of gaining enlightenment. But we might describe him as ' putting the teacher to the test'. It is a test in that, were the teacher unable to answer the questions, he would have displayed a lack of competence. It would be *as if* he had taken a test and had failed it. In my discussion of Hegel, I spoke as if the denial of rights involved in crime was purposive and intentional. But there is no need to speak in this way. The denial of rights exists as an aspect of crime in so far as failure to punish it would be tantamount to admitting that an explicit denial would have been correct.

The second objection is this: let us admit that the existence of rights is only established if some action is taken against those who infringe putative rights. But why should this action take the form of punishment? Why should it not take the form of public denunciation, for example? If not, there must be further explanation of why the form should be that of punishment. The first point to note is that Hegel does distinguish between punishment and annulment. He says ' if crime and its annulment (which later will acquire the specific character of punishment) . . .'[52] Thus he does not think that punishment is necessarily the sole means of annulment. Indeed, as we have seen, he does admit of cruder, less satisfactory forms – such as those employed by the heroes and knights-errant of

[50] § 97 Addition, p. 246.
[51] § 99, p. 69.
[52] § 99, p. 69.

old. However, he clearly thinks that punishment is the form that annulment must take in our society. And here we might surely defend him. The action taken against criminals must, according to our previous argument, be at least as strong as is required to establish the paradigmatic existence of rights. Now it seems, as a matter of empirical fact, that only punishment possesses the required strength. If the authorities merely denounced crimes against, say, a racial minority, there would be good reason to suppose the authorities did not take these rights seriously. Certainly members of this minority could complain : ' You say we have rights and you denounce those who violate them. But such rights are a mockery. What sort of rights are they which men can violate and then remain free to violate again and again? ' Of course, it is imaginable that there should exist a society in which denunciation was regarded as the ultimate disgrace one could suffer, and was as feared and as effective as punishment is today. I do not think Hegel need deny that possibility. But he could insist, quite rightly, that such an alternative procedure is highly unlikely to gain the strength that punishment has. Alternatively, he could say that if denunciation did become as unwelcome, generally, as punishment, then we simply have a new form of punishment. We used to speak of our headmaster, for example, as punishing us by exposing us before the rest of the school and giving us a dressing-down.

It should now be clear how Hegel can reply to a utilitarian. At the end of section 1 I mentioned a nagging question the utilitarian is wont to ask – a question it is very difficult to answer in the negative. Would not a society in which punishment was quite ineffective in preserving rights be better off without it? Hegel does not answer this question in the negative. He shows the question is faulty. To ask that question is like asking ' Wouldn't it be better to get married without going through any form of ceremony? ' Just as one cannot get married without going through a ceremony, there cannot be rights, felicitous ones at least, unless we punish violators. To justify rights is *ipso facto* to justify punishment, with the qualifications I have made. What justifies rights, if anything, is another question.

Hegel's account of war

D. P. VERENE

Hegel's account of war, although primarily given in a few statements in the *Phenomenology of Mind* and the *Philosophy of Right*, has been the subject of some of the most divergent interpretations of his thought and has engendered some of the strongest feelings regarding it. It has been a point on which the interpretation of Hegel's theory of the state has often turned. Opinion has varied from the view that Hegel advocates a nationalistic, totalitarian state and regards war as a fundamental and glorious activity [1]; to the view that Hegel is a conservative, reflecting the political situation of his time and acknowledging the fact that war plays a role in the actual life of nations [2]; to the view that Hegel's political philosophy is essentially compatible with the liberal constitutional model of the state and hence is not an enemy of the pursuit for peace. [3] These interpretations of Hegel's statements on war involve the scholarly interest in developing a consistent reading of a major figure but they have behind them a larger need, dictated by the conditions of our own time, to understand the problem of war itself.

My intention is: (1) to assess the views that can be taken of Hegel's statements on war; and (2) to decide what they indicate for the problem of war in general. Questions concerning Hegel's account of war cannot be answered apart from an assessment of their place within Hegel's philosophy as a whole. Hegel's statements on war, if approached primarily within the context of his political philosophy, can lend themselves to either a militaristic or a non-militaristic inter-

[1] For example, Karl R. Popper, *The Open Society and Its Enemies*, vol. II, *The High Tide of Prophecy : Hegel, Marx and the Aftermath* (London, 1945), ch. 12. See also Hans Kohn, ' Political Theory and the History of Ideas ', *Journal of the History of Ideas*, xxv (1964), 305. Kohn's criticism is directed against the defense of Hegel's views on war in John Plamenatz, *Man and Society*, vol. II (New York, 1963).

[2] I take this to be the standard or most frequently held view. See, for example, F. S. Northedge, ' Peace, War, and Philosophy ', *The Encyclopedia of Philosophy*, vol. VI (New York, 1967), 63–4; George H. Sabine, *A History of Political Theory* (New York, 1937), pp. 664–7, 753; J. N. Findlay, *Hegel : A Re-examination* (New York, 1962), p. 331.

[3] See Shlomo Avineri, ' The Problem of War in Hegel's Thought ', *Journal of the History of Ideas*, xxii (1961), 463–74. That Hegel's political thought is part of the mainstream of Western European political theory not incompatible with that of Hobbes, Locke, Montesquieu, and Rousseau is argued by Z. A. Pelczynski in his introductory essay to *Hegel's Political Writings*, trans. T. M. Knox (Oxford, 1964). See the exchange over Pelczynski's interpretation between Hook and Avineri: Sidney Hook, ' Hegel Rehabilitated? ', *Encounter*, xxiv (Jan. 1965), 53–8; Shlomo Avineri, ' Hook's Hegel ', *Encounter*, xxv (Nov. 1965), 63–6. Reprinted in W. Kaufmann (ed.), *Hegel's Political Philosophy* (New York, 1970).

pretation. The commentators have approached Hegel's views on war primarily within this context and have engendered a dispute that in principle can have no resolution. Beyond the textual question is the larger question of what Hegel has shown or not shown about the problem of war itself. Has Hegel shown war to be a necessary part of the relations between nations or is his view in some way compatible with the concept of permanent peace? The answer to this question depends upon a decision regarding what Hegel's political philosophy is fundamentally about. It is my intention to deal first with the question of the interpretation of Hegel's statements on war and then, using this as a base, to inquire into what Hegel offers for the understanding of the nature of war itself.

Hegel's statements on war range from remarks in his early writings such as *The German Constitution*, written and revised between 1799 and 1802,[4] to the *Philosophy of Right* (1821) and his lectures on philosophy of religion, philosophy of history and philosophy of fine art during the latter part of his career.[5] Hegel's fullest statements on war are contained in his treatment of the initial stage of spirit (BB. *Der Geist*) in the *Phenomenology of Mind* and his theory of the state in the final section of the *Philosophy of Right*.[6] Hegel's views on war do not appear to have undergone any substantial change from his first to his last writings. In fact, in explaining his view on war in the *Philosophy of Right*, Hegel quotes from his essay ' On the Methods of Scientific Treatment of Natural Law ' (*Über die wissenschaftlichen Behandlungsarten des Naturrechts*), from the same early period as *The German Constitution*.[7] Two themes are evident in Hegel's statements on war: (1) the relevance of war to the relationship of individuals to the state; and (2) the role of war in defining the state as a distinct political entity or a politically organized nation and its relations with other nations. These two themes run side by side throughout Hegel's statements on war and appear as essential parts of his discussion of the state.

Hegel regards war as something to be explained. It is, for him, one of the phenomena of human affairs, having a particular content and structure comprehensible by human reason. Hegel states:

War is not to be regarded as an absolute evil and as a purely external accident, which itself therefore has some accidental cause, be it injustices, the passions of nations or

---

4 *Political Writings*, pp. 143–4, 208–10. See also the quotations from ' The System of Ethics ' (*System der Sittlichkeit*) and ' On the Methods of Scientific Treatment of Natural Law ' (*Über die wissenschaftlichen Behandlungsarten des Naturrechts*) in Avineri, ' Problem of War in Hegel's Thought ', pp. 463–4.

5 For a compilation of quotations on war from Hegel's lectures, see H. G. ten Bruggencate, ' Hegel's Views on War ', *Philosophical Quarterly*, 1 (1950); and Constance I. Smith, ' Hegel on War ', *Journal of the History of Ideas*, xxvi (1965), 284–5.

6 Hegel's views on war in the *Philosophy of Right* are also stated in the third part of the *Encyclopaedia*. See William Wallace, *Hegel's Philosophy of Mind* (Oxford, 1894), §§ 545–7.

7 *Hegel's Philosophy of Right*, trans. T. M. Knox (Oxford, 1942), § 324. See also Herbert Marcuse, *Reason and Revolution : Hegel and the Rise of Social Theory* (Boston, 1960), p. 55.

the holders of power, &c., or in short, something or other which ought not to be. It is to what is by nature accidental that accidents happen, and the fate whereby they happen is thus a necessity. Here as elsewhere, the point of view from which things seem pure accidents vanishes if we look at them in the light of the concept and philosophy, because philosophy knows accident for a show and sees in it its essence, necessity.[8]

For Hegel the task of philosophy in general is to explain that which has occurred. Philosophical explanations involve the analysis of particular forms of experience and the showing of how they are interrelated with each other such that experience itself can be viewed as a whole.[9] For Hegel the task of political philosophy is to analyze and relate together those forms of experience through which ethical and political life occurs.[10] War, being one of the forms of political life, must have a place in the philosophical account of the political. War can no more be regarded as accidental to the activity of the state than can peace. War and peace are both modes of activity in the actual life of states and are to be part of the philosophical analysis of the state. The state along with the forms of the family and civil society comprises the general structure of the ethical–political world.

(1) Hegel regards war as an important factor in the relation of the individual to the state. War makes the individual citizen realize that his existence is bound up with a larger whole. War, by having within it the possibility of the destruction of the existing social order, forces the individual citizen to realize that his private world of family, marriage and property ultimately exists because of the public world of the state. Through war or its threat each citizen is made to realize in concrete terms that the future of his private world is inexorably tied to the future of his state. Hegel asserts:

While, on the one hand, war makes the particular spheres of property and personal independence, as well as the personality of the individual himself, feel the force of negation and destruction, on the other hand this engine of negation and destruction stands out as that which preserves the whole in security.[11]

War is the security of the state in that it forces its citizens to experience the state as a particular entity. In order to defend his state the citizen must experience his state as something more than the general context in which he pursues his private goals and holds property. In order to defend his state the citizen must internalize the general character of his state and see it as a particular state set off against other states. War also makes the individual experience himself in a new way. War makes individuals feel the finitude of their own existence; they ' feel the

---

[8] *Philosophy of Right*, § 324.

[9] See the concluding comments to the preface to the *Philosophy of Right*, especially the owl of Minerva metaphor, pp. 12–13, and also Hegel's description of the purpose of philosophy in *The Phenomenology of Mind*, trans. J. B. Baillie, 2nd ed. (London, 1949), pp. 80–91.

[10] *Philosophy of Right*, §§ 1–2.

[11] *Phenomenology of Mind*, p. 497.

power of their lord and master, death '.[12] War makes the individual realize not only the nature of his citizenship in the state, it also makes him realize the temporal character of his own existence.[13]

(2) Hegel regards war as an important factor also in the relation of state to state. War is an activity that originates in the clash of wills and interests of individual states: ' It is as particular entities that states enter into relations with one another.' [14] States relate to each other not in terms of a common context but in terms of their own customs, peculiarities, and passions. Thus the realm of international relations is one of abiding contingency in which war is always in the background, residing as the means for ultimately settling any dispute. War can occur as the result of any incident, for a state may regard its honor and interests at stake in any of its activities no matter how small.[15] War, once resorted to by states, however, does not entail the abandonment of their recognition of each other as states. War is undertaken as a limited action with peace as its end.

Hence in war [Hegel states], war itself is characterized as something which ought to pass away. It implies therefore the proviso of the *jus gentium* that the possibility of peace be retained (and so, for example, that envoys must be respected), and, in general, that war be not waged against domestic institutions, against the peace of family and private life, or against persons in their private capacity.[16]

War in Hegel's account is not an act of total destruction undertaken by one nation against another. War arises from the fact that politically organized nations act as individuals without a common superior; thus no treaty or agreement is ultimately binding. Any treaty may be broken when it is not in the interest of one of the parties. The relation of each nation to others is contingent on the advancement of its own interests. Thus the world of nation-states is characterized by the cycle of war and peace and the return to war.

How are we to understand Hegel's views on war? The alternatives presented by Hegel's commentators noted at the beginning of this essay – that Hegel can be taken as either a totalitarian, conservative, or liberal – can be viewed as responses to the question of whether Hegel in his statements on war is *prescribing* or *describing*.[17] The totalitarian view takes Hegel's statements as prescriptive.

---

[12] *Ibid.* p. 474. See also *The German Constitution* in *Political Writings*, pp. 143–4.

[13] *Philosophy of Right*, § 324 and Addition. Hegel's discussion of war in the *Phenomenology of Mind* (pp. 466–99) and in the section of the *Philosophy of Right* titled ' Sovereignty *vis-à-vis* foreign States ' (§§ 321–9) seems primarily directed to the relation of the individual and the state. His discussion of war as a feature of the relations between states occurs primarily in the section on ' International Law ' in the *Philosophy of Right* (§§ 330–40).

[14] *Philosophy of Right*, § 340.

[15] *Ibid.* § 334.

[16] *Ibid.* § 338.

[17] Smith, ' Hegel on War ', applies this distinction to Hegel's statements on war to show that at least in his later works Hegel's intent was to describe, not prescribe. I agree with Smith that this

Hegel is regarded as advocating war and nationalism and as providing a theoretical basis for the twentieth-century fascist states. The conservative view takes Hegel's statements as essentially descriptive. Hegel is regarded as reflecting the actual state of affairs between nations; his view is regarded as prescriptive only to the extent that he may have reflected some of the positive attitudes toward war of his own day. It is often said on this view that Hegel's statements on war hold only for a limited or conventional war and would probably not have been made if Hegel could have known of the possibility of a global war or war of total destruction. The liberal view is most frequently cast as a reaction to the view that Hegel is a supporter of totalitarianism. The liberal view finds Hegel's statements on war insufficient to support the claim that Hegel advocates war. Yet it does not hold that his political philosophy contains a plan for peace. The liberal view takes a strong stand on the point that Hegel is not an enemy of the constitutional form of government and the open society, and generally takes no definite stand on the interpretation of Hegel's statements on war.

The difficulties concerning a decision on the meaning of Hegel's statements on war arise from the procedure of approaching them wholly or largely within the confines of Hegel's *political* thought. I contend that no amount of concentration on nor dissection of Hegel's statements on war can solve the problem of their meaning. Such an approach seems to result in nothing better than the current antinomy between a prescriptive and a descriptive reading. The zealous tone and strong phraseology of some of Hegel's statements, particularly in regard to the effect of war on the individual's awareness of the finitude of his own existence and the importance of war in solidifying the citizens of the state, give support to the view that Hegel's statements are prescriptive. The somewhat factual and neutrally cast statements Hegel makes concerning the way war functions in relations between states give support to a descriptive interpretation. The traditional way out of this dilemma – to regard Hegel as a conservative, claiming that his views are the result of the political situation of Germany of his time and the international situation of the Napoleonic era – is too superficial to be satisfactory. It is no more satisfactory to explain away Hegel's political views by an appeal to the historical conditions of their formulation than it would be to explain away his epistemological views by such an appeal. Hegel's political views and especially his views on war are integral parts of his philosophy and must be met on their own terms. The solution to the problem of the oscillation between a prescriptive and a descriptive interpretation rests not on a closer reading of the texts but on a placing of Hegel's statements on war in their proper relation to his philosophy in general. In order to solve the problem of what Hegel's statements on war mean we must ask what philosophical statements themselves are for Hegel.

distinction is useful for structuring approaches to Hegel's views on war, but for the reasons that follow below do not find it, as does Smith, a sufficient mechanism for solving the problem of the logical status of Hegel's statements.

The philosophical proposition, for Hegel, aims at the presentation of actuality (*Wirklichkeit*). Philosophy, Hegel points out in the preface to the *Phenomenology of Mind*, is neither the production of edifying discourses, construction of proofs, nor the formulation of inductive generalizations. Philosophy aims at a dialectical presentation of experience and thus derives its method directly from a reflection on the oppositional process inherent in consciousness's own act of knowing the object.[18] The philosophical proposition is itself internally dialectical as is consciousness. In the proposition the predicate brings forth an aspect of the subject and in so doing alters the subject so as to produce a new subject. The predicate stands to the subject as one of its determinations.[19] The attaching of subjects to predicates in the philosophical or ' speculative proposition ' is a formal expression of the way in which philosophy builds its total account of experience. Such an account is morphogenic. It distinguishes the various forms or frameworks in which the mind (*Geist*) apprehends its object and orders these in a developmental scheme from the least determinate to the most determinate. Mind is shown to be an internally systematic process that forms itself in a manner analogous to the relationship internally expressed in the philosophical proposition.[20]

The presentation of actuality, for Hegel, is accomplished neither by prescribing nor by describing. Philosophy neither formulates imperatives, whereby states of affairs may be judged or actions directed, nor does it generalize from facts. The philosophical proposition fits neither of these modes; instead it portrays the frameworks of mind that are to be presupposed in order that prescribing and describing are possible. Philosophy accomplishes this by taking the most general form of human consciousness and analyzing it into further forms until the entire system of experience is before us. This is as much a process of analyzing one form out of another as it is a process of taking all the forms actually before us and ordering them in a development. Hegel's statements have a descriptive element in that they grow from reflection on actual states of affairs. They have a prescriptive element in that they cause us to consider alternatives. Hegel's statements, unlike descriptions, do not form facts but form the frameworks through which facts can be formed; and, unlike prescriptions, they do not form actions but form the frameworks wherein actions can be formed.*

In order to solve the problem of the status of Hegel's statements on war, the status of his philosophical statements generally must also be considered in relation to the works in which his views on war occur. The *Philosophy of Right*, the basic work of Hegel's political philosophy, comprises a section of the second part

---

[18] *Phenomenology of Mind*, pp. 139–45.

[19] *Ibid.* pp. 84, 120–1.

[20] *Ibid.* pp. 88–91.

* *Editor's note* – A similar account of Hegel's philosophical method is given by R. N. Berki, p. 200.

of Hegel's total system of spirit.[21] It is thus part of a continuous construction of thought, traceable back to the *Phenomenology of Mind*. The *Phenomenology* presents mind as a series of stages of consciousness wherein the concept is uncritically or un-self-consciously joined with its content. This series terminates in the stage of Absolute Knowledge, or the realization by consciousness of its ability to give itself form wholly in terms of concepts divorced from specific content. The *Science of Logic* retraces the ' schema of movement ' of the *Phenomenology* from the standpoint of Absolute Knowledge, that is, as a conceptual progression.[22] The result is the Absolute Idea or the concept self-consciously joined with content. When this joining occurs in the way of science the Absolute Idea is formed as nature (*Philosophy of Nature*); when this joining occurs in the social world the Absolute Idea is formed as culture (*Philosophy of Spirit*).

The fact that Hegel's political philosophy as presented in the *Philosophy of Right* can be assigned a definite place within his system provides an answer to the question of the status of his statements on war. If Hegel's political philosophy is systematically derived from the rest of his system,[23] his statements regarding the state will have a status consistent with those in the earlier part of his system. Hegel's statements about the state and its functions, like the statements in his philosophy generally, can neither be regarded as prescriptive nor descriptive, neither as imperatives nor as empirical generalizations.[24] It would be as much a mistake to take Hegel's views on war stated in his account of the initial stage of

---

[21] The first part of the system is presented in the *Phenomenology of Mind* (see pp. 95, 806–8). The second part of the system is presented in the *Science of Logic* (trans. W. H. Johnston and L. G. Struthers (London, 1929), vol. I, p. 37) and the *Encyclopaedia of Philosophical Sciences* (the first book being a restatement of the larger logic and the second and third books being the *Philosophy of Nature* and the *Philosophy of Spirit* or *Culture*). The *Philosophy of Right* is an expanded statement of section II of the *Philosophy of Spirit* and, Hegel states, is intended systematically to present those remarks he would normally present verbally in lecturing on that section of the *Encyclopaedia* (*Philosophy of Right*, p. 1). Hegel regards the *Philosophy of Right* as based on an extension of the principles established in the *Science of Logic*, the foundation work of the second part of the system.

[22] *Science of Logic*, p. 37.

[23] In speaking of Hegel's political philosophy here, I am not including his shorter political writings which are not directly part of his system and are generally empirical in character. As Z. A. Pelczynski argues in his introduction to *Hegel's Political Writings*, these show a different side to Hegel's political thought (see pp. 134–7). However, as mentioned earlier, the content of Hegel's statements on war in these shorter writings does not differ from those made in the works of his system.

[24] The importance of not approaching Hegel's political theory as a set of empirical generalizations is well realized by Irving Louis Horowitz, ' The Hegelian Concept of Political Freedom ', *The Journal of Politics*, XXVIII (1966), 3–28. Horowitz states: ' The Hegelian approach assumes completeness in that all relevant concepts and relations which would be required in empirical undertakings are worked out. This special sense of methodology as ideal typification should be kept in mind when examining Hegel. What we are provided with is a systems approach rather than empirical analysis. Few commentators have viewed the directly political and social writings of Hegel as an extension of his more abstract works ' (p. 3).

spirit [25] in the *Phenomenology* as equivalent to the position of his political philosophy as it would be to take his views on the nature of the thing in the second stage of consciousness as equivalent to his epistemology.[26] In both cases Hegel is portraying a particular form of the mind's relation to its object and it is a principle of his philosophy that no one form of mind is equivalent to the whole of mind nor to his philosophical position. In like manner Hegel's discussion of the state in the *Philosophy of Right* and its relation to war is a portrayal of how the idea of right, determined in the form of the state, is joined in a particular way with its content. The quandary over the status of Hegel's statements on war in the *Philosophy of Right* arises only if we approach it as a kind of independent work. If we regard Hegel as having first written a metaphysics and a theory of knowledge and then having gone on to write a political philosophy, with only a rather broad connection between them, in short, if we approach Hegel's political thought much in the way we approach that of Locke or Hume, then the question arises about the status of Hegel's statements on war. If, however, we see that Hegel's political philosophy proceeds from his philosophy in general with systematic rigor, the status of his statements on war is not a difficulty as such. The question of their status resolves itself into the question of the status of what Hegel calls the philosophical or ' speculative proposition '. One cannot do justice to Hegel's political thought by approaching it as a relatively independent set of ideas having goals apart from the goals of his system.

The question which was stated as the second concern of this essay remains : what light do Hegel's statements on war throw on the problem of war in general? This question is closely tied to Hegel's comments on Kant's *Perpetual Peace*. Kant and Hegel appear at two ends of a spectrum on the question of war. Kant in *Perpetual Peace* proposes a set of principles whereby war may be overcome and a federation of free states or league of nations established. Hegel, in the *Philosophy of Right*, seems to regard war as something necessarily rooted in human existence. Hegel states that Kant's idea

presupposes an accord between states; this would rest on moral or religious or other grounds and considerations, but in any case would always depend ultimately on a particular sovereign will and for that reason would remain infected with contingency. It follows that if states disagree and their particular wills cannot be harmonized, the matter can only be settled by war.[27]

Hegel maintains that international law as such ' does not go beyond an ought-to-be ' [28] and criticizes Kant's statement that perpetual peace is possible because of the working of providence in history.

---

[25] (BB.), vi, A. ' Objective Spirit: the ethical order.'
[26] (A.), ii. ' Perception, Thing, and Deceptiveness.'
[27] *Philosophy of Right*, §§ 333–4. See also § 324 (Remark).
[28] *Ibid*. § 333.

The difficulty in Kant's theory of peace to which Hegel's criticism points is that Kant fails to face the problem of the reasons for the existence of war. The paradox that is posed for ethics by the existence of war is that men can bring themselves together under law as states but seem unable to extend the process beyond the bounds of states to the creation of genuine international law. The response to this problem from the standpoint of Kant's theory is to regard the failure of men to establish international peace as residing in an inability to conceive properly the principles whereby it could be established. The elimination of war from the Kantian view is essentially a conceptual and organizational problem. War is regarded as an unnatural state of affairs that exists because of man's present inability fully to grasp the means for peace. The fact that mankind — although in possession of the idea of peace — seems not to be ready to institute peace does not worry Kant, who optimistically appeals to providence to solve the difficulty. Kant states:

The guarantee of perpetual peace is nothing less than that great artist, nature (*natura daedala rerum*). In her mechanical course we see that her aim is to produce a harmony among men, against their will and indeed through their discord. As a necessity working according to laws we do not know, we call it destiny. But, considering its design in world history, we call it ' providence ', inasmuch as we discern in it the profound wisdom of a higher cause which predetermines the course of nature and directs it to the objective final end of the human race.[29]

On Kant's view war is dealt with in the same way evil is dealt with on the traditional solution to the theodicy problem. War is regarded as nothing in itself, as a privation having no positive content.[30] War becomes a delay in the working of providence rather than a moment of its development in history.

Hegel's criticism of Kant derives from the general principle of his thought affirmed at the beginning of the *Philosophy of Right*, that the rational is actual and in turn the actual is rational.[31] For Hegel: ' History is mind clothing itself with the form of events or the immediate actuality of nature.' [32] War, being actual, cannot be regarded by philosophical reasoning as an unnatural state of affairs or as mere chaos. War must be understood as a form of the state's activity. Kant's view leaves us with a conception of the principles of peace that ought to be followed by men and a hope that the working of providence will soon be fully manifest in the actualities of history. Hegel's view indicates that the possibility of peace must depend not upon a faith in the ultimate order of history, but upon the analysis of the structure of one of its specific moments – war. War, for Hegel is a moment in the development of social consciousness and action; war is an activity of the state as an independent nation. ' A nation ', Hegel asserts, ' does

[29] *Perpetual Peace*, ed. Lewis White Beck (New York, 1957), p. 24.
[30] *Ibid*. pp. 17 and 46.
[31] See Preface, p. 10 and § 29.
[32] *Philosophy of Right*, § 346.

not begin by being a state. The transition from a family, a horde, a clan, a multitude, &c., to political conditions is the realization of the Idea in the form of that nation.'[33] Hegel, following his dictum that every philosopher is a child of his own time,[34] terminates his account of the state with the conception of the state as a politically sovereign nation. The Idea exists in the form of a world of nations related to each other through the contingencies that surround their cycles of war and peace. Kant offers us directly a theory of peace. Hegel offers us directly a theory of war. Kant's theory, although admirable in design, is under-pinned by a view of history that in principle forbids a theory of war. War remains a sojourn in the irrational. It asks human consciousness to overcome a mode of its activity without understanding the roots in its own structure from which the activity it is to overcome has stemmed.[35] The question now to be faced is whether Hegel's theory of war and the metaphysics of history from which it derives can engender a theory of peace.

From Hegel's position any theory of peace would need to follow from an understanding of the phenomenon upon which war is based. War must be seen as having its roots somewhere in the very structure of human consciousness. Karl Jaspers in *The Future of Mankind* states:

Fighting – risking one's life so as either to meet force with force or else to use force to win power and booty – is a primordial phenomenon of human life. The primordial element is the fierce fighting spirit. Unleashed, it engenders the self-transcending lust of flinging one's life away and the savagery that rates other lives no higher, vents itself in pillage and rape after victory, and finally abates in the climactic feeling of power: to spare the conquered and let him serve as a slave. This abatement led Hegel to interpret the productive meaning of life-and-death struggles. *The warrior is a human type, but not everyone is a warrior.*[36]

In the full context of this statement Jaspers regards the warrior as a particular way of engaging in the master–slave relationship which Hegel portrays in the *Phenomenology of Mind*.[37] His statement captures the point that follows from Hegel's treatment of war – that war exists not because of man's inability to conceive the principles whereby to organize for peace, but because the warrior is a specific way in which men relate to their own existence. Any solution to the problem of war must rest on a solution to the problem of warriors; and this is particularly difficult since the style of life of the warrior is rooted in one of the basic structures of consciousness, the master–slave.

---

[33] *Philosophy of Right*, § 349.   [34] *Ibid.* p. 11.

[35] It is interesting to note that Kant in the *Critique of Judgment* makes comments similar to Hegel's regarding the stagnation of nations during prolonged periods of peace that are quite in contrast to his approach in *Perpetual Peace*. See the *Critique of Judgment*, sect. 22 (83). For remarks on these passages, see Albert William Levi, *Humanism and Politics : Studies in the Relationship of Power and Value in the Western Tradition* (Bloomington, 1969), pp. 268–9.

[36] Chicago, 1951, p. 45 (italics mine).

[37] (B.), IV, A. ' Independence and Dependence of Self-consciousness : Lordship and Bondage.'

In his theory of the warrior Jaspers further draws out a point that illuminates Hegel. Jaspers maintains that the warrior depends upon the phenomenon of self-sacrifice.[38] Hegel points to this in his discussion of the military as a class. The military, Hegel maintains, are men who realize the nature of their own freedom through courage and their courage is manifest in their willingness to sacrifice themselves for the sovereignty of their state. Hegel states: ' The work of courage is to actualize this final end, and the means to this end is the sacrifice of personal actuality. This form of experience thus contains the harshness of extreme contradictions: a self-sacrifice which yet is the real existence of one's freedom . . .'[39] It follows from Hegel's view that war exists not because nations reach an impasse in their relations with each other; war exists because armies exist. The military exists because the warrior is a human type and the warrior is a human type because the act of self-sacrifice, of meeting force with force on behalf of an ideal, is one of the ways men apprehend themselves as free agents. The genuine threat to peace is not that diplomatic relations will break down and the technical problems of such negotiations will be taken up in the physical conflict of war. The genuine threat to peace is the fact that the warrior is a type of life. Wars are the result of the frustrations that peace brings to the warrior in his drive to act out the freedom of his own being. When such frustrations are sufficiently felt by the warriors of two nations, the actual conditions for war are met and the technical, diplomatic justification will soon be found.[40]

If, in the *Phenomenology of Mind*, Hegel has shown the master–slave to be one of the fundamental ways whereby human consciousness structures itself and realizes its own freedom,[41] and if the *Philosophy of Right* has shown that the warrior is the type upon which the state's ability to make war depends, then an end to war lies in a transformation of the warrior's existence. The realization of freedom that the warrior experiences in his act of self-sacrifice, of risking his life by meeting force with force, must be carried to a new form in which the same goal is reached but the violence of its means is overcome. It is not enough to encourage all men to adopt the slave side of the master–slave relation and advocate the realization of their freedom in their work as does the conquered slave.[42] To advocate the replacement of the evil of war with the good of work, to view work as a moral equivalent of war, is to misconstrue the nature of the warrior and view him simply as an energetic man. The warrior must be taken

---

[38] See *The Future of Mankind*, ch. 4.

[39] *Philosophy of Right*, § 328. See also the Addition to § 327.

[40] As Hegel points out, the honor or interest of the state may be seen by it as at stake in any of its dealings with other states. See *ibid*. § 334.

[41] See *Phenomenology of Mind*, p. 233. For a discussion of some of the perspectives from which Hegel's master–slave relationship can be viewed and some of the difficulties of developing social hypotheses from it, see George Armstrong Kelly, ' Notes on Hegel's " Lordship and Bondage " ', *Review of Metaphysics*, XIX (1966), 780–802.

[42] See *Phenomenology of Mind*, p. 238.

more seriously. If he were simply an energetic man we could have expected warriors long ago to have turned to organized sports and dangerous occupations. The courage of the warrior is not simply the courage of risk but the courage of risking one's life for the sake of an ethical ideal.[43] Any attempt to transform the warrior must account for this ethical element.

Given the direction in which Hegel's account of war takes us, it is difficult to believe that peace depends upon the institution of a set of principles for the actions of nations. In the realm of practical political affairs it is difficult to believe that the United Nations can ultimately be more than organized good will unless we come to grips with the roots of the activity it is dedicated to overcome. Once it is seen that war is grounded in one of the ways consciousness structures itself, in a type of life, the problem of peace becomes one of the redirecting of warriors. To formulate prescriptions for peace apart from the realization that war is not a lapse in the natural state of affairs but is an integral part of their structure is to foster illusion. Hegel's theory, by focusing on the analysis of war rather than advancing prescriptions for peace, does in no way glorify war. His philosophy, being in largest terms the portrayal of the self-alterations of consciousness, would allow for the warrior to be superseded. The grounds for him to be superseded lie in Hegel's placement of art, religion, and philosophy as forms of mind that lie beyond the state.[44] The state to which the life of the warrior is tied has above it the forms of art, religion, and philosophy which could, like the state, be said to entail types of lives, the task of which is the apprehension of other human types. Thus from the perspective of Hegel's philosophy it is in the activity of artists, religious men, and philosophers that the possibility of comprehending and transforming the warrior lies. It does not lie with politicians. The solution to the problem of peace, which is properly the solution to the problem of warriors, cannot lie with those whose existence is tied to the form of the state.

In conclusion, I have intended to show that Hegel neither endorses war nor simply reflects the fact of its existence. For Hegel, war, as anything else actual, is something to be understood philosophically and cannot be regarded as something accidental. His approach in the *Phenomenology of Mind* is to show the relationship of war to human consciousness and in the *Philosophy of Right* to show its relationship to the state. Hegel's insistence on showing the role war plays in human affairs reveals the difficulty of regarding the elimination of war as a matter of correctly conceiving the principles of peace and organizing around them. War exists not because of the weakness of our conception of peace nor our slowness to adopt international order. Our inability to carry the process of law

---

[43] For an analysis of the mode of being of the warrior, see J. Glenn Gray, *The Warriors : Reflections on Men in Battle* (New York, 1959), esp. ' Conclusion '.

[44] See Ernst Cassirer, *The Myth of the State* (New Haven, 1946), p. 274.

beyond the perimeters of nations rests on the existence of warriors. The warrior's style of life constitutes a particular orientation toward the problem of human freedom which has its roots in the master–slave relationship wherein consciousness discovers one of the fundamental ways of structuring itself. Hegel's philosophy offers no specific solution to the problem of how the warrior's act of self-risk that lies at the base of war can be overcome. Hegel's analysis, however, if correct, does show that if war is to be eliminated, efforts must be directed to the development of alternative ways of relating to the state than the warrior's.

Principle and prejudice in
Hegel's philosophy of history[1]

W. H. WALSH

In this essay I want to approach Hegel's philosophy of history from a point of view which is different from that of most modern critics: I want to consider it as philosophical history rather than philosophical meditation on history. Hegel began his lectures by distinguishing three ways of writing history (his own manuscript contains the words: ' Ich unterscheide dreierlei Weisen des Geschichtsschreibens '),[2] and one of these is what he calls ' philosophical '. Philosophical history cannot be written without benefit of philosophy, but equally it does not itself belong within philosophy. It is, if I may insist on the obvious, itself a form of history, an attempt to present the history of the world from the philosophical point of view. Hegel's course had the title ' Lectures on the philosophy of world history ', but this designation is misleading if it suggests, as a similar title might today, second-order reflection on the activity of *composing* a history of the world. There is in the lectures a certain amount of second-order reflection on what world history *involves*, but the bulk of the course is given over to a first-hand account of the history of the world as Hegel saw it. This account, which despite the generality of the subject often goes into considerable detail, is of interest for its own sake as well as for the light it throws on Hegel's philosophy.

1 For the purposes of this discussion I shall refer very largely to J. Sibree's translation of Hegel's lectures, published originally in 1857 and made from a reprint of the text of the second German edition, which was produced by the philosopher's son Karl Hegel in 1840. Karl Hegel's text corrects that of the first edition, by Eduard Gans (1837). Sibree translated the prefaces of both the original editors, and each explains the principles on which he composed his text. It seems clear that, as later editors have alleged (see in particular the remarks of Georg Lasson, reproduced in Johannes Hoffmeister's volume *Die Vernunft in der Geschichte* (Hamburg, 1955), pp. 272 ff.), neither Gans nor Karl Hegel was altogether competent or even altogether scrupulous as an editor. Gans by his own admission wrote out the entire volume in his own words, though on the basis of manuscripts of Hegel's own as well as of students' notes; Karl Hegel altered the language and transposed passages arbitrarily in order to put in new material which he thought his predecessor had mistakenly left out. How much they compressed the available matter can be seen if their versions are compared with those in the Philosophische Bibliothek edited by Hoffmeister and Lasson respectively. It seems to me even so that they reproduced the essentials of what Hegel had to say, and that their work can therefore be safely used in a general discussion such as this. As for Sibree's translation, I take it to be free, idiomatic and generally reliable. I shall indicate a few points where I differ from it below.

2 *Die Vernunft in der Geschichte*, p. 3. Karl Hegel has ' der Arten, die Geschichte zu betrachten, gibt es überhaupt drei ' and this is rendered by Sibree by the phrase ' methods of treating history '. Philosophical meditation on history is a method of treating history, but not a way of writing it.

World history, according to Hegel, consists of the transactions of world-historical peoples, which play their part successively on the historical scene. It begins with the nations of the Oriental world, China, India and Persia; proceeds through the contrasted worlds of the Greeks and the Romans, and finds its culmination in the Germanic world of modern times. The theme which gives it unity is that of the development of the reality and the consciousness of freedom. The Oriental world, especially in its original form in China, had a rational structure of a sort and through that was able to provide conditions in which men could live, to some degree, on the human level; it was, however, a world in which no importance was attached to subjective freedom, with the result that its members had no sense of making their own lives. In the conditions of ancient Greece this deficiency was in part overcome, for free men at any rate (Hegel is never tired of emphasizing that Greek civilization rested on slavery). But though the individual counted for altogether more in Greece than in any Oriental country, he did not, during the main period of Greek history, live a fully self-determined existence. His life was governed by moral and social rules which he inherited and took over uncritically rather than imposed on himself. Morality as we know it became possible only after the Sophists subjected accepted ways of going on to criticism; it was in fact invented by Socrates.[3] But its invention was fatal to Greek society and Greek civilization, which collapsed and had to be replaced by the dour world of the Romans. The Roman state was stronger than the Greek in providing conditions of objective freedom; it was better organized and in particular it had a rational system of law. But though it thus did some justice to the claims of personality, it failed to acknowledge them explicitly. It was only with the advent of Christianity that the value of the individual soul was insisted on, and only at the Reformation that the right of the individual to determine his own life according to rational principles was fully recognized. The Germanic peoples of Hegel's own day were thought by him to enjoy conditions which, taken as a whole, combined objective and subjective freedom: that is to say, put men in a position to live orderly and civilized lives, and at the same time let them feel that they were doing so not as a result of external direction but through their own efforts. It was not Hegel's thesis, as I read him, that the ideal of free self-development was fully realized in the modern world. But he did think it was realized there as never before in human history, and believed in effect that world history was a rational process because it led up to this result.

If we now consider the developments just sketched as Hegel himself saw them, namely as crucial stages in the overall history of humanity, certain comments immediately suggest themselves. I shall say nothing at this stage about Hegel's assumption that world history can be viewed as a single process; that

---

[3] G. W. F. Hegel, *Lectures on the Philosophy of History*, trans. J. Sibree, Bohn's Libraries edition (London, 1858), p. 281.

assumption was, after all, common at the time and is far from abandoned even today. But I think it is worth remarking that he regarded history not just as a unity, but as a unity of a special kind. It got its unity from the fact that it consisted of a series of attempts, by no means independent one of another and increasingly successful as time went on, to achieve a certain desirable result, what Hegel called the realization of freedom. In a previous discussion of this subject * I called attention to the *moral* nature of the goal of history as seen by Hegel and other speculative philosophers; here I want to point out something which concerns not its form but its content. History as Hegel explains it involves the progressive realization of what may be called the European ideal, and written history at this level is in consequence the success story of modern European man. What is more, ' modern European man ' in this context means man as he is, or rather was, to be found in the Germanic countries, as opposed to what Hegel called the ' Romanic ' nations, France, Italy and Spain. The European ideal as Hegel interprets it is the ideal of protestant Europe; the catholic sector was, in his view, precluded by its commitment to an authoritarian church from doing full justice to subjective freedom, despite the important connection between such freedom and Christian conceptions. Hence world history makes sense, for Hegel, not, as is commonly said, because it culminates in the Prussian state, but because it leads to the wider society of northern Europe of which Prussia was a part, a society which embraced Britain and Scandinavia as well as large parts of Germany. It was in this society, and only in this society, that man was able to realize his potentialities and so to be truly himself.

It is worth looking at this question from the other side, by noticing what Hegel excludes from world history. His section in the introduction entitled ' The Natural Context or the Geographical Basis of World History ' is of particular interest in this connection. On the first page of this section he tells us that ' the locality of world-historical peoples ' [4] is confined to the temperate zone. ' In the extreme zones man cannot come to free movement; cold and heat are here too powerful to allow Spirit to build up a world for itself.' [5] The ' true theatre of history ' [6] is in fact a highly restricted portion of the earth's surface, the more so because only the northern temperate zone comes seriously into the reckoning. Only in that area does the earth ' present itself in a continental form, and has a broad breast, as the Greeks say '.[7] There are important contrasts between the flora and fauna of north and south, Hegel adds, though how this is supposed to bear on the possibility of world history is not evident.

Hegel now passes to the division between the Old and the New Worlds. The New World may well have emerged from the sea at the same time as the Old,

---

* *Editor's note* – Cf. W. H. Walsh, *An Introduction to Philosophy of History*, 3rd ed. (London, 1967), especially ch. VII.

4 *Philosophy of History*, p. 83.   5 *Ibid.* p. 84.
6 *Ibid.*   7 *Ibid.*

but in all other respects it is markedly inferior. Hegel knew of the existence of the native American civilizations of Mexico and Peru, but dismissed them as unimportant. The information we have about them, he said, ' imports nothing more than that this culture was an entirely natural one, which must expire as soon as Spirit approached it. America has always shown itself physically and psychically powerless, and still shows itself so '.[8] The term ' America ' in this connection means the land of the American Indians, the aboriginal population of the continent. These aborigines were, it appears, weak both in physique and in intelligence, and Negroes were imported into America because the natives were simply unable to perform the tasks which Europeans required of them. Negroes were capable of becoming clergymen, doctors, etc. as well as labourers whereas, according to an English traveller quoted by Hegel, ' only a single native was known to him whose intellect was sufficiently developed to enable him to study ' and he ' died soon after the beginning, through excessive brandy-drinking '.[9]

It is not surprising in these circumstances that Hegel declares that ' what takes place in America is but an emanation of Europe '.[10] For the purposes of world history America can be treated as an extension of Europe and nothing more. I should perhaps emphasize that this verdict is intended to apply to history up to Hegel's own time, and not to anything that has happened subsequently. Hegel makes some acute remarks about political conditions in contemporary North America, the upshot of which is that the lack of a definite frontier to the west prevents it from being a fully-formed state. In a rash moment he permits himself to prophesy that America is ' the land of the future, where, in the ages that lie before us, the burden of the World's History is due to reveal itself – perhaps in a contest between North and South America '.[11] But strictly such prophecies are not open to him: on the basis of the knowledge available he could not have said whether future developments in America were likely to involve a new phase of spirit, distinct from the European phase, or not. We can be fairly confident all the same that he would want, if alive today, to treat the civilization of North America as fundamentally a product of the Old World. What he might have made of twentieth-century South America is another and more interesting question.

Passing now from the New World to the Old, ' the scene of the World's History ', Hegel begins with the astonishing declaration that the three continents that compose it ' have an essential relation to each other, and constitute a totality '[12] because they all lie around a single sea, the Mediterranean. Without this feature ' the history of the world could not be conceived: it would be like

---

[8] *Ibid.* p. 85. The Bohn edition misprints ' national ' for ' natural '.

[9] *Ibid.* p. 86.

[10] *Ibid.*

[11] *Ibid.* p. 90. I have substituted ' is due to ' for Sibree's ' shall ' (the German is ' *soll* ')

[12] *Ibid.* p. 91.

ancient Rome or Athens without the forum, where all the life of the city came together '.[13] Civilized life developed round this centre, and it marked an epoch in human history when Julius Caesar opened up the area beyond the Alps. Hegel points out that the Mediterranean embraces the civilizations not only of Greece and Rome, but also of Carthage and Alexandria and Syria, with their connections with Mecca and Medina. But he makes only brief and inexplicit references to the farther parts of Asia. At one point he says that ' the extensive tract of eastern Asia is severed from the process of general historical development, and has no share in it '.[14] A little later we read that ' what lies on the far side of Syria constitutes the beginning of world history, which yet remains outside the course of its development without movement '.[15] I take these cryptic words to mean that the East impinges on history but does not strictly participate in it. Hegel's defence of this view can be found in his detailed picture of China and India as fundamentally static societies: they begin human history but are no real part of it because they do not change in any important particulars.[16] But even if this were true the same could not be said, on Hegel's own evidence, of Persia, which also belonged to the Oriental world. ' With the Persian empire we first enter on continuous history. The Persians are the first historical people; Persia was the first empire which passed away.' [17] The Persian Empire certainly extended to the Mediterranean, but the latter was in no sense at its centre, only at its periphery.

After this attempt to demonstrate the unity of the Old World Hegel proceeds to a survey of its various parts. He devotes most space to Africa, perhaps because this is the only point in his lectures where that continent gets serious consideration. His treatment is, to put it mildly, not very sympathetic. He begins by remarking that geographically Africa falls into the three parts: the upland south of the Sahara desert, which was in Hegel's time almost unknown to Europeans; the Nile valley, and the northern coast territory from Morocco to Tripoli. This last part ' was intended to be and had to be attached to Europe ': [18] it looks towards Europe, and ' the interests of Europe have always striven to get a footing in it '.[19] As for Egypt, this certainly has a part in history, but not, in Hegel's view, as part of the history of Africa. It belongs, odd as this may seem, to the history of the Persian Empire, and thus ' to the passage of the human mind from its eastern to its western phase '.[20] There remains Africa proper, and about this Hegel pronounces with confidence, despite what he said before about the difficulty of getting information on the subject.

13 *Ibid.*

14 *Ibid.*

15 *Die Vernunft in der Geschichte*, p. 211. This passage is not in Sibree.

16 Compare Sibree, p. 180, where the translation should read ' The Chinese and Indian empires can enter the context of history only potentially and as viewed by us.'

17 *Philosophy of History*, p. 180.

18 *Ibid.* p. 97. The German is ' *sollte und musste* '. I have changed Sibree's translation.

19 *Ibid.*   20 *Ibid.* p. 103.

' The peculiarly African character ', he begins,

is difficult to comprehend, for the very reason that in reference to it, we must quite give up the principle which naturally accompanies all *our* ideas – the category of universality. In negro life the characteristic point is the fact that consciousness has not yet attained to the realisation of any substantial objective existence – as, for example, God or Law – in which the interest of man's volition is involved and in which he realises his own being.[21]

The African, on this account of the matter, has no sense of anything to which he must conform his will, and this affects his religion, his morals and his political life. Religion, says Hegel, ' begins with the consciousness that there is something higher than man '.[22] But the African has no such consciousness, and religious practices in Africa are accordingly magical practices, through which man seeks to control or manipulate the forces of nature. Negroes do indeed recognize the existence of supernatural powers, and think of them as embodied in fetishes. But these are simply projections of their own arbitrary imagination, as is shown by the fact that the fetish is discarded if it fails to produce its expected results. Hegel mentions one feature of African religion which seems to point to something beyond the will of the individual, worship of the dead, only to add that here too ' the power in question remains substantially always in bondage to the living subject. Death itself is looked upon by the negroes as no universal natural law; even this, they think, proceeds from evil-disposed magicians '.[23] The powers of the dead are thought of as manageable in the same way as other supernatural powers, and this state of affairs is quite inconsistent with the religious attitude proper.

If man recognizes no higher being than himself, ' it follows that he has no respect for himself ',[24] with fatal results for his morals. Hegel's picture of the moral life of the native Africans could scarcely be blacker. Lacking any conception of a higher being, and with no knowledge of the immortality of the soul, they assign no value to humanity. Hence ' tyranny is regarded as no wrong, and cannibalism is looked on as quite customary and proper '.[25] Slavery too is a natural part of African life, and excites no special repugnance. ' Parents sell their children, and conversely children their parents, as either has the opportunity.' [26] It is true that Africans seem to have some virtues: for example, they display great courage in war. But Hegel sees in this ' not so much a despising of death as a want of regard for life ': [27] it is all of a piece with the general ' contempt of humanity ' [28] shown in this society.

It is hardly surprising after this to learn that the whole nature of the African

[21] *Ibid.* p. 97.
[22] *Ibid.*
[23] *Ibid.* p. 99.
[24] *Ibid.*
[25] *Ibid.*
[26] *Ibid.* p. 100.
[27] *Ibid.*
[28] *Ibid.*

set-up precludes there being any political constitution. There can be no constitution, as Hegel understands the word, where the rule of law is totally absent, as it is here. ' The standpoint of humanity at this grade is sensuous volition with energy of will ',[29] and the word translated here as ' volition ' is *Willkür*, which always has about it the suggestion of arbitrariness. It follows that such political arrangements as there are in Africa must depend on force and mere personal self-assertion. A chief will impose his rule as best he can, but his subjects will always strive to throw off his yoke. They have no proper respect for a king as king, but will if occasion arises have him put to death. In these conditions the office of executioner ' is regarded as of the highest consideration ':[30] the king uses it to put suspected persons to death, and his opponents in their turn may use it to despatch him. Hegel remarks at this point on a feature of negro life which he regards as wholly inimical to settled political conditions, its fanaticism.

An English traveller states that when a war is determined on in Ashantee, solemn ceremonies precede it: among other things the bones of the king's mother are laved with human blood. As a prelude to the war, the king ordains an assault on his own metropolis, as if to excite the due degree of frenzy. The king sent word to the English Hutcheson: ' Christian, take care, and watch well over your family. The messenger of death has drawn his sword and will strike the neck of many Ashantees; when the drum sounds it is the death signal for multitudes. Come to the king, if you can, and fear nothing for yourself.' The drum beat, and a terrible carnage was begun; all who came in the way of the frenzied negroes in the streets were stabbed.[31]

These people are normally quiet, but when aroused can suddenly become beside themselves, whereupon ' plunder and carnage run riot '.[32] They live in fact in the state of nature, a state which Hegel describes as one of ' absolute and thorough injustice '.[33]

Africa, says Hegel, ' is no historical part of the world; it has no movement or development to exhibit '.[34] Spirit exists in Africa only in an undeveloped natural state; we have here the possibility of human life proper, but no more than that. And this is fundamentally because rational principles have no real hold in this type of society; everything depends on passion and caprice. Hegel does not say that Africa never can be part of history. But clearly he thought that it could do so only if radically transformed, perhaps as a result of contact with Europe.

Hegel proceeds next to consider Asia, which he treats altogether more briefly in this introductory section. After distinguishing the main physical features of the continent – the massive central uplands, the river plains of China, India and Mesopotamia and what he revealingly calls Anterior [35] Asia, which comprises

---

29 *Ibid.*, omitting ' mere ' before ' sensuous '. 30 *Ibid.* p. 102.

31 *Ibid.* 32 *Ibid.*

33 *Ibid.* p. 103. 34 *Ibid.*

35 ' *Vorderaisen* '. For Hegel ' Europe presents, on the whole, the centre . . . of the Old World ' (*ibid.* p. 104).

Syria, Asia Minor and Arabia – he points out that the economy of the first is pastoral, that of the second agricultural and industrial, whilst the third has some share in commerce and navigation. ' Patriarchal independence is strictly bound up with the first condition of society; property and the relation of lord and serf with the second; civil freedom with the third.' [36] The peoples of the Asian uplands generally lead a ' calm habitual life ', but are also ' swayed by a powerful impulse leading them to change their aspect as nations ' [37] from time to time; as a result of this, although they have not themselves ' attained an historical character, the beginning of history may be traced to them '.[38] Hegel says no more about them at this point, but passes on at once to the inhabitants of the plain, who strike him as more intrinsically interesting just because ' agriculture . . . demands foresight and solicitude for the future ' [39] and so fosters a more enduring and more rational set-up. However, he finds that the peoples of China, India and Babylonia have remained shut up in themselves, the sea having had little or no influence on their culture, and concludes from this that they can have a relation to the rest of history only ' through their being sought out, and their character investigated by others '.[40] In other words, these countries play a part in history only because of the exploratory enterprises of Europeans. As for Anterior Asia, this combines the physical features of both the other parts of the continent and has a special relation to Europe, in so far as it exports to Europe ideas which it originates but cannot itself develop. This area sees ' the beginning of all religious and all political principles ', but ' the development of these happens first in Europe '.[41] Hegel must have forgotten about the Moslem religion, which he elsewhere treats with some sympathy, in writing these arrogant words.

The geographical background to European history is dealt with still more briefly, and perhaps the only points worth notice here are, first, Hegel's comment that the Slavonic peoples appear only late on the historical scene and retain their connections with Asia; and second, his perceptive observation of the different part played by the sea in European and Asiatic life. In India religion positively forbids sea voyages, whereas the European state could not be what it is apart from its connection with the sea.[42] Whatever charges of parochialism we can bring against Hegel, we cannot accuse him of having looked at history with the eyes of a middle European, though it was in that part of the continent rather than near any coast that he was born and brought up.

Enough has now been said to document my main thesis that Hegel looks at world history from a point of view which is distinctively, indeed aggressively,

[36] *Ibid.* p. 105.   [37] *Ibid.*
[38] *Ibid.*
[39] *Ibid.*
[40] *Ibid.* p. 106.   [41] *Ibid.* (emended translation).
[42] *Die Vernunft in der Geschichte*, p. 241. This passage is **not** in Sibree.

European, and appeals to European standards and ideals in judging the significance of historical conditions and happenings. If more support were needed it
could readily be found in the part of his lectures where he deals with the Oriental
world in detail. He is certainly interested in that world and anxious to find out
more about it, but he sees its history as primarily and properly no more than a
prelude to the history of Europe. Hence the harsh judgements he passes on the
'servile consciousness'[43] of the Chinese and the moral depravity of the
Hindus;[44] hence again the hostile account of the Indian caste system and the
failure to offer any serious treatment of Indian philosophy and religion, whose
ideal of the total annihilation of ordinary consciousness struck him as merely
escapist.[45] But here we touch on points which connect with Hegel's being not
just a European but a northern European and a protestant, and about this we
need more documentation.

The individual heroes of Hegel's history of the world, if it can be said to have
any, are Socrates and Luther. Pericles, Julius Caesar and Alexander the Great
are all mentioned with respect, but none of them has quite the importance of the
two great teachers. Socrates, as we have already mentioned, was thought by Hegel
to have invented morality; that is, to have insisted that moral principles be freely
subscribed to rather than passively accepted. Luther was responsible for putting
an end to what Hegel calls somewhere 'the long, eventful and terrible night of
the Middle Ages',[46] a period whose 'life and spirit' were constituted by 'infinite
falsehood'.[47] He thus achieved substantial, if not complete, recognition for the
principle of free personality which was implicit in the Christian religion, and in
so doing marked an epoch of major importance in the development of human
history.

Hegel devoted ample space to the Middle Ages in giving his lectures; his
picture of them is well defined, if not very attractive. He begins by describing the
workings of the feudal system, which he sees as a series of essentially private
arrangements, put in the place of a system of universal law which had prevailed
briefly under Charlemagne. The 'noble and rational constitution' of the latter
was 'superficially induced – an *a priori* constitution like that which Napoleon
gave to Spain'[48]; it was not surprising that it disappeared with Charlemagne
himself. Men at this time were not capable of appreciating the importance of
guaranteed rights, and in their absence they could only make private arrangements to protect themselves, by submitting to the authority of powerful individuals. Hegel writes as if there were no true state in the Middle Ages, only
an aggregate of particular individuals, more or less personally powerful. This
account of the medieval state is complemented by an account of the medieval

[43] *Philosophy of History*, p. 145. [44] *Ibid*. pp. 165–6.
[45] *Ibid*. p. 155.
[46] *Ibid*. p. 428.
[47] *Ibid*. p. 380. [48] *Ibid*. p. 383.

church. Hegel represents the latter as having reacted against the confusions which prevailed in the eleventh and twelfth centuries by withdrawing into itself and putting its house in order. The result of this move, carried out by Pope Gregory VII, was to transform the church itself into a powerful institution on the secular plane. At the same time the doctrines professed by the medieval church were in Hegel's view thoroughly unsatisfactory. The design of the mass ' involves the error of isolating the sensuous phase ' [49]: Christ is taken as being present in the Host apart from the disposition of the faithful. The sharp separation between clergy and laity puts ' the highest of human blessings in the hands of others '.[50] Faith in these circumstances becomes ' a matter of external legislation ', and ' compulsion and the stake ' [51] follow. The three vows of Chastity, Poverty and Obedience preached by the church are inimical to good morals. Society rests on respect for the marriage relation and on diligent activity by its members; both were degraded in medieval teaching. And though an individual must obey the moral law as the embodiment of rationality, his obedience to it must not be unthinking or blind. Yet it was exactly this kind of obedience which was recommended as pleasing to God, according to Hegel's account.[52]

The feudal system was already giving way to monarchy as the Middle Ages came to an end, and the destruction of the medieval structure was completed by the Reformation. Hegel emphasizes what may seem relatively trivial matters: he speaks of the ' slavish deference to authority ' [53] shown by the pious, denounces their credulity, declares that their moral teaching is such that ' in actual life, nothing is left . . . but avoidance, renunciation, inactivity '.[54] He also serves up a lot of stale stuff about the general corruption of the church, which was not, he assures his audience, ' an accidental phenomenon', but ' a native growth ', arising, surprisingly, from the fact that ' the specific and definite embodiment of Deity which it recognises, is sensuous '.[55] But despite this he seizes firmly on what from his point of view was the all-important aspect of this process: the fact that it put an end to the sharp distinction between church and state. It was and remained part of catholic teaching, according to Hegel, that secular life is irretrievably corrupt, the church alone being holy. Against that the reformers proclaimed that the secular sphere too is ' capable of being an embodiment of truth '. ' It is now perceived that morality and justice in the state are also divine and commanded by God, and that in point of substance there is nothing higher and more sacred.' [56] These are strong words, but like the famous claim that ' the state is the divine idea as it exists on earth ',[57] they perhaps suggest more than their author intended. Hegel was not saying that the state is a sort of divinity, which deserves worship;

[49] *Ibid.* p. 392.
[50] *Ibid.* p. 393.
[51] *Ibid.*
[52] See *ibid.* pp. 395–6.
[53] *Ibid.* p. 430.
[54] *Ibid.* p. 431.
[55] *Ibid.* p. 429.
[56] *Ibid.* p. 440.
[57] *Ibid.* p. 41.

his point is that it must be seen as the product of rational activity, brought about by men's efforts and embodying their ideals. It is not the case, on this view, that right and wrong depend solely on the pronouncements of God or of his self-styled ministers; human reason can discern what is true or false in morals, and must do so if the central moral principle of autonomy of the will is to be preserved. The repudiation of ecclesiastical claims by the reformers was thus seen by Hegel as a move towards a state of affairs in which men achieve self-determination. To put it in his own words: ' This is the essence of the Reformation: Man is in his very nature destined to be free.' [58]

It must be admitted that Hegel seldom mentions the catholic religion without denouncing it. But he can also, on occasion, point out unattractive aspects of protestantism, as when he speaks of the ' self-tormenting disposition ' [59] which became characteristic of even ' the most simple souls ' as they grew ' accustomed in painful introspection to observe the most secret workings of the heart '.[60] Nor did he claim that the Reformation of itself brought in the golden age of liberalism: he mentioned the Anabaptists and commented that ' the world was not yet ripe for a transformation of its political condition as a consequence of ecclesiastical reformation '.[61] The Reformation was only a step in mankind's progress towards the goal of history. But it was a vitally necessary step all the same, which explains the stress Hegel placed on it and his tendency to understand the European ideal in protestant terms.

At this point I shall abandon exposition and turn to comment. And first I should like to ask what happens to the old charge that Hegel writes history *a priori* when we approach his work as I have in the foregoing pages.

The complaint that Hegel construes history *a priori* is part of a very general criticism of his philosophy. It is alleged that he thought that the fundamental truth about reality was embodied in the categories of the Hegelian logic, and that given knowledge of these categories it would be possible to deduce truths about particular things. On this view Hegel could have known the plot, and indeed the details, of history without consulting a single empirical source. Whether in fact he was committed to any such absurdity I shall leave without discussion now. On this occasion I want to point out that in practice he made a very different use of philosophical ideas in writing world history. He used them not to supply details but rather to set up criteria by which to judge the importance and memorability of historical events. His central notion of spirit as involving activity which is at once self-contained and self-directed gave him the idea of a state of affairs which would be morally and philosophically satisfactory; he supposed, in part on the basis of his general philosophical principles, that history could be seen as the

[58] *Ibid*. p. 434.
[60] *Ibid*. p. 442.
[59] *Ibid*. p. 443.
[61] *Ibid*. p. 436.

progressive bringing about of such a state of affairs. But quite apart from this supposition he employed the idea as a standard by which to estimate different epochs: he looked at the life and achievements of past peoples with this idea in mind, and was able to command a clear view of them just because of that fact. There was, however, no question here of deducing facts of any sort from the idea: on the contrary, the latter could come into play only when historical evidence was forthcoming. Hegel certainly made considerable use of his philosophy in writing his history of the world; he says himself that satisfactory history ' presupposes not only a disciplined faculty of abstraction, but an intimate acquaintance with the Idea '.[62] But he would surely not have denied that it also presupposes the existence of historical data. What Hegel says about parts of the world like India and Africa shows that he had consulted a variety of travellers' accounts of conditions there. He may not have treated these accounts very critically, or again he may have picked and chosen among the observations they offered in a prejudiced manner. But he nevertheless knew something of what they contained, and was aware that without such knowledge no sort of history would be possible.

It is no proper objection to Hegel that he came to history with preconceptions, provided that these concern only what is of ultimate historical importance. Quite unphilosophical historians do just this, as I have tried to show elsewhere.* But of course there are preconceptions and preconceptions. And here we must consider a second and, on the face of things, more serious criticism of Hegel, that the principles he used in constructing his philosophical history were no more than vulgar prejudices. I have already said that Hegel's philosophy of history could be described as the success story of modern European man; a less kind way of putting it would be to say that he arrogantly assumes the superiority of white Anglo–Saxon protestants. The term ' Anglo–Saxon ' would doubtless have to be taken fairly broadly here, but it is not all that far from what Hegel meant by ' germanisch '.

Let me begin my discussion of what could be an emotionally-charged subject by making clear that, whatever his faults, Hegel was not any kind of a racist. It is true of course that he had a poor opinion of the abilities of the American Indians, and that the picture he offers of Negro society in Africa is far from attractive. But he has, so far as I know, no tendency to divide mankind into superior and inferior races, and indeed he rarely makes use of the term ' race ' itself. He is fond of contrasting modern Europeans with the age-old Chinese, just as he elsewhere contrasts the classical Greeks with the Persians they fought against; but neither in the one case nor in the other does he speak of racial differences. The contrasts as he sees them are between different peoples or

[62] *Ibid.* p. 67.

* *Editor's note* – Cf. Walsh, *Introduction to Philosophy of History*, pp. 169 ff.

societies. The history of every people is the expression of a distinct national spirit. Different nations contribute to world history in different degrees, and some succeed in making virtually no contribution at all. But this, so far as I can discover, is a matter of fact, not of destiny; all at least start with an equal chance.

It might be said in reply that, so far from reflecting credit on Hegel, my remarks simply emphasize his shortcomings, since they show that he unconsciously assimilated men of other cultures to himself, and in so doing failed to pay them the compliment of examining them for their own sake. In Hegel's day Herder and others had begun to insist on the diversity of human nature and the independent interest of distinct civilizations; Hegel, despite the wide sweep of his history, shows few signs of having taken Herder's main point. Hegel was aware of historical diversity to the extent of recognizing and indeed emphasizing the many important differences between, say, life in the Oriental world and life in early nineteenth-century Europe; he nevertheless thinks of the former as *prefiguring* the latter. The real hero of his history is after all spirit, and by this term he means something which is active in all cultures and peoples, something which has to do with humanity. The different manifestations of spirit are indeed distinct, but this is not to say that they cannot be seen as steps in a single process. Hegel was quite sure that they could be so seen, and that the process reached its culmination in modern Europe.

I think it is true that Hegel retained something of the eighteenth-century belief in a common human nature, and that he had little use for the extreme historicism, or historical relativism, which was coming into fashion in his later years under the influence of Romantic historians (compare with this his attacks on the school of historical law in the *Philosophy of Right*). It is not, of course, self-evident that he was wrong to take this view. But whether he was or not, is there not something suspect in the conception of human nature he works with? When we come down to fundamentals, was it not simple prejudice on his part to assume that man fulfils his potentialities when he lives as he does in protestant Europe, and then to use this as a yardstick by which to judge other societies?

It was not *simple* prejudice, as it may have been on the part of some of the travellers he quotes, since he does more than simply *appeal to* the European ideal in its protestant form; he tries to justify it as *rational*. His arguments in justification move on two levels, ethical and metaphysical. At the ethical level Hegel seeks to show that it is only in conditions approximated to in modern protestant Europe that men can realize the different sides of their personality and live a coherent and harmonious life. At the metaphysical level he adds that the free life of spirit which is possible in such a community is a microcosm of the universe at large, which is best understood as the self-expression of mind.

Setting aside this metaphysical claim as too complex as well as too remote to discuss here, let us concentrate on the ethical question. Quite clearly, the most potent influence on Hegel in ethics was Kant. Hegel agreed with Kant that moral principles, to be satisfactory, must possess two apparently contradictory characters: they must be objective, that is, valid without reference to particular persons, and they must be self-imposed. Kant himself held that both require-ments would be satisfied if the moral law were seen as the law of reason, in which all moral agents can be said to participate. What I am morally called on to do in a particular situation is not peculiar to me, since anyone else similarly situated would be under the same obligation. But I need not conclude that I am coerced in so far as I act morally, for the law to which I conform my will is not an alien law, but one to which my own reason freely assents. I am subject to the moral law, but I am also in a sense my own moral legislator. Now Hegel was prepared to accept the main lines of this theory, but he objected to some of the assumptions involved in Kant's version of it. He thought in the first place that there were serious deficiencies in Kant's moral psychology, with its sharp contrast between moral reason and the inclinations and its implication that man is a being com-pounded of two utterly disparate elements, spirit and flesh. In the conditions imagined by Kant reason could be satisfied only if the inclinations were sup-pressed. Secondly, Hegel argued that moral reason as conceived by Kant would be impotent, since it would enunciate an eternal ought-to-be. I take this to mean that Kantian morality would lack any institutional standing, and would be ineffective just because of that. Hegel's own ethical theory sought to remedy these defects by the expedient of seeing the moral law as part of the life of a living community constituted by free persons.* Because they were intimately bound up with such a community – because the community in a sense made them what they were – they would not see the restraints it imposed as alien; because they were persons and recognized as such they would not be merely conditioned or habituated to behave morally, as were the ancient Greeks accord-ing to Hegel, but would have opportunities to modify and develop moral prin-ciples as well as to hand them on. Nor would it be a case of morality consisting in the suppression of one side of human nature, for the object of the institution, if one may speak that way, was not to suppress but to liberate. The state, like the family, multiplied opportunities for the individual to do what he wanted, even if it also brought pressure to bear on him to forego some immediate satisfactions for the sake of a wider good.

I do not wish to claim that Hegel's ethical position is free of difficulties; it is easy to think of objections and I have discussed some of them elsewhere.* It is easy again to argue that the community Hegel thus claims to be imbued with moral qualities is no actual community, and conversely that the European states of Hegel's own day were ludicrously remote from satisfying the ideal he sketched. Hegel repeatedly said that the world of the Greeks was morally defective because

* *Editor's note* – Cf. J. Plamenatz's essay, sect. III.
* *Editor's note* – Cf. W. H. Walsh, *Hegelian Ethics* (London, 1969), especially pp. 49–53.

it depended on the institution of slavery; the Greeks knew only that some are free. One does not have to be a very advanced political thinker to wonder if the same was not true in principle of the world Hegel admired. Formal slavery was in process of abolition, and certainly did not exist in the Germanic countries themselves. But the conditions of early capitalism reduced men to servility if not to actual slavery; with the work they had to do they could scarcely feel substantive members of the community. At the same time, as Hegel himself acutely pointed out,[63] the most advanced countries of Europe were increasingly being driven by the need to export surplus goods to seek colonies overseas: so far as they secured for their citizens the opportunity to make their own lives, they did it by keeping others in a state of permanent inferiority. To suggest, as Hegel seems to do in his more sanguine moments, that the millennium had actually arrived in protestant Europe is in these circumstances insulting at the best.

Yet these criticisms do not after all destroy the essentials of the Hegelian case. They alert us to Hegel's complacency, but they do not challenge his ideal. We know in any case that many of his particular judgements may well have to be abandoned in the light of information which has become available since his time: there can be no question of a modern Hegelian's sticking to every detail of Hegel's philosophical history. The important thing to ask, however, is whether the central insight is correct. And it seems to me that the critics in question clearly share Hegel's central insight: they not only believe in his ideal of a self-determining society, but think that it is embodied in some degree in the Germanic world, or at least is on its way to being embodied there. This is certainly true of the most important of these critics, Marx. Hegel and Marx differed in many important ways in their approaches to history. Hegel was primarily interested in what gives unity to a culture: he wanted to characterize an epoch, and then to pinpoint its specific contribution to human development. Marx, by contrast, was occupied with efficient causes: he wanted to find out what makes cultures rise or fall, or again what brings about specific changes within them. But the two agree, even so, in seeing history as a unitary progression, and though Marx puts its goal in the future, he sees its path as proceeding through modern European society, particularly the industrial society of northern Europe. Moreover, his conception of the goal is the same as Hegel's: it is a civilized community in which men make their own lives. To look at history with Marxist eyes is thus not to break with Hegel, but simply to argue that Hegel was not true to himself when it came to applying his ideas.

A more interesting and more contemporary way of attacking Hegel would be to suggest that, despite everything he says about it, he does not really believe in freedom. A free society, as Hegel understands it, is one which guarantees its members certain liberties and commands their subjective assent. Objective free-

---

[63] *Hegel's Philosophy of Right*, trans. T. M. Knox (Oxford, 1942), §§ 246 ff.

dom requires an institutional framework, and this of course means that the persons concerned must forego certain satisfactions they would otherwise pursue, when for instance they pay their taxes or submit to compulsory military service. But Hegel thinks that in the conditions of the modern nation state, at least in its protestant form, they will do this willingly or at least not unwillingly. The authorities will treat them as persons entitled to consideration in their own right, and they in turn will accept the direction of the authorities as a necessary condition of what they really want. But what if they do not? What if they insist that the social whole, so far from being an instrument of liberation, is an instrument of tyranny? Hegel condemned Plato's republic on the ground that it contained too little subjective freedom: its members perhaps got what was good for them, or at least for the community as a whole, but had to put up with their roles whether they liked them or not. A lot of people today take a similar view of the modern nation state and its constituent institutions. They regard it as something under which they are condemned to live rather than something they voluntarily accept, an evil to be endured if it cannot be destroyed. And they insist that it is a necessary condition of any acceptable society that its members shall choose to belong to it, and shall be free to opt out if it fails to retain their approval. This is in effect to reverse Hegel's emphasis, to play down or indeed dismiss the institutional framework in which liberties are exercised, and to make freedom consist in nothing but the power to do what one wants, without let or hindrance.

It is certainly true that Hegel did not believe in *that* concept of freedom, obviously correct as it seems to so many of his critics. On the contrary, he argued explicitly against it. He maintained in the first place that freedom and organization in many respects go together. The civilized man is free to do many things just because society affords him these liberties; the savage may, if he is powerful enough, be able to act without restraint, but the range of actions open to him is pitifully restricted. So far from its being the case that the natural man is free and the civilized man in bondage, the precise reverse is true, the natural man being to a large degree prisoner of an environment he cannot control. About this I can say only that I myself find it a powerful argument; I do not know any critic who has met it satisfactorily.

Hegel's second reason for rejecting the subjectivist account of freedom is perhaps more controversial. He believes that its supporters are committed to the view that subjective freedom is not merely a necessary condition of a tolerable society, but also a sufficient condition: any society in which it is present must be accepted. And this strikes him as the advocacy of total anarchy. Hegel himself discusses the question with particular reference to the moral situation, asking whether a man could choose anything which appealed to him as a moral principle, and again whether the appeal to conscience will justify any action as moral. His answer to both questions is a decisive negative. Conscience claims to be true, not arbitrary, and as such must be open to correction; a moral principle is ' the rule for a mode of conduct which is rational ',[64] and hence cannot depend on individual whim. In a revealing comparison Hegel says that the state cannot give recognition to conscience in its private form any more than ' science ' can give recognition to ' subjective opinion ' [65] : no one could justifiably claim the right to believe what he chose in the sphere of knowledge, and equally no one can justifiably claim the right to think what he chooses in the sphere of morals. I doubt if many philosophers today would say it was as simple as that. But I do not believe that we can properly dismiss Hegel's comparison without careful consideration. It is true, after all, that there are forms of moral conduct – behaving justly and not taking advantage of the weak would be examples – which seem to be in no sense optional; without some respect for them society would be not merely intolerable, but perhaps not possible at all. These ways of behaving could be said to be rational in the sense that experience shows that we could not do without them. But if this is correct, the Hegelian position is also correct in principle : we are not free to promulgate any law we choose in the moral sphere, but must conform to objective requirements. I do not say that Hegel worked out a satisfactory argument on these lines; on the contrary, he seems to me sadly slipshod over this point. But I suggest that the general position for which he was arguing has more to be said for it than might immediately appear.

All this has taken us a long way from Hegel's philosophy of history, and I must return to that in conclusion. I have been maintaining that Hegel's view of world history stands or falls with his ethics, and have been trying in the foregoing discussion to show that his ethical position at least deserves serious consideration. To accept this view is not, of course, to endorse everything Hegel says in his lectures : we can take it that prejudice as well as ignorance comes into them at some points, without having to deny that the main judgements are based upon principle. Nor is it to argue that no other approach to world history is possible. One can think of what might be called a non-activist view of history, related to eastern ideals, or again of an interpretation of the past which judges cultures and peoples by reference to individual spontaneity rather than conditions of objective and subjective freedom (in such an interpretation Viking society would count as significant because it had so much life in it). But it should be added that Hegel himself would have rejected these alternatives. The eastern ideal as he saw it involved a turning away from the world, instead of an attempt to master it and realize oneself in so doing. And to insist on spontaneity as the sole mark of a good society would be like insisting on good intention as the sole criterion of a good act : it would open the door to any amount of nonsense. In neither case could the ideals involved be stated as part of a coherent philosophy, whilst the opposite was true of the ideal Hegel himself commended.

---

[64] *Philosophy of Right*, § 137.
[65] *Ibid*.

If we want to take a unitary view of history, Hegel's philosophy offers a firm and well-argued basis on which to build. What he says in the lectures needs revision to cope with more recent knowledge as well as more recent developments, but for all its extravagances it is not unplausible even as it stands. But do we need a unitary view of history at all? Most professional historians would undoubtedly say that we do not. History is a matter of diversity, not of unity, and to search for a single path of development in human history is grossly unscientific. We can all appreciate the attraction of this point of view. But I think if we are honest we will also acknowledge the attraction of the Hegelian type of alternatives. There are moments when, whatever the difficulties, we all want to see the past entire and to extract some sense from it. To do so is part of that elusive activity, constructing a philosophy of life.

Perspectives in the Marxian critique of Hegel's political philosophy

R. N. BERKI

I

Marx has quite a lot to say about Hegel in practically all of his works, either indirectly or in the form of isolated *obiter dicta*. But there is surprisingly little in his writings that would pass as direct, systematic criticism of definite aspects of Hegelian philosophy. In fact, only two manuscripts of Marx would fall into this category, both written in the 1840s. One is Marx's critique of Hegel's dialectic and his concept of man, with particular reference to Hegel's *Phenomenology*. This critique is a part of the famous *Economic and Philosophic Manuscripts of 1844*, where the exegetical limelight (justifiably) has been focused on the substantive Marxian notion of the ' alienation of labour ', this being the *fons et origo* of the subsequently elaborated mature Marxian system. The other, constituting the subject matter of the present essay, is an incomplete but lengthy manuscript written in either 1842 or 1843,[1] which has been given the title ' Critique of the Hegelian philosophy of state '.[2] It is, for all intents and purposes, the only Marxian work directed principally, and involving detailed arguments, against Hegel as a *political* philosopher. A consideration of it, therefore, affords us a unique opportunity of looking at some of the characteristic Hegelian and Marxian political conceptions in immediate juxtaposition, and even of offering some perspectives in regard to the wider issues involved.

I would like to begin by making a few remarks on Hegel's political philosophy, considered as a whole and in isolation from Marx's critique, though anticipating the latter's main lines of attack. I want to draw three analytical distinctions, which, albeit considerably simplifying some of the issues, will serve the dual purpose of facilitating an understanding of Marx's criticism of Hegel and of making some kind of an evaluation of this criticism possible. Hegel's political philosophy will then, on this analysis, be considered in relation to three main features it displays. In the first place, it embodies a certain view of philosophy. Secondly, it formulates a certain basic political principle, or ideal. Thirdly, it contains an elaborated translation of this political ideal. Marx's criticism is directed against all these three aspects of Hegel with equal force. It seems to me, however, that whereas much credit can be given to Marx for his critique of the

---

1 1843 seems the more probable date, at least according to a recent historical commentary on Marx's development. D. McLellan, *Marx before Marxism* (London, 1970), p. 106n.
2 In K. Marx, *Die Frühschriften*, ed. S. Landshut (Stuttgart, 1953). (References in the present essay will be to this version.)

Hegelian *translation*, the assumptions behind his criticism of the Hegelian political *principle* are open to serious questioning. Regarding the Marxian critique of Hegel's *philosophy*, I would like here to reserve judgement.

Hegel's conception of philosophy is of obvious importance to his political ideas. Philosophizing about politics can mean a number of things, from the elucidation of single meanings to the working out of normative goals, and whatever is said substantively about politics in a text of political philosophy has to be understood in the light of what a philosopher conceives his method, his philosophy, to be in the first place. In Hegel's case this view is fairly simple and straightforward. Philosophy is retrospective rational construction. It is the final, and highest, touch of reason on its object, the most comprehensive and satisfactory explanation to be given of every subject matter. In the stark, succinct phrase of the philosopher: 'To describe that which is, is the task of philosophy, for that which is is reason.' [3] From the point of view of politics the significance of this view, of course, is its emphatic rejection of utopianism, the rationalistic pursuit of distant ideals. In Hegel's view political philosophy should not, and indeed cannot, do more or less than to show that the real is rational, good and necessary. It starts out from and finishes up in reason, but it never leaves reality behind. Two more points about this. Though for Hegel philosophy is retrospective and self-consciously rooted to the existing, real world, it does not follow that it purports to be a mere 'description', in contradistinction to 'prescription', in the empiricist and positivist sense of the dichotomy. Hegel's political philosophy is 'prescriptive' as well as 'descriptive', only that its normative ideals appear in the form of embodiments, concretizations, the institutions of 'objective spirit' in the real world. Secondly, to qualify this point, it does not follow either that Hegel's political philosophy is sheer, unabashed conformism to what happens to exist, an attempt at 'idealizing the existing', in Haym's renowned phrase. Hegel's philosophy, and in particular his political philosophy, purports to be the rational formulation of a definite historical period, and Hegel refuses to look further ahead into the future. His detailed political recommendations, though not necessarily the principles behind them, are meant to be precepts for his age only. Posterity can certainly learn from them but it is not Hegel's purpose to leap over his time.

Hegel's basic substantive political principle follows, as does his view of political philosophy, from his fundamental metaphysic. It is, of course, impossible to do here more than to indicate its principal outline. For Hegel ultimate reality is reason and reason is seen as the dialectical unity of opposites. It reconciles, 'sublates', apparent contradictions in the empirical world by giving their rational explanation. Reason, therefore, is not a dumb, vague, abstract entity, but a

---

[3] G. W. F. Hegel, *Grundlinien der Philosophie des Rechts*, in *Sämtliche Werke*, ed. G. Lasson, vol. VI (Leipzig, 1921), p. 15.

differentiated, structured whole in which ' unreason ' does not vanish but is taken up and made rationally to abide by and coexist with reason itself. In the realm of politics also, Hegel insists on there being a rational structure, a community which is united through internal differentiation. His underlying political principle is based on the recognition that perfection in the state coincides with and is dependent on imperfection. ' It is reason itself that recognizes that contingency, contradiction and appearance have their own limited sphere and right, and it does not strive to eliminate these contradictions.' [4] In his political philosophy imperfection, contradiction, is lifted up through being institutionalized, through being preserved in a sphere which is kept separate from the state. In this community the ' rational ', highest freedom of the state reposes on the ' natural ' freedom of the citizen, and the common interest is arrived at through the dialectical ' mediation ' of opposed particular interests. The ideal state of Hegelian political philosophy is one where the subjective and particular consciousness of the citizen is not crushed by the objective and universal will of the community, but is reconciled to it through the mediation of the state's rationality, i.e. its structure. With a narrow focus and attention fixed exclusively on detail, we might not recognize in this ideal more than the classical ' constitutional ' or ' liberal ' state. I do not, however, think that it would be impossible or ill-advised to set our aims higher and to attempt to see the general application and inspiration of Hegel's political wisdom that reach beyond dated historical forms. The general Hegelian maxim that the community should have such a rational structure is prior, both logically and from the wider standpoint of political philosophy, to any claims as to the particular kind of structure that may be thought optimal by anybody at any one time.*

Thirdly, however, Hegel's political philosophy also consists in the detailed elaboration of such a rational structure, the one that he considered the most appropriate explanation of the modern state as he knew it. It is the structure outlined in the *Philosophy of Right*. There is no need to go over its categories here, as we shall have an opportunity to take a glance at some of them in the mirror of Marx's criticisms.

II

As regards the view of philosophy held by Hegel, the view of the apparatus with which a student of politics should approach his subject, Marx's rejection is total and uncompromising, and the alternative put forward by him is almost directly the opposite of Hegel's. The point here concerns Hegel's alleged mystification of reality in philosophy and his panlogism. The charge of inverting the human ' subject ' into a lifeless attribute, a ' predicate ', and vice versa, attributing subjective being to a lifeless abstraction, was first levelled against Hegel by Feuerbach

---

[4] *Ibid.* p. 214.

* *Editor's note* – On Hegel's philosophical method, see also D. P. Verene, p. 173.

in his programmatic *Preliminary Theses for the Reform of Philosophy*,[5] a more dramatic application of his arguments first presented in the much more renowned *Essence of Christianity*.[6] Marx's critique of the Hegelian philosophy of the state appears, incidentally, to be his first work where these characteristically Feuerbachian tools of analysis are employed in a systematic manner.

The Feuerbachian charge consists, basically, in a frontal attack on philosophy itself. Philosophy, abstract thought, is alienation, an unconscious projection of real human powers on to an abstraction, be it the Hegelian ' reason ' or the Christian God, with the result that in the process the human being appears as impoverished, dependent and dominated by the abstraction. In religion the lifeless abstraction, God, appears as the ultimately real, all-powerful, creative ' subject ', and the human being its creature, a mere ' predicate '. Feuerbach's main concern, of course, remains religion. Marx, however, applies the analysis to political philosophy. The ultimate explanation for Hegel's fundamental political mistake, argues Marx, lies in his being an idealist philosopher in the first place, in his making everything in his philosophy revolve around reason, or the ' Idea '. The Idea is his starting-point, his principle of explanation, his agent. What follows? The outcome is, according to Marx, that existing political institutions are made to appear as the emanations of this Idea, with the ultimate result that the human being, who in truth is the progenitor of these institutions, is presented as a predicate, as an abstraction himself. The accusation is repeated by Marx at several points, and is made to apply to all the basic categories which for Hegel constitute the Idea's development in the realm of politics.

Thus in Marx's presentation Hegel, in the first place, develops the idea of the state from this elemental, primary, philosophical Idea. The state, therefore, is afforded a being which is prior to and independent of the existence of empirical men and women. It is ' rational individuality ', the being that knows itself to be ' free '. From the idea of the state we see the mystical and seemingly inevitable development of its subordinate ' moments ', the categories of family and civil society. These latter, in Hegel's philosophy, are regarded as abstractions from the state, spheres of life that depend on the state for their very existence. The transition in Hegel from one category to the next, at all levels, is in terms of the universal relationship of the philosophical categories of freedom and necessity, in terms of logic, and not in terms of the separate, empirical necessity contained in the separate, empirical being of these categories. The development that Hegel regards as necessary is therefore necessary only from the viewpoint of his abstract logic of the Idea. Determinations appear in his philosophy of state that can be explained and justified only in terms that have been merely smuggled in, and have, therefore, nothing to do with the actual subject matter. One conspicuous

---

[5] L. Feuerbach, *Sämtliche Werke*, ed. W. Bolin and F. Jodl (Stuttgart, 1959), vol. II, *Vorläufige Thesen zur Reform der Philosophie* (1842).

[6] *Das Wesen des Christenthums* (1841) (*Sämtliche Werke*, vol. VI).

example is Hegel's logical justification of an individual ruler in the state, a monarch. ' Individuality ' in Hegel is an aspect of reason itself, a logical category. The state, he asserts, reaches individuality in the person of the monarch. But this, argues Marx, is an arbitrary selection. Why should individuality exist at that point only? he asks, why not develop the idea of the state at other points, for example, in the legislature? [7]

We have, however, to take note of the real thrust of Marx's arguments. It is not for mere idle, innocent speculation, for arbitrarily toying with logical categories in a realm that demands other methods of analysis, that Hegel is called to account by Marx. The point of the critique, on this level, is that Hegel's ' logical, pantheistic mysticism ' leads necessarily to an uncritical acceptance of existing political reality. Now I have said that realism does indeed figure very prominently in Hegel's political thought, realism in the sense of finding normative ideals in the realm of the concrete achievements of reason. Marx's accusation, however, is much more severe, and as the alleged connection between such an idealism and such an uncritical conservatism is not entirely self-evident, Marx's point deserves more than a moment's attention. Artificial persons or subjects, so runs his criticism, are accepted by Hegel as real, independently existing persons, and not taken for what they are, the realizations (*Verwirklichung*), that is, creations, of empirical human beings. This confounding of the object with the subject amounts to asserting that human activity is the result, and not the origin, of the being of political institutions like the state.

So, Marx says:

This inversion of the subjective in the objective and the objective in the subjective (which stems from the fact that Hegel wants to write the life-history of the abstract substance, the Idea, that therefore human activity must be shown as the activity and result of something else, that Hegel wants to show the essence of man as an imaginary individuality, instead of allowing it to come forward in his *real, human* existence), has the necessary result that *uncritically* an *empirical existence* is taken as the real truth of the Idea; for what is concerned here is not that empirical existence be brought to its truth, but that truth be brought to an empirical existence, and so here an immediate existence is developed as a *real* moment of the Idea.[8]

We should not fail to notice the interesting fact that Marx's critique is not merely humanist and radical, but also rationalist as well as, in a certain obverted manner, Hegelian.

The Marxian argument can be paraphrased in this way. What has to be described, what has to be shown, is *development*, the turning of one form of being into another, and it has to be presented as a necessary process. So far Marx is in agreement with Hegel. Now the question is: where do you start, what are

---

[7] Marx, *Die Frühschriften*, p. 43. Emphasis in all subsequent quotes from Hegel and Marx is in the original, unless otherwise stated.

[8] *Ibid.* p. 47.

you considering this development the development of? Hegel, Marx contends, is concerned with the development of his ' abstract substance '. However, as a philosopher of politics, he cannot remain with his abstractions, but has, at some point, to come down to the level of existing political realities. In so far as he started out from his Idea, he has to arrive at that which appears, at first, as the opposite of this Idea, and which must, therefore, be explained ultimately in terms of this Idea. It is the Idea that must be found an earthly dwelling-place and Hegel seems to find just that. But where does he find it? He finds it at the only place possible, in existing political institutions. But in so far as these institutions are to be explained, accommodated according to the requirements of ideal determinations, it follows both that you have to present them as the necessary results of the philosophical Idea, and that once they are thus explained you cannot proceed any further. You end up by attributing ideal essences to empirical existences, in this case political institutions, which means that instead of criticizing them, lifting them up into the higher realm of reason, you bring reason down and arrest its development in the swamp of empirical existence. From the height of speculative fancy to the depth of unimaginative falsification. The idealist philosopher vulgarizes reason in that he remains necessarily blind to the irrationality of the existing world. In Marx's wonderfully cryptic sentences:

Hegel is not to be blamed for describing the essence of the modern state, as it is, only for giving out that which is as the essence of the state. That the real is rational is revealed precisely in the *contradiction* of *irrational reality* that is at every angle the opposite of what it asserts, asserting the opposite to what it is.[9]

Marx at this stage, it may be noted, is not unequivocally hostile to every one of the actual institutions described in Hegel's political philosophy, and least of all to the state; his concern is to point out that Hegel's reasoning about them, his attempted derivation, proceeds the wrong way round. Hegel's way is from reason to institutions and finally to man as he is shaped by his political environment, appearing as the ' bourgeois ' and the ' citizen '.[10] Marx's way is from man, to reason, and consequently to the critical understanding of institutions. His main concern is not yet with the elimination of the state, but with the correct way of conceptualizing about it. Rightly seen:

Man always remains the essence of these essences, but these in turn appear also as his *real* universality, hence also as *community*. On the other hand, if the family, civil society, state, etc. are determinations of the Idea, substance as subject, then they must have an empirical reality, and the human mass in which the Idea of civil society develops itself is the bourgeois [*Bürger*], the other being the citizen [*Staatsbürger*]. As it is merely an *allegory*, as it concerns merely the addition of the *meaning* of the realized Idea to some empirical existence, so it is obvious that these forms [*Gefässe*] have achieved their determination as soon as they have become a determinate incor-

9 *Ibid.* p. 74.
10 *Ibid.* p. 54.

poration of a life-moment of the Idea. The universal therefore appears everywhere as something determinate, particular, as the individual can never reach its true universality.[11]

Thus the Marxian view of the role of the political philosopher appears as the opposite of Hegel's. With the latter explanation and justification are in the forefront. With the former it is critique. And, as we have seen, the Marxian conception of criticism is, as it were, immanently related to the basic mould of Hegelian thought itself. In Marx's eyes Hegel achieves a false penetration and deduces a fanciful dynamic; for Marx too, however, there must be a penetration, the critique must achieve an understanding of its subject matter in depth, and it must perceive the process whereby one form of existence turns into another. Marx's comparison of vulgar and correct criticism reveals here an important insight. The vulgar critic, he argues, falls into a dogmatic error himself when pronouncing on political institutions. For example, he would criticize a constitution by calling attention to the conflict prevailing among its various parts. He would confirm that there are contradictions all over, but he would not be able to reach beyond the level of institutions; he would be engaged in a struggle with the immediate object of his criticism. Marx likens this to earlier critiques of the Christian religion, which would attack the concept of the Trinity by focusing on the contradictions between the numbers one and three.

The true critique, on the other hand, shows the inner genesis of the holy trinity in the human brain. It describes its birth. In this way the truthful philosophical critique of the modern constitution not merely shows contradictions as they exist, but *explains* them, grasps their genesis, their necessity. It comprehends them in their own *peculiar* meaning. This *comprehension*, however, consists not in the universal re-cognition of the determination of the logical concept, as Hegel thinks, but in the grasping of the peculiar logic of the peculiar object.[12]

Instead, therefore, of trying to present a ' constitution of concepts ',[13] Marx's self-appointed task is to show the real concept, real genesis of the constitution and other political institutions. In this essay the task, of course, is not completed. But Marx says enough to reveal the main contours of what remained, by and large, his own substantive political principle.

III

Marx's point is that the philosopher of the state ought to concern himself with concepts peculiar to the state. Thus at first glance it may appear that a general metaphysic would be entirely irrelevant to his purposes. This, however, is not the case. The view that metaphysics is irrelevant to a critical inquiry into a

[11] *Ibid.* p. 53.
[12] *Ibid.* p. 111.
[13] *Ibid.* p. 35.

restricted subject matter is itself a metaphysical view, and it can, either explicitly or implicitly, be supported by a general metaphysical doctrine. The point here is that the Marxian stand is, in fact, supported by some rudimentary views on metaphysics which Marx condenses in a few paragraphs. These points have been generally neglected by critics. This is regrettable, because, although the arguments in Marx's essay are sketchy and inconclusive, it is one of the very few places where Marx does engage in metaphysical speculation, and besides, these arguments explain Marx's insistence on the ' peculiar logic ' of ' peculiar objects '.

The issue arises out of the Hegelian notion of ' mediation '. In Hegelian metaphysics this concept plays the role of effecting dialectical unity: the unity of reason and its opposite is ' mediated ', that is, structured. In Hegel's political philosophy the concept has the role of explaining the co-existence and peaceful functioning of seemingly opposed institutions in the state, for example, the mediation of the executive between the crown and legislature, or the mediation of the estates between civil society and the political authorities. Mediation, for Hegel as well as for Marx, stands for peaceful bargaining and accommodation, for the legitimized playing out of conflicting relationships. But Marx's attitude to mediation is hostile in the highest degree. He pours scorn on this process in politics, whereby decisions are deferred and roles constantly exchanged, with a view to maintaining a precariously balanced system and at the expense of radical changes. Mediation is a process without results; in political relationships, in the last resort, it reveals itself as a tangle of ' irreconcilable contradictions '.[14] Mediation, argues Marx, is comparable to the case of the doctor who intended to mediate between a man and his wife but ended up as being a protagonist of both the wife and the man, with the wife having to mediate between him and her husband, and the man to mediate between her and the doctor.[15] Mediation, of course, assumes that there are oppositions, and the continued existence of mediation is dependent on the maintenance of opposition. But one can take different attitudes to this. When, in a slightly different context, Marx finds it a defect in the Hegelian state that the bureaucracy here fights *against* its own presupposition, the corporation, fighting simultaneously *for* it,[16] the point can be taken as a singularly apt illustration of both Hegel's and Marx's political principles.

The reason, according to Marx, why this process of mediation in society cannot be presented as the ' speculative mystery of logic ', is that it is impossible to mediate between ' real extremes '. He goes, in other words, beyond the actual political details of the Hegelian position, and opposes to Hegel's metaphysics the outlines of a metaphysical doctrine of his own. We can, he argues, come across three kinds of extremes. Firstly, there are real extremes, ' opposed essences '. These do not allow for and do not need mediation. They do not yearn for one

[14] *Ibid*. p. 103.
[15] *Ibid*. p. 106.
[16] *Ibid*. p. 59.

another, do not anticipate one another. Such extremes are, for instance, ' pole ' and ' non-pole ' or ' human ' and ' non-human '. Secondly, there are opposed existences of the same essence, such as North and South Pole, or man and woman, but these are merely differentiated appearances of an essence at the highest stage of its development. Thirdly, there is the opposition between an essence and its abstract concept, such as the opposition between matter and spirit. But these, again, cannot be mediated, for their relationship is asymmetrical; philosophy, for example, does not unite with religion through mediation, but grasps the latter in its illusory reality. Hegel is accused of confusing these three kinds of extremes, thereby committing the threefold error: (1) attempting to reduce different principles to one principle; (2) regarding the sharpening of opposition and the struggle to resolve contradictions as something detrimental or harmful; (3) endeavouring to mediate between them.[17] ' Mediation ' is thus dismissed by Marx altogether. It is either impossible (in the realm of thought), or unnecessary (in the realm of life), or positively harmful, in the case of abstractions, like political institutions, having come to dominate human beings. Here struggle, not mediation, is the answer.

This is the general context then, in which to explain the characteristic Marxian position in political philosophy: Marx's insistence that ' man ', with the exclusion of a more comprehensive reality, should be seen as the operative principle of political institutions, and his avowed intention of replacing the strife-torn, contradictory, ' mediating ' state of Hegel with a community of universal harmony, free of contradictions. As he dispenses with the macrocosm of a universal reason, so he throws overboard the idea of an internally structured state. His substantive ideal in this early essay is called ' democracy ', which he contrasts to Hegel's constitutional monarchy. Monarchy, he argues, ought to be merely the form of the state, but it falsifies its content. In it the people belong to the constitution, in democracy the constitution belongs to the people. The democratic constitution is rooted in the essence of man. In monarchy the people are subsumed under one determination, the political, whereas in democracy the political constitution appears as the self-determination of the people.[18] Marx sees the ' republic ' as merely the abstract negation of monarchy, within the same framework. It is, however, still debatable as to whether his notion of ' democracy ' in this essay means the total absence of any form of political organization, i.e. whether or not he envisages the complete abolition of the ' state '. Although an interpretation along these lines has been advanced recently,[19] there is still room for argu-

---

17 *Ibid.* p. 108.

18 *Ibid.* p. 47.

19 Shlomo Avineri, in *The Social and Political Thought of Karl Marx* (Cambridge, 1968), argues that Marx's ' context makes it clear that any radical, institutional conception of democracy will be inadequate to express ' his meaning (p. 35). Both he (p. 34) and McLellan (*Marx before Marxism*, p. 115) are of the opinion that Marx could not at this stage be called a ' Jacobin democrat '.

ment. Marx draws a clear distinction between the 'political state' (a body separated from the rest of society) and the 'state' as the 'totality of the being of a people'.[20] His employment of the term, 'democratic constitution', and his remark that man is not for the law but the law is for man,[21] all tend to suggest that he does not yet regard the 'law' itself as an expression of alienation. (This position is reached only in the *1844 Manuscripts*.) When, later in the essay, Marx claims that the reform of the franchise is the demand for the abolition of the abstract political state as well as of civil society,[22] he means, of course, the state only in its restricted sense.

Marx appears here a firm advocate of popular sovereignty, not in the legal, but in the deeper political sense of believing that the 'people' can and should form a united community without the instrumentality of an individual sovereign ruler, that they can control their destiny through conscious direction of the constitution, and that the people should all be concerned with deliberation and decision-making. Hegel's position on these questions – the traditional concerns of political philosophy – is moderately conservative. Marx appears as a radical, sometimes tinged with individualism.

Sovereignty is a difficult concept and its discussion in both Hegel * and Marx does not present the issues sufficiently clearly. Hegel's argument is lumbered with metaphysical ballast and the two vital aspects of the question, that is, the necessity of structured unity in the state, and the individual monarch as the necessary expression of this unity, are conflated. In a recent commentary on Hegel, the interesting point has been put forward that as Hegel has an exaggerated, almost Hobbesian concern for unity and integration within the community, which he considers can be achieved only in a single individual, he is careful not to endanger this unity by conceding too much to popular representation.[23] However that may be, Marx's attitude appears, on the other hand, unduly cavalier. Hegel, having arrived at the concept of the monarch as the 'moment of individuality' and the concrete expression of sovereignty in the state (in § 279 of the *Philosophy of Right*), goes on to explain and to dismiss various conceptions of popular sovereignty. He considers it meaningful in the sense of external sovereignty *vis-à-vis* other peoples, and internally only if by 'people' one understands the 'whole state'.[24] Marx regards the first as trivial [25] and answers to the second: 'As though the people were not the real state. The state is an abstraction. The people alone are concrete.'[26] But, Hegel goes on, if by popular sovereignty

[20] Marx, *Die Frühschriften*, p. 94.
[21] *Ibid.* p. 48.
[22] *Ibid.* p. 145.
* *Editor's note* – On Hegel's concept of sovereignty, see also section VII of K.-H. Ilting's essay, and Z. A. Pelczynski's concluding essay, starting on p. 230.
[23] R. K. Hočevar, *Stände und Repräsentation beim jungen Hegel* (Munich, 1968), esp. chs 1 and 4.
[24] *Philosophie des Rechts*, p. 229.
[25] *Die Frühschriften*, p. 44.   [26] *Ibid.* p. 45.

we understand sovereignty opposed to that of the monarch, we are confronted with a 'wild' and 'confused' notion.[27] Marx poses the question here: is the sovereignty of the monarch not, after all, an illusion? And he proceeds by drawing a distinction between two conceptions: '... here we are concerned with *two entirely opposed concepts of sovereignty*, of which one is such that it can come to existence only in a *monarch*, the other only in a *people*. Just like the question: is God the sovereign, or is man the sovereign? One of the two is an untruth, even if an existing untruth '.[28]

But the argument here takes a more serious turn. Hegel says: 'The people, taken without its monarch and without the *structuring* of the whole, which is the necessary and closely connected feature of monarchy, is a formless mass, no longer a state and without the determinations that are present in a whole internally organized.'[29] For Marx all this is a tautology. *If* the community is organized as a monarchy, with monarchical institutions, *then* to abstract these institutions from this community yields us indeed a people that is nothing but a formless mass.[30] He then goes on to outline his sketch of democracy. Now, although we are not primarily concerned here with a criticism of Marx, a few remarks may perhaps be permitted at this point. Marx, on the one hand, seems to be correct in arguing against Hegel's identification of monarchy with a developed structure of the community. On the other hand, however, Marx seems to take it for granted that in a democracy the unity and integration of a people would be somehow natural and spontaneous. Hence, he dismisses the question of definite form and definite institutions in too lighthearted a manner. The implications of the Hegelian position are by no means tautological – they have a very practical, political significance. In the Marxian picture of democracy (as in the later vision of communism), there is no mention of internal determination, institutions that would concretize the community. Does Marx conceive of the people in democracy as a 'formless mass'? And if not, what does he say of the 'form'? He calls democracy the 'solved riddle'[31] of all constitutions, the 'free product' of the people. What he does not appear to give sufficient consideration to – and what is the fundamental truth behind Hegel's proposition – is that internal structuring is necessary to all communities. This can be shown at two points. A community, whether monarchy or republic or Marxian democracy, has to have internal differentiation in the shape of lesser, particular institutions. And it has to have a 'unitary will', articulated in an individual. It is no doubt

[27] *Philosophie des Rechts*, p. 230.

[28] *Die Frühschriften*, p. 46.

[29] *Philosophie des Rechts*, p. 230.

[30] *Die Frühschriften*, p. 46.

[31] *Ibid*. p. 47. Cf. 'Communism is the riddle of history solved, and it knows itself to be this solution ', K. Marx, *Economic and Philosophic Manuscripts of 1844* trans. M. Milligan (Moscow, 1961), p. 102.

possible to move away from the narrowly conceived Hegelian position, but not so easy to spirit away the principle underlying it.

This leads us to the next point and here again a close comparison between Hegel's caution and Marx's confidence sheds an illuminating light on their respective positions in political philosophy. The question here turns on the relationship of the constitution to the legislature. Which is prior to which? In § 298 of the *Philosophy of Right* Hegel puts the problem in an authentically dialectical perspective. As the legislature itself is a part of the constitution, the latter falls outside its sphere. However, it is in the development of laws and the 'progressive character of legislative business' that we find the further fate of the constitution determined.[32] And Hegel adds in the Addition that though the constitution must not be created, it not only 'is' but just as essentially 'becomes', and that its advance is invisible and lacks the 'form of change'.[33] Marx retorts first by pointing out that the laws which are presupposed by the legislature had themselves to be made in the first place.[34] And in so far as our attention is to be focused on an existing state, where the question of origin does not arise, Marx's endeavour is with laying bare the contradiction contained in this Hegelian dictum. The legislature is both outside and within the constitution. How is the antinomy to be solved? It can be looked at in various ways; we can say that the constitution directly lies outside the legislature, but indirectly inside it, or that the legislature is able to do factually, materially, what it is not formally and legally entitled to do. But this amounts merely to pushing the antinomy further and further, without ever solving it. Finally it appears as the contradiction between the constitutional activity and the constitutional determination of the legislature.

Marx, as can be expected, takes particularly strong objections to the Hegelian belief that the future emerges but is not consciously determined. The constitution, in Hegel, is allowed to change, but it has to change in an unconscious manner. Its appearance, therefore, contradicts its essence. The appearance is conscious, but the essence is unconscious. The law does not pronounce on what is necessary according to the nature of things; it is the very opposite of what its real nature demands. Characteristically, here Marx strikes an extreme rationalist note, appearing himself as a hyper-Hegelian, criticizing Hegel for not living up to his own previously formulated principles. Hegel calls the state the 'free essence' of reason in the realm of objective spirit. But can this state, this constitution, be called free? We see that here, where self-conscious reason should be able freely to determine itself, only blind natural necessity dominates. How can this contradictory dualism be maintained? Hegel wants to present the state as the realization of free spirit, but he cannot resolve contradictions except by

[32] *Philosophie des Rechts*, p. 243.
[33] *Ibid.* p. 364.
[34] *Die Frühschriften*, p. 63.

appealing to natural necessity which stands opposed to reason. This realization of free will is an unconscious, accidental act, similar to the ' mediation ' between the private and the public interest.

Further, Marx points out that the gradual, imperceptible change of the constitution is not only conceptually inadequate as an explanation, because of the unresolved contradiction it contains, but that it is also historically false. Gradual changes can only be changes within an existing framework, only particular alterations which at the same time also serve to maintain the existing *status quo* in all essentials. But real changes, which become necessary with the emergence of new human needs, demand entirely new constitutions, and these can come about only by revolution. What, therefore, is needed is that the people themselves should undertake consciously what in the Hegelian state appears only as one aspect of an unconscious process.

So that the constitution be not just merely changed, so that therefore this illusory appearance be not in the last resort shattered violently, so that man may do consciously what he is otherwise forced to do by the very nature of the thing, it is necessary that the movement of the constitution, *progress*, be made the *principle of the constitution*, that therefore the real bearer of the constitution, the people, be made its principle. Progress itself is then the constitution.[35]

Marx's example is the French Revolution which was the work of the legislature, representing the will of the people. The right and relevant question for Marx is therefore: have or have not the people the right to make a constitution when the existing form of the state has become a practical illusion, no longer expressing the people's will? And he concludes this topic by pronouncing that ' the collision between the constitution and the legislature is nothing but the *conflict of the constitution with itself*, a contradiction in the very concept of the constitution '.[36]

Again, a few words of appreciation may be added. However much one may sympathize with Marx's demands for popular determination of the law and constitution, and however willingly one may agree with him regarding the periodic necessity of formal changes, revolutions, there is again a feeling that Marx treats some matters too lightly, and that in certain respects the cautious Hegelian formulation still has the edge over him. The question is not merely about anybody's ' right ' to make the constitution, whether it be the ' people ', the legislature, or any other, more accurately defined, body. The question also concerns the *ability* of any such group or institution really to achieve what it sets out to achieve. We do not need here to emphasize the argument of traditionalism that the constitution is never entirely made anew, but is always resting on existing notions of propriety, and that these notions can never be reduced to the level of free, conscious ' will '. This may or may not be the case and its importance can

[35] *Ibid.* p. 66.
[36] *Ibid.* p. 67.

easily be exaggerated. The point is that even if we allow for the possibility of a people making freely, consciously a constitution that has the sole purpose of providing for the people's needs, it will still not result in the community's becoming a 'free, self-determining essence'. The people's constitution is 'posited' in the same way as the monarch's. Once made, it inevitably assumes a form, a rigidity, and when new needs arise these can be incorporated in legislation only at the expense of engineering a conflict between form and content, between the constitution 'as it is' and 'as it becomes'. The conflict between the constitution and the legislature may very well be called a 'contradiction in the principle of the constitution', but this so-called 'contradiction' is not confined to monarchical states. And it does not follow that recognition leads necessarily to elimination, and that the contradiction can be resolved in such a way as Marx seems to suggest. The French Revolution and its aftermath is only one, and not the most important, example to serve as a negative illustration of Marx's thesis.

The third issue here is popular representation. The question comes up in connection with Marx's critique of the Hegelian notion of 'estates' and I shall mention the latter again in the last part of this essay. Here I am taking it up for the wider interest it affords in relation to Hegel's and Marx's respective political principles. Hegel touches on the problem of representation in § 308 where he says that the commercial and industrial sector of society (agriculture we shall mention later) can take part in the political life of the state only through representatives who are appointed (*abgeordnet*) by society as the representatives of functions, not of individuals. Hegel does not consider it rational to demand that all members of the state should take part in deliberation and decision-making. The 'democratic element' should be allowed in, but not without a 'rational form'. Being a member of a state is dismissed by Hegel as an 'abstract determination'. There are, in fact, three issues here and Marx considers them all, though not equally satisfactorily. Should all participate in legislation? Should all take part in appointing, i.e. electing, representatives? Should election take place along functional lines, or on the basis of some other principle?

Marx accepts Hegel's point about the membership of the state being an abstract determination, but argues that here the fault lies partly in Hegel's way of developing the concept of the state, and partly in the actual conditions of modern life which assume the separation of the state and civil society. Marx believes, on the other hand, that the democratic element should become not merely the formal, but also the real basis of the state, and that the democratic element would then give the state its 'rational form'.[37] Further: 'In a really rational state one could reply [to Hegel] : "The people *should* not *all* as *individuals* take part in deliberation and decision-making in the general concerns of the state," for the "individuals" do this as "all", within society (*Sozietät*) and as its members.

[37] *Ibid.* p. 136.

Not all of them as individuals, but the individuals as all [as members of the whole].'[38] Hegel's dilemma, that is, whether to allow civil society political influence through representatives or to allow individual participation, is seen by Marx as an opposition of existence within an essence (see above for Marx's distinction between these categories). The existence concerned is 'number'. This consideration, seen by Hegel as merely 'external', serves as the best argument against the direct participation of all. In any case, Marx argues, the question itself arises only on the assumptions of the abstract political state, it is therefore itself an 'abstract political question'. Marx appears here an individualist:

All the individuals do this [that is, participate in politics] or the *individuals* do this as the *few*, as *not-all*. In both cases allness remains as the *last* sum or totality of the individuals. Allness is no essential, spiritual, real quality of the individual. Allness is not something through which the individual would lose the determination of his abstract individuality; allness is only the total *aggregate of individuality. One* individuality, *many* individualities, all individualities. The one, the many, all – none of these determinations alters the *essence* of subject, individuality.[39]

If, Marx goes further in the vein of conceptual analysis, by the state we understand the 'common concerns' of a people, then being a member of a state means being concerned with public matters. In this case it is not only true that the members are parts of the state, but the state likewise is a part of them. 'To be a conscious part of something is to take part of this something consciously, to participate. Without this consciousness the member of a state would be merely an animal.'[40] This designation of membership by Marx is, of course, the application of the famous Feuerbachian concept of man as the 'species-being' (*Gattungswesen*), used by Marx to such a great effect in his *1844 Manuscripts*. Here Marx proceeds by stating that the real question, therefore, is not whether or not all members of the state should participate in public affairs, but whether or not all should be members. On account of 'number', he himself seems to reject the possibility of direct participation in deliberation and decision-making. He is, however, emphatic in arguing in favour of the participation of all through elections. When it comes to the problem of the modern representative constitution, he declares, the real concern is not with deciding on representation or universal direct participation, but with 'the *extension* and in the highest possible degree *universalization* of the *franchise*, both *active* and *passive*. This is the actual debating point of political *reform*, in France as well as in England'.[41] The election is the only real link between civil society and the state, and it is therefore only through the abolition of the limits on franchise that civil society, that is, the members of the state seen in their real, material living conditions, can become fully political.

[38] *Ibid*. p. 137.
[40] *Ibid*. p. 139.
[39] *Ibid*. p. 138.
[41] *Ibid*. p. 143.

There is, however, still one question left to decide. In what capacity should, or can, the members of the state participate in politics? The point assumes importance in that here Hegel's solidly grounded arguments in favour of corporate, functional representation * have in the course of time fallen by the wayside together with his more dated pronouncements on the subject, and also on account of Marx's interesting, but inadequate and cryptic remarks in this connection. The substance of the Hegelian argument, to the effect that the member of the state can be considered politically only through and by his membership of occupational groupings, that is, social classes, is as relevant now as ever before. What is Marx's attitude?

In the first place, Marx argues, it is the presupposition of the modern political state that the members of civil society should take part, or indirectly influence, legislation as individuals. Here the legislature does not present itself as the emanation, or function, of the actual, social life of the state's members, but concerns only the organization, the form, of civil society. It is a direct requirement of the organization of the legislature that members of society should look upon one another as separate individuals. Their membership of the state is abstract because on this level it does not express their real life-activities. It is, of course, impossible that all should be members of the legislature, as this would mean the surrender of civil society to the state. The participation of civil society in politics through representatives is ' precisely the expression of their separateness and merely dualistic unity '. And what if we consider civil society as *real* political society?

Then it is nonsense to demand that which is only a corollary of the notion of the political state as an existence separated from civil society, of the theological notion of the state. In this situation the meaning of the legislature as a representative body entirely disappears. Here the legislature is representative in the sense that every function is representative, as, for example, the cobbler, insofar as he furnishes a social need, is my representative, as every determinate social activity as species-activity only represents the species, i.e. a determination of my own essence, as every man is the representative of every other.[42]

One can surmise here, but unfortunately one cannot divine the precise meaning of Marx's remarks. Representation, of course, is one of those issues that are never taken up in a positive manner in the Marxian works. The nearest Marx comes to discussing the points he seems to be making in the passage just quoted is in *Capital*, in connection with the ' social quality ' of labour. But there, of course, the argument does not concern political representation. The central problem of his position in the early essay seems to lie in this, that whereas on the one hand he appears to reject individual, territorial representation on the grounds that

---

* *Editor's note* – See G. Heiman's essay, pp. 129–32, for an exposition of Hegel's arguments for corporate representation.

[42] *Ibid.* p. 141.

this makes sense only on the assumption of a separated, purely ' political ' state, on the other hand he does not consider it necessary that representation in ' civil society ' be given a *political* form. In other words, he appears to believe that once civil society becomes synonymous with political society, representation, as it were, becomes immediate and an expression of harmony among the several ' species-activities '. He does not envisage the possibility of continuing conflict, and hence the necessity of ' mediation ', among the several social functions. This belief of his, especially when seen in the light of the more circumspect Hegelian formulation, appears unduly optimistic.

IV

I propose now to turn briefly to the Marxian critique of Hegel's political philosophy on a more concrete level, with reference to actual political configurations prevalent in Hegel's day, the existence of which is justified by Hegel and duly denounced by Marx. In the previous section of my essay I inflated somewhat the discussion of the more esoteric general points to be found in Marx's critique. My reason for doing so lies in the belief that it is only these issues, the still unsolved ' riddle ' of political philosophy and popular sovereignty in particular, that make the Hegel–Marx relationship a living, exciting subject even in our own day, both in an academic and in an ideological sense. However, I have thus correspondingly to condense my remarks on the last count. The justification for this is, on the one hand, that Marx's concrete arguments advanced in the 1843 essay have been superseded in his later works, and on the other the fact that in respect of these concrete issues the Hegelian position seems considerably weaker than it is on the level of general political principles. Hegel's *Philosophy of Right* sets out to defend a particular *kind* of ' separation ' and ' mediation ', and to outline the structure of a state with definite, concrete institutional characteristics. The state retains the institution of the ' estate ', a relic of the medieval political framework of European communities; it includes a strong bureaucracy holding the reins of government; it postulates hereditary monarchy as the most rational form of sovereignty; and it reposes on the landed nobility as its stablest, most ' substantial ' section, or estate.

On this level the critical onslaught of Marx's essay goes in two directions. Marx is, of course, highly critical of the actual society and state of which Hegel's *Philosophy of Right* purports to be the expression. It is the actual, material, earthly separation of economic and political life, the diremption of the human being into various unrelated aspects of his whole essence, that is given the heavenly gloss in Hegel's logical categories. In the modern age the human being appears as an emotive, sensitive creature whose relation to his fellows is experienced as love; he comes before us as a self-seeking, self-assertive individual whose only concern is to get the better of his fellows; and he makes his appearance also as the rational being who can – but only in thought – rise above his worldly concerns. Hegel's categories of the family, civil society and the state are the reflection of this situation, and of course Marx's point is precisely to expose the reprehensible, inhuman character of this separation. For Marx, then, to the extent that Hegel speaks the minds of this society, presupposing universal separation and the alienated ' citizen ', Hegel's political philosophy appears correct. Naturally, this does not endear him to Marx whose attitude to this society is irreconcilably hostile. Marx's exposure of the world of the fragmented human being culminates in his classic critique of capitalism, which is castigated for its political shortcomings in *On the Jewish Question* [43] (in many ways the most incisive *political* tract ever written by Marx), for its psychological effects in the *Manuscripts*, and for its exploitative character in the whole subsequent Marxian literary output. The Marxian strictures on bourgeois society as elaborated in the 1843 essay, therefore, have only a secondary, purely scholarly significance.

The other prong of the Marxian critique of Hegel, however, is more interesting in that it presents some complications for the subsequently stereotyped Marxist view of Hegel as the last authentic representative of bourgeois philosophical thought. It is, actually, Marx himself who in his published *Introduction* to his critique asserts that even though the German political *status quo* is an anachronism,[44] Germans are yet ' philosophical contemporaries ' of the present,[45] and that the German philosophy of state and right has ' achieved its most consistent, richest and last formulation through Hegel '.[46] Yet it is the case that in large parts of his direct attack on Hegel's political philosophy, Marx takes Hegel to task not so much for speaking the mind of bourgeois society (he even receives a grudging appreciation for it), but much more emphatically for not even rising to the level of reasoning appropriate to this stage of historical development.[47] It is not that Hegel makes bourgeois fragmentation look respectable through his metaphysical fancies. It is that he makes it look respectable by the employment of concepts that even this bourgeois consciousness repudiates. It is interesting to observe that Marx's vehement denunciation of Hegel's medievalism appears sometimes in tone and style not too dissimilar to the writings of liberal philosophers, though, of course, his assumptions are far more radical.

---

[43] *Zur Judenfrage* (1844).

[44] ' If we wanted to start out from the German status quo itself, even though in the only suitable way, negatively, the result would still remain an anachronism. Even the negation of our political present reveals itself as a dust-covered affair in the historical lumber-room of modern nations ', *Zur Kritik der hegelschen Rechtsphilosophie. Einleitung* (1844). Marx, *Die Frühschriften*, p. 209.

[45] *Ibid.* p. 214.   [46] *Ibid.* p. 215.

[47] It may be noted that Engels' mature appreciation of Hegel is more in line with Marx's critique than Marx's own remarks in the *Introduction*. In *Ludwig Feuerbach and the end of Classical German Philosophy* (1888) (Moscow, 1950), Engels does assert that ' with Hegel philosophy comes to an end ' (p. 22), and that ' the German working class movement is the inheritor of German classical philosophy ' (p. 91). He makes it clear, however, that in terms of a Marxist analysis the *Philosophy of Right* articulates a view justifying an anachronistic political configuration (*ibid.* p. 20).

There are two points to consider here. In the first place, it is pointed out by Marx that Hegel's attempt at establishing the unity of civil society and the political state through the mediating function of the estates falls to the ground because it tries to reconcile two opposed principles, that of the Estate and that of the representative constitution.[48] The estates belong by type to the medieval community, prevalent at a time when the private and the public interest were in fact coincidental.[49] It was a period of democracy, of unity.

In the Middle Ages the political constitution is the constitution of private property, but only because the constitution of private property is the political constitution. In the Middle Ages the life of the people and political life are identical. Here man is the real principle of the state, but it is the *unfree man*. It is therefore the *democracy of unfreedom*, fully consistent alienation. The abstractly reflected opposition belongs only to the modern world. The Middle Ages is the *real*, the modern age is *abstract dualism*.[50]

In modern times, of course, the restitution of estates, or their formal incorporation in the political constitution of a community which rests on different material presuppositions, would be a contradictory and inherently impossible as well as thoroughly undesirable undertaking. The constitution of estates, where it does not linger on as a tradition of the Middle Ages, is the attempt to force man back into his limited existence even on the level of his political being, and to make his particularity to be the substance of his consciousness.[51] Whereas modern society is the highest expression of ' private man ', the ' individual ' who is abstracted from his real, social life, the Middle Ages also separated man from his ' universal essence ' by making him a particular being, an animal who coincides with his immediate determination. The Middle Ages form the stage of zoology in the history of mankind.[52]

The second point, and it is here I think that Marx's pen is the most devastatingly effective, concerns his attack on the hereditary principle. It is in asserting this concept to be a necessary aspect of his ' rational ' philosophical construction of the state that Hegel falls farthest behind the characteristic formulations of bourgeois thought. The latter, as exemplified in the thought of Hobbes, Locke, the eighteenth-century European Enlightenment and the political manifestoes of the French Revolution, stands on the basis of equality at birth and personal merit as the criterion of political and social advancement. The bourgeois principle is thoroughly ' rational ', even though, according to Marx, it remains ' abstract '.

---

[48] Marx is credited by Hočevar (*Stände und Repräsentation*, p. 15) with being the first to grasp this duality in Hegel's political philosophy. Hočevar's interpretation of Hegel's notion of representation, stressing its derivation by Hegel from medievalist, conciliar sources, bears out Marx's critique in many important respects.

[49] Marx, *Die Frühschriften*, p. 87.

[50] *Ibid*. p. 50.

[51] *Ibid*. p. 98.

[52] *Ibid*. p. 99.

Hegel, of course, accepts this as a general principle, and applies it, amongst other things, to the membership of the bureaucracy, which, he says, is to be open to talent wherever it comes from. Yet Hegel also insists on retaining heredity as the basis of political position at two points in his political philosophy: with the constitutional monarch as the head of state, and with the so-called 'agricultural estate'. Marx discerns a primitive 'naturalism' to lie beneath these assertions, and he condemns both, as slavery to the body and to the soil respectively. The monarch, he argues, represents arbitrary, personal will which Hegel imposes on the state arbitrarily, ostensibly deriving it from the principle of 'individuality' in his philosophical concept. The monarch is designated by Hegel as the moment of 'absolute self-determination'.[53] What does this self-determination consist in? asks Marx and he finds the answer in the monarch's natural person.

The heredity of the monarch stems from his concept. He should be a person specifically differentiated from the whole species, from all other persons. Which is then the final, definite distinction between one person and all others? The *body*. The highest function of the body is *sexual activity*. The highest constitutional act of the king, therefore, is his sexual activity, for it is through this that he *produces* a king and perpetuates his body.[54]

And further:

The interesting point about it is that that which can be the product only of the self-conscious species is seen as the immediate product of the physical species. I am a man by birth, without the agreement of society, but this particular birth becomes a peer or a king only by general agreement. It is the agreement that makes the birth of this man to be the birth of a king; it is, therefore, the agreement, and not the birth, that makes the king. If birth, in distinction to other determinations, gives a man immediately a position, then it is *his body* that makes him to be *this determinate* social function.[55]

The political status of the landed nobility as hereditary members of the legislature is based by Hegel on their independent position, as owners of land and a will, which, similarly to the monarch's, 'reposes on itself'.[56] Marx has no difficulty in pointing out that this will, in fact, reposes not on itself, but on the ownership of land. What especially arouses Marx's wrath is Hegel's further insistence that the 'substantiality' of this estate must be safeguarded by the institution of primogeniture, which takes priority even over the love of family.[57] Here Marx's critical broadsides are assured of an easy target. What this reveals, he says, is that the apex of the Hegelian political edifice is not reason, but private property, and moreover property that is presented as a quality more basic to man than any other quality, including personality and the freedom of the will. Family

---

[53] *Philosophie des Rechts*, § 275, p. 225.
[55] *Ibid.* p. 126.
[56] *Philosophie des Rechts*, § 305, p. 250.

[54] *Die Frühschriften*, p. 54.

[57] *Ibid.* § 306, p. 250.

life itself appears as a spiritless illusion over which the barbarity of private property takes precedence. The inalienability of landed property signifies the rule of property over the political life of the state. It means that property is our veritable ' subject ', and reason, man, is mere appendage, predicate again. And how hypocritical, how misleading it is for Hegel to describe this institution as a ' protection against human weakness '.

It is precisely this *romantic* itching of primogeniture, that here private property, hence private arbitrary will in its most abstract form, the *wholly ignorant*, immoral raw will appears as the highest synthesis of the political state, as the highest alienation of the arbitrary will, as the hardest, most arduous struggle with *human weakness*, for here the *humanization* of private property appears as *human* weakness.[58]

Yet, though Marx's tone here is unmistakably that of the enraged nineteenth-century liberal democrat, it should be noticed that his vistas reach further than a ' humanization ' of property in the shape of a superficially more enlightened system where property is held freely but still in private.[59] Marx's conclusion here has its undying echo in all his later writings:

As opposed to the *raw stupidity* of independent private property, the uncertainty of business is elegic, the pursuit of profit pathetic (dramatic), the instability of ownership a serious fate (tragic), dependence on the state's wealth moral. In short, in all these qualities the *human* heart beats through property; it is the dependence of man on man.[60]

---

[58] *Die Frühschriften*, p. 120.

[59] In a narrow sense, McLellan's opinion, that it is not obvious that Marx at this stage was arguing for the abolition of private property (*Marx before Marxism*, p. 125), appears certainly correct. On a different level, however, Avineri is also right in maintaining that in this early essay of Marx we see the first appearance of the famous notion of the ' fetishism of commodities ' (*Social and Political Thought of Karl Marx*, p. 30).

[60] *Die Frühschriften*, p. 121.

The role of the individual
in pre-revolutionary society:
Stirner, Marx, and Hegel

EUGÈNE FLEISCHMANN

The 'great refusal' of Herbert Marcuse is clearly prefigured in Max Stirner's work, *Der Einzige und sein Eigentum* (1844) (*The Individual and his Property*).[1] We therefore propose to view the problem of the rebellious individual in its original setting, then to glance at the reactions of Marx and Engels to the questions raised by Stirner, and finally to compare their polemics with some of the ideas of Hegel, whose philosophy gave rise to the entire Young Hegelian movement.

I

The first part of Stirner's sole important work is only of very moderate interest to us. Criticism of philosophy and political ideas at that time had become a polemical contest, often descending to the level of demagogy, and was thus ultimately of limited scope. Yet we do well to observe that Stirner brought with him into this field a radicalism of attitude which could not be exceeded without a complete change in philosophical orientation. Thus, for example, Stirner's treatment of the two great subjects of his critique – the spirit and liberalism – makes a complete mockery of these two ideas in Hegel, and yet at the same time makes use of the Hegelian conceptual apparatus. The spirit is originally that of man, but by becoming a concept, an isolated philosophical entity, it can no longer be identified with him. The spirit, or, for that matter, any abstract concept, must transcend every human limitation, otherwise it would be man and not spirit. Spirit is transcendent for it remains, while man dies; spirit represents universality, while man is always individual; and it is spirit which is ideal, while man is always but one single instance of its incarnation. After the invention of the notion of spirit, no reconciliation with it can ever be possible: either it is spirit, or it is man: a third term is scarcely possible. The philosophers (Hegel, Feuerbach, etc.) and the theologians have chosen spirit to the detriment of man, and it is in this that the greatest alienation of philosophy consists.

The same goes for the idea of liberty. For Stirner, to be free means to be free *from* something. Consequently, from the moment that I wish to be free from a thing, I am involved in a vicious process which stretches to infinity, for having

---

[1] I have used the edition of P. Lauterbach (Leipzig, 1892). [For an English version, see Max Stirner, *The Ego and His Own*, trans. S. T. Byington (New York, 1907; London, 1912) – *Editor.*]

rid myself of one thing, I will desire to be free from a second, then from a third, then from a fourth . . . and I shall never succeed in breaking out of this vicious processs. The sole means of liberating myself from this vicious process is to rid myself of the idea of liberty itself. The ideologues of liberty, political or otherwise, incur a greater loss for man than do his philosophical or religious benefactors.

But it is not so much Stirner's criticisms which will interest us in this context as his own proposals for helping man out of this condition of alienation by putting him at one with himself. At this point we must consider the subject of his philosophy: it is the human self which so obsessed the Hegelians of his time, and which means for him the individual in all his indefinable, empirical concreteness. The word ' unique ' (*einzig*) means for Stirner man as he is in his irreducible individuality: always different from his fellows, and always thrown back on himself in his dealings with them. Thus, when he talks of ' egoism ' as the ultimate definition of the human ' essence ', it is not at all a question of a moral category (whether positive or negative), but of a simple existential fact. A man is always himself, whether he wishes it or not, and it is simple ignorance to suppose that he can become different through his actions, or renounce himself in favour of some other human being. Stirner simply wishes us to take account of this existential fact, in order to make all conceivable forms of alienation, conscious or unconscious, impossible. Thus liberty becomes not an ideal stretching away into infinity, but the coming into possession of himself by each individual man.

For what in effect Stirner calls ' property ' (*Eigentum*) is not the appropriation of some good or other, but rather it signifies the identity of a man with his manifestations, and above all with his own individual existence. This idea is purely Hegelian in origin, and it sends us back to the beginning of his *Philosophy of Right*: the first and most immediate manifestation of right (that is to say, of liberty) is the possession by man of his body and of his bodily functions (work, etc.). It is virtually superfluous to point out that the possession of vassals by noblemen is thereby criticized. With Stirner – who takes his stand on the minimal degree of liberty advocated by Hegel – we will see that man's taking possession of himself implies an entire political programme for the non-conformists and the uncommitted.

His analysis of the political situation following the French Revolution is made from the point of view of the individual and is very different from the Hegelian or Marxist diagnosis. True, he says, the feudal political system was far from being an ideal set-up, but at least it carried with it the advantage of being a pluralist one: when a man was not happy with his prince, he could always turn to the bishop; when the bishop proved too exacting, he could solicit the protection of the city; and against the city he could request the aid of the corporations; and so on. But what is a man to do in a state which is based on a single principle, on an idea (as, for example, with Hegel, whose state is the active reality

(*Wirklichkeit*) of the moral idea)? Here the individual is declared a citizen whose moral obligation it is to put himself at the service of the state, to respect the law, and to obey the authorities. As more ideas are introduced, so more obligations are imposed, and finally the individual finds that he is being sacrificed to an abstract philosophical idea. This too bears out Stirner's thesis that the individual and the spirit are mutually exclusive entities, and that he who espouses the idea subjugates the individual man.

The nascent socialism of his age likewise falls a victim to this criticism. Under the old form of society there were at least rich as well as poor. Modern socialism, however (at this point Stirner is thinking mainly of Proudhon), proposes to abolish all property, thus making everyone poor. For if, in effect, the state possesses everything, then a new ' principle ' is interposed between the individual and the property of all, namely, the socialist notion of ' social justice ', a notion which is just as open to arbitrary interpretation and just as oppressive as, for example, that of ' divine grace '. In Stirner's eyes, Marx demonstrated the direction in which this new form of social justice, founded on the notion of labour, might tend. I can work for myself if the spirit moves me, or if I need to, but what am I to make of compulsory work done in the service of society? Such work, with its divisions and subdivisions, seems to Stirner rather like a new system of conceptual clockwork directed against the individual. And it matters little if at this point the opposing camps become confused because Marx, too, a little later, proposed to emancipate man from alienated labour.

Now what will be the attitude of the individual amid so many forms of alienation? He has only to ' recapture ' his property from the hands of the usurper, to ' reappropriate ' his creative strength and activity, and he will be able to depend quietly on himself again. Thus – just as in Hegel – true, concrete individuality (*Einzelheit*) is a return from alienation and leads to the individual's taking stock of his central importance, of his own ' absolute value '. First of all I must regain from the state my power (*meine Macht*) which it had expropriated by erecting a fictitious juridical system the purpose of which is to dispossess individuals of their possessions. Stirner is thinking, of course, of that part of Hegel's political philosophy where he treats of ' Abstract Right ', which is private law based on the notion of property. The goods appropriated by the state are not only of a material kind (confiscation, arbitrary taxation, disinheritance, fines, etc.), but also of an intellectual order. The products of the human intellect may serve only the interests of the state; anything else is ' criminal '. It is in this context that Stirner's famous ' apology for crime ' is embedded, and it is a reaction to a heated contemporary debate. For him crime is not a sign of the malfunctioning or rottenness of the state. On the contrary, it is in the nature of the state to assert its power to the detriment of individuals. An individual automatically becomes ' criminal ' when he asserts his personal interests against the interests of the state. Of course, there are ' legitimate ' personal interests recognized by the state, but their possession is not truly enjoyed by the individual, because they depend on a ' principle ', namely that of right, which, as we have seen, is a spiteful fiction. And that is why Stirner so violently attacks Proudhon for whom property is robbery. But robbery itself already implies the principle of legitimate acquisition, and this is inadmissible: one cannot steal something unless there is a ' legal ' owner. It may further be the case that the official ideology interposes yet other abstract notions between itself and the individual (apart from the juridical fiction of ' person ') such as, for example, the ' interest of the people ', the ' public good ', the ' national cause ', etc., which are just so many imaginary justifications for the more efficient oppression of the individual. The worst of all evils occurs when, as was the case in the Prussia of Frederick William IV, the state dons the robes of a religious ideology and preaches ' Christian love ' the better to subdue its citizens; and this is a trap into which a good many Left Hegelians likewise fell. But Stirner barricades himself in the Great Refusal: the individual owes precisely nothing to the state, and there can be no compelling him to collaborate with it until such time as he himself would profit from it.

The chapter on ' My Social Relations ' (*Mein Verkehr*) complements this attitude in the realm of society, and such a view could not but irritate those militant socialists of all kinds who were rife in Germany at that time. Even the principle, of political ' engagement ', the belonging to a party, is a form of alienation. The party is nothing but a *partie prise* adopted by the individual for some reason or another, a one-sided and rigid attitude which tends to be self-perpetuating and to become an obligation for its members. Such a political attitude will never countenance the belief that its adherents, all its adherents, may change their minds; in short, that it may lose its entire *raison d'être*. For Stirner it is the very image of that society to which we belong not by choice, but by birth, and which does not allow of our departure. Just as Hegel, in his *Philosophy of Right*, sees the vocation of the family in its dissolution, so Stirner regards society as a sort of natural framework – not to say a necessary evil – which is bound to disappear as soon as its members attain their majority, that is to say, become individuals aware of their uniqueness. Stirner does not, however, advocate anarchism. Playing with certain ideas of Proudhon (in his *Création de l'Ordre*), he proposes an ' association of egoists ' (*Verein der Egoisten*) in which each man may live his life without self-abnegation. The ' association ' offers the most elastic form of relations between individuals because it is neither a social tie, nor an ideological prison, but quite simply a community of interests which, moreover, does not exclude the possibility of its members using it to their advantage. Here, then, a man is complete ' owner ' of himself, and no sacrifices are demanded of him. But this is just Stirner's utopia, inspired by the other utopian writers of that era. The judgement he passes on existing society is very much more sombre. He foresees for society not a ' revolution ' – which is merely the replacement by violent methods of one set of political fictions by another – but a ' revolt '

(*Empörung*), that is, the complete unleashing of individual passions and energies against every social and political tie. It is the most powerful form of individual dissent conceivable, and a radical complement to more or less passive resistance to the state.

But Stirner is far removed from violence, and his philosophy – not without similarities with the classical philosophical systems – comes to rest in an almost contemplative attitude which he calls 'My Pleasure in Myself' (*Mein Selbst-genuss*). I say 'almost', because just at the end of his theory, Stirner introduces a sort of dialectic which runs counter to what he has understood to be the final position of Hegel. First of all it must be said that man cannot take pleasure in himself when he is placed under obligations. By recovering my individuality from philosophy, from the state, from society, from religion, etc., I have eliminated all forms of transcendence or, to put it another way, all idealist fictions (*Sollen* in German) liable to subject me to something other than myself. But this being said, I am not thereby reduced to a solely vegetable existence. The single individual remains a double-faceted entity: he is not anything, or rather, he *is nothing* inasmuch as he is capable of rejecting everything. But yet at the same time he is *everything*, because the things he rejects need him, in effect, in order to exist. And so there resides in him a creative power which is, in the last analysis, the key to an understanding of the whole of reality. His intellect creates fictitious but effective abstractions, while his senses present him with an image of the material world. It is therefore not surprising that Stirner's thought ends on an ambiguous note: the reduction of everything to the single individual is just as much an end – the end of all philosophy and ideology – as a beginning, the beginning of a human life uniquely creating its own non-alienated nature. But in the end Stirner does not permit himself any speculation concerning the future, and he is content to reduce his unique individual to his true proportions, that is, a creature depending on itself and consuming its forces until it disappears: immortality is only a sinister theologico-philosophical farce. The motto which he sets at the beginning of the second part of his work sums up his own point of view as well as the much earlier one of Foucault:

No-one has noticed that man has killed God in order that he himself might now become 'the sole God on High'. The *Beyond outside us* has indeed been swept away . . . and yet the *Beyond within us* has become a new Heaven which exhorts Us to renewed attempts at taking it by storm: God has had to make way, yet not for Us, but – for Man. How could you believe that the God-Man has died without both Man and God first dying through him?

II

Marx and Engels' critique of Stirner is notoriously misleading.[2] It is not just that ridicule of a man's person is not equivalent to refutation of his ideas, for the

---

[2] In *Die deutsche Ideologie, Marx-Engels Gesamtausgabe*, vol. v, sect. i.

reader is also aware that the authors are not reacting at all to the problems raised by their adversary. The principal misunderstanding consists in the fact that Marx and Engels regard Stirner as just another doctrinaire ideologue who must at all costs be eliminated from the field. But this was not at all the case. From the brief résumé given above, it should already be clear that Stirner wishes to break out of the vicious circle of critical invective common at that time, in order to express his *own* feelings and his *own* perfectly concrete historical place in a situation where to *think* revolution was the fashion. And so the *Individual and his Property* can easily be conceived as a sociological document of the first order, namely, the testament of a dissenting intellectual (*unintellectual contestataire*).

Along with so many others, Stirner was the prototype of the drifting intellectual to whom the doors of an academic career were closed and who did not succeed in gaining entry into any of the existing political organizations. Moreover, as is well known, the consolations of family life and material well-being were likewise denied him. He was, to quote a phrase of Karl Löwith's, a sort of 'neutral point between bourgeois and proletarian ',[3] an anticipation of the intellectuals who stand outside organized classes and are, according to Marcuse,[4] the probable heralds of a social upheaval. Marx, who was well aware that ' revolution begins in the minds of intellectuals ', did not accord this credit to Stirner because at that time (1845–6) he was already thinking in terms of classes and no longer took account of individuals.

The reply to Stirner, which is made in the boring form of a running commentary, is a magisterial lesson in historical and economic facts. Marx simply emptied his well-stocked Paris filing-cabinet over his unfortunate opponent, and cared little if Stirner's ' philosophy of history ' was merely an ironical reply to the historical speculations of the Hegelian school. The same is true of the economic categories implied in this polemic. When Stirner speaks of revolution, party, association, property, labour, money, state, etc., it is not for him a question of universally valid scientific analysis; on the contrary, he wishes to reduce these abstract concepts to their significance for the individual, the sole acceptable criterion in an anti-philosophical framework. To what good teach history to men who are suffering from it? To what good expound economics to men dying of hunger? In this particular instance, the example of Marx bears out all Stirner's objections to the doctrinaire ideologues who sacrifice individuals on the altar of ideas.

Proof of this lies in the fact that it is precisely Stirner whom Marx uses to illustrate his theory of abstract intellectuals. Abstraction is made from reality, and reality is the process of production based on the division of labour, etc. Stirner's reality is the world of his immediate experience, while Marx's reality is that of universal labour, and it is not surprising that these two worlds, the particular

[3] *Von Hegel zu Nietzsche* (Zürich, 1941), p. 332.
[4] *One Dimensional Man* (Boston, 1964), pp. 256–7.

and the universal, never meet. Yet Marx, in so far as he is a disciple of Hegel, nevertheless makes an effort to 'reconcile' these two worlds, and here, too, he falls into the trap previously set by Stirner. I am alluding to Marx's doctrine of the individual consciousness which is mediated by the social consciousness. That the individual consciousness is never completely autonomous and independent is a fact explicitly admitted by Stirner himself, a truth, indeed, which is the common coin of the age. The real problem is to what degree the individual consciousness is necessarily determined by its social ties. At this point Marx has not yet completed his transformation of Hegel's philosophy – where the individual consciousness is independent of its epoch but not of society – and consequently he is unable to furnish a definitive answer, thus bringing grist to Stirner's mill. If consciousness is completely determined by society, then there is nothing to be done, and an upheaval in the minds of men is not possible either. If on the other hand the individual consciousness preserves a sort of autonomy, then it is Stirner who is right, for in that case it is quite possible, as we read in the *Individual and his Property*, for the individual to reject his society while yet remaining in it – in other words, he can become a non-conforming dissenter. And so this example shows that Marx, at least at this stage of his development, was philosophically unable to conceive of any possibility of an 'oppositionist consciousness' on which, quite obviously, one must always and necessarily count if one entertains ideas which are intended to transform political reality.[5]

It is just this confrontation with Stirner which throws into relief a disagreeable characteristic of the 'young' Marx: he was unable to understand any possible opposition to *his* revolution. To revolt against his revolution you must either be mad or else a corrupt product of bourgeois society, and this, in effect, is the reproach he made against his adversary. Stirner, on the other hand, poses a truly Hegelian problem, which still preserves its vital importance: can the dialectic or 'negativity', once it has been set in motion, ever be halted for any conceivable ideological reasons?

And here we reach the crux of the problem, Marx's fundamental difficulty *vis-à-vis* Stirner. What will man be like once he has been rid of his various forms of alienation? Stirner speaks of the individual's taking pleasure in himself, and Marx too, at this time, does not aim at any other goal: the total individual who is no longer a miserable slave of the division of labour, and who does exactly as he wishes. Stirner commits only one 'ideological' error which is inadmissible from a Hegelian point of view: he wishes to realize this pleasure of individual self-possession immediately, without first of all passing through the intermediate stage of total alienation of consciousness as it is found among the proletarian classes – a process which, naturally implies revolution. And so here, too, there is

[5] H. Arvon, *Max Stirner* (Paris, 1954), p. 167.

a characteristic misunderstanding between the two antagonists. Marx has a very clear notion of his own revolutionary tactics and sees clearly the tendencies of the future in the present age (the dialectical tension between exploiters and exploited), but he has no doctrine for the immediate present, and least of all for those whose lives are led on the margin of the economic process. It is precisely Stirner who fills in this gap. When Marx reproaches him with retreat into atomistic isolation like any petty bourgeois Germans of the time (*die vereinzelten Einzelnen*), he is only too right. For what, indeed, is to be done by the dissenting members of a society which has not yet become socialist and can only be endured with great difficulty? Until the dawn of a new order, they have nothing but the passive yet radical resistance so well described by Stirner. Marx is wrong in thinking that the Stirnerian egoism is a new form of morality while his own doctrine is purely scientific; this would be to underestimate the role of discontent in the unfolding of historical events, an error which Hegel and Stirner did not themselves commit. In analysing the notion of liberty, it is Stirner who has most closely followed the Master by establishing that, in order to create an explosive situation, individuals do not have to know what they want; it is sufficient for them to know what they want to free themselves *from*.

III

What are the sources in Hegel's work of this acrimonious dispute between his antagonistic disciples? Among the vast number of subjects cast pell-mell into the controversy, we will take up only the role of the individual consciousness, the pivot about which all the other problems revolved.

This problem, which has its origins in Kant and Fichte, dominates the *Pheno-menology of Spirit*, a work which bridges the gap between the ' young ' and the ' old ' Hegel. The difficulty for the reader (and also for Marx) stems from the fact that Hegel here treats together three different aspects of the problem – metaphysical, political, historical – which are best separated if they are to be made intelligible. From the metaphysical point of view, the individual con-sciousness represents ' subjectivity ' or ' negativity ', that is to say, that aspect of reality which is active and creative, and which consequently gives meaning to things, and enables us to understand the purely objective aspect of reality which rests solely on itself. Work and language are for Hegel – in the context of the *Phenomenology* – the two fundamental principles of creative human activity,[6] the one transforming the world of objects into a human world, and the other, in the form of representation (*Vorstellung*) educating and transforming the individual into an ' interiorized ' creature, that is, into an intelligent human being whose actions are determined by preceding acts of reflection. It need scarcely be said that for Hegel a reality which is determined by reflection and

6 *Phänomenologie des Geistes*, ed. J. Hoffmeister (Hamburg, 1952), p. 229.

comprehension becomes a function of that comprehension – the more we know the better we act – and that is why he proposes to elaborate systematically the concepts by which man understands the world and himself; this is the programme of his *Logic*. In such a system there cannot, of course, be any *individual* subject, for the latter will always and necessarily be but a part of a system without ever being able to serve as that system's fundamental principle. Hegel thought, rather, that a global system of understanding can only be the intellectual product of *all* those who create valuable and valid ideas.*

So we can see at a glance, even from this schematic exposition, where the difficulty lies for the post-Hegelian generation. They more or less accept the structure of individual consciousness in its practical and even its reflective aspects (conceiving the world in the form of representation), but they reject all speculation which causes the individual act to pass over into an a-historical process. For it is quite clear that for Hegel, just as for Spinoza, logic, which enables us to understand all reality, cannot depend upon history, which is itself a portion of this reality. But Hegel, too, had his own problem: while allowing that human actions are always individual and historical, they cannot be *merely* that, for after death of individual men and the disappearance of historical epochs there is always something which *remains* and which does not belong to the realm of transient things. We will see in a moment the importance this restriction has for the political utilisers of Hegel's doctrine.

Throughout his political evolution, Hegel never ceased to be intrigued by the political aspect of individuality. Ironically, it is on this very topic that he has been most often, and most unjustly, attacked. In the *Phenomenology* we already encounter in its finished form his theory of the ' moral ' individual who, in the name of moral consciousness (*Gewissen*) and personal conviction, is opposed to the existing social order. He shows, primarily with the example of Greece (here Antigone, elsewhere Socrates), that the questioning by individuals of established injustice is the end of an epoch and the beginning of another, more just, age.*
Is not what is common – and best – in the theories of Marx and Stirner the attribution to the individual consciousness of this ' negativity ', this capacity to reflect on social and political reality while at the same time rejecting it? By constantly citing the sacrifices which Hegel demands of the citizen in his philosophy of the state, one easily forgets that the negating powers of the individual are not in the least forgotten by him. Hegel is the first to say that there are social and political situations in which the moral degradation of individuals makes discontent both inevitable and intolerable, as is the case, for example, with social poverty and political tyranny. Indeed, Hegel's state is a moral entity, an ' idea ', but its precarious equilibrium depends on the satisfaction of individuals in and

* *Editor's note* – This point is stressed by J. N. Shklar, p. 74.
* *Editor's note* – Another view of Hegel's interpretation of Antigone is given by J. N. Shklar, pp. 83–7.

through their liberty. Phenomena like Stirner and Marx are thus foreseen by this philosophy, and it is only natural that the exacerbation of such problems in the historical context of the age should have brought with it a radicalization and concretization of thought, and exposed its negative effects.

But this generation had another account to settle with Hegel, which lies in the realm of philosophy of history. The issue is that of the celebrated Hegelian theory of ' world-historical individuals ' (*weltgeschichtliche Individuen*) and the ' cunning of reason ' (*List der Vernunft*), a theory posterior to the *Phenomenology*. Is it really so unacceptable? Stirner, who along with others gave up philosophizing on this subject, has no need of a historical theory. Marx, on the other hand, is well and truly entrenched in Hegel's historical vision. For, in this too, Hegel was the first to assert that through and beyond individual action there unfolds a process of which the individual actors are unaware and which yet prevails in the end. Individuals always and necessarily act under the impulse of passion and selfish considerations in their attempts to attain satisfaction and happiness, but history, history itself, brings nothing of any special interest to either one individual or another; at most, it realizes freedom for *all*. All this is not very far from the Marxian conception of history with its process of alienation, awareness of this process, and final liberation from all trace of servitude *as rapidly as possible*.

These last words separate in perhaps the most radical fashion the philosopher Hegel from his political disciples. Hegel's thought possesses, as we mentioned earlier, an a-temporal dimension – that of pure contemplation – which can be affected neither by individual passions nor by the fracas of history; there the philosopher retires to meditate on the individual and on history. Thus we are faced with a true form of ' transcendence ' which has been so often and so loudly decried by all the activists. Confronted with this position, we are able to understand rather better the mentality of the Hegelian school. Hegel was the last philosopher to possess the secret of contemplation, which after his death became a lost paradise. Stirner reverted to the resigned attitude of a simple mortal who must find his entire satisfaction in his own life; Marx elaborated a universal theory of action where contemplation is replaced by the impatience of those who aspire to a better state of things. With the irruption of time into Hegel's a-temporal framework, classical philosophy became but *one* of the forms of spirit.*

* *Editor's note* – Translated from the French by Roger Hansheer.

Hegel's political philosophy: some thoughts on its contemporary relevance

Z. A. PELCZYNSKI

The Hegelian concepts examined in this book are bound up with a definite political and constitutional theory about the character of the governmental authorities which the modern state must necessarily have in order to perform its complex tasks *vis-à-vis* the ethical and the civil order, while at the same time safeguarding the integrity and independence of the body politic itself. The political and constitutional theory has already been treated from different viewpoints in some of the essays.[1] It is nonetheless worth while at the end of this book raising the question of the contemporary validity of the theory, and the wider question of the distinctive contribution of Hegel's political philosophy to contemporary political and social theory. There is obviously much that is questionable in Hegel's political philosophy and it cannot all be excused on the ground that he was born in 1770 and died in 1831. One must also remember that his concepts and theories were thought by him to have validity for a whole historical epoch, and not merely for the times in which he formulated them.

His theory of sovereignty is open to objections even without the benefit of hindsight. Hegel proceeds from the view that the different organs of 'the state as a political entity' must be seen as branches of a single public authority, and must be prevented by the constitution from becoming 'self-subsistent', that is, functioning with excessive independence. This unified character of the public authority he calls 'sovereignty' – or, more strictly, the domestic or internal aspect of a state's sovereignty since he also distinguishes a state's sovereignty *vis-à-vis* foreign states. It would seem to follow from this concept that the constitutional power of the monarch is limited by the equally legitimate powers of the other organs (the executive, the legislature, the electorate and the lower public authorities) which together with the crown form the 'organism' or the constitution of the political and civil state. However important and powerful, the crown as an institution is only one of the elements of the whole differentiated constitutional structure, which is logically prior and legally superior to him. Not the crown but only the constitution as a whole is able to 'actualize' sovereignty in the Hegelian sense.

But the position of the crown changes radically when Hegel begins discussing sovereignty in a conventional sense as the ultimate source of the validity of all

---

[1] Especially in those of K.-H. Ilting, G. Heiman, J.-F. Suter, R. N. Berki and my own introductory essay.

legal acts and rules in a state, as the basis of a particular, positive legal system. In this sense sovereignty seems to Hegel to be necessarily vested in one part of the constitutional system, and in § 279 he attributes it to the crown. It follows from this concept of sovereignty that all the constitutional organs of the state are inferior to the crown, derive their power from it, and may be deprived of their power in certain circumstances.[2] Hegel thus seems to arrive at a doctrine of monarchical absolutism which is contrary to his belief that the rational form of the modern state is a constitutional monarchy. The doctrine of monarchical sovereignty is modified only partially by Hegel's expectation that modern monarchs will in normal circumstances play a limited constitutional role and increasingly restrict their personal political influence.[3]

In §§ 279 and 280 of the *Philosophy of Right* Hegel is clearly preoccupied with the need for a single formal head of state to represent a state *vis-à-vis* other states. He also sees clearly the necessity of what he calls ' the culminating point of formal decision ' within a complex constitutional structure. This is, presumably, the sense in which, in the United Kingdom, bills passed by Parliament become valid laws when signed by the monarch, or individuals become government ministers, army commanders or ambassadors when formally appointed by the monarch. It is misleading, however, to regard such acts as an exercise of sovereignty and still more as a justification of absolute sovereignty being vested in the crown. Such actions as the above are prescribed or sanctioned by the constitution, which need not derive its validity from some absolute, ultimate right of the monarch. Apart from an obscure metaphysical argument about the personality of the state being fully actualized only in a concrete, natural person, Hegel can only justify his preference for monarchical sovereignty on the not very strong grounds of expediency.

One can appreciate Hegel's desire to avoid the disadvantages of collective sovereignty, which over two centuries earlier also haunted Hobbes. At times when a country's survival as an independent state is at stake, division, strife and disunity within the public authority may be highly injurious, and may be overcome if all authority can be temporarily concentrated in the hands of one man.

---

2 In wartime ' the sovereign is entrusted with the *salvation of the state* at the sacrifice of these particular authorities whose powers are valid at other times . . .' (*Hegel's Philosophy of Right*, trans. T. M. Knox (Oxford, 1942), p. 187; my italics). Cf. with this idea Article 16 of the Constitution of the Fifth French Republic: ' If there is a serious and immediate threat to the institutions of the Republic, the Nation's independence, its territorial integrity, or the fulfilment of its international undertakings, and the constitutional machinery of government breaks down, the President of the Republic takes the measures that the situation demands . . .' (P. Campbell and B. Chapman, *The Constitution of the Fifth Republic : Translation and Commentary*, 2nd rev. ed. (Oxford, 1959), p. 19.)

3 See §§ 274 and 278 and Additions to §§ 279 and 280 of the *Philosophy of Right*. Cf. also *Hegel's Political Writings*, trans. T. M. Knox (Oxford, 1964), pp. 234, 250, and *Lectures on the Philosophy of History*, trans. J. Sibree (New York, 1944), p. 456.

But such 'constitutional dictatorship' is logically quite compatible with parliamentary or popular sovereignty; it may be established by an act of parliament
or be written into a constitution adopted by popular referendum. Hegel himself
admitted that Britain suffered no disadvantages over other countries in wartime,
although effective sovereignty was vested in the British Parliament, and not in
the crown. He also admitted that in Britain patriotism extended beyond the
landed aristocracy to all sections of the people, which might indeed be an argument for bringing the whole British people ' within the pale of the constitution '.
Hence only temporary and specific circumstances, such as lack of patriotism or
political immaturity in the representative assembly or the nation at large, justified
the vesting of sovereignty in the monarch; Hegel's general and philosophical
arguments are invalid.[4]

In 1831 it remained, of course, to be seen how far the spirit of ' civil society '
would be modified through the operation of the traditional institutions of the
state power and whether the representative bodies would develop among its
middle-class members and the population as a whole that ' sense of state ' or
' political consciousness ' which he regarded as absolutely essential to the proper
functioning of the ' political state '. Hegel feared that it might not do so very
quickly, and in a sense partially abandoned his own conviction that political
liberties were the best, indeed the only, means of political education of the masses,
capable of forging strong links between ' particularity ' and ' subjectivity ' on
the one hand, and the universal values of the ethical life on the other.

Equally open to questioning are Hegel's recommendations of hereditary
monarchy with strong governmental prerogatives as a means of strengthening
the executive vis-à-vis ' civil society ' and the legislature exposed to its influence.
There is nothing in the nature of hereditary monarchy which makes it necessarily
independent of the pressures or influences of particular interest. Indeed its
dynastic interest might itself become one particular interest among many, and
the monarch's prerogatives over foreign policy and the army may be used as an
instrument of dynastic aims as well as of national influence or defence. Only an
effective constitutional limitation of the monarch's role to one of reigning rather
than ruling can avoid those dangers. This is, of course, quite compatible with
wide prerogatives of the crown, which are then at the disposal of a government
responsible to the people. Once the monarch is stripped of actual governmental
power and exempt from political criticism, he may perform a useful function as a
symbol of national unity; but his specifically political functions can be equally well

---

[4] Hegel's low opinion of his compatriots is well illustrated in the following passage: ' In the
English people . . . the sense of national honour has permeated the different social classes more
generally. Hence parliament's right to sanction taxation annually has a meaning totally different
from what it would have in a people brought up [like the Wurtembergers] to a sense of merely
private concerns, and being remote from any political standpoint, gripped by the spirit of
narrow-mindedness and private self-seeking ' (Political Writings, p. 268).

exercised by an elected president. On the other hand a president may be invested with many of Hegel's monarch's powers provided he is responsible for their exercise.[5]

Hegel's ideas about the Assembly of Estates are questionable on the ground that they are too favourable to particular interests. Landed nobility, as Hegel explicitly acknowledged in the case of Britain, can easily become a bulwark of particular interests and a barrier to rational reform.[6] Functional representation in the lower house and indeed any kind of parliamentary system sensitive to local or other pressures encourages bargaining between sectional interests instead of furthering coherent national policies. But while Hegel was therefore wrong in making the legislature the special preserve of the various particular interests, his belief that these must be recognized and integrated into the governmental process

---

[5] Hegel recognized that at least one large contemporary country – the United States of America – was a republic with an elected president at its head. This, however, did not lead him to reconsider his political theory, and still less to see North America as a model of future development in Europe. He regarded the U.S.A. as an immature state, without significant external enemies or serious social problems. ' North America will be comparable with Europe only after the immeasurable space which that country presents to its inhabitants shall have been occupied, and the members of the political body shall have begun to be pressed back on each other . . . pursuing town occupations, and trading with their fellow citizens; and so form a compact system of civil society and require an organised state . . . For a real State and a real Government arise only after a distinction of classes has arisen, when wealth and property become extreme, and when such a condition of things presents itself that a large portion of the people can no longer satisfy its necessities in the way in which it has been accustomed to do ' (*Philosophy of History*, pp. 85, 86). In another passage Hegel suggests that the United States is thoroughly imbued with the spirit of civil society. ' Universal protection for property, and . . . something approaching entire immunity from public burdens [in the United States], are facts which are constantly held up to commendation. We have in these facts the fundamental character of the community – the endeavour of the individual after acquisition, commercial profit, and gain; the preponderance of the *private* interest, devoting itself to that of the community only for its own advantage ' (*ibid.* p. 85. Hegel's comments on North America are to be found on pp. 80–7). Hegel wrote those remarks in 1830 for use in a course of lectures on world history which he gave at Berlin University in the winter semester 1830–1. It is not altogether surprising, therefore, that some of his views on America strongly resemble those of Alexis de Tocqueville who stayed in the United States between May 1831 and February 1832.

[6] As Hegel grew older he seemed to become more aware of the influence of economic factors in history. His comments on the United States have already been mentioned in the previous note. In his essay on the English Reform Bill written shortly before his death, Hegel comes close to a consistent Marxian viewpoint in his analysis. He treats the struggle for the Reform Bill as one between the urban middle class and the agricultural upper class, attributes the imperviousness of the landed class to reform ideas to its class interests, treats the state power in Britain as an instrument of class domination, and questions the possibility of a peaceful resolution of the class struggle. Throughout the essay he tends to use the term *Klasse* (class) rather than the usual *Stand* (estate), and even applies the Marxian term *herrschende Klasse* (ruling class) to the landed aristocracy and gentry who dominated Parliament and the executive. But from this analysis he draws the anti-marxist conclusion that a strong and independent executive power, centred on the king rather than on Parliament, would have defused the revolutionary situation by pushing through necessary reforms and pacifying the middle class.

has been strikingly confirmed by the growth of government consultation with organized interest groups in modern industrial states. Using ' corporation ' in the widest possible sense to describe all sorts of organized interests, one might say that the modern state is as ' corporative ' as Hegel believed it had to be. Also the notion of ' estates ' has still some meaning today even if the terminology itself has been abandoned. One might apply it to any social class or sub-class whose members have special juridical and political status. In this sense the unionized working class of today is an ' estate ' since it enjoys certain legal immunities, has representatives on various public bodies and is officially consulted about government policies.

But of course the main basis of legislative bodies today is neither ' estates ' nor ' corporations ', but mass political parties. Hegel knew and approved of party divisions inside representative bodies,[7] but he did not foresee the extension of the party system to the electorate. It is mass parties which today articulate and aggregate social interests, counteract political ' atomization ' of the electorate, modify particularism by devising and carrying out when in power *national* policies, and supply the supreme public authority with a trained political elite to fill legislative and executive posts. Also the split and hostility between the two main branches of the public authority is minimized (or as in Britain virtually eliminated) by the party system, which also helps to ensure just the kind of strong governmental leadership by the executive which Hegel regarded as essential. His fears that a wide democratic electorate might behave irresponsibly, and use its political power to the detriment of long-term community interests, have proved rather exaggerated though by no means groundless. But again it is the party system which has at least partially remedied that danger by increasing people's trust *vis-à-vis* the government and the government's means of convincing the people of the necessity of unpopular measures. Other remedies have been the educative influence on public opinion of a responsible press and other mass media, and the gradual spread of ' political consciousness ' among the masses, brought about primarily through the world wars and economic crises of this century. It has to be admitted, however, that this ' political consciousness ' has drawn much of its strength from nationalism rather than from the rational patriotism based on ethical life which Hegel had in mind.

The necessity of a permanent, highly qualified civil service as an essential element in the public authority of the modern state has become too self-evident to need discussing. The higher civil servants of today may in some countries fall short of the ideal immunity from the pressures of civil society, but there is no doubt that no modern government could function without them. Almost equally self-evident has become Hegel's view that the supreme public authority must exercise a supervisory and regulatory function over civil society, and that it must

[7] Cf. *Political Writings*, pp. 258, 326.

step in and take over the activities of individuals and associations when other forms of control fail. The enormous growth of ' police ' powers (in Hegel's wide sense of the word ' police ') in the modern state, although not specifically foreseen or advocated by him, is perfectly compatible with his general position.[8] All in all, when purged of the element of historical conditioning and personal bias present in all political philosophy, his political and constitutional theory provides a fairly far-sighted, perceptive model of the functioning of the modern state.

Hegel's political philosophy has suffered heavily from the scathing critique of Marx and Engels.[9] And yet, if one limits one's historical horizon to the period up to the 1914–18 war,[10] there cannot be any doubt at all which theory of the modern state – the Hegelian or the Marxian – fits reality better. This is despite the fact that Marx and Engels outlived Hegel by some fifty to sixty years and witnessed such important developments as the transformation of ' civil society ' into a mature capitalist economic system, the growing influence of the bourgeoisie over the state power, the creation of a mass industrial proletariat organized into trade unions and political parties, and the spread of democratic ideas. Hegel believed that the public authority, in which monarchy, landed aristocracy and bourgeoisie (entrenched in the lower chamber of the Estates' Assembly as well as in the civil service) shared power, could and would successfully cope with the problems posed by the dynamism of civil society. They would be able to preserve sound elements in the ethical life of the country by a policy of thorough reforms of traditional laws and institutions, by concessions to ' subjectivity ' and ' particularity ' through the gradual widening of civil and political rights, and by the piecemeal mitigation of social evils brought about by economic forces, through the extension of government controls and welfare measures. This in fact is what happened, and the soundness of Hegelian ideas was proved in 1914. Contrary to the Marxist slogan that the workers have no country, the socialist parties of Western Europe, and the bulk of the working class which they represented, supported their national governments with a great deal of truly Hegelian patriotism even if it was not entirely free from emotional nationalism.

After the First World War the picture becomes more complicated, and neither Marxism nor Hegelianism can account for the rampant nationalism, extreme left and right polarization, political and economic instability, and the rise of one-party dictatorships, equally remote from the dictatorship of the proletariat and the monarchical state power of Hegel. Neither the total character of the two world wars, with their mass slaughter, atrocities and widespread suffering of the

---

8 Cf. *Philosophy of Right*, §§ 236–49 and Additions.

9 Beginning with Marx's critique of the *Philosophy of Right* written in 1843, which is the subject of R. N. Berki's essay.

10 On the ground that the outbreak of the Bolshevik Revolution and the establishment of the soviet state in Russia introduced a new element into world history.

civilian population, nor the totalitarian character of Stalin's Russia or Hitler's Germany fits into the Hegelian or the Marxist framework of political and historical theories. On the other hand, in countries where constitutionalism survived before 1939 or was restored after the Second World War the idea of popular sovereignty has become respectable, even among the upper classes and institutionalized in universal or near universal franchise. But this does not discredit Hegel as completely as it might seem at first sight. Wartime conscription and national service in peacetime, the contribution made by women to the war effort during both world wars, improved education, and the gradual transformation of the 'rabble of paupers' described in the *Philosophy of Right* into the fourth estate of respectable and increasingly prosperous blue- and white-collar workers – all these phenomena can be interpreted as proof of the spread of 'political consciousness' among the masses, which would amply justify their enfranchisement on Hegelian grounds. Although the people is nominally sovereign, it exercises its authority only through a system of established, interacting and interdependent institutions. An interlocking combination of classes, organized groups, parties, and an elite of civil servants and professional politicians, though wider and more complex than a century and a half ago, still dominates the 'political state' and 'civil society'.

Marx and Engels were aware that the modern state did not always have to act as the agent of the bourgeoisie; state power could maintain some independence from 'civil society' as it did in the France of the Bonapartes or in Bismarck's Germany. But they thought of this as an exceptional and temporary situation, in no way invalidating the prediction of a successful workers' revolution. The idea that 'the bourgeois state machine' could control capitalism, protect the economically weak from its evils, and distribute its benefits throughout society according to some fairly generally shared principles of social justice, they would have dismissed as utopian and unscientific because contradictory of the very nature of capitalism. Yet these things have happened to a large extent in the major industrial countries. One need not assert that they function perfectly. Social harmony does not reign in every country all the time, and 'particular interests' have a steady and at times powerful influence over governments. But they have sufficient community of interest to prefer the *status quo* to its violent overthrow, and sufficient consensus about fundamental social and national values to work out fair compromises or accept those worked out for them by the government.[11]

---

[11] The rise of communism in Russia and its spread elsewhere are of course not a vindication of Marxism; it is impossible to explain them in classical Marxian terms. On the other hand the Hegelian theory provides for the possibility of a fanatical and well-organized minority, imbued with a 'subjective' ideal of an egalitarian and stateless community, seizing power in a politically and socially disorganized system. Such disorganization or disintegration might itself be due to the system's failure to satisfy the material and ethical aspirations of the masses. Hegel's explanation of Jacobinism and Terror is partly along these lines. But Hegel could not foresee the technological

One of the greatest merits of Marx as a social and political theorist was to sever the connection of the theory of society and the state with philosophy, especially with metaphysical and speculative philosophy. By developing Feuerbach's criticism that Hegelian metaphysics was merely historical reality seen in a distorting mirror, Marx radically emancipated social and political science from the tutelage of philosophy, and based it on a thoroughgoing empiricism.[12] But in one respect Marx and Engels proved themselves far less empirical than Hegel. They had sought to transcend the historical reality of their time and place and to prove the inevitable emergence not just of the next historical epoch (socialism), but also of the one after that (communism), together with an outline of their corresponding social and political systems. Hegel on the contrary flatly refused to look beyond his own epoch to a radically different world. He confined the task of political philosophy to ' the apprehension of the present and the actual, not the erection of a beyond, supposed to exist, God knows where . . . It is just as absurd to fancy that a philosophy can transcend its contemporary world as it is to fancy that an individual can overleap his own age, jump over Rhodes '.[13] This standpoint did not in the least preclude criticism, prescription and recommendation from being legitimate parts of social and political philosophizing. But it did exclude those kinds of philosophical criticism and speculation which ignored the wealth of available social experience and indulged in far-reaching historical prophecy.

It is possible to interpret economic, social, cultural and political developments of advanced contemporary capitalist countries from a basically Hegelian point of departure and arrive at a set of radically different conclusions – as has been shown by members of the ' Frankfurt school '.[14] One must certainly acknowledge that social and political theory owes a great debt to the Frankfurt school for regarding Hegel as a great seminal thinker of the nineteenth century and continuing to treat his ideas seriously despite so much neglect or just ill-informed and politically biased writing on the subject. But the Frankfurt school's critique of modern industrial society presupposes that it is possible to transcend the

and organizational developments which enabled such a revolutionary minority to establish its rule on a permanent basis and to transform the economic basis, social structure and political consciousness of the masses to the degree that communism has done.

12 This, however, was more of a programme than an actual achievement. The metaphysical element in Marxism is far larger than many sociologists (not to mention communists) like to admit. Cf. R. Tucker, *Philosophy and Myth in Karl Marx* (Cambridge, 1961) and S. Avineri, *The Social and Political Thought of Karl Marx* (Cambridge, 1968) for support for this point of view.

13 *Philosophy of Right*, preface, pp. 10, 11. Karl Popper's classification of both Hegel and Marx as ' historicists ' is, in one respect at least, based on a fundamental mistake.

14 By this I mean such writers as Th.W. Adorno, A. Gehlen, J. Habermas and H. Marcuse who share a similar conception of socio–cultural criticism and a distinct social philosophy. As their major works are in German, the point of view of the school is known in the Anglo–American world largely through the works of Marcuse.

historical limitations of man's intellectual horizon in an essentially Marxist way. Its Hegelian paternity is therefore illegitimate, and its attempt 'to jump over Rhodes' would undoubtedly have been disowned by Hegel. Had Hegel been alive today he might have recoiled in horror from the weakness of the American state (in his special sense) *vis-à-vis* American civil society, but he would have refused to contemplate reforms which transcended elements at least partially present in the idea of 'the American way of life'.

However, it is not with Marx and Engels – prophets of social disintegration and of the total re-structuring of modern society – but rather with later sociologists that Hegel can more fruitfully be compared. He shares with them three fundamental and related viewpoints: the search for the sources of stability and cohesion in society, the importance of the concept of community, and the conviction that the analysis of social and political life is inadequate unless it takes into account the concepts, values and ideals actualized in that life.

Hegel's three concepts of the state correspond to the three main ways in which modern societies may be said to be integrated into stable and cohesive wholes. The first one, corresponding to his concept of 'ethical community', is through the influence of moral rules and principles, firmly rooted in the history, culture, customs, laws and institutions of a country, which are transmitted from one generation to another by an educative process that begins in the family and continues in the various social and political activities of adult life. The second form of integration, corresponding to Hegel's 'civil society', is through the pursuit of private interests, typically though not exclusively of a material kind, which produces a social division of labour, the exchange of goods and services in the market economy, and a network of cooperative and associative institutions. The third form of integration, corresponding to Hegel's 'political state', is through the system of central governmental bodies enacting general laws or acting on the basis of prerogative powers vested in them by the constitution. While the first two types of integration are predominantly spontaneous, the third one is inherently conscious and deliberate, and is backed by the organized might of 'the political state'. Provided that the supreme public authority is properly constituted it can remedy the defects of the other two and hence reinforce their methods of integration. The idea of integration does not, of course, exhaust the meaning of the three terms. They are also, from the standpoint of the individual, different types of activity in which he plays different kinds of role. They impose different duties or secure different rights, and they make freedom in different senses possible. But the categories of cohesion, stability and integration certainly express one of Hegel's central concerns in drawing the distinction between the different concepts of the state.

We have it on the authority of a leading Weberian scholar that Hegel's ideas on social integration have had a profound influence on Max Weber and through him (one might presume) on many other sociologists.

Weber recognizes the importance of the problem of integration. He attempts to solve it through an adaptation of Hegel's theoretical synthesis, the second intellectual tradition that greatly influenced him . . . He believes, like Hegel, that not only the coalescence of interests on the market but cultural norms and conventions produce a degree of social cohesion . . . Like Hegel, Weber believes that social stability depends also on government and the exercise of authority.[15]

Hegel cannot be credited with the discovery or even recovery of the concept of community at the turn of the eighteenth and the nineteenth centuries. Nor was he unique among his contemporaries in conceiving the state as a community, and attributing to it pre-eminence over other communities. Burke and Coleridge in England, Bonald and de Maistre in France, and several German Romantic thinkers of the era of revolution and reaction shared many of Hegel's ideas on the state as a politically organized community. Nevertheless, of all his German contemporaries he alone produced in the *Philosophy of Right* a work of outstanding intellectual calibre. There he incorporated, together with the social, political and ethical insights he shared with his contemporaries, an analysis of modern European culture in world-historical perspective, and a more sympathetic and profound evaluation of economic, social, political and cultural individualism than most of them could achieve. His thought was also free from the Romantic idealization of religion as an essential prop of society and the state; Hegel may have attributed divinity to the state, but for him, as for Kant, the state was a secular deity, which could do perfectly well without the aid of theology or organized religion.[16] In a century which became progressively secularized as well as influenced by individualism, Hegel's standpoint had a better chance of being appreciated even though the metaphysical formulation of his political philosophy was increasingly out of tune with the positivistic influences in social and political theory. The significance of Hegel's political *chef d'oeuvre* was recently summarized as follows: ' In Hegel the influence of community is seen most strikingly in his *Philosophy of Right*, the work which, above any other single piece of writing in early nineteenth-century German philosophy, created the effective setting within which German sociology was later to arise.'[17]

15 R. Bendix, *Nation-Building and Citizenship : Studies of our Changing Social Order* (New York, 1964), pp. 27, 28. Cf. also the same author's *Max Weber : An Intellectual Portrait* (London, 1960), ch. 9, where Weber is said to have recognized ' three overlapping dimensions of social life – authority, material interest, and value-orientation ' (p. 290).

16 Cf. *Philosophy of Right*, p. 285, and the long Remark to § 270.

17 R. A. Nisbet, *The Sociological Tradition* (London, 1967), p. 54. The same writer makes the following interesting comment about the concept of community on p. 47 of the book:

' The most fundamental and far-reaching of sociology's unit-ideas is community. The rediscovery of community is unquestionably the most distinctive development in nineteenth-century sociology, a development that extends well beyond sociological theory to such areas as philosophy, history and theology . . . It is hard to think of any other idea that so clearly separates the social thought of the nineteenth century from that of the preceding age, the Age of Reason.'

Many of Nisbet's own ideas about ' the normative order in society ' and its connection with

One of the distinctive contributions of Marxism to sociology was its recognition of the great importance of material interests in the functioning and structuring of society. But Marx's view that all social concepts, values and ideals were merely reflections of class interests, and formed part of the ideological superstructure of society shaped by the prevailing mode of production, has for long been abandoned by most sociologists as dogmatic and inadequate. Max Weber, in *The Protestant Ethic and the Spirit of Capitalism*, decisively modified Marxism by arguing that it was ideological forces – protestantism and its secularized bourgeois ethos – which made the accumulation of capital, and therefore capitalism, possible. Emile Durkheim maintained that what he called ' objective social morality ' – a concept strongly resembling Hegel's *Sittlichkeit* – pervaded human relations and formed a framework within which political, economic, and all other social activities took place.[18] The view that value systems can shape social relations to a significant extent, and can therefore be a starting-point for the investigation of social reality, is shared by many contemporary sociologists. ' That a system of value-orientations held in common by members of the social system can serve as the main point of reference for analysing structure and process in the social system itself may be regarded as a major tenet of modern sociological theory.' [19]

S. M. Lipset's *The First New Nation* (1963) is an interesting example of such an analysis of the American social and political system in terms of America's two basic values – equality and achievement.

Lipset's type of approach to America can be traced back to Tocqueville's *De la démocratie en Amérique*, and Tocqueville was under the strong influence of Montesquieu. But so was Hegel, and this is one reason why he shares with Tocqueville the fundamental belief that the spiritual – that is, moral, intellectual, religious and cultural – forces operating in a society profoundly affect its political

culture are strikingly similar to Hegel's. See, for example, R. A. Nisbet, *Tradition and Revolt : Historical and Sociological Essays* (New York, 1968).

[18] ' Each people at a given moment of its history has a morality, and it is in the name of this ruling morality that tribunals condemn and opinion judges . . . I postulate, then, supported by the facts that there is a general morality common to all individuals belonging to a collectivity ', E. Durkheim, *Sociology and Philosophy*, trans. D. F. Pocock (London, 1965), p. 40. In his work *Moral Education*, Durkheim admitted that at the present stage of humanity's evolution the nation-state was the highest group to which men could owe moral allegiance. In *The Division of Labour in Society* Durkheim was chiefly concerned about the breakdown of moral and legal norms regulating human relations in the economic sphere of advanced industrial society, and with the urgent necessity of creating such norms. This is rather similar to Hegel's concern about the weakness of ethical life and the strength of individualistic tendencies within civil society. Cf. also the chapters on the state in Durkheim's *Professional Ethics and Civic Morals*.

[19] Talcott Parsons, *Structure and Process in Modern Societies* (Glencoe, Ill., 1960), p. 172. Parsons' ideas about how values and other cultural facets are shared by individuals, internalized in their personalities, institutionalized in the social structure, and influence the regulation of social relations, all seem to have been anticipated by Hegel.

life. But it was mainly to the ancient Greek philosophers that Hegel owed his insight into the close connection between ethics and politics. As he remarks in the preface to the *Philosophy of Right*, ' Plato's *Republic* . . . is in essence nothing but an interpretation of the nature of Greek ethical life.' Paradoxically, it was a return to antiquity that helped Hegel to take a stride towards modern political and social theory. By his insistence that the state and society of modern times must be explained in terms of men's shared cultural concepts and ideals he has deserved to be considered one of the first sociologists. By his contempt for all knowledge of man's social and political life which was not founded on speculative philosophy like his own he has voluntarily banished himself from their ranks.

Index

*Numbers in **bold** type refer to essays in the book dealing with the subject listed.*